TRADE SECRETS

Young British Talents Talk Business

Cynthia Rose

Thames & Hudson

Designed by Simon Emery

British Library Cataloguing-in-Publication Data

A catalogue record for this book is available from the British Library

ISBN 0-500-28083-5

Printed and bound in Hong Kong by C&C Offset

Dedicated to the memories of my friends
Gavin Hills and **Tony "Agent" Cooper**

OPENING HOURS

A.M. TO P.M.

OPENING HOURS

A.M. TO P.M.

CHAPTER 1

1

Introduction

Trade Secrets

"People always want you to think it's crowded at the top. But there's always plenty of room at the top. There's room for everybody. It's crowded at the *bottom*!" Judy Blame, stylist.

For British leisure and those things it fosters (music, fashion, advertising, concepts of "youth"), the '90s have been explosive. Following a renaissance of the club and the dancefloor came mass rave culture and the "E Generation" - named not merely for the drug known as Ecstasy, but for their fresh and pan-European focus.

What began with kids on cheap package holidays has entirely re-drawn the map of youthful leisure. It now leads from the West End to Eastern Europe, from the beaches of Jamaica to Berlin's Love Parade. It celebrates many different sorts of star, from DJs like Sven Väth to ensembles like The Orb; from figures like Bally Sagoo to Eric Cantona. What their ascent can reveal to culture pundits is a watershed change in communications.

For decades, pop and style have been global and multinational. But they are now linked around the world by something else: digitization, or content reduced to bytes. Existing industry structures continue to favour packages - hence the success of Oasis and the Spice Girls. But most industries are learning from digital change. It sends UK newspapers around the world on the Web; it makes superstars out of suburban DJs. In 1994, the critic Hugh Gallagher wrote, "There are different DJs for every music style - techno, acid jazz, hip-hop, ambient - but all of them are essentially doing the same thing: manipulating information. Recorded music is stored information and the best DJ has the best information."

"In a world where information plus technology equals power, those who control the editing rooms run the show. DJs are editors of the street, using technology to structure an alternate sonic reality. They are the first musicians to turn a medium into an instrument - a natural step for a society that spends increasing time interfacing with communications technology."

In the '90s, "interfacing with communications technology" means more than capturing your 21st on a camcorder. It means using automatic cash dispensers, passing through electronic Tube barriers and - for a growing number of young Britons - communicating with the world via satellite, e-mail and the World Wide Web. It also means learning how these things have changed your neighbours.

Journalist Gavin Hills once told me, "My first visit to Sarajevo seemed to like going to Peckham. Everyone was just smoking dope and talking about the football. Plus, they all had bloody great attack dogs. I was more afraid of those dogs than the snipers." There are also DJs spinning in Bosnia, just as there are nightclubs and bands with punkish names such as "Fuck Off". Most of them know the sound they want to imitate. But it's not Oasis, it's Seattle's Nirvana.

In many ways, digital progress and its changes have emanated from the United States more than elsewhere. Certainly, rapacious US conglomerates - from Time-Warner to Disney, Microsoft to MCI - aim to conquer Europe. But the tools of digital revolution are unusual, in that they empower more than they limit.

Thus, the "social imperialism" Europeans have loathed for years is beginning - albeit slowly - to change. England, long a depthless fount of style and image, has discovered these assets can be valuable exports. In the '90s, there are even different role models. John Galliano and "Lee" McQueen rule Paris; Kate Moss and Naomi Campbell have become icons. So, in different ways, have musician Goldie, actor Ewan McGregor, Prime Minister Tony Blair. The music for Hollywood's "MTV-era" *Romeo & Juliet* comes from Nellee Hooper, once of Soul II Soul. The cult movie of 1995 was *Trainspotting*, a double-edged tale of down-and-out Scottish junkies. The fashion editor of America's *Vibe* magazine is Derrick Procopé, once a window-dresser for London's Woodhouse chain.

Young Britons now clearly feel more "in the world"; part of a single scene which moves from Seattle to Spain, from Amsterdam to Manhattan's Amsterdam Avenue. Yet they are proud (and aware) of what it means to be British. In this respect, many are far ahead of their elders.

This book traces a few paths by which some Britons got there, mentions some antecedents, tells a few stories which happened as the '90s flowered. More importantly, it aims to listen - as separate kinds of talents tell their histories and detail their strategies. Whether they are making fashion or furniture, political statements or pop records, all have something in common: a particular brand of imagination. It is one which fuses style and music with pragmatism, hard work and attitude. It is a wonderful, very British quality; in the years to come, I hope it can flourish.

Cynthia Rose

2

1. Daniel Pemberton
In his studio
2. Cyber Collection
Design: Dane Goulding
Photo: Will Berlin
3. Book cover "Kate"
Design: Phil Bicker
Published by
Pavilion Books Ltd
Photo: Corinne Day

WITH ME, IT'S ALWAYS BEEN THE PEOPLE IN MY LIFE, MY FRIENDS, THAT I GAIN MY INSPIRATION FROM.
(→PAGE 32)

I LIKE SECONDHAND THINGS, SEEING THE POTENTIAL IN WHAT'S CHUCKED OUT.
(→PAGE 34)

3

CHAPTER ONE

1

Enter the '90s:

a neo future

Back at the start of 1993, no one ever thought the Velvet Underground or the Sex Pistols would re-form. No one thought punk-era stars such as Debbie Harry or Phil Daniels would ever resurface. Yet, that year, punk made a telling mini comeback - both as a style and an operational strategy. It went from the streets of Camden to the European catwalk. This strange revival held the seeds of another change - one that would teach young Britons do-it-yourself marketing and help some shape their singular creative skills into strategies.

That autumn, punk hijacked Europe's *haute couture* shows. Azzedine Alaïa sent models down the runway wearing shoes inscribed "Sid" and "Nancy" in *faux* graffiti. Versace chose to replicate the clinging, punctured lycra done fifteen years earlier by Camden's Swanky Modes. Jean-Paul Gaultier revived the white gauze T-shirt - as he had seen it worn by Johnny Rotten.

It was hardly fashion's first glance backwards; punk had never actually been allowed to die. The "do-it-yourself ethic" and proud techniques of recycling were perennial staples of the British style mags - one print genre to which punk helped give birth. Ten years on, however, in 1986, London was exploding with pirate stations, warehouse parties and indigenous black music. The obligatory punk memorial features ("Ten Years After") felt both stale and strange. And their vintage slogans - such as "DESTROY!" and "No Future" - when resurrected, sounded both dusty and quaint. Individual recollections appeared equally arcane, running as they did alongside pieces with titles such as "Age of the Microchip".

Still, great claims continued to appear. Long-time punk hagiographer Jon Savage wrote in *The Face*, "What is omitted from most accounts of punk rock is its humour, its poetry and expansiveness of vision. It's a mistake to regard punk as a local, music industry phenomenon... Regard it rather as an ambitious cultural movement that connected, as so few do, with the world outside, and like Dada and Surrealism, sought to turn it on its head. Or, even better, regard it as an attitude that can be captured at any time, in a laugh, a toss of the head and a refusal to accept anything less than total possibility." This vision of punk saw a coalition of British strengths: attitude, visual resource, wit as strategy and use of the street as theatre.

The punk fashions in that '86 *Face* were lurid and ugly. More importantly, they were out of step with their times. Savage was right: it was the spirit,

2

1

2

not the duds, which finally mattered. Besides, much of Britain's business structure was shifting. The once-illegal radio stations had altered broadcasting. Black stars from Soul II Soul and Massive Attack through Omar changed the content and style of British music. Even warehouse raves would engineer lasting change, moving UK leisure from the coterie arts back to mass entertainment.

As the '90s dawned, styles of recreation changed again. Britain's growing drug culture pushed all before it, changing the habits, the language and the health of leisure. Soundwise, techno music was engulfing acid, and young ravers paved the way for consumer Britpop. This would do more than bring back the guitar, moving hits away from live turntable decks and dancefloors. Britpop would produce a highly saleable export, a double cult of pop personalities and nostalgia. It brought back the late '60s, early '70s concept of celebrity, and it returned control to the record companies. It was at this very moment Europe seized on "couture punk". Was that significant or simply total accident?

Certainly, the style was no copy of its predecessor; *faux* punk used its signifiers in very different ways. British street style, as it demonstrated, was now European - both in its reach and its impact. More than this, it had gone completely global. The referencing of punk, of style-as-aggression, was now a synonym for youth, which could supersede cultures. It was "punk" all right, but it was punk as marketing.

This was a preview of the coming decade, when almost every style would become commodified - then sent forth via advertising and the Internet.

Yet the D-I-Y strains remained important. They would prove the key to young British business, allowing the inventive to live by what they loved.

First, however, *faux* punk began as a trend, snatched - like so many others - from the streets of London. At the very inception of the '90s, tartan, kilts and bondage gear surfaced once again. In Old Compton Street, this fashion was male and gay: boys with shaven heads pairing boots with "bondage kilts". On the dancefloor, in the clubs, the look turned more towards fetish; back were a punkish rubber and assorted kinky undies, albeit married to the new fads - tattoos and piercings.

Punk even made its way into another industry, that of "new-wave beauty", better known as make-up. Early '70s personalities, such as Jordan and Siouxsie Sioux, had used punk face and eye makeup as their tribal markings. They extended eyeliner out to their ears and painted on cheekbones, adding chains and pins.

Nineties designers like Martine Sitbon now mimicked that look, using models with punkette crops and ragged, dyed-bright locks. In part, it was a response to one magazine feature. Seven years after the critics hymned its anniversary, punk's whole dynamic was being re-adjusted. This was crystallised in the feature

3

4

Previous pages:

1. From i-D
The Outlook Issue
"Scared Stiff - sewing seeds on the crow road"
Stylist: Judy Blame
Photo: Donald Christie

2. Flyer: Torture Garden - Demask, '97

1. Flyer: Torture Garden - *MERIC*N*

2. Flyer: Torture Garden

3. The Face - Zip It Up
(no. 59 Aug '93)
Stylist: Judy Blame
Photo: Jean Baptiste Mondino

4. The Face - Destroy!
(no. 70 Feb '86)
Photo: Nick Knight

A POSE IS TO DO JUST WITH CLOTHES. AND, SURE, CLOTHES ARE IMPORTANT. BUT IT'S MORE THAN THAT, IT'S GOT TO DO WITH BRAINS.

(→PAGE 18)

THE STYLIST SHOULD BE INVISIBLE. BECAUSE IF IT LOOKS STYLED, YOU'RE NOT A GOOD STYLIST.

(→PAGE 33)

Both images from i-D
The Outlook Issue
"Scared Stiff - sewing seeds on the crow road"
Stylist: Judy Blame
Photo: Donald Christie

MY DESIGN JUST STARTS FROM SEEING A PIECE OF FABRIC. I GET MY IDEAS FROM FABRIC RATHER THAN SHAPES.

[→PAGE 35]

"Head Hunters" (*The Face*, August 1993) which was styled by inventive veteran Judy Blame. Here, Blame saw punk as minimal and conceptual. He used D-I-Y totems from the '70s craze - zippers, dog chains, paper clips and safety pins - to update and anchor all the looks which followed. These included hip-hop's baggy jeans, rare groove's platform shoes, and Soho body piercings.

Blame, née Chris Barnes, was a certified punk participant - but one who, unlike many, still moves with changing times. He enjoys an uncanny sense of the moment - one which ensures him work from a top-shelf client roster. It can range from Karl Lagerfeld to Kylie Minogue; Neneh Cherry to Euro-queen Björk; Jean Baptiste Mondino to Donald Christie.

In music and fashion, stylists like Blame comprise much of British exportability. They are the invisible, inexhaustible, image-makers who choose clothing, props and a look for models and pop stars. Stylists can make or break a musical act or a video and, from *haute couture* to sportswear, they help take a trend to the high street.

In the worlds of advertising, record sleeves and MTV, such shaping of pop style goes largely uncredited. Yet the stylist is a star's unsung therapist - a colleague who deals with fears from weight to fashion smarts and cleavage. Stylists strive to make each client feel like a million bucks, to imbue their image with a constant freshness - and to give their work a special, individual edge.

Blame ran away from his home at 17, to become "the classic starving artist". His fashion training came from the free spirits of punk, those whose work soon helped establish the UK style press. They included talents like the late Ray Petrie who, in the mid-'80s, founded Buffalo, a fashion-based collective which handled a range of projects. Buffalo did fashion features and styling for *The Face*, but they could also mix a record or design their own clothing. Blame says he was their enthusiastic graduate: "First the people, then the photos, then the clothes. That's what Ray Petrie taught me. Those are styling's priorities."

The "Head Hunters" spread returned Blame to these roots - and to what he sees as a British legacy. "It's a strong attitude but it's not a pose. A pose is to do just with clothes. And, sure, clothes are important. But it's more than that, it's got to do with brains."

"I think", he adds, "that's what people want from styling like mine. They want to know it's not just some fashion scam. They want to know that it's not elitist, that there are hundreds of others out there wearing that T-shirt. I mean, when I was growing up and I had my spooky orange hair, I wanted to see someone whose hair was inky-blue. It was like a wonderful dream, you know? Like, 'Look, there's *another* one!'"

Yet "Head Hunters" drew on more than communal longings; it was sensitive to a special '90s vibe. These punk revisions embraced a newer stance, one advanced by changes in fashion photography. Apparently both natural and casual, they were actually complex. They were sparked by the work of one young woman, Corinne Day.

Led by Day, Britons started photographing punk detritus, the "no future" they observed in teenage faces. Day discovered an unseasoned model, Kate Moss, whose downbeat aura captured her personal sense of the era. With Moss, as with others near her own age, she would pioneer a whole new view of glamour.

Day took Blame's persistent punkish ethos to a new place, keeping a sense of theatre but junking most of its props. Basically, she returned to the movement's bottom line: a searching re-evaluation of daily life - and a questioning of what it actually means to be British. Day found punk's prophecy realised in shapes and faces; her photographic subjects were seen in mundane haunts. Plus, they appeared as seemingly unvarnished. It was less "fashion" than something more compelling. And, certainly, it appeared to be something timely.

Just as a Blame shoot could distil order from chaos, Day showed Britain's youngsters in a world devoid of glamour. It looked as if they coped, or failed to cope, exactly like the young viewers who perused them.

Graphic designer Phil Bicker knows both Day and her work. He was for many years Art Director at *The Face*, then he went on to found a design firm, Village. Bicker has consulted on graphics for MTV Europe and, in 1995, he designed "Kate, a book about Ms. Moss". He is a long-time supporter of young British talent.

In 1990, it was Bicker who had the idea of choosing one girl as "the face" of *The Face*. Kate Moss as seen by Corinne Day intrigued him. He felt Moss was fresh - and almost anti-model ("Or, at least opposed to the whole of that industry"). Hence Day's now-famous ultra-natural photo spreads, pics of a giggling Kate running nude along the beach, squinting because of the sun, smiling with a wrinkled nose. It was the post-punk face of a raver's culture - UK suburbanites discovering drugs, freedom, Europe.

Moss was 15 then and Day was ten years older; the Moss face was only one in the Day portfolio.

But, rapidly, Moss moved into the commercial fold, becoming a symbol for Calvin Klein and Versace. Placed there, her looks lost much of their initial subversion. In 1993, with 'punk' back in a culture's lexicon, *Interview* magazine ran a profile of Corinne Day. It included her stylist Melanie Ward and Kate Moss - now referred to as Day's "superstar discovery". Moss was already moving towards a traditional glamour which, as Bicker notes, "she had certainly helped to change".

But the same world which embraced Moss would not take Day, as the pioneering photographer quickly discovered. Though it likes to play with tokens and images from the margins, fashion cannot afford to make them its whole reality. At the end of the day, its single task is selling - which became the lesson in the international rise of Moss. Says Bicker: "Even early on, it was something like that; because no one really nurtured what Corinne was embarked on. Partly, she was just that little bit too early. More to the point, her work really threatens people. With a Judy Blame spread, even if the underlying message is aggressive, you can still very clearly see the work is styled."

"With Corinne, lots of the images are awkward - which helps make them much, much less accessible.

1

1. The Face (no. 22 July '90) "The 3rd Summer of Love" Photo: Corinne Day
2. Tara - Blue Ketamine '95 Photo: Corinne Day

WE HAD REALLY WEIRD MODELS, GUYS WITH ONE LEG SHORTER THAN THE OTHER, OLD PEOPLE WITH FALSE TEETH. I LIKE ECCENTRIC PEOPLE, I LIKE INDIVIDUALS. (→PAGE 34)

2

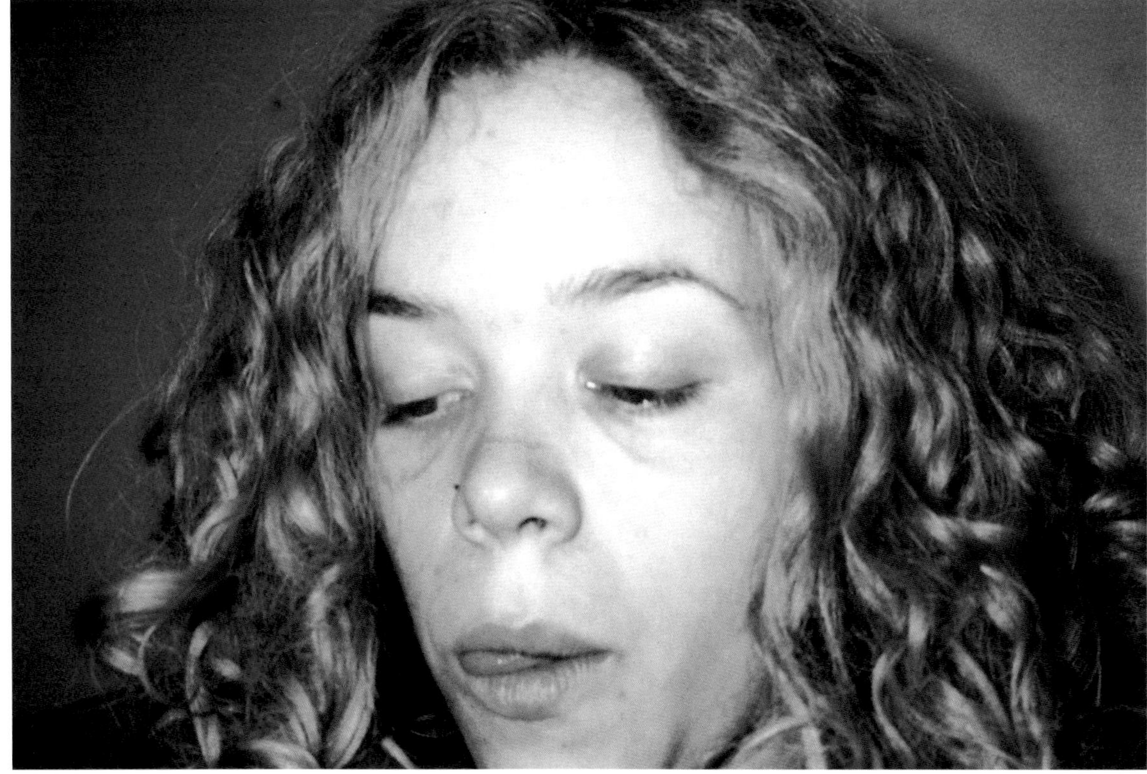

Tara sitting on the toilet '94
Photo: Corinne Day

She's manufacturing something, but it's quite direct. It doesn't really entail a whole lot of irony. People think, 'Hey, what's that guy doing; we do that at home!' But: do they really? How much of it is constructed?"

Probably more, reckons Phil Bicker, than what "looks constructed". ("That's what makes Corinne's work so hard to analyse.") "Take the pictures of Kate. People actually thought that was Kate. But it wasn't, it had all been styled. There was an agenda, whether it was conscious or not."

In 1996, punk celebrated two decades. The Sex Pistols, The Ramones and Iggy Pop played concerts. Blondie resurfaced, roughly, as Courtney Love - and, more sweetly, in a clutch of Britain's girl-led groups. Patti Smith, too, returned: with a tragedy and an album. With punk clearly now a controlled commodity, Corinne Day's work was hailed for its acumen. This recognition also followed on Kate Moss' transition, into a jet-setting superstar and celebrity. Day was given exhibitions in New York and Paris. And, in a valentine published by the *New Yorker* magazine, the critic Hilton Als lavishly hailed her startling vision. He claimed Day's work marked "the end" of a dictatorship: that of fashion editorial's rule over youth imagery.

Wrote Als, "Unlike the work of many of her predecessors, which relied on the usual contraptions of fashion photography ("genius" makeup and hair; improbable girls and improbable situations), Day's pictures - of models clothed in the low-budget, mismatched outfits of youth - were about her subjects' unabashed narcissism, and how it sheathed them in the glow or the gloom of self-love. Day's world unfolds in broad expanses of grimy nature, or in dingy council flats that one associates with post-Thatcherite Britain..."

This was the very landscape wherein '70s punk was born. Yet, essentially, punk remained an outsider art, one of fashion and design's faddish novelties. Day's work, like that made by some of her subjects, both entered into and affected the marketplace. So did the imagery of those who caught a similar vibe: notably, Kurt Cobain's world-beating group Nirvana. Most remarkable was their effect on advertising. (Much of the Als piece carried in the *New Yorker* focused on how adverts have now usurped the editor's power - and how those ads were changed by Corinne Day's images.)

Certainly, Corinne Day defrocked punk's English legacy. Her work captures social decline while making it viewable. Her pictures may seem extreme, filled with ominous tones. But they do not show a youth fed its image by the media. They are about young Britons in the '90s, real individuals, and the beauty that Day sees in them.

The whole equation, as Phil Bicker notes, is large. "Her early work is a true reflection of that time. But Corinne's photography is no cartoon; it's actually dangerous. And the fashion world most certainly saw it that way. In 1997, things are just a little bit different. With people like Lee McQueen and Galliano working, maybe Corinne can once again return to working in fashion. Maybe she can once again make her statements in that arena."

Whether she does or not, Day helped rejuvenate the "style mags". Britain's young leisure press is a complex animal, given to making pronouncements in every paragraph. But its scrappy attitude is not an accident; its task, month by month, is to provide young Britain with a sense of self. Mostly, this has to be accomplished in opposition - for the pages are heavy with American imports. Still, because it was punk which initially shaped these magazines, they retain a mocking and offhand arrogance.

Added to which publications like *i-D* and *The Face* are pressure cookers: highly competitive slots which pay very poorly. While they push an aspirational vision to the readers, leisure mags don't bring it within the reach of their contributors. To use their showcase, one has to make one's living elsewhere.

When Day's photo shoots appeared in the style mags, she showed youngsters dealing with reality - not with those toys and dreams the magazines usually retailed. She inspired a generation to start again: kids who felt she had brought them real glimpses of themselves. Says Jefferson Hack, who at 19 started *Dazed & Confused*, "Our first office was right below Corinne's flat, and I used to go up there almost every week. We'd have a smoke, and she'd play me tapes. And we'd spend hours and hours talking about magazines - all about what was what and what was wrong with 'em."

"I really did enjoy those conversations, because they reinforced my sense of mission. She made me feel that there was potential for change. And some room for a younger kind of reality."

By 1993, Hack and his age group were busy carving out their own arena. It turned out to be distinguished by a taste for fusion. The rave generation, it seems, wants an access to everything. They want dancefloor style with its multiple black traditions; they want punk's '70s ironies and attitude - plus they want the usually white world of pop.

Their easy embrace of such disparate legacies was soon personified in a single figure: Iceland's Björk, with her smash solo CD "Debut" and her watershed video, "Violently Happy". Formerly an

1 

2 

1. Björk, May '95 One Little Indian publicity shot
2. Flyer: Dazed & Confused Launch of Issue 1

THE REGGAE, HIP-HOP, MULTI-RACIAL MOMENT. THIS WAS NOT JUST IN MUSIC AND STYLE, BUT IN LIFE. IT WAS THE BEGINNING OF A MASSIVE CHANGE, OF THE MOVE TOWARDS TRULY GLOBAL IDENTITY. (→PAGE 33) indie cult-queen with the Sugar Cubes, the European ex-pat became a prophetic icon. "Debut" was produced by Nellee Hooper, a veteran of Bristol's Wild Bunch and the Soul II Soul posse. With Björk, he created a new brand of indie-pop: kind of a '90s "world music" with a twist. Its full aesthetic required the help of an Asian Briton (Talvin Singh, later a star DJ, player and producer), producer Howie B (one of "Debut"s engineers) and two image veterans: Judy Blame and Jean Baptiste Mondino.

Blame's "Head Hunters" spread was done the year he styled "Debut". It recycled all of punk's signature totems, but it added important touches of raggamuffin. Here, ragga style meant Gaultier trousers and braces - just as, for Björk, punk turned into a mohair sweater. Both Blame vehicles used theatrical rhinestone tears.

"At the time", says Judy Blame, "I was against all that hippie business, all those rave flares and flowers everyone else was into." During the 1993 UK Fashion Awards, establishment punk Vivienne Westwood cornered Blame about "Head Hunters". It was the only *punque nouveau*, she told him, which she felt offered anything.

Blame says he knows why each young Briton's legacy - conscious or unconscious - continues to involve punk. "The real thing, the '70s moment, didn't involve that many people. But the *ideas* involved in it were very big. They hit a broad spectrum - and they just keep on moving."

What's in Judy's own "blood", he says, is basic and positive. Centrally, there's the idea that you 'do it yourself' - maybe with little money, but with a family of friends. Blame: "I've spent lots of time in New York and Tokyo. But I never went to college, I never studied. I came at my work with ideas but not necessarily with a brilliant method. Meeting special people was my whole education." This kind of bond remains a British resource. The sound system, the young magazine staff, the graffiti crew - all become a similar kind of surrogate family.

But Blame sees '90s London as chaotic and changing. "It's a difficult time; some people are going under. At the moment punk appeared, everyone did what they wanted. A young black movement surfaced; kids started really mixing. Twenty-one years later, it's changeover time again. Once again, young people want that collective feeling."

It's a British legacy, he says, which unites their spirits, one that still fuses music and graphics, dress and attitude. In the looming world of high-tech interactivity, this can only serve as an asset. "One thing which keeps our fashion scene so high-focus is that here music and clothes and daily life are inseparable. That's why a designer with no financial backup will still receive real commercial attention. Even if it comes off a hoarding or a pop star's back."

Blame remains a happy friend to controversy. He greeted Corinne Day and her followers with enthusiasm. In 1997, he works easily with new designers - and young photographers such as Donald Christie. "All the clinging to nostalgia, all the retro fashion, seems so hollow whenever it's set against what's happening. For me, the present always has a lively quality. I want the sense of what's alive, what's happening now. Whether it's a visual, a beat or a piece of slang. To me, they're all parts of the same thing. People call it image, but it's much more far-ranging."

Corinne Day's *oeuvre* fuelled a huge shift in fashion, both as editorial and advertisement. It was also the source of intense debate: over "objectification", anorexia, "victimisation" - even what some have called "flirtations with death". But respect for her work now flourishes round the world and, like Judy Blame, she changed fashion's self-perception. Still, after Day, many spreads caricatured her vision. Her "bruised eyes" launched vast pools of purple make-up; her hint of the confessional led to melodramatic set-ups, with models weeping, sprawling and cringing.

It is a virtual circus of imitators, whose work is often crass, extreme and amazingly charmless. As Phil Bicker says, theirs is "a cartoon version". But it did place a face on the early '90s: one which thumbed its nose at conventional portraits.

And, subliminally, a corner was turned. The new punk had become a '90s property, owned by a young culture with its own views of the past. They created global punk personalities - from Nirvana to Björk to Marilyn Manson. Through their icons' highly-publicised problems and actions, that young world culture also found shared concerns. Kurt Cobain, in particular, fuelled a singular stardom: one more accessible in Internet newsgroups than on video; one which lives on after his death in debates, allusions and anecdotes. Björk and Courtney Love (and, later, Patti Smith) also managed to create "looks" which bridged cultures - while remaining freighted with genuine history and feeling.

Young Britons like Jefferson Hack have helped live all these changes. At the time he talked magazines with Corinne Day, Hack was orchestrating *Dazed & Confused*. Both the precedent of her work and the Britain around it, he says, helped shape what he and

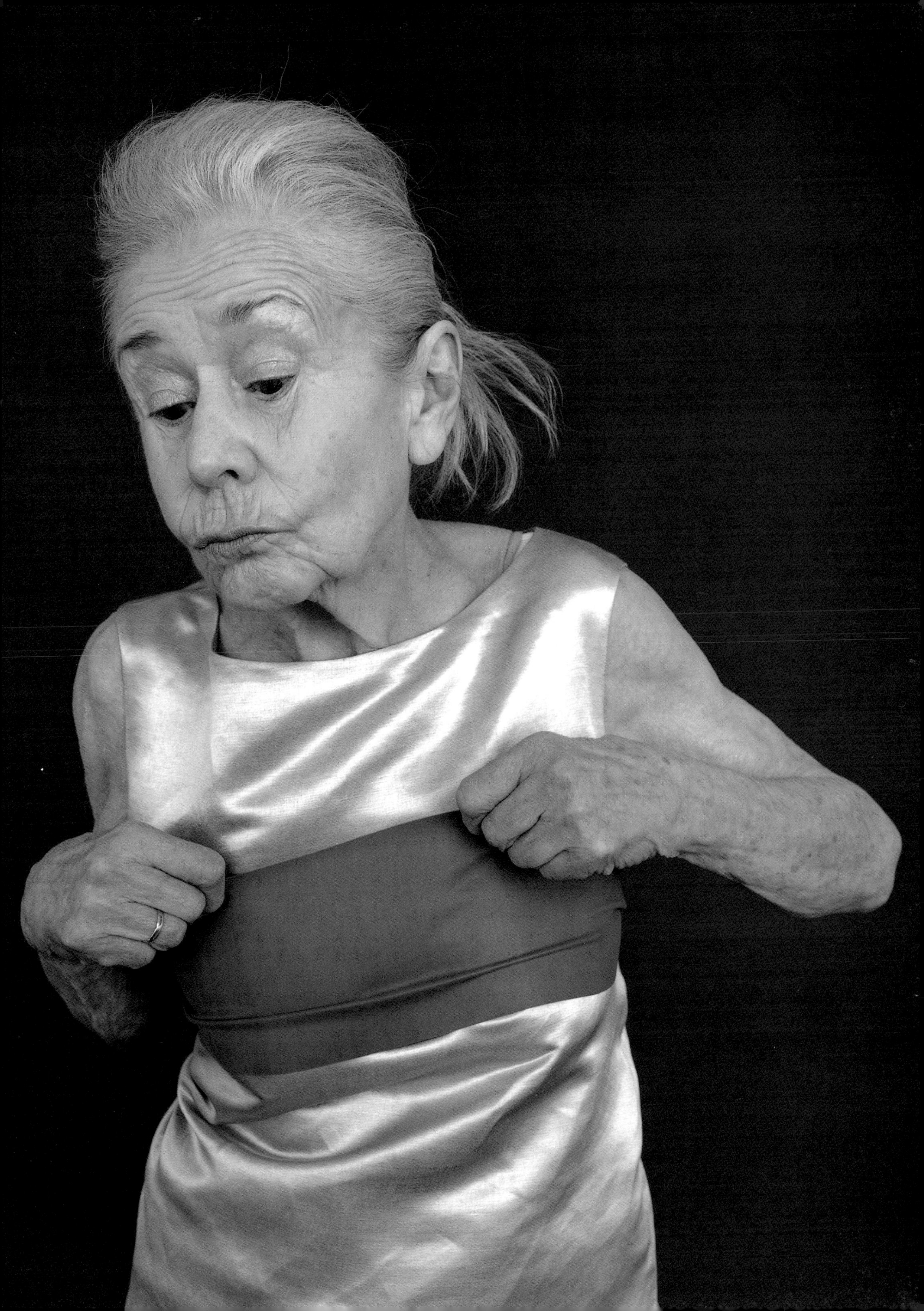

his friends now do. "For our tenth issue, we had a cover called 'Weep' and we carried a fashion spread inside which matched it. Rankin Waddell shot them and they were very conceptual. There was no pretence of realism in either one; it was very clear that all the models were acting. Neither was there any kind of real emotion present. It was just like *Cosmopolitan* shooting a pout, making it 'sexy', making it phony, and airbrushing it. We just went to the opposite end of the spectrum."

"Corinne's work", he adds quickly, "isn't at all like that. It's very organic. It's much, much more real. But even in that difference there's a common factor. Both of us try to shove 'fashion' in your face - to make you view the whole thing very differently."

What does such a punk mutation mean? Is it another fashion moment or a workable strategy? Is punk only old pins in changing garments? Or has it learnt from its own abortive past - has it changed to declare a new, British identity?

Mainstream critics disavow the possibility. For many who rule the media, punditry on youth is a job. Some once started out as putative rebels, only to find themselves firmly establishment pundits. London fashion guru Iain R. Webb is one such talent. He began at the style-mag *Blitz* but then graduated to jazzing up the staid *Evening Standard*. The same month as Blame's "Head Hunters" appeared, Webb wrote in *The Times*: "Today the image [of punk] is more refined. The essence of the punk ethos may now simply mean a flash of fluorescent colour in a scissored haircut or makeup which is little more than a gash of bruised purple lipstick or blackened eyes... [Yet] even after the experience of punk the first time round (and all that has followed), it is still not what we are used to, or what we accept as beautiful."

Webb's view of Day's world, and of Hack's, was generic. Punk meant shrink-wrapped rebellion and iconic imagery - not "what we are used to", maybe, but hardly earthshaking. The new '90s point of view, according to Webb, echoed "the ripped edges it sees in society", and "its potent message shows the way forward". Young women were rejecting conventional glamour - but only to give themselves "the power to be whatever they want".

Webb was discussing a real street phenomenon. Yet the looks which ran alongside his comments were very controlled. They were not the new young choices Day and Blame reflected, but the choices of stylists from a mainstream press. The media had commodified a change which frightened it - and it would keep on doing so throughout the '90s. In 1995, after Nirvana had shaken an industry, mainstream fashion responded with grunge makeup. With lines entitled "Urban Decay" and, later, "Hard Candy", it took the "ugly punk" look to retail counters.

This encapsulates a central '90s dilemma - how to have both sincerity and attainment? With the worlds of imagery global and electronic, questions of intent and control become dominant. What does it mean to "communicate around the world"? Is that necessarily hollow - or can it be meaningful? What is the human, the individual, toll, when one reconciles underground with overground?

A new generation experienced such questions writ large through the life of the icons around it. There was Kurt Cobain's precipitous suicide, Richey Edwards' disappearance from the Manic Street Preachers. There are conundrums such as Eric Cantona (French philosopher or ex English footballer? International pitchman or nationalistic avenger?). Meteoric careers like Alexander McQueen's - gay street designer made Head at the House of Givenchy - took off at the same moment as did Tony Blair's.

1

Previous page:
Margo Pillon, wearing Isaac Mizrahi
Photographed for Dazed & Confused by Rankin Waddell

1. Flyer: Dazed & Confused

Facing page:
La Philosophie de Cantona
Edited by Michael Robinson
Illustration and design:
Joe Magee
Published by
Ringpull Press Ltd, '95

Next page:
Trainspotting by Irvine Welsh
Published by Minerva, '95

la philosophie de

CANTONA

United

EDITED BY MICHAEL ROBINSON

In a '90s spurred by sampling and mixing and Ecstasy, punk's real UK legacy has grown complex. The issues mid-'70s music and fashion always meant to address - rage, class, power, hypocrisy - have become central to a different generation. And their cities have become changed places; one where even tourists see the evidence of "No Future".

It can be read in the genuinely bruised faces - the visages of the elderly and the homeless. It can be felt in the thickening air pollution, sensed in the booming rush for escapist drugs. Once unthinkable, guns are sometimes visible. As the '90s began, disaffected youth even had a symbol sport, the form of car theft known as "ram-raiding". Briefly, ram-raiding married larceny and joyriding. Teens nicked cars, then used them to break and enter - driving through a shopfront to get at the goodies it advertised.

Like many such "outrages", ram-raiding was by and large conceptual. Its real effects were headlines, stories and legends; whether or not it actually happened (and where) became irrelevant. Most would-be ram-raiders did well to grab a car. But the sport emerged as an early symbol of the decade, creating one bad film (*Shopping*) and a notable resonance. Why? Because it married breakdown to revenge.

The romance of ram-raiding resurrected punk's old landscape: the soulless tower block, housing estate and shopping precinct. Later, the book and film of *Trainspotting* carried this further, as did the world-wide sales of the "Prime Suspect" series. When exported, even decay could seem exotic.

This landscape meant little to Versace or Helmut Lang - two of the first whose '90s clothes were hailed in Britain as punk. (Versace's evening dresses with "safety pins" did launch one career - that of Elizabeth Hurley. Fittingly, Hurley shot to fame as a cosmetics spokesmodel, known for what tabloid papers soon dubbed *that dress* and, later, for boyfriend Hugh Grant's indiscretions.)

Britons who helped engineer these changes sniffed at labels. To most, any mention of punk was passé. Journalist Catherine Wilson, just out of art college, covered fashion's '93 shows for the *Guardian*. She called the European punk "calculated" and "plastic". Said Wilson, "Since '91, fashion's made massive changes. People now don't care if clothes are creased or rumpled. So this fashion isn't anything like real punk anger. It's a planned progression from the inside-out thing - which, in itself, is a movement forward from grunge."

Wilson did, however, connect these shows with Britain's climate. In young designers like "Lee" McQueen - then 24 and presenting his first non-college show - she (and other critics) saw true punk allusions. Says Wilson, "His clothes were wet; there was body-painting. There were pony-tails done up like Mohicans. But McQueen's is a British vocabulary. He's responding to the changes in this country."

As with olde punke, that change was "from the street". Catherine Wilson: "That's still where it starts. Three of the best designers I know sell off market stalls. One does satin clothes with the seams exposed. But I wouldn't call it 'punk'; that term's irrelevant. It could just as easily be 'travellers' or 'deconstructionist'."

Whatever the title of choice, one thing was clear early on. To punk's English canon, '90s work would add two things. One was an embryonically global connection - a sense, as Judy Blame said, that kindred souls were "out there" somewhere. Only, this time, *out there* truly meant anywhere. The world had suddenly opened - from Europe to Africa to Manhattan, via cyberspace.

The second addition was one already defined by the late '80s: the realisation of Britain's own black aesthetic. Or, as Catherine Wilson put it then, "There's another way to see this whole punk revival. There's another side to it, both here and abroad. Even with the European couture, those rips and roughness - plus the different shapes - quite clearly come from raggamuffin. It's a fact."

For many years, Phil Bicker art directed *The Face*, before founding Village, his own design studio. At *The Face*, he worked with photographer Corinne Day. Eventually, through her discovery of Kate Moss, her unique commercial campaigns and her pictures in magazines, Day revolutionised photography in the '90s. Bicker is now Art Director of *Hommes Vogue International*. Day continues to advance photography, and is now starting to work with film. Here, the pair discuss their past and present - and talk about the price of preserving a personal vision.

Phil: When you started doing pictures, what was it like?

Corinne: The first photographs I took were of my boyfriend and friends. When I started working with you for *The Face* magazine, I didn't know the people I was going to photograph. I also didn't know many people in London cause I had been living abroad. It was very voyeuristic photographing people I didn't know. I didn't like that feeling. When I met Kate (Moss), we became friends. The photographs I took of her were on a personal level, the pictures were about us.

Phil: But magazines like *Vogue* live in a different world. Even *The Face* and *i-D*, they don't seem to understand fashion as personal experiment.

Corinne: *The Face* has changed a lot since you and I worked there. We had a lot more freedom. The art directors at *The Face* and *i-D* now tell the photographers what they want and how they want it. There's no freedom of expression in the magazines. Now there are the same advertisers in *The Face* magazine as there are in *Vogue*. The editorial pages are manipulated to please the advertisers. It's more about business. When I moved to London in 1991, I was unemployed and on the dole. Kate and I loved clothes but I couldn't afford designer labels. We subverted our own personal style - second hand clothes - on the pages of *The Face* magazine. Grunge became mainstream fashion and everyone could afford it. Grunge was not a style that could be labelled with a price tag.

Phil Bicker talks to Corinne Day:

on pictures that matter

Phil: There are two kinds of motivations for our kind of work. There can be money and there can be fame. But the other kind of motivation is more difficult. For me, I want to help people make good pictures, give them a platform to work from, provide a showcase. With you, it's much harder. Because people don't want to give you full control. They're happy just to say, "Corinne Day's working for us". They don't actually want you to do what you really do.

Corinne: The photographs I like to take are of actual experiences between friends. Experiencing life itself is more exciting to me than the taking of photographs. Commercial photography is all about setting up, forcing emotion and faking it. The times I have been asked to take these kind of pictures is usually for money. I have tried to subvert ideas in photographs through the context they're seen in, e.g. when working for *Vogue*, I took pictures of Kate in her home where she lived wearing underwear. The underwear was cheap and tacky. This was a style that had not been seen in *Vogue* before. I thought this was funny. Commercial photography does not change - it tends to be romantic and glossy, the people always look so beautiful. The repetitiveness of seeing images like this has made me want to break away.

Phil: You're a woman in a field that's male-dominated. You know if a male photographer is difficult, people just say, "oh, he's charismatic". But if a woman starts giving her opinions, people don't expect it. They don't like it; it threatens them.

Corinne: My photographs reflect the world around me. My influences come from outside the fashion industry. I have tried to subvert reality on to the pages of fantasy. People feel threatened because of their lack of freedom and their inability to change. Most fashion photographers are men and most stylists are women. My ideas of style often do not agree with those of a fashion stylist.

Phil: I remember when I first met you, seeing your pictures of Kate [Moss]. Those images really challenged the whole fashion industry: its view of clothes, of how a model should look - even of makeup. At that time, everything was very glamorous, very glossy, very superficial. You went straight against that.

Corinne: I became very satirical. I had not long stopped modelling myself. I always felt that my model friends looked more interesting just being themselves than they did in the magazines. I was into the hippy revival in the late eighties and early nineties. A lot of that had to do with the music at the time. Some of the clothes Kate wore were my own. I never wore makeup and neither did Kate. I wanted to capture her presence naturally. I wanted to take photographs in a documentary way, showing the highs as well as the lows.

Phil: When you first met Kate, what did you think?

Corinne: When I first met Kate, I thought she was short and skinny like me. She was gawky with long hair a bit like me. I knew how hard photographers strived for that perfect picture and that flawless studio lighting. I felt if I took a documentary snap shot image, the photo would be more spontaneous, more about Kate and not the photographer. I was curious to know if photography could make someone famous.

Phil: You shot Kate in a very, very natural way.

Corinne: Kate was a fifteen year old girl from an estate in Croydon. I wanted to blur the eyes of what is considered beautiful and ugly. But the main thing I wanted to capture was Kate's presence, something felt and not always seen.

Phil: Those last things you did with Kate for British *Vogue*, they upset a lot of people. They led to a lot of unfair criticism. Do you think it was the fact that they appeared in *Vogue*, in that kind of bastion of glamour?

Corinne: Kate and I were both past the age of consent. I was commissioned by Alexandra Shulman, *Vogue*'s editor, to photograph Kate for eight pages of fashion. I photographed Kate where she was living at the time. I bought some cheap underwear from Anne Summers Sex Shops and some American tan tights. I wanted the photographs to be everything *Vogue* was not - cheap and tacky. I've often been accused of glorifying some social problems. This misinterpretation comes when my work is seen next to an air-brushed and manipulated, glossy fashion image. Magazines seemed to only show a sterile version of life. The thing about fashion magazines is that there are so many of them and they all look the same and are so unwilling to change.

Phil: But it was the last time you worked for *Vogue*.

Corinne: I found working for *Vogue* and most women's magazines very boring. When I first started working for *Vogue* I could choose who I wanted to photograph. Obviously, I chose to photograph friends but it was uncomfortable having to ask them to wear the clothes the magazine supplied because they weren't very nice.

Phil: Were you surprised those images became notorious?

Corinne: I was surprised that a fashion magazine would be taken so seriously.

Phil: That brings up something else. With the first big story on Kate, the "Summer of Love" *Face* cover story, a lot of people simply thought that "was" Kate. They didn't think that she had been styled in any way. Yet Melanie Ward was working as your stylist.

Corinne: Melanie and I worked very closely together on styling Kate. The clothes were very much what we were wearing at the time. Well, maybe not the feather head dress...

Phil: For Kate, was this a kind of a discovery process? Like you were offering her something she could take or leave?

Corinne: Kate wanted to be a model. Her model agency didn't like the pictures I took of her. They tried to persuade me to photograph Kate in a more classical way. There wasn't much interest in Kate from other photographers at the time. Over the years Kate and I became good friends. She didn't really pay much attention to her agency, until she started earning money. She is beautiful. I hope I helped give her the confidence to recognize it.

Phil: What you two did together wasn't easy. Spending three years of your life photographing someone. Certainly, that's not taking an easy option.

Corinne: It wasn't easy trying to get a magazine to publish my photographs when they were the complete opposite of what a fashion photograph was seen to be at the time.

Phil: You also used your friends as stylists.

Corinne: I've known Tara about six years. I met her with George when they were sixteen at Tooting Beck Lido in Streatham with Sarah Murray. We thought George was really cute. Sarah asked if I could take a picture of him. I've taken loads of pictures of George since then. Tara was George's girlfriend. I loved the way she dressed. She was on the dole and when Melanie Ward went to America, I asked Tara if she was interested in using her clothes to style some pictures. We've worked together ever since. She's my closest friend.

Phil: How do you manage to survive, doing what you like?

Corinne: I'm the kind of person that needs my freedom. I like music and I work with musicians. I have directed some videos and I get by. I am not motivated by money or fame.

Phil: But the work hasn't necessarily come from where you'd expect. Not from the big fashion campaigns or whatever.

Corinne: I have pissed a few people off in the fashion world, which isn't hard to do. And you know how they love to gossip.

Phil: For me, it's been frustrating on your behalf. Because you did all the things you needed to do to reach the top. I don't think there's any doubt people thought your work was amazing. Yet certain media, and certain magazines, used their power to make sure you were sidelined.

Corinne: I like working for magazines. It's a great medium to subvert ideas through. But unless I'm given the freedom to do this, there's not much point. Fashion magazines and advertising try to mimic real emotion. But in my opinion when it's contrived it looks fake, same as the Spice Girls. I think that simulated emotions have become a marketing tool to sell products.

Phil: Still, if you get beaten down by that, you don't lose anything. Not as long as you have your own values.

Corinne: My photographs are not an effort to document in any real sense, but a collision of experiences with friends. I like to be spontaneous, curiosity motivates me. I think if you know the outcome, then, what's the point. I feel creativity can be very powerful because you can inspire people you don't even know.

Phil: Or, if you always think, "Where is this going to get me?", your work is never gonna go anywhere. Usually, the best stuff isn't even the stuff you're paid for.

Corinne: If I get paid for doing what I like, that's great. If I get paid for doing something I don't like that's great as well. I took this picture recently of a friend of mine called Emma. We'd both been drinking a lot of red wine and I saw it left stains in the cracks of her lips. I thought she looked beautiful. I laughed to myself, I saw this as a makeup tip that I've never seen in any magazine. Things just come along by accident.

With the rise of Corinne Day and Alexander McQueen, the stylist's work has been brought out of the shadows. Day's compatriot Melanie Ward, McQueen's aide-de-couture Katy England, each has received kudos in their own right. But, when it comes to stylists who have stayed the course, Judy Blame is the top of Britain's list.

In the '90s, stylists move between clients and industries: working on adverts, films, pop videos and couture shows. More and more, the designers are looking to them. It's no news to Blame, whose vision has often sparked the spirit of visual changes. Blame has worked for stars such as Boy George, Lisa Stansfield, Neneh Cherry, Massive Attack; worked with couture in both Paris and London. But he has also kept styling for 'street' magazines, like *i-D* and *Time Out*. He talks about what he does, who influenced him, how he sees styling and how he survives.

How did you start your career?

The first thing I really did was make jewellery. Just after the era of the Blitz kids and all those clubs, when Boy George was starting his career, all these young designers were starting out in Kensington Market. A lot of New York fashion PRs took their stuff over to America, which kind of made people sit up here in London. They came back with loads of orders: I had $30,000-worth. But - when we approached a bank for backing, it wasn't quite grown up enough for them. Still, we kept it going through shows in Tokyo and New York. A lot of my stuff has always been one-off and handmade. Because I set up direct relationships with the stores, and I never tried to expand on it, I made enough that way to pay the rent.

So, from the very beginning, you were connected abroad?

I spent quite a lot of time abroad, in New York, France, Japan. Meeting Ray Petrie [the late fashion editor] and Marc Lebon [the photographer] really was my education. With Ray, of course, I didn't need a college. Also I was introduced to Chris Nemeth [the UK designer who now lives in Japan]. He was very into re-using things, re-using fabrics. Marc literally saw him from a taxi. He made the cab stop just to find out who made such stunning clothes. Marc was really a focus, because he worked at *i-D*. He was established there and he encouraged me to do some editorial.

Blame it on Judy:

stylist extraordinaire

Did you like working as a stylist more than making fashion?

What I enjoy about styling is having access to other people's clothes and re-inventing them the way I want to. Most stylists have a successful idea and just repeat and repeat it. My challenge is to make each project completely different - and not just for the sake of money. I really try to maintain my enthusiasm, my sense of humour, while I'm doing it. I'm a fan of gimmicks, but gimmicks in clothing, not emotion. With me, it's always been the people in my life, my friends, that I gain my inspiration from.

You're known as the guru of UK street fashion.

England and London, that's my heart. I've certainly tried both America and Japan, but when I tried to leave here, it was too much like working in a vacuum. People aren't so frightened of failure here. In the US, if you fail once, they dump you. Something like "street fashion" is so misrepresented. Even when, financially, British fashion has rocky times our creativity is a separate thing. You just have to walk down Oxford Street to see it: kids with the most brilliant kind of personal style. And maybe they were inspired by my *Time Out* cover, or a page in *i-D* or a video that I helped make. But that's the whole idea. That's the educational facet of my work. If anything, that's what I do: educate. Let young people know they can go out and express themselves. Even if it's just down to a haircut with your carvings in it.

Is there a difference in attitude with the people you now work among and the people you started with?

Yeah, because when I started it was just post-punk. There was a kind of aggressive, each person-makes-their-statement feeling. It's moved on towards something more collective. We managed to take it into the commercial arena, even though a lot of the ideas themselves started out as a flyer, a T-shirt, a piece of music. That's one thing about me, my ideas come from everywhere. One will be a video, one will be an LP sleeve. So it's hard to quantify on an invoice. But that is the way creativity works. To me, it doesn't matter if a budget is ten quid or ten thousand. That's not what it's about.

Was your work with Neneh Cherry a turning-point?

In a way, yes. Because Cameron [photographer Cameron McVey, Neneh's partner and manager] and Neneh came to me before anyone even thought of a record. They said, "We're gonna go to the company with the whole idea and get creative control", which is what we did. But the agreement we finally got said, "OK, but if things even start to fail, then our people will come in and take over."

They certainly didn't fail.

Well, there were lots of reasons. With Neneh, I had a really brilliant canvas. But I also need that constant feedback, that family thing. I mean, Neneh became a pop star, which is the last thing I want to be. But I did like being involved in it all. And it's a kind of trust, it really is about teamwork. Plus, that happened at a particular moment, the reggae, hip-hop, multi-racial moment. This was not just in music and style, but in life. It was the beginning of a massive change, of the move towards truly global identity. And, of course, it was the solution. British pop and fashion were ahead of politics! That came home to me when Neneh went to America. At the time, all they saw was a black Madonna, a black Paula Abdul - just a woman with upfront imagery. We came away from that jaunt disillusioned.

You've done a lot to publicise black British aesthetics.

I'm a massive cheerleader of black style. Because I really believe the West has raped Africa enough times to know how many ideas have come from it. So, as far as I'm concerned, it's payback time. There's something in that struggle I really rate, so I feel proud when black artists ask me to work with them. A lot of them, too, who are black and are British, they're coming from my culture, my own history. In that sense, everyone has this mixed-blood mentality. Now, black style has taken over America. It's the black kids who are changing it. A black aesthetic pushes our frontiers, too. Often, it brings us a new sense of purpose, community.

You really move, not just from circle to circle, but between ideas. No one has ever captured each moment like you do. How do you manage to keep up?

Well, it's not all hair and makeup, you know what I mean? Which a lot of styling is, just a lot of hair and makeup and a fake reality. To me, it's much more about communication. That's the whole club thing I came out of. It's not about building up a fake aesthetic, something everybody has to aspire to. It's dealing with what's actually out there happening. And promoting that, rather than using fake imagery. When I do it, I hope people rip me off. I hope they copy me, that's what I want - to encourage some 13-year-old in Wolverhampton.

Luckily, I've got a varied career. Sometimes it might get a bit haphazard. But I do at least have the opportunities. I can do a magazine page or a video or a bit of clothing for Japan. Or, you know, I'll style for the catwalk. I think that's what always kept me going. I mean, I'm in quite a privileged position, people need to understand I'm aware of that. But it's not at all unobtainable - and I don't want anyone to think so.

In another era, fashion had its old-boy network. You once dubbed yours the "new homie network". How does it work, in terms of doing business?

Well, it's not done in an office and it's not done with blue suits on. And it's not that whole investment mentality - getting to know someone so they will help you out. A lot of it comes out of social situations. It comes out of dancefloors, clubs and social events. You don't actually do your business in nightclubs but if I went out to some place and I saw oh, Björk or...oh, anyone, an artist or a photographer or another stylist, I could find the next day I'd be working on something. Again, this goes back to Ray Petrie. He built a whole image and got attitude into business. Which is really, in the end, important. Because you need strong attitude.

What is the nuts-and-bolts reality of professional styling? What are your professional criteria?

Well, number one, I think the stylist should be invisible. Because if it looks styled, you're not a good stylist. Two, I think a stylist has to grab the moment and understand the moment - both at once. Know who to bring in, who not to bring in. That is really the important thing. It's not just the clothes that make the stylist, it's the moment and the action: making people work together. The whole white, mainstream Western view opposes it. But they're wrong about that. You can't separate fashion from ideals.

From coats and dresses made from decaying material, to those spreads he does for the slick magazine *Skin Two*, Richard Royle personifies design and styling as outsider arts. He prefers the one-off to the collection - and prefers recycling to beginning from scratch. Here, he traces his artistic odyssey.

How did you start in fashion?

I could sew by the time I could write. I used to sew things for my mum when I was five. It's quite natural for me, and I think it's a very underrated form of expression. I did go to Goldsmiths; I did fine art textiles and screenprinting. When I left college, I did exhibitions of quilts. That was all about gay sexuality, and dress codes, and lonely hearts columns - all mixed up into these big hangings. Then I started working for Leigh Bowery, who invited me to do some clothes for a show. I put together a collection of shirts based on the AIDS scare coming out in Britain: newspaper headlines, men kissing, Rock Hudson. We had really weird models, guys with one leg shorter than the other, old people with false teeth. I like eccentric people, I like individuals.

I was quite surprised, however, that clothing could still shock. The reaction to that first show was horror. I got thrown out of Marks & Spencers for wearing one of my shirts, not to mention several clubs and pubs. Even gay pubs! I mean, I'm gay, I went in wearing this shirt, and they said, "You can't come in." It was very strange, the strength of the reactions, when it was nothing which hadn't been in the papers.

Is it similar now with your *Skin Two* styling?

No, I don't think that sort of stuff is underground any more. I mean, in '95, Kit Kat used it for adverts! I do like the materials and that you can be a lot more theatrical. I've done a bit of theatre as well, and my *Skin Two* styling is sort of in that vein. But the clothes themselves, it's become a fashion crossover. You see some guy in a camouflage outfit and it's blue and pink camouflage - it just looks like a clown. It doesn't look remotely erotic or sexual. Because it's in a club, too, it's vaguely in public. If it was seriously sexual, it would be behind closed doors. That's a very English attitude, but I'm very English.

Inside-Out:

Richard Royle on styling

What came after your début shows?

Well, I styled the first show and did the photo shoots. Then I got involved with an Oxfam project. I was working as a chef in a restaurant. A friend, Jeanette Swift, had this idea of setting up a group called Reactivart, which was, in the beginning, five people who made things out of junk - sculpture, painting and fashion - and set up shops. We had our first show in the restaurant and it was on MTV Europe and got loads of press. So, over 18 months, the group grew until there were about 150 people. It was the first time the environmental thing had been treated that way. Then, the big-name fashion designers started doing environmental ranges. But we had kick-started all that off.

When we first started the Oxfam shop I got a bag full of junk, sat down and thought, "What can we do with this?" That's where my first accessories came from: jewellery, embroidery, beading. It just happened because the things were available. I thought, "I'll make a bra, and sew on badges and things. I've got a dummy to work on and an old bra, so I'll do that." It transformed it into something quite odd. It's not especially practical, but sometimes things that aren't practical work.

What did you do next?

Some clothes I called No Logo. But I was also doing pop videos, selling to people like S-Express. It was mostly word of mouth, rather than in a shop. I have also done a couple of rooms in people's houses. The thought of going into production fulltime, it was always like - not for me; I can't cope with it. I'm much happier doing one-off things for specific ideas, which is why, now, I do more things with advertising or with the Boy shop in Soho.

Recycled materials are one of your trademarks.

I always work with found stuff. I like secondhand things, seeing the potential in what's chucked out. Like the stuff I've done with Davies & Davies' military underwear: that was something I just found in government surplus. I like the detailing on it, the fabric is old and the stitching's old. I like things that have those marks. I made one jacket out of Masonic banners from the 1860s. They're made from silk, and they were pretty much rotting. But I managed to get the jacket out of them - I think Adam Ant had that - and it got worn three or four times. The whole thing is disintegrating, but I lined it and backed it so it could hold together. The whole point was I knew it would disintegrate, because that silk is 130 years old. The more you wear it, the more it's going to rot. But I like that idea: things falling to pieces on you. You could wear it 'til it's an absolute rag, and it would still look good.

Has recovered stuff always intrigued you?

Sure. I just found a postman's sack on the street in Camden and made a shirt of it. I used to make bits of jewellery out of broken glass. It's just putting things together in unusual ways. I've used everything: bits of carpet underlay have been in my jewellery. I've chopped up old Naval duffel bags and made waistcoats, used this silver stuff which is butcher's aprons from Smithfield Market. That was a bit nasty because, when I got it, it had bits of cow on it. So I had to scrub it. It's nice, though, because it's good on the female form. It's got good movement. I've made jackets of remnants, curtains, old furnishing fabrics. I used to make stuff out of paper as well, from hospitals. That is interesting because it's layered - and sewn together in a sort of quilting. So you can actually wash it and dye it. But, again, it would disintegrate. I really like that idea.

What's at the heart of transforming things?

The idea of using something quite obviously intended to be something else. I do a lot of work for *Skin Two*, styling, because I quite like underwear and the shapes of it because it's figure-hugging, shows off the body's contours. I'm into playing around, turning things upside down and putting them in the wrong place. I do like extremes: either really skin-tight fitted things, or baggy loose ones. Things that take the body's shape or go against it. My design just starts from seeing a piece of fabric. I get my ideas from fabric rather than shapes. I don't use patterns, either. If I do, I copy them. I like messing up, putting things where things shouldn't be.

I think the secondhand thing is important now because of the environmental message. It doesn't have to be really glamourous, it's just a question of what you can find. Just use a bit of imagination to adapt it. I've made very glamourous clothes out of recycled clothing, but I've made very unglamorous clothes as well. It's just trying to make the material true to itself. I do see it as an artform, like painting or sculpture. I prefer dealing with the fabric and clothing - or parts of clothing - as raw materials.

Who are your favourite clients?

I particularly like working with Björk. I made her a dress I loved, out of old, rotting fabric. I think designing for women is easier. Men with a strong sense of a look are rarer than women; they're just not prepared to go as far. But I make things as things in themselves, without any thought as to who's going to wear them. It could be men or it could be women.

Most of the stylists I know can't even sew on a button. They see their work in completely different terms. They're all interested in fashion as fashion, they know what's in, what shop is where, what things cost. I don't think like that. I see it more as putting colours and textures together. But, with styling, you make it suit the person. That's quite interesting, if you've got a model - you can change them a lot with hair and makeup; they can also act. Whereas, if you're dealing with someone in a band, it's a lot more difficult. They already have a set personality.

Your styling is singular, partly because you can design whatever extras you need. Do you design for yourself?

I still make clothing for myself occasionally. But I'd like to try other mediums, like rubber, things that are more moulded and sculptural. The very simple things are often the hardest. I mean, it's easy to chuck a load of beads on something and make it interesting. But to do something that's very refined and sculptural, that is really difficult. I might do some pattern cutting, so I can understand more. If you do mainstream fashion, pattern cutting is the thing, because it has to fit in a conventional sense. My clothes, I just hope they'll find somebody to fit *them*. As to business, I don't really think of it in those terms. I can make a living doing a styling job, but the only way it really works is to get backing, to be really committed. A lot of it's luck, just being in the right place at the right time. I've got quite an outsider's view, that's what I feel about fashion. I don't really want to be part of it. I don't have the mentality to be part of it. But I quite like nipping round the outside, and throwing little things in now and then.

CHAPTER 2

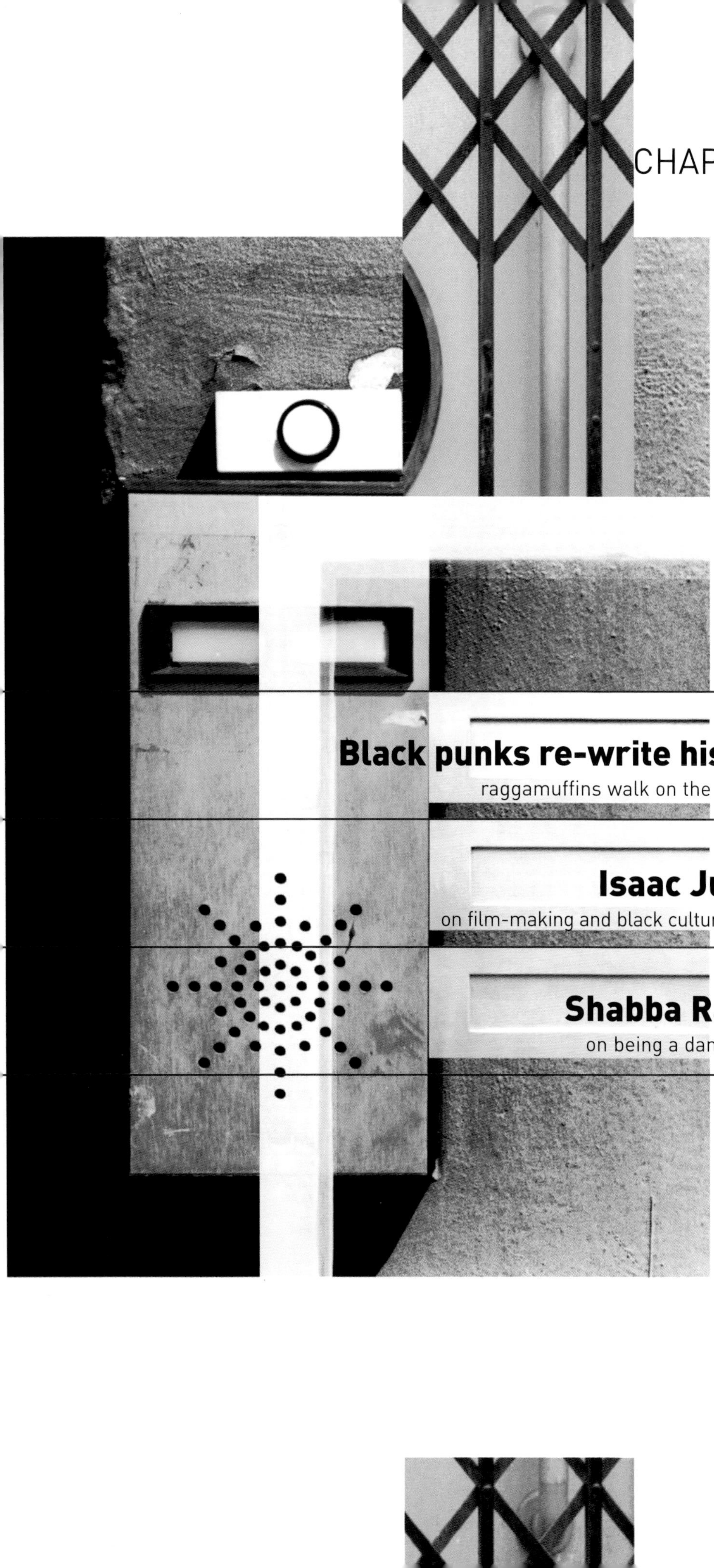

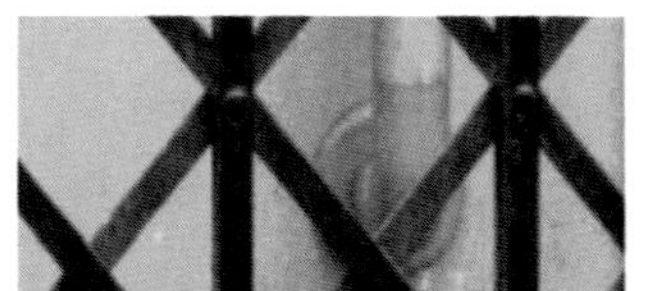

1

2

CHAPTER TWO

Black punks re-write history:

raggamuffins walk on the dark side

Sandie Duncan is another Londoner working in fashion. In the fall of '93, she was a partner in the black PR firm Scott-Duncan. She saw the new incarnations of punk as a frank admission, an over-due confession about street-style and its sources: "I don't think that punk is coming back as such. I don't think it could influence the way people portray either themselves or their music. Because, to the mainstream, 'punk' is still a white movement. They never have understood our role in it."

"Black kids", she adds, "really lead style in Britain. Now - it's just a fact - ragga style has taken over. The influences for that come from Jamaica and the States. But here it's very much worn in a style of our own." By ragga, Duncan meant reggae's bad-boy, street-hustler edge - fashion's spinoff from dancehall reggae and, later, jungle. All emphasised a rough and ready look, but one that was fond of jewellery and flamboyance. Ragga had a lot of ties with hip-hop; followers of each would borrow from the other.

Ragga-wise, Sandie Duncan too noted Versace's penchant for ripping and pinning - as well as John Richmond's "spiky shoes" and Jean-Paul Gaultier's bondage trousers. "But, for Chanel, Karl Lagerfeld has oversize dungarees. That's not punk at all, that one is pure ragga. Gaultier with his tribal headgear and body-painting...it's all exploitation, which is nothing new."

Duncan is not the only one aware of such thievery. By spring of '94, it was even more established. Jungle and ragga were only two British street styles, yet the European and American catwalks fetishised them. Critic Cathy Horn critiqued it in the *International Herald Tribune*. After noting how would-be Afrocentric labels like Cross Colors failed to win over teens, she went on to echo Sandie Duncan:

"...just as the youth market was moving on to something else...Karl Lagerfeld tried on baggy jeans at Chanel, and the tracksuit found its way into the collections of Isaac Mizrahi and Anna Sui... Five years ago it was easy to draw connections between what surfaced in clubs and what eventually found its way to high fashion, but as black dance music has stratified into narrower grooves - techno, gangsta, hardcore - so have the associated styles of dress."

Ragga style was, of course, an English form of punk. Even in the '70s, as a film like *Young Soul Rebels* (1990) notes, punk was a testament to

Britain's new mixed blood. By incorporating her black and her brown heritage - as well as some of England's gay sensibilities - punk had denoted a nation coming out of the closet.

Set on the day of the Queen's Silver Jubilee, Isaac Julien's *Young Soul Rebels* raised these avoided facts; it showed punk had affected black youth, too. This was not conjecture; it came straight from memory. For one location, producer Nadine Marsh-Edwards re-discovered a Deptford club she remembered frequenting. (In the '70s, it was called "The Crypt.") There, disco records mixed with emerging punk tracks and disco fashion fused with pins and mohair sweaters.

Says Marsh-Edwards, "Punk was made in Britain, but funk and disco were not. There were only two or three places fans could buy those as imports. If people knew the same record, it was a shared experience, an experience that was very precious." This applied, she says, to both punk *and* funk.

For black youth, punk also marked a hopeful moment. Marsh-Edwards: "There was also an optimism. Very rarely, for instance, was there fear of having no job. Seventeen-year-olds now have very different problems. They've seen unemployment, job schemes, huge recession. The attitude now is 'no job, no self-esteem'."

Isaac Julien, too, remembers this era as "optimistic". While making his film, he said:

"I was a teenage soulboy. It was the start of London club culture and I was going to a pub disco in Ilford. I'd be wearing winklepickers you bought from Brick Lane market, fluorescent socks from SEX [Malcolm McLaren's punk shop], a mix of punk gear and my soulboy look. Like fluffy mohair jumpers. I had my hair dyed blonde on one side, striped like a badger on the other. About six earrings in one ear and a fluorescent feather in the other one."

These are not the only black Britons who view punk as a watershed. Founding Kiss-FM DJ Norman Jay was a part of the same underground. Years later, he would help stage-manage "rare groove", using the same funk tunes Marsh-Edwards had heard in The Crypt. He would also serve as one of the first, and still most lasting, bridges between young Britons of every race.

In 1987, as a pirate jock, once again operating from outside the mainstream, Jay recalled punk as an upbeat moment. "And, when I say that, I think I have some authority. Because I've always been a follower of various styles, various fashions and cults. I'm a person who lived it all, so my accounts

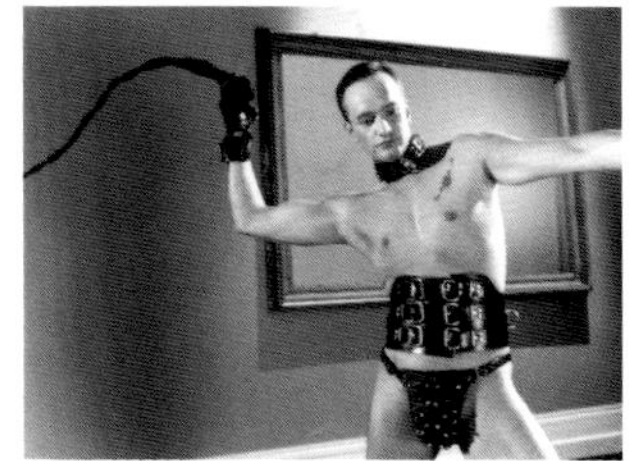

3

4

1. Young Soul Rebels
Photo: D. A. Bailey
Directed by Isaac Julien
2. Isaac Julien
Photo: The Voice, Nov '89
3. The Attendant
(Normal Films, '93)
Directed by Isaac Julien
4. Looking For Langston
Directed by Isaac Julien, '89
5. Young Soul Rebels
Directed by Isaac Julien
Photo: Sunil Gupta

Following pages:
Young Soul Rebels
Directed by Isaac Julien
Photo: Sunil Gupta

I'VE JUST HAD TO LEAVE BRITAIN IN ORDER TO MAKE A LIVING. MY COMPANY, WE'VE BECOME NOMADIC PEOPLE. IT'S LIKE WE'RE OPERATING FROM A BASE IN LONDON. (→PAGE 43)

THE MARKETING OF NIHILISTIC PLEASURE IS ALWAYS GOING TO WORK - SIMPLY BECAUSE IT SELLS. IT IS PLEASURABLE. JUST LOOK AT SOMETHING LIKE THE WHOLE NIRVANA THING. (→PAGE 47)

5

are eyewitness accounts: how I saw things evolve and where they led. The beginning of punk, I was a part of it. And not just from a London point of view. I always travel the country, I go to clubs everywhere."

Adds Jay: "The black community understood punk differently. Because, like all social movements, it started in trendy places, where the reason for it was to be 'alternative', which is why the black music press always knocked it. Because if you had spiky hair, or you were jumpin' around to it, you were just seen as a bandwagon-jumper. Whatever came along, you would be into it. That's how they saw punk; that's why they disapproved."

1

Jay felt the '90s punk renaissance missed the point. It co-opted trends - namely raggamuffin - which were not breaking, but already established. Plus, it wrested these out of their proper context. "In London, always being hip means always moving. And black Londoners, we're the modernists. We always want new things, we're ahead of the 'movements'. London's whole marriage of fashion, pop and society: that's been led by the black kids who grew up here. At the time of punk, ever since, that's been bloody obvious."

It took years, though, to state this fact upfront; it was only done at the outset of the '90s. *Young Soul Rebels* was made 14 years after punk's Jubilee summer. Punk may have inspired kids to shape their own experience. But it was less about that self-expression than about art as a business. Not until the very end of the '80s would young black Britons start to accumulate business clout; even today, only 2% of Afro-Caribbean Britons can claim a membership in the "professional classes". Black Britain is largely a working-class population. Punk rebellion involved class divisions, but it also emphasised their reinforcement. Most of all, this happened through the media.

When he made *Young Soul Rebels*, Isaac Julien was 27. He was a product of both punk politics and an East London upbringing. Well known as one of the capital's most fastidious dressers, Julien studied film and painting at St. Martin's School of Art. There his student movie, *Who Killed Colin Roach?*, marked him as an artist of unusual promise. Colin Roach, the victim of an infamous death-in-custody, had lived on the same housing estate as the would-be film-maker. But, says a lecturer who knew Julien then, that piece was not conventional agitprop. "It was a documentary, yet it pushed formal boundaries. Doing that without ever trivialising its subject; it was an early indication of a special talent."

Very soon, something else became apparent about Julien: he despised the ghetto slots on offer to both black and gay film-makers. In 1984, as an effort to avoid them, he co-founded Sankofa Film & Video: a production company of black and Asian Britons. Under the Sankofa aegis, he started honing his skills, making *Territories* (1985), *This is Not an AIDS Advert* (1987), *The Passion of Remembrance* (1987) and *Looking For Langston* (1989). It was the latter, a homage to the Harlem poet Langston Hughes, which first brought him real attention. Much of that came from far outside the UK.

A pop promo Julien made for Peter Gabriel ("Shaking the Tree") gained him something of a profile abroad. But *Langston*'s New York début made him a minor celebrity. Critics gushed ("Law-abiding or lawless, Julien is never boring"), and sold-out showings launched him on a tour of lectures and festivals. Eventually, *Looking for Langston* won seven awards, in sites as far apart as Copenhagen and Ohio. It helped pave the way for the making of *Young Soul Rebels*, a tale of friendship which aimed at the teenage audience. Although interracial friendship was a part of the film, this time black protagonists were in the foreground.

Rebels was made for a mere £1.2 million, a fraction of the budget Julien had initially planned. At Cannes in '91, it took the *Prix de la Critique*.

Few British critics congratulated Julien on this; even fewer grasped his version of punk's "Englishness". Subtleties in the film (such as the tensions between black siblings) captured an evolving, multiethnic Britain. But UK critics saw its gays and blacks as "issues", bearers of various socio-political points. Wrote one, "the message of the film outweighs its story."

Critics outside the UK disagreed; many saw a new and interesting take on a social phenomenon. Others simply felt it was a well-told teenage story. Enthused one from Cannes: "He knows how to weave a tale with gusto, how to incorporate music and a roving camera to great storytelling advantage. Those who have their eyes squarely focused on Spike Lee...would be well advised to redirect at least one eye in the direction of Julien."

Nowadays a veteran of America's PBS network, as well as his native BBC TV, Isaac Julien smiles at the contrast in reactions. He is the first to note that his début film has flaws. "But when you're black", he says, "the pressures are multiplied. You are carrying a lot of people's fantasies. Most especially white people's fantasies of 'black British film'."

In the '90s, Julien has tackled a wide range of projects. He helmed the two-part *Black and White in Colour*, a critically acclaimed look at race on British TV. Then he turned his hand to an "art short", *The Attendant*, which played the UK cinema circuit with Derek Jarman's *Wittgenstein*. He then filmed the feature *Fanon*, but not before he had to earn his keep in America.

In New York, Julien was recruited for a PBS project called *Breaking the Boundaries*: a "gay version" of civil-rights history. The job took him away from Britain for most of a year. But his company, Normal Films, had already presented UK networks with seven separate proposals. When they were all rejected, Julien felt he had little choice. "That's continued right through the '90s. I've just had to leave Britain in order to make a living. My company, we've become nomadic people. It's like we're operating from a base in London.

Those who travel between Europe, Britain and the States understand the problems faced by UK talents such as Julien's. Most are better connected than Britain's media czars - and more deeply engaged in global debates on culture. As the World Wide Web and Internet grow more accessible, their position can only strengthen. In Julien's flat next door to the British Museum, a telephone and fax are constantly in action - whether he is here or in South

2

3

4

1. Norman Jay - '76
2. Territories (Frame Enlargement) '84 (Sankofa Film and Video) Directed by Isaac Julien
3. Frantz Fanon: Black Skin, White Mask (Normal Films, '96) Directed by Isaac Julien
4. Frantz Fanon: Black Skin, White Mask (Normal Films, '96) Directed by Isaac Julien
5. The Attendent (Normal Films, '93) Directed by Isaac Julien

IN LONDON, ALWAYS BEING HIP MEANS ALWAYS MOVING. AND BLACK LONDONERS, WE'RE THE MODERNISTS. WE ALWAYS WANT NEW THINGS, WE'RE AHEAD OF THE 'MOVEMENTS'. LONDON'S WHOLE MARRIAGE OF FASHION, POP AND SOCIETY: THAT'S BEEN LED BY THE BLACK KIDS WHO GREW UP HERE. AT THE TIME OF PUNK, EVER SINCE, THAT'S BEEN BLOODY OBVIOUS.

(→PAGE 42)

5

Africa. Ditto the e-mail flooding his Powerbook. These messages come from New York, Tokyo, Paris, Prague. And they hold a lesson for the British establishment: try and value your artists as much as the rest of the world does.

Julien's work does get exposure in the UK media. But here, its emissaries are almost totally white. Plus, their offices are bastions of a certain class - with a certain outlook. This creates problems for most young black Britons. Says Julien, "Either you're ignored or you're trashed. And it's almost always out of ignorance." Plus, he adds, there is now the role of political correctness, which can function as a useful smokescreen for liberals. "They want black art to remain something they can *grade*."

In 1994, for BBC2, Julien tackled something central to Britain's evolving moment: the wave of popular, anti-gay dancehall reggae. Those artists he wanted to query were the stars of its dancefloor, with tunes every hip club-goer knew. But homophobia seemed to be part of the trend, featuring in songs like Buju Banton's "Boom By-By", Capleton's "Buggerin'", "Batty Boy Fi Die" by Red Dragon. To discover their genesis, what human places they came from, Julien researched, then filmed, in the UK, the US and Jamaica. The story he found was complex; it involved close ties and crossing paths, but also wide gaps in culture, politics and understanding.

He shaped it into an hour-long documentary, produced by Normal with the Black Audio Film Collective. They entitled it *The Darker Side of Black*, for it dealt with hip-hop as well as reggae. The film tackled nihilism in black-based, popular culture. There was the gun as a visual and a lyrical symbol; homophobia both in the street and among the stars. Like all Julien's work, the piece was rich and evocative. Yet, as usual, it scorned easy judgments.

It was the contradictions of the trend which most intrigued Julien. He knows how few images still convey black power, so he can understand both genres' grip on young black consciousness. "In the '90s, both reggae culture and hip-hop offer a package. Each has a whole mode of dress, a style, an attitude. The message is, 'It may be tough out here - but it's *glamourous*'." Just as seductive are the most contentious tunes. Says Julien, "No one can deny a lot of that music sounds brilliant."

Julien is not someone who demands role models. He agrees there is a crisis in black leadership and many questions surround what it means to be black and British. ("And working-class and British, or gay and British.") But, he asks: why look to teenage artists for one's politics? What really bothers him, what *Darker Side* investigates, is the spiritual toll exacted when a choice is made to merchandise pathology. In a marketplace already ruled by ritual machismo, values such as tolerance and love literally lose all worth. "In both hip-hop and reggae, there is always controversy: over an artist, over a feud, over one song or another. There's always a Snoop Doggy Dogg, a Tupac, a Shabba Ranks. But the mainstream media avoids the real, the harder questions. *Why* are those things so powerful? How does such a trend happen?"

The answers Isaac Julien found are complex ones. They involve class, marketing, fundamentalist faith, views and fears about masculinity. In Jamaica, for instance, where dancehall music was born, US gun culture has exerted a wide influence. Yet Jamaica's "lyrical gun" has an image all its own.

By the mid-'90s, dancehall music was "popping" in Britain, via her pirate radio stations and flourishing club circuit. It went hand in hand with techno's offspring, jungle, and its presence was even felt at raves. But Julien's film on it was inspired by a New York conference. There, in 1991, the black theologian Cornel West gave a speech in which he spoke out against "black nihilism". Twelve months later, young Britons were dancing to "Boom By-By". This was a dancehall hit by a youngster (Buju Banton), who was 17 when he cut the record. Its lyrics launched abuse at women and threats at gays. (Those who called it "just a song" might cringe at the actual words: "Girl bend way back/And accept the peg/And if it really hurt/You know she still no go fled/And some men still no want the panty red/Bare

1

botty business them love... Send for the automatic and the UZI instead/Shoot them now/Come let me shoot them".)

Besides, as Julien knew, much of hip-hop and dancehall (and jungle) were not mythic and removed from daily life. Even if one didn't hear the lyrics, one might encounter their echoes. It happened to photographer Vernon Adams, 25, as he walked home.

"I walked past Cato Road", says this white skateboarder, "maybe three minutes after a policeman was shot there. I saw some guys who ride bikes and hang around telephones. So I asked them what had happened. And, when this one guy opened his mouth, he had solid gold teeth. They just *glistened.* But, instead of answering me, he sang a line from 'Boom By-By'. He just sang that, and rode off on his bicycle - laughing."

This happened three summers *after* the song's release, after the catchy hit had broken dancehall's "flex rhythm". The song's popularity had fed off several trends: hip-hop's multifarious death

1. **7" pre single label:**
   Boom By-By
   Artist: Buju Banton
2. **The Ragga & The Royal,**
   by Monica Grant
   Published by The X press, '94
3. **Yardie by Victor Headley**
   Published by The X press, '92
4. **Shabba Ranks**
   Sony Music publicity shot
5. **The Harder They Come**
   Arthouse Productions

HERE, THESE BLACK CULTURAL MUSICS - DANCEHALL, RAGGA, JUNGLE - THEY'RE ALL STILL RELATIVELY MARGINAL. HIP-HOP, IN AMERICA, IS NOT AT ALL MARGINAL. THERE WE'RE TALKING ABOUT VERY BIG BUSINESS. (→PAGE 49)

4

2

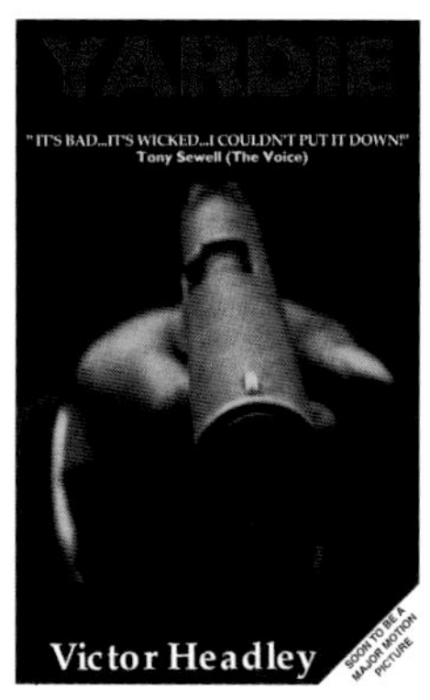

3

allusions; "gangsta" films like *New Jack City*; dancehall's Bogle step; and bombastic ragga threats (many directed at "batty boys"). "Boom By-By" played on the phobic fears - and fantasies - of both whites and blacks about maleness and blackness.

In the manner of "God Save the Queen", the song became a legend. When ragga superstar Shabba Ranks graced Channel Four's "The Word", he supported Buju Banton's views. Shabba called for gays to be "crucified". Black Lesbians and Gays Against Homophobia in the Media sprang into action on a global level - sending cassettes of this to activist groups in New York. They soon reached the desk of

5

Harlem Congressman Charles B. Rangel and US television's *Showtime at the Apollo*. Shabba was booted off that popular prime-time show and - until he made an "apology" - was dropped from a slot as support act for Bobby Brown. Banton himself said he would never "apologise to a gay".

The uproar over "Boom By-By" drew from a number of things. There was the moral panic which - worldwide - accompanies AIDS. There was the pre-Stonewall state of Jamaica. And there was the increasing visibility of queer culture. London activist Ted Walker-Brown helped lead the campaign. But, after he appeared on "The Word" to argue with Shabba, Walker-Brown was beaten up - by "some builders who had seen me on the broadcast".

He remains adamant about anti-gay sentiments. But, like Julien, Walker-Brown knows ragga's consumption is complex. "Number One, it's made in a Third World country. Two: it's like punk music, in that it's engineered controversy. Three: the UK media implications are different. Here, they easily become: 'Look: blacks and wogs are at each other's throats.' I mean, Guns and Roses are homophobic, too. Marky Mark was racist *and* homophobic. Yet, at the same moment, he was a gay pin-up."

In raggamuffin music and rap, Julien sees the parallels. He was exploring a '90s phenomenon: one, increasingly, shared around the world. It may be explicit in Buju Banton's lyrics, but it's also present in Nike's Michael Jordan - the potent combination of bodily worship and phobia. Says Julien, "Gay communities share with black cultures certain ideas of the body - very hard-core and masculinist views. The white beefcake pin-up, buffed and musclebound, mirrors the black macho-man with his B-boy clothes and gun." He pauses. "In gay communities we don't see much debate about *that*."

Britain's gay cultures and her black communities share a search for vehicles in which to locate freedom. Especially in music, both constantly generate difference. It was gay aesthetics which created the disco continuum - pop as producer's medium built around the female voice. One year, this might mean Kym Mazelle and Jocelyn Brown; in another, Björk singing "It's So Quiet".

But, gay aesthetics also helped lead to post-rave techno - which, in turn, mutated into jungle. Liberals are comfortable with some of these connections. But, just as his public balked at probing Marky Mark, there is resistance to coming clean about jungle music's early drug connections.

The mixture of hypocrisy with hidden history can be powerful. As Walker-Brown notes, it has its *own* history. "Look at something like the *Twist* craze in America! That dance came out in '62, in New York. It was a direct response to laws targeting gay bars, a way for men to dance close without really touching. Now, that's hardly how social histories tell it."

If one doubts Ted Walker-Brown's assertion, one has Chubby Checker, novelty music's Lord of the Twist. Checker spilled the beans himself, to *The Advocate* magazine.

In the final analysis, says Isaac Julien, neither black or gay agendas should look for help to mainstream culture. Nor will it provide an answer for the serious question. Why? "Because, as we know too well, it's the straight editor, it's the white straight producer, who is always going to make the real decisions. That is who decides the nature of representation. What's 'controversial' remains up to them. When you hear and see what's *really* all around you, then you can't help but begin to notice that."

When film-maker Isaac Julien wanted to practise his craft, he had to set up a collective to do so. But his path has never been easy. He uses work to explore cultural issues as well as questions of form - and, sometimes, he's had to leave Britain to do so. Here, he talks about using film to investigate dancehall, hip-hop and ragga musics.

Just before the jungle deluge "Boom By-By" was quite a story. Was it the lyrics alone?

Well, the music was central. At the time, everybody was into something new called the flex rhythm. Buju Banton did this song, 'The Bogle', and suddenly there was this whole new dance. Along with that, you had the release of Victor Headley's books, like *Yardie*, the beginning of the real British crack epidemic, and films about all these kinds of black gangsters - with hip-hop soundtracks. It was a whole move within black culture which explicitly intended to sell black nihilism. People are still selling black nihilism - and why? Because it makes money. People are into abjection, especially black abjection. It continues to be very highly marketable, because it plays on fears and fantasies. Fears and fantasies about blackness and maleness.

When did you start having critical thoughts about it? And why did you think it could be dealt with on film?

Well, it didn't happen when I first heard "Boom By-By", because, *I* couldn't understand what was being articulated. I had to slow it down; then, someone showed me the words. Sly and Robbie developed the flex rhythm on "Boom By-By"; they'd been tryin' to push this rhythm in dancehall for a long time before it really caught on. The whole development of hardcore in dancehall - which we here call ragga - emphasises the bass and applies technological treatments. It's a technologically treated version of dub plating. And it's an even sound, the so-called flex rhythm. So, when I first heard it, I thought "Hey, what a catchy tune!"

Isaac Julien:

on film-making and black cultural musics

The marketing of nihilistic pleasure is always going to work - simply because it sells. It is pleasurable. Just look at something like the whole Nirvana thing. What intrigued me, really, was something more. Which is that, before now, great black artists were able to transcend that mere fact, to do something with it. I'm speaking here of Billie Holiday, Bob Marley, James Brown. Plus, the psychological crisis this change betokens - for art and for music and for society - isn't just in the West alone. You know? It's also in the South, it's in Third World spaces. I think that dancehall comes out of all of that.

Also once we started filming and were actually in Jamaica, I learned things I didn't know about dancehall. I discovered very quickly it's a working class culture. It's a statement against the country's *petit bourgeoisie*. And the audience for it is extremely wide and varied. I mean, we found obviously gay people at all the concerts. It just simply could not be clearer.

Are they really allowed to express it, though?

You bet! One guy, for instance, had this see-through plastic mac with these postcards of Jamaica sewn all over it. He had a homemade hat and it was just fantastic. We couldn't film it, because it was too dark. And, anyway, we wouldn't have done it justice. But the amount of creative stylin' is profound. This is like punk rock meets glam rock meets showbiz - but done in poverty, with no resources. Everything is made up, improvised. Someone will have a net curtain wrapped around them, and somehow it looks incredible. We discovered it's really profound.

What about the sounds?

Dancehall is *audibly* exciting. This whole thing about guns and weapons turns out to be - well, people do carry guns into dancehalls. But if you were found with a gun on you, you'd be arrested. It's illegal there for civilians to carry a firearm. But, usually, if there's a really good song, they'll fire rifles into the air. It's a recognition of the excitement. But, dancehall culture in Jamaica takes place in open spaces; it's all open-air. So it's hot, but it lacks the claustrophobia of a club in Britain. I'm not legitimising this, but when I was there, I heard no guns fired. I heard bullet sounds in the records, but that was all.

But it exists, and admiration for it crops up in the lyrics.

There is violence in Jamaican culture and there is gun culture in the country. There is something else too, but it's not about guns. It's about a different kind of violence, it has to do with human rights, and the fight for decent living conditions. When we interviewed *some* gay people there, they said "Boom By-By" and all those songs were the best things that ever happened. Because it finally articulated and gave a language to something which had been taboo. It enabled them to have a debate on these questions. I'm not saying I agree with that. But it was a widespread viewpoint we discovered. Other people, of course, felt it did great harm.

Did you find the same thing in gay circles outside Jamaica?

What it did to gay and lesbian communities around the diaspora - at least in the West and New York and London - was to highlight that there is no bill of rights for gays or for lesbians. People like Outrage in Britain, or Gay Men and Lesbians Against Defamation in New York, that is what they responded to. There isn't a UK Sex Relations Act like there is a Race Relations Act. If you incite hatred or violence there's no law to apply. What "Boom By-By" did was focus people on that problem. Of course the moral panic around AIDS has been projected onto gays and lesbians. But there's also the delusion that you can police sexuality.

As a film maker, as a documentarian, how do you feel about censorship?

I rarely interview anyone who calls for censorship. But, in Britain, quite a few people do that. Quite a few liberals, quite a few gay white men, make calls for censorship. The censoring of black speech - to put that on Buju Banton or on Shabba Ranks - it's not what I try to do with my work. That's not gonna solve their problem. All it would do, ironically, is to silence black gays and lesbians. I do, however, think these people should be contested; I aim for that. But another thing which will contest them, automatically, is the marketplace. Because in the West, at least, gays and lesbians have a stake in the marketplace. So if people like Shabba and Buju want to get over, they'll have a problem. At least if they hold on to those points of view.

One excuse people fail to challenge is their religious fundamentalism. During our interview, you know, Shabba got his Bible out, and he waved it around. But many clerics we spoke with contested him. To them, that whole use of the Bible is quite suspect. People prise things out of the Old Testament, but they take some things out and leave others in. Reverend Jones of New York's Unity Fellowship Church put it very well. He said when we look at it carefully, people don't know what God says - and, in fact, they don't care. Not until it comes to this particular issue.

Isaac, how widespread do you feel this problem is?

Oh, everybody concentrated on "Boom By-By". And it kicked off a series of songs which are openly homophobic. But the same could be said of hip-hop, where that impulse has been present since the outset. Basically, it just became *fashionable.* "Boom By-By" was exceptional just because of the press. Most people didn't actually understand what it said. That summer, I was at the Notting Hill Carnival, and I heard lots of homophobic songs. And there were lots of people just dancing away to them, white people who simply heard it as groovy. They can't understand what the hell it's *saying.* So it's like a coded thing. But sometimes I also think the white gay and lesbian's experience is not at all what I've had living in Britain.

What about the whole question of scapegoating?

A lot of stuff's been postulated here about an increase in violence against gays and lesbians because of dancehall music, ragga and hip-hop. I don't buy that, I just don't buy that at all. It sounds quite close to those arguments made by the women's movement, that pornography causes violence against women, which I think is really dangerous and, in some instances, a racist argument. I think if there are such increases, it's to do with the AIDS crisis. It's also about lesbians and gays finally being more visible in UK culture. I mean, this is like white culture going, "Hey, we've got these black men using words like *batty boy*!" Well, maybe they always used those words, but white people just never knew it. Whether or not this is because of Buju or Shabba Ranks is a whole other question. How many white people - gay *or* straight - really know or give a fuck about dancehall? On the whole, it's a different audience.

In the film you made with Black Audio, "The Darker Side of Black", it's clear things are different outside Britain.

In Jamaica things *are* different. There, dancehall music is very much a part of gay and lesbian culture. In America, hip-hop music is central to black youth culture. I'm not giving an argument which is for either, but it's more contradictory than it seems. This "us" and "them" divide is much, much too easy. It says, "Let's position this marginal music right here" - this is *black* music, right? "Let's say it's all bad." You have to look more closely at the contexts. Where in each case does the music come from? Is it not read differently in different contexts?

Do you find Britons understand this? Do they understand the initial reggae roots of jungle?

No. There's very little understanding of the complexities of its original audience. Dancehall, for instance, *exists* to be controversial, partly by talking a lot about sex. Also, dancehall music is reggae music, which is a kind of national cultural music. It may not be the high point of the genre; because it's market-driven, and it sells to youth. But, very basically, in terms of its audience, going to Jamaica's dancehalls is like going to Taboo. It's very outrageous, the women are very exhibitionist - to a certain degree, people are really out for a laugh. A lot of it is just masquerading. A lot of parody. And people enjoy doing it.

Here, the questions of diaspora get quite intriguing. Somehow, if you're into dancehall outside Jamaica, it's like "This is what *real* black people are into". It becomes all about authenticating black identity. People feel like you're really "down" if you're buying dancehall or gangsta hip-hop - this is like some real, hardcore "blackness". Therefore, it also demands an exclusionist posturing. It's against gays and lesbians. That has pursued the music through its every mutation. Well, the truth is - dancehall culture is *camp*. It's borrowed an iconography from a lot of different subcultures; whether or not it wants to acknowledge that.

Camp as in British club style?

Sure. In terms of how it looks, the culture is camp. Men are wearin' these really shiny costumes and these lavish clothes, sort of Liberace-ish. But in these contexts, of course, that is seen as glamour. First and foremost, it's working-class styling. It works against the labels and designer clothing worn by upper-class Jamaicans. But, in London, in terms of black people here, I feel the way all these musics are used politically - and I mean people writing about them, making films about them - that's a very different stance. To me, that stance is very much pretending to be down with the folk. It's very much aping and using and *pimping* from that culture. Just in order to make your statement.

Jamaican culture is not British culture, it's very different from *our* West Indian culture. Believe me, it is nothing like the same. Of course, people have a tough time in Britain, but Jamaica is a Third World country. In Jamaica, there are no rights for poor people, no protections. So there are hardly gonna be any for gays and lesbians.

But there are huge cross-overs, not just musically, but culturally?

Whenever something happens in black cultures - around the world - it's interpreted differently everywhere. In Britain, what is interesting in our culture, in the people who become interesting - such as Soul II Soul or Massive Attack - is they show there are certain things that we're very good at. One is taking on the hybrid aspects of black culture, of black music, and remoulding them. Doing something else with them.

The other thing, of authenticating, of taking on black identities from other spaces? I think it bespeaks a black European inferiority. It's a negating activity. I mean, it doesn't matter how Yardie or street-like some black clubs are here. They're nothing on JA, because the context is different. This whole thing also really applies to hip-hop. There, you're talking about the US gun culture, which is a thriving thing; we've all seen the consequence. Here, these black cultural musics - dancehall, ragga, jungle - they're all still relatively marginal. Hip-hop, in America, is not at all marginal. There we're talking about very big business. And a lot of very white consumers.

You've filmed around the world, you work many places. Has that altered your sense of diaspora?

I'll tell you, to be honest, it's been one of those things which worries me. The idea of the limits of black identity. But, then, we never were all the same just because of the colour of our skin. There are definite limits to diasporic unity - and "Boom By-By" is certainly one of them! I have a problem with collapsing us down, into one supposedly homogeneous thing. And making that the so-called "black community". No one who does that really looks at context, looks at economics, looks into complexities. I mean, when we talk about hip-hop, or we talk about the problems of dancehall, we are talkin' about black cultural production. About black male voices who, for the main part, are heterosexual. I don't see too many white pop stars who are out. And plenty of white pop stars are gay. But *that's* not ever framed as a controversy. The controversies are always based around questions of race.

Take one other aspect of 'diaspora': the misogyny of American hip-hop.

That is speaking to a certain constituency, but it's not the entire "black community". If you look at those kind of attitudes towards women, the things you see in rap, it's pretty much how adolescent boys view women. Well, adolescent boys are part of the community. But I have to question the idea of letting them speak for the community. It's a very racist idea - and it's quite destructive. It's a thing that black people should be the first to oppose. After all, rap is an art form, which has great things to offer.

Above all, remember, we don't make the laws. Black culture very rarely gets to make the laws. In Jamaica, for instance, the law that makes homosexuality illegal? It comes from 17th-century English law. I'm not sayin' this removes the blame from black people. Because some of them are homophobic. I just find the fact of it interesting.

1

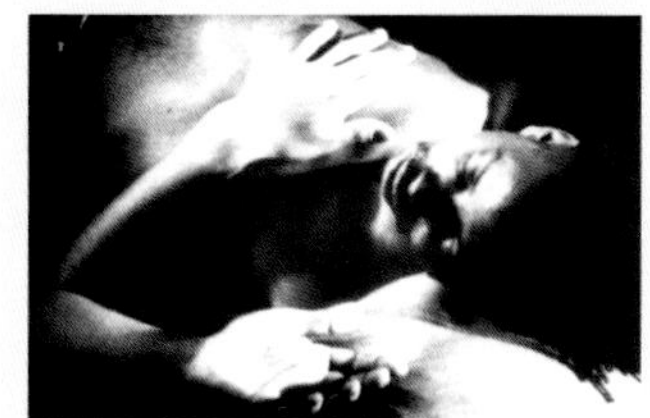

2

3

4

5

6

1. Who Needs A Heart
Directed by John Akomfrah,
B.A.F.C. '91
2. Twilight City
Directed by Reece Auguiste,
B.A.F.C. '87
3. Handsworth Songs
Directed by John Akomfrah,
B.A.F.C. '86
4. Testament
Directed by John Akomfrah,
B.A.F.C. '88
5. Seven Songs For Malcolm X
Directed by John Akomfrah,
B.A.F.C. '93
6. Mysteries of July
Directed by Reece Auguiste,
B.A.F.C. '89
7. Martin Luther King
Days of Hope
Directed by John Akomfrah,
B.A.F.C. '97

The Black Audio Film Collective

The Black Audio Film Collective, co-producers with Normal Films of Isaac Julien's "The Darker Side of Black", are the most prominent black production company in Britain. Now headquartered in Camden, north London, they were established in the '80s. The company is comprised of producers Lina Gopaul and Avril Johnson, directors John Akomfrah and Reece Auguiste, writer Edward George and assistant producer David Lawson. They have made numerous acclaimed documentaries and features, which include "Handsworth Songs", "A Touch of the Tarbrush", "Twilight City", "Mysteries of July", "Testament", "Who Needs A Heart", "Seven Songs for Malcolm X" and "The Migrant's Tale: A Symphony for Our Time."

7

Shabba Ranks is one of the premier DJs of dancehall, a controversial bad boy and style-setter. When he supported Buju Banton's anti-gay stance, film-maker Isaac Julien spoke to him about it. In Jamaica, for Normal Films and the Black Audio Film Collective, they talk about his art and some of its political meanings.

Isaac: Shabba, we're going to talk first about your childhood. Can you describe the part of Jamaica you grew up in?

Shabba: I grew up in a very rough neighbourhood. It was just like Vietnam, see, because of political violence. There was always a dead body to be stepped over, found in the early mornings. Rough times, real bad times. But prayers and deliverance be out there, give thanks. Good bad, real rough, real rough. Rough side of town, Kingston city.

Isaac: Can you tell me what made you want to be a DJ?

Shabba: I wanted to be a DJ because the DJ was just a great sender from God. I grew up seeing DJs dealing with people and he was just like Jesus in that method. I mean, wherever he go, there was always a lot of people around him. He was always at the top of the spotlight. I be watching U Roy, Yellowman, Josey Wales - because Josey Wales, he was in my neighbourhood. You be poor, music can help you; so I choose the music; give praise. But I be a DJ because the way I see people treat an artist or a star.

Isaac: Can you give Britons a description of what the Jamaican dancehall is? What does it look like? What could I expect to see if I went to a dancehall?

Shabba: If you should go to a dancehall in Jamaica, you would see that it's a place where it's like a mini-stadium or arena, with one or two sound systems being played. And there be a lot of patrons there. In Jamaica, put it like this, we ain't got no clubs. Clubs is for the rich cats, the clubs is for the people who have things. Dancehall is for we who go for fun, it's like our funland. One sound system, two sound system, three sound system, four sound system. You get old music, new music, every music.

Shabba Ranks:

on being a dancehall DJ

Isaac: What is the role of the DJ in a dancehall?

Shabba: The role of a DJ within a dancehall is to get the place much busier. I go to a dancehall, I'm there to sweat up the people, OK, they be there and they be doing real cool at a normal temperature. When I go there, I lift the temperature, so that everyone be boiling, keep sweating. When a DJ in command, you look, you listen, and you move, because that's what we be there to do. We be there to get the musical listeners in gear, musically that's what we be there for, go there, mash it up, nice it up.

Isaac: Does any responsibility come with this role of the DJ in the dancehall?

Shabba: Yeah, it should. Dancehall should have some responsibilities. But it's like this: younger youth listen more to the DJs than older heads. So my factor is to keep myself clean so that someone wishing to be like me be clean. When I say clean, I mean my education first, then be drug-free, because if you be drugging, you ain't gonna be a star, you be bugging. You're licking your own spirit so every star out there or every DJ out there has got a responsibility because many younger generation be looking up to you, wanna be like you. I make sure that my head is clean at all times, because Jamaica is my biggest responsibility and, if I slip, then Jamaica is gonna slip.

Isaac: Can you tell us the main themes in dancehall music?

Shabba: Main themes in dancehall music: break down the barriers, break down barriers, they be for each and every individual they have their own theme. My theme is once males used to act dominant over females, they be saying "I'm the king and you're the queen so you've gotta listen". It ain't like that any more. That's what I'm preaching, we be equal, because is a rib from a male is formed to create a lady. Then the womb of a lady is there to form babies so it be equal. Man must take care of his woman, do not disrespect. Love her at his best; truth and rights; roots and culture.

Isaac: Why is dancehall so popular in this moment of the '90s?

Shabba: Because it's younger generation time, yeah! Whenever people judge things with an undermine that thing gets powerful. When I say undermine, that mean it be right in front of you but you discredit it without even taking time out to learn what is it about, where it is coming from, you just get up and follow everyone and say "I don't like it; I can't take it".

It's like you be one of the critics. The motion of this music has been facing a pressure. Well, this is the time that the pressure has been exploded on all the people who be putting the pressure on the music. The music has turned loose out of the pressure. Younger generation be hip to dancehall, because you know this is the time for dancehall. Yeah, most definitely it is dancehall time; if you be hydraulically pressing me down, you think I'm gonna stay there? No, I'm going to try and go bigger than the pressure you have me under. It's time for it, it is the time for dancehall.

Isaac: There seem now to be a lot of songs about sex and guns. Why is that?

Shabba: There seems to be a lot of those songs within the circuit of dancehall because we be tired of guns, see most dancehall artists who be preaching about the gun, they themselves never went to store to buy a gun, they never make a gun, they ain't using a gun. They be just preaching about the gun, because we see the gun do so much damage in our circle and our society. So we talk about the gun, what else can we do? We can't do nothing but talk about it. OK; it's all about the gun but we never make none. I just tell you, we be of the ghetto, we see the gun do so much damage. But bigger heads, they be responsible for the motivation, the distribution, of guns.

Isaac: What about sex in dancehall?

Shabba: Sex, sex. We talk about sex because sex is overall. Sex is within everyone, so we talk about sex. Whosoever is alive love to have sex, but we ain't preaching you must derogatorily have sex, protect your sex, that's it. They say I'm preaching sex and that dancehall is sex. No it ain't, dancehall isn't sex. Sex is people. The people within themselves, they have sex. Why don't critics say it to *Penthouse* magazine? Isn't that more damaging to the kid brain or the kid eyesight than music? Sex is within us all, if it wasn't for sex I would never be here. I follow that line because I deal with multiplication. The Bible says that sex is multiplication, so protect it.

Isaac: What is slackness?

Shabba: Racism is the biggest slackness this world could face. Apartheid is another drastical slackness. Using drugs is slackness, child molesting. Music could never be slackness. Many people say slackness is talking about sexual issues, but slackness to me is much more than that. For me, the biggest slackness is racism, because it is an act against God and an act against human righteousness.

Even hating your brother that is slackness or if you're coveting your sister that is slackness. Parents who do not show respect for their children that is slackness, children who do not show respect for their parents, that's slackness. Music ain't slackness, this world is full of much more slackness than the music. People of the world, they do not support slackness and whatsoever we were doing was slackness, I would never be here, for real. If I know that slackness is over there, I'm not gonna go over there. Slackness is bigger than me myself and I and the music; so, pow! Hotness. Hotness, not slackness.

Isaac: Do people really understand dancehall music?

Shabba: Many people they don't know what is the music. I'll let you know something about this music. Dancehall music helps me and it help another young generation of people out of Jamaica. We be of the ghetto and youths of the ghetto, people check them out as being criminals minded of the ghetto. That's the first impression people get whenever they see a ghetto kid strolling - that he is criminal-minded.

OK, I never wanted to be a criminal, I never wanted them to label me criminal-minded. So I take my music and I elevate myself with my music and bring my music to the world. I could be down there popping people, leaking blood, which is very much wrong in the sight of God Almighty and the son of David. We tried many things in order for people to absorb our music.

Isaac: Tell me how you talk about women in your music.

Shabba: Well, I talk about ladies within my music just like this: you gotta make good love to them, that's all I'm saying. I ain't telling no male to brutalise or ill-treat their lady out there. I just say you better make real love to them, because no matter what you're giving a lady, if you ain't loving her with the schooling type of method, you're gonna lose her, yeah.

You could be giving her the world but as soon as you be out another brother be jumping through your window. I am not talking about just going around sexing and sexing her, I mean, Yow! Appreciate her as a woman, remember she's just as significant as your mother. The only difference is she's your lover. She's as significant as your sister, but the difference is she's your lover, so love them, take care of them, that's what I am here trying to tell a brother.

Isaac: What does dancehall have in common with hip-hop?

Shabba: They undergo the same pressure. People don't take time out to listen, everyone say that it's violent or it's dealing with sex. That's the most thing that dancehall and hip-hop face pressure, critics, critic - not saying that critics ain't on other styles or the other type of music, but the way how people treat these music or label these type of music is like its coming from the heart of the Devil, which it's not.

Isaac: There was recently a whole furore over some comments you made on a television programme about some gay people - for which you apologised. Tell us what happened.

Shabba: Well, I face the camera again I never apologise. People do, not me. Personally, let me tell you, me do not apologise because or why do I have my opinion? And if somebody is gonna kill me or hate me for my opinion, then go ahead, kill me. I'm gonna die for my statement. I never make a statement to please no-one, I make my statement to please God Almighty. So if you feel like, or you want to hate me for my opinion, then you'all bring it on, sling it on, hate me. But I tell you now, personally, I never apologise.

Because I quote from the Bible, I do not live by the words of man, I live by the words of the Bible. And this say I must multiply, and another to another is an abomination to this. And this is what I live by, the words of the Bible so, if you want to hate me for saying you'd be unjustified in the sight of the Almighty. I hold my opinion and my opinion is to please God, not mankind. We don't apologise for no statement out of the Bible.

You must be crazy. Niceness. Love you all. Me, if I apologise, I lose my pride or I lose my sanity. It would be like I am joining the bandwagon of other people. Yow! I am out of Jamaica and whatever Jamaicans die for, Yow, I die for it... And if I should die for anything else, it would be the belief of an African. I went to Africa and that's not the progress in Africa. They ain't dealing with that, and Africans love women. Eight wives! So I'm with them and die with the Africans. No, I can't have eight wives. It ain't gonna work. I'll keep one wife. That's it.

CHAPTER 3

NOW ON HERE

CHAPTER THREE

1

Slackers, idlers

and some hot stuff for hooligans

Until his untimely death in 1997, critic and journalist Gavin Hills had a proto-'90s career. He began on the fringe, as a fanzine editor. But by the time he died, Hills had moved into - and sometimes subverted - mainstream British institutions. He had moved from writing on skateboarders to editing *England* magazine; from MTV Europe in Bosnia to BBC2 in Lebanon. Working through Zone Publishing, Hills even looked set to be the decade's Felix Dennis - Dennis being the '60s *Oz* magazine rebel who built an empire through Omnibus Press.

Whereas Dennis helped run *Oz*, however, Hills co-founded *Bomber Terrorzine*. He came of age in the late 1980s, publishing his first piece in '88. The following year, he co-authored a skater's manual, "Skateboarding Is Not A Book", with the photographer Vernon Adams. Adams was the other half of *Bomber*.

For Zone, Hills helmed magazines on phenomena from football to the Spice Girls. But he was also embarked on a novel for Hodder & Stoughton (working title: "My Life in Disco").He was also scheduled to co-present a series of Rough Guides for the BBC. Just weeks before he died in a fishing accident, Hills decided life was feeling good. First, he was over the moon about the Labour landslide. Plus, he felt his work was "finally amounting to something."

"You know how it is. For years people meet you and it's always, 'Oh, yeah, I think I read something by you'. These days, it's got better. It's got funnier, too. It's like 'Oh! *Hiiiiii*!' Last year, being frank, I was earning jackshit. I still wrote for free. But, in 1997, I can't complain." Hills had already written for a range of publications, from "quality papers" such as the *Observer* and the *Guardian* to youth mags like *G-Spot*. His thoughts were sought-after and his travelogues usually hailed from war zones, places like Sarajevo, Somalia and Northern Ireland. Yet the first lines Hills ever published made a scathing attack on the media:

"Statistics will always be found to 'prove' that youth like youth TV. But what do statistics really say? Just that teens watch the programmes because they're all that is on - or instead of Italian cookery."

"The bigger question is what we're being sold. And that is a version of our own lives which has been re-thought, re-packaged and re-directed: sanitised and rendered safe. Not for the family viewing audience of yore - more for the media men who control our access in today's electronic world."

"Those company types are also tightly controlled, and they direct Britain's perceptions of youth into non-confrontational models. This may not be true to life. But it works very well for both business and government. A passive, faddish, consumer-conscious youth brigade is always certain to do one thing - grown up the very same." ('Wipeout on the Juve Tube', *City Limits*, Oct 1988, with Vernon Adams.)

When punk re-surfaced as a theme for the '90s, Gavin Hills was no less skeptical. He felt the whole phenomenon left a double-edged legacy. Yes, the famous do-it-yourself ethic had brought empowerment; it was present in hip-hop, in the proliferation of bedroom studios, and in the always-resilient culture of the streets. "Rave culture, sound systems, they have no real stars. And their main attitude is still 'Let's tackle authority'."

But the movement's downside, he contended, was as large. Hills: "Those were the people who made *heroin* cool! Punk helped bring the whole crap phase of post-modernism. Level everything, just reduce everything to one level - that's another punk legacy. After all, the classic punk slogan was 'No Future'. And, in the end, where is that gonna leave you?"

Like many Britons his age, Hills always fought an official veneration of punk. Said he, "What annoys me most is: people who were part of it and who now have power, won't see punk for what it really was at all. Their line still is, 'It was great, then it ended'. During 1976, they started saying 'Fuck You'. In the '90s, they're still saying 'Fuck You' - only this time, it's to us. Their lack of idealism is astounding."

Whether one called it "punk" or not, the impulses battling for the soul of youth in the '90s - give in and give up, or strike back and endure - were pre-figured twenty years earlier. Accelerated decline only honed their double edge, even as it emphasised their talent's resilience.

Nothing about young life in London is now easy or safe. After the '80s, nothing is alternative, either. But, just as punk had re-envisioned the dole and pirate radio re-drew racial boundaries, rave culture transformed turntables and modems.

The "summers of love" which preceded the Criminal Justice Act had their own generically punkish aspect. Then, as rave culture exploded in the decade's centre, Douglas Coupland's book *Generation X* became a cult. The catchy terms this US author used for '90s apathy ("*McJob*", "*Option Paralysis*", "*Dead At 30, Buried at 70*") became trendy updates of the old punk slogans. Those (like "*Anarchy is the Melody*" or "*Modernity Kills*") had a similar ring, albeit a distant one.

1. Phat magazine HQ '93
Photo: Tim Leighton-Boyce
2. Generation X
by Douglas Coupland
Published by Abacus, '93

WHAT ANNOYS ME MOST IS: PEOPLE WHO WERE PART OF IT AND WHO NOW HAVE POWER, WON'T SEE PUNK FOR WHAT IT REALLY WAS AT ALL. THEIR LINE STILL IS, 'IT WAS GREAT, THEN IT ENDED'. DURING 1976, THEY STARTED SAYING 'FUCK YOU'. IN THE '90S, THEY'RE STILL SAYING 'FUCK YOU' - ONLY THIS TIME, IT'S TO US. THEIR LACK OF IDEALISM IS ASTOUNDING.
(→PAGE 57)

2

Gavin Hills summed up the impact of both: irony. "Punk introduced irony as a cover for British fears. And the end results have been diabolical. That's had a stronger appeal, at every level of society, than any thing punk ever meant or accomplished."

At the time Hills spoke, he was involved with a magazine which bore out his theory. It is a "little literary publication" founded by Hills' friend, Tom Hodgkinson. The bi-monthly is entitled *The Idler* (and subtitled *"Literature for Loafers"*). *The Idler* devotes itself to ultra-English roots, and its first "cover boy" was Samuel Johnson. "But," the magazine noted on its very first page, "Idlers are not nostalgic or sentimental: we live in the modern world. We embrace the computer, the fax, interactive TV." (Cover boy number two was TV's Homer Simpson.)

1

The Idler, says Hodgkinson, sprang from D-I-Y roots. But it makes a fetish of ironic ambivalence. (Features have covered a history of video games, London's toilets, ruminations on the Underground, plus the praises of croquet, heroin, and Douglas Coupland.) Said its founder on the eve of publication, "All that nihilistic slacker McJobs stuff, half of me really does find it quite attractive. But it means you abnegate responsibility. The initial idea of punk - just react against things - that idea has lost all its power. And part of the reason was it's been put on the catwalk."

The Idler could not be further from a fanzine - those smudgy, stapled sheets rife with Xeroxed clip art. It is printed on heavy, high-quality paper, with a colour cover and deliberately retro feel. *The Idler*'s print run started out at 1,000 - yet trebled itself within the first three issues. Some of its gambits demonstrated public-school savvy (Hodgkinson spent his student days at Cambridge). One, a young *Guardian* editor friend was drafted to help. Two, each issue was "launched" - separately - with a private party.

2

These dos were first held at the "Salon des Artes" near Kensington High Street; an eccentric, semi-private, would-be Chelsea Arts Club. Initially, they were filled with twentysomething friends. By issue four, however, they were crammed with the media. All were keen to meet some "genuine young people". Before long, the *Guardian* and *Observer* were actually publishers of *The Idler*. (Later, publication was taken over by Zone.) Says one old friend who contributed photos, "I went in to see them at the *Guardian* office. And, all of a sudden, it was 'Can we see your book?'"

Hodgkinson saw his magazine as one in a chain, schemes young people were hatching in loose collectives - a '90s D-I-Y strategy for gaining direction. Said he, "Right now, in London, everything is up for grabs. The positive side of that is how you can easily carve your niche. That's why I'm interested in these kids starting businesses, managing to express themselves while making money. They do it by being both operators and idlers."

Although the non-middle class "kids" were hardly "idlers", the roll-call of underground business bears out his statement. In an era moving slowly out of recession, their cheek and their spectrum defied the cynical. Early-'90s London had clothing labels, from Insane and Sign of the Times to Against All Oz and Hassan Haji's Rap; art and fashion teams such as BKS (Best Kept Secret) and The Watchmen Agency. There were also new magazines such as *Graphotism*, *Jihad*, and *Nubian*. When it came to the realm of indie vinyl, things were even hotter: with names such as Cold Sweat, Kongo, Cowboy, Go for the Juggler, Bite It!, Azuli, Mo' Wax, Instinct, Zoom, Greedy Beat, Elevation Inc, XL, Oh-Zone, Perfect Taste, Fresh and Warp.

All of these were separate endeavours, each destined to flourish or fall. But, even when their founders disavowed the label, threads from the punk movement still linked its past to their present. Fresh Records, for instance, was founded by Vicky Aspinall, her partner Dave Morgan and Frankie Goes to Hollywood ex Peter "Ped" Gill. Aspinall, once a member of punk trio The Raincoats, started a bedroom studio in her Notting Hill home. From 1990 to 1992, it introduced the team to artists, mixers, and producers. By 1993, thanks to a helpful bank manager, Aspinall, Morgan and Gill were the proprietors of Fresh Records.

By its eighth release, Fresh had distribution (through 3MV Sony) and was licensing all over Europe. They had various *noms du turntable*, such as Eden and Lovestation. In 1994, due to interest

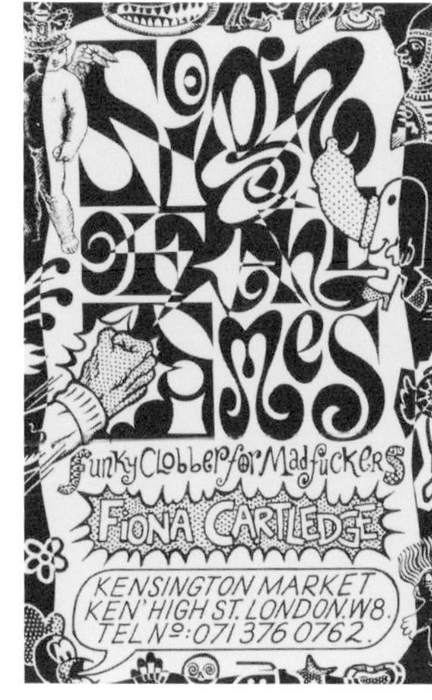

3

1. The Idler magazine Issue 1, Aug '93
2. The Idler logo Design: Ged Wells, '93
3. Flyer: Sign Of The Times Funky Clobber for Madfuckers Design: Fiona Cartledge
4. Insane - skate supplies shop, 5 Pratt Street, Camden Town Photo: Ged Wells
5. Ged Wells, '98

ALL THAT NIHILISTIC SLACKER MCJOBS STUFF, HALF OF ME REALLY DOES FIND IT QUITE ATTRACTIVE. BUT IT MEANS YOU ABNEGATE RESPONSIBILITY. THE INITIAL IDEA OF PUNK - JUST REACT AGAINST THINGS - THAT IDEA HAS LOST ALL ITS POWER. AND PART OF THE REASON WAS IT'S BEEN PUT ON THE CATWALK. (→PAGE 58)

4

5

from Nirvana, Aspinall's initial punk trio re-formed. She, pregnant with her son Nathan, declined to participate. Instead, Fresh architected three straight hits, claiming #31, #24 and #6 in the national charts. Strike, their new project, ended up at #4, having racked up sales of a quarter of a million.

Aspinall may eschew revivals. But she's certainly stuck to the punk ethic. She still believes in passion, and the power of perseverance. "You just have to believe in yourself. It comes down to that. If you lose faith in what you're doing, no one can help you."

She also still believes in a real team effort. "Plenty of times we've been in serious debt. Then it's helped that we've had each other to lean on. It sounds corny, but it's a family thing. The artists who come here are treated like that. So it's like a disservice to them to give up." The day she gave birth, Aspinall was hard at work; later, she took Nathan along to meetings.

Fresh is not the only punk spinoff of the present era. A similar case in the realm of print is AK Distribution. AK allows many radical mags their only sales outlet. They capitalise on youth's desertion of bookstores by selling in record and comic-shops or, occasionally, on the road with bands. AK began life in 1990; three years later, they were Noam Chomsky's publisher. Now, they keep a linked trio of offices; one in London, one in Scotland, one in San Francisco. At home, their expertise is specialist outlets, and they handle 100 independent titles, from *Girl Frenzy* ("a feminist glossy") to *Bad Attitude* (a "tabloid parody").

Yet who founded AK Distribution? Ramsay Kannan, once part of a punk band called Political Asylum. "All of us", a colleague concedes, "used to run about in Mohicans."

Even as they grew to an establishment status, London's rave and techno scenes also existed cheek by jowl with a string of retro-punk clubs. The most revivalist of them all was Stupid, held in an Oxford Street basement. It was run by David Rosen, a committed social worker. His views of punk differed widely from Gavin Hills'. Says Rosen, "It mattered to me as I grew up. I was the little kid in Lewisham, into records and jumpers. I was doing it all alone. But punk taught me a lot about self-expression."

Rosen never claimed his childhood inspiration was perfect. On the contrary, he says, punk "withered into packaged anger". But, unlike others, he is happy using the term. It is more enduring, he feels, than the fashions. "OK, I will grant you the clothes came back. Shops like Sign of the Times and Boy made a fortune in bondage strides. The average gay boy in the street is into tartan kilts. But my club, it's a forum, not just a hangout. It's not only about 'Let's dress nostalgically'."

Why? "Because that font of anger, it's still there. There's more reason for it in the '90s. This time, what we're gonna do is turn it around."

His nightclub's scheme - a literal, activist place for everyone - was the movement's unsung legacy. It was as visible at some raves as down in Oxford Street. Even as Britain took the path to insular anger, or to that escapism hymned in *The Idler*, Rosen's stance as the picky consumer was accurate. "Now, it's all about what kind of choices we make. Not being prepared to buy just any clothes; not being prepared to listen to just anyone's records. Not being prepared to say 'My vote doesn't matter'. We want our own moment and we're going to make it. Those drugs people took in punk times, they were passive. People still take those and we need to break the cycle."

Rosen spoke on the eve of Ecstasy Nation - but also as punk's nemesis, heroin, made its comeback.

For black cultural critic Paul Gilroy, words like Rosen's stir hope as well as memories. "When I think of punk," he says with a smile, "it's always, 'Here's an E Chord; so go form a band!'

1

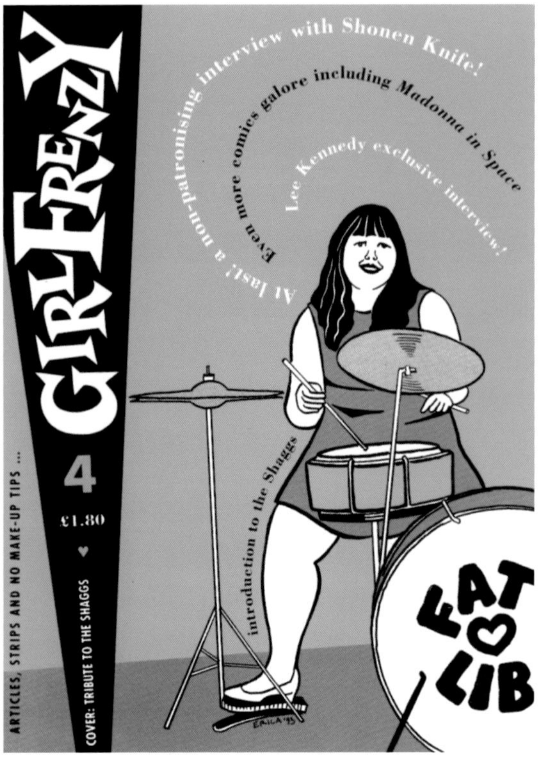

The idea of punks turning into something like Beefeaters, no one of that era could ever have thought of it."

Postcard punks, "crusties" and beggars are now '90s icons. But Dr. Gilroy, too, updates his image. "When I think of what might be '90s punk, I guess I think first of Apache Indian. More specifically, of the logo used on his posters." This was a parody of the campaign to 'Keep Britain Tidy'; its graphic featured dropping a swastika into the litter-bin. Who designed it? Stylist Judy Blame.

"The link between 'No Fun' and 'No Future'", says Paul Gilroy, "was a device, by which people declared there had to be a future." So there was, which explains punk's '90s presence, from skateboarding to hip-hop, raves to jungle, hackers to cyberpunks.

Everyone now aims to cover that sprawling landscape - from the *Electronic Telegraph* to Channel 5. But the first organ which really did it well, which managed to be part of the change rather than just chase it, lasted only six elusive months. It fell victim to a tabloid witch-hunt, a tradition of censorship which will not die.

Up until the beginning of 1993, a team of young Britons handled the publication *RAD* - an acronym for *Read and Destroy*. Initially based around BMX biking and skateboarding, "the *RAD*-mag" became a British cult. Its sales attracted a succession of owners, until it ended up in Robert Maxwell's empire. After Maxwell died, staffers were offered the chance to buy it.

The offer they submitted was not declined - just ignored. (To their surprise, *RAD* was already sold.) But, using fresh plans and shared experience, the same team launched a different magazine. It debuted July 1993 with the title *Phat* - which was raggamuffin slang for "hot".

Phat was designed in four separate parts: one cover feature plus three additional "modules". Each module's brief was very deliberately different. One covered "culture in the 21st century"; another, consumer affairs; a third, clubs, sport and leisure. Thirty thousand copies were placed in high street stores.

Or, at least, some high street stores. Once an "advance exposé" appeared in the *Sunday Telegraph*, *Phat* was locked into a battle with newsagents John Menzies. Some advertisers, like the Midland Bank, pulled out. Why? Because of the magazine's initial cover. Tag-lined "Teenage Gangsta!", it showed a weedy teen - clad in a sweatshirt - aiming a handgun.

3

2

1. Girl Frenzy
   Tribute to The Shaggs, no. 4
   Aug '93
2. Insane stickers
   Design: Ged Wells
3. Design from "Flirt"
   T-Shirt catalogue
   Design: Ged Wells

RIGHT NOW, IN LONDON, EVERYTHING IS UP FOR GRABS. THE POSITIVE SIDE OF THAT IS HOW YOU CAN EASILY CARVE YOUR NICHE. THAT'S WHY I'M INTERESTED IN THESE KIDS STARTING BUSINESSES, MANAGING TO EXPRESS THEMSELVES WHILE MAKING MONEY. THEY DO IT BY BEING BOTH OPERATORS AND IDLERS.

(→PAGE 58)

1

2

1. to 4.

Phat magazine

Photo: Tim Leighton-Boyce

Facing page:

Phat magazine facts (fax) '93

YOU JUST HAVE TO BELIEVE IN YOURSELF. IT COMES DOWN TO THAT. IF YOU LOSE FAITH IN WHAT YOU'RE DOING, NO ONE CAN HELP YOU.

[>PAGE 58]

OUTSIDE LONDON, IT'S NOT SO EASY. IF YOU COME TO LONDON AND WORK HARD ON AN IDEA, AT SOME POINT, SOMEBODY WILL PICK UP ON IT. AS LONG AS IT'S GOOD, SOMEBODY WILL PICK UP ON IT.

[>PAGE 71]

C21 Publishing Ltd
Broadway Studios
28 Tooting High Street
London
SW17 0RG

Phone + Fax: 081 682 2414

PHAT FACTS

PHAT MAGAZINE — HOT STUFF FOR HOODLUMS

Published by C21 Publishing

TARGET READERSHIP

* Teenage boys 13-16 years old
* Into HipHop/Rap music, HipHop/Skate clothing, computer games, street culture
* Not into team games, mainstream activities, authority!
* No direct competition: currently read music or computer magazines or R.a.D

FORMAT

* Monthly, first issue on sale 15th July
* 64 pp A4 32 pp colour
* Cover price £1.50
* Modular concept:
  - C21: articles on street culture
  - Buzz: where to go/what to see/where to hang out
  - Products: catalogue and reviews of latest products

CONTACT DETAILS

* Editorial:	Tim Leighton-Boyce
* Advertising:	Laurence Stubbs
	Broadway Studios, 28 Tooting High Road, London SW17 0RG
	Tel & Fax: 081 682 2414
* Accounts:	Peter Collins
	The Old Church, Chittoe, Chippenham, Wilts SN15 2EL
	Tel: 0380 850334 Fax: 0380 850335

Stuck in the gun's muzzle was a daisy, a fact lost in subsequent discussions. Inside, the captions noted it was "a replica Beretta", wielded by a model called Matt Stuart. Under Stuart's credit, *Phat* ran the following line: "He doesn't like guns. His holiday in LA was ruined when he saw a traffic warden get shot. We thought you should know."

Gavin Hills, then 25, was *Phat*'s Editor. He wrote the cover story himself: as a reasoned, streetwise argument against "gun culture". Hills was already an author, *Face* writer and gossip columnist. For an article he had written on Somalia, he was given an Amnesty International award.

Within a week of the *Sunday Telegraph* piece, however, Hills was vilified by the very same media. He faced radio hosts, columnists, pundits, e-mails and faxes. Or, as he puts it, "All of a sudden I'm on the air. And Mothers Against Murder and Aggression are telling me I'm unfit to have children."

Amidst the uproar, *Phat* actually hit the shops. Effortlessly, it mixed skateboarding, consumer jokery ("Shopping with Satan: Barcode of the Beast"), Japanese manga comics, Britain's latest trends in graffiti, "Movie Musts" and UFOs in Belgium. There were some clear echoes of "No Future" (the "Career Guide For Losers" and the town-by-town index called "Getting A Life in Boring Britain"). But the energy of its young staff was palpable.

Above its masthead, *Phat* ran a manifesto: "Our mission is clear. *Phat* magazine is for hoodlums, by hoodlums. Together we'll take publishing into the twenty-first century by sinking it to depths

Is Satan In Your Shopping Basket?

Barcodes are now on every product you buy. From chewing gum to Durex, those strange patterns of lines appear. But are they in any way involved in the ultimate fate of mankind? Yes indeed, according to the latest tale of the apocalypse going the rounds.

The story is that if you take a close look on all barcodes you will see that there are three sets of lines that are longer than the others, at the beginning, middle and the end of the main barcode section. Each section of lines represents a number, but you will see that these three longer lines have the same format on all barcodes. They also have the same numeric value: six. On every barcode the only thing that is constant is those three sets of lines. The only thing that ever reads constant on a barcode is: 6 6 6.

As anyone who has ever read Revelation, or seen the film the Omen, can tell you, six hundred threescore and six is the number of the beast. As we come up to the end of the millennium we are informed that this is to be the time of the second coming. If that is true then the beast, the anti-Christ, Satan, must surely soon be amongst us and the number of the beast appearing at every shopping transaction is very worrying indeed.

For, as it says in Revelation XIII 16-17:

"And he caused all, both small and great, rich and poor, free and bond, to receive a mark in their right hand, or in their foreheads: And that no man might buy or sell, save that had the mark, or the name of the beast, or the number of his name."

The story continues that in Western Australia a small town called Balimore is already experimenting with doing away with cash and replacing it with a personal barcode which is worn on the wrist and run through the till to pay for things. Revelations makes it very clear that the first thing the anti-Christ will do is take over trade. While all this could of course be just mystic mumbo-jumbo, it's very hard to think of a better way for Satan to conquer than to control the shopping habits of the world. A hi-tech high prince of darkness would indeed be a dangerous thing. Keep 'em peeled: you heard it here first folks.

Barcode Battlers code includes '666'

Is Satan in your shopping basket?
Phat magazine, issue 1
Aug '93

Facing page:
Phat magazine, issue 1
Aug '93

"ALL WE ENDORSE", SAID HILLS, "IS FACING UP TO THE FACTS. YOU'RE NOW BOUND TO BE UNEMPLOYED AT SOME POINT. YOU'RE PROBABLY NEVER GONNA HAVE A CAREER FOR LIFE. SO LEARN TO BE FLEXIBLE, LEARN WHAT'S WORTHWHILE. AND LEARN HOW TO USE YOUR ANGER BEST."
(→PAGE 68)

Hot Stuff for Hoodlums
£1.50 monthly. Issue 1
Phat
magazine
new!
Top Manga Action
Girls & Robots!
Shopping with Satan
Barcode of the Beast
Tank Girl
goes to Hollywood
Graffiti
Britain's new school
UFO Watch
Calling Occupants
Top Cult Films
Video classics not to miss
teenage gangsta!
You've got the look
Do you really need the guns?
Phat blows the myth away
Three Great Mags in One:
Module 1:
C21
Journey into the next century:
Paranormal
Anti-culture
Wierd Science
& Attitude
Module 2:
buzz
Region by region guide to Britains top spots
Shops
Clubs
Events
& Hang-outs
Module 3:
produx
Consumer durables for undesirables
Ultra-Fashions
Jap Imports
Games
Music
Free Skate Supplement
Edinburgh, Bristo Square
Frank Hirata
The New Generation
Sequences
new boards & wheels
Hot Babes
Cicciolina,
Swimsuit comics plus our top five to lust after
Win the latest labels
before the Kevs get 'em
08
£1.50
August
Version 1
9 770969 740002
International Info Overload!

1

previously unimaginable. Seven years, four months, sixteen days and counting. Read us and weep." It was a teen bravado, raggamuffin-style.

At the time, Hills said he expected something of a flap. "I went out to lunch with that *Telegraph* guy. And we chatted about everything from drugs to joyriding. I said, 'OK, sure, all this stuff happens. But here, from my point of view, is what you can do.' He was pretty straight with me, however. He said, 'I'm afraid you already know what we're gonna run'."

"*Phat*-mag", as the staffers referred to it, was more sophisticated than its critics admitted. Hoping to draw readers from 13 to 16, it was a boys' mag which was both clear-eyed and modern. "It was to do with truth," noted editor Hills. "If you tell kids the truth, they're likely to believe you, take what you say on board. And the truth about guns is: thanks to movies and hip-hop, kids really think they're sexy."

He was not being alarmist. "Britain has no gun epidemic at the moment. But someone's friend of a friend might easily have one. So we need to say, 'Look, guns may attract. But they kill people too, which isn't cool'."

This was just what *Phat*'s "Gun Special" said. It began with the words, "I've always wanted to shoot somebody". But it then spent pages deconstructing the urge, checking out its social roots ("Five Gun Songs", "Guns'n'Rap", "Pukka Gun Movies") and exploding myths ("Spraying from the hip looks good but you won't hit a sausage"). Then, it finished with an unequivocal paragraph:

"Practically all this world's problems are caused by men with guns. Life may be tough and we all might want to be cool, but shooters are strictly for losers. Because the thing about guns is: they kill people. From Moss Side to Sarajevo; from Somalia to south LA: Bang-bang and you're *dead* sucker."

Newsagents John Menzies were "reluctant" to handle the cover, yet distributors COMAG fanned the controversy. Says publisher Tim Leighton-Boyce, a *RAD* alumnus, "They wanted a lot of promo, so we did ads and flyposters. We had a PR send our press release." But the latter was inoffensive, consisting of "*Phat* Facts" like the following:

"The first issue of *Phat* examines gun culture and the frightening implications of gun-law: in America, 12 people under 16 are shot every day; in all, 27,000 people a year die from gunshot wounds. Movies and music reinforce the image of the gun as a desirable object in most teenage boys' heads. In reality, most boys who do end up with a gun get little respect, a life of hassle, and rarely get a second chance."

1. Photo-shoot for cover of Phat magazine, issue 1 Aug '93

2. Phat magazine, issue 2 Sept '93

NO MATTER WHAT THE FACTS, WHAT THE PRODUCT, HOW GREAT ITS INITIATIVE, INSTITUTIONS HAVE THE FINAL SAY. WHEN IT COMES TO BUILDING A BUSINESS - TO DOING ONE'S OWN THING ON ONE'S OWN TERMS - A MUCH SAVVIER STRATEGY IS REQUIRED.

(→PAGE 69)

2

IT'S JUST OUR OWN DESIGN GROUP; BEING REPRESENTED AS A GROUP HELPS A LOT. IT TOTALLY MAKES SENSE. SO MANY PEOPLE IN BRITAIN ARE OUT THERE WORKING FREELANCE; IT GETS LONELY AND THERE'S NO SUPPORT. NOWHERE YOU CAN ACTUALLY TURN FOR INFORMATION.

(→PAGE 72)

"Encouragingly, the *Phat* poll also revealed that a further quarter of 'Gangster Culture' boys don't rate guns at all - they dismiss the subject, joking that they'd rather have no gun or a water pistol, certainly nothing that fires bullets."

"*Phat* Magazine is a revolutionary new magazine for those who will be 21 in the 21st century. It is the only one of its kind available in the UK catering for the tastes of teenage boys covering a wide variety of subjects - techno gadgetry, clothing, style, where to go, what to do, food and places."

Despite the upbeat PR, *Phat* was pilloried; questions on it were even raised in Parliament. But most who spoke the loudest read only its media pack. Nor did they understand it was prophetic: *Phat* was a hip precursor to both the *Wired* and *Loaded* phenomena. Its young designer, Steve Hicks, came from traditional publishing. For *Phat*, he used slick, fast computer layouts.

It was the first British magazine to use the Internet, both for reader surveys and for contributors' copy. (Staff also used the cix network for memos and conferencing.) In addition, Hicks fed Hi-8 video straight to page make-up. "The reason we started doing that", says Leighton-Boyce, "was to help us analyse movement in sport. Then, we found it generated exciting imagery."

In short, *Phat* was put together almost without paper. It included contributors from Japan, Eastern Europe, America and Malaysia. Even the regular staff often eschewed its office. They were linked by modem, cellular phones and e-mail.

But detractors claimed the budding techies were "junior deviants" (as *Media Week*'s Simon Waldman put it on Radio One). In his interviews, Gavin Hills fought back staunchly, saying the magazine's audience deserved respect: "*Phat* is realism, it's not nihilism. All our readers know Britain's current situation. They know perfectly well why we've ended up where we have. We want to discuss it, but with a positive slant."

"All we endorse", said Hills, "is facing up to the facts. You're now bound to be unemployed at some point. You're probably never gonna have a career for life. So learn to be flexible, learn what's worthwhile. And learn how to use your anger best."

Phat turned No Future into Techno Future - and it was, accordingly, extremely popular. Years before Web mania could arise, before Britain sprouted companies like Rise, Obsolete or WebMedia, *Phat* did more than predict online linkups. It courted the video and computer game mindset and looked towards a burgeoning electronic culture. Moreover, it knew they had a total identity - they belonged to a different, fresh generation. There have since been many attempts to do the same thing, from *UK Wired* to television's "The Net". None, however, have had either *Phat*'s assurance or style. They are aimed at an audience; *Phat* was made for peers by peers.

Regardless, both Britain's corner shops and news chains shunned it. And, in the midst of the controversy it engendered, Steve Hicks was poached by American giant Time Publishing. They made him art director of a new mag, *Mouth 2 Mouth*.

Said Hills, "That just symbolised the whole hypocrisy. We had such a good product everyone could see it. So America came in and stole our man. One day, Steve's in our dodgy little office; next week, he's out in Malibu in the sun with his green card. While, here at home, we're being forced out of business."

It was true. As *Phat* struggled, Hicks went on to become a US success. He moved from *Mouth 2 Mouth* to the more mainstream *Self* - where, within a year, he was Art Director. Before long, he left that for new technology, at Avalanche Systems, where he spent another year. In the late '90s, as a designer for Poppe Tyson Interactive, Hicks works largely on the World Wide Web.

Says he, "I do lots of big, corporate accounts. But that early training was invaluable. Going from being edgy and on the fringe to the opposite - it's a very cool way to study applying one's skills. I get quite a kick out of what I do now, trying to stretch technologies on a daily basis."

America, says Hicks, can teach valuable lessons. "Just being a good designer, knowing how to 'sell yourself', it's just not sufficient. You need an in-depth course in marketspeak, so you can really communicate with businessmen. Then they know why your choices are right for them. In England, there's too much dancing around those questions. Plus, there's not enough respect for skills."

Certainly, this was the case with *Phat*. As the magazine started to produce a third issue, Leighton-Boyce drove to Scotland to placate John Menzies. The newsagent chain had insisted on seeing every page. Then, says Hills, W.H. Smith "delivered the death-blow". After Issue Three had already left the printer's, Smith's announced that none of their shops would stock it.

Phat's staff started scrambling for a way to survive, but no D-I-Y ethos could save their baby. Says Leighton-Boyce, "We never did what we were accused of. But we certainly did suffer for it."

One professional tried hard to save the mag. This was Jim Heinemann, circulation manager for Time Out Distribution. The alternative agency was four years old, one of several offshoots of London's *Time Out* magazine. *Time Out* was the veteran London listings weekly - and Heinemann, too, saw himself as a veteran. A can-do bloke with a laid back temperament, he saw small magazines as "Frankly, a total headache".

Yet his company handles up to 40 a time, and Heinemann sees himself as the trade's diplomat. "I mediate between a very staid, conservative business and this cottage industry where nothing is predictable." He and his team wanted *Phat* very badly; they saw it, Heinemann says, as "a real original. *Phat* truly caught the spirit of its era. Which rarely happens, we very rarely see it."

But their research revealed the title's case was hopeless. "We found all the newsagents had this huge resistance. They had the wrong idea, but they wouldn't budge. Once this happens, there's just no way around it. You can even ship them magazines, but they won't be opened".

Today, *Phat* remains a collector's item - roundly praised by everyone who read it. However, there are few better illustrations of "D-I-Y creativity" meeting its match. No matter what the facts, what the product, how great its initiative, *institutions* have the final say. When it comes to building a business - to doing one's own thing on one's own terms - a much savvier strategy is required.

It arrived too late for *Phat*, but *Phat* paved the way.

Phat magazine, issue 3
Oct '93

YET NOTHING OUTSIDE YOURSELF CAN MAKE YOU FEEL WHOLE. NOT FAME, NOT DRUGS, NOT SEX, NOT MONEY. YOU HAVE TO COME TO A POINT WHERE YOU REALISE THAT - NONE OF THOSE THINGS WORK, NOTHING CAN FILL YOU UP.

(→PAGE 75)

Ged Wells was part of the early *Phat* posse; he also does illustrations for *The Idler*. Until summer, 1997, he also ran a Camden skate shop. It bore the same name as his company, Insane Productions & Distribution, Ltd. Wells has evolved it from a set of skateboard stickers into an independent, self-owned business, distributed in Britain, in Europe and Japan. In addition to Insane, he also founded Flirt: a self-created collective of visual artists.

You started out on the Isle of Wight?

Yes, that's where I'm from. I joined the Enterprise Allowance Scheme there. You had to have £1,000 in the bank to do it. I tried to get an overdraft from my bank manager. But they tried to make me take out lots and lots of loans. In the end, I borrowed it from my parents. Then the Scheme sent me on an "Awareness Day", which was especially bleak. It was full of builders and women hoping to sell knick-knacks.

What happened then?

I moved up to London, where I used the Enterprise money for rent and food. I also got the idea for Jim-Jams, which were this sort of line of skateboard shorts. I mailed all my Jim-Jams designs back home; there, my Mum sewed and printed them. I came up to London for work, I wanted to be an illustrator. But I found it very, very hard to get work. No one really liked my style much. But I really like doing my own kind of drawings. So, I messed around. I just sold Jim-Jams to a couple of skate shops.

How did Insane happen?

Well, on the Isle of Wight I had worked on fanzines. They were just good fun, you know, lots of friends would do one - just on photocopiers. From that, I had started doing stickers, which could be put onto skateboard decks. I would draw this special little face, it looked a bit mad and someone said to me, "You should do stickers with that on and call them Insane". So I did that, and people seemed to like them.

I was still going back to the Isle of Wight, making a few clothes at a time with help from my Mum. We'd just print a few shirts here and there, with no real intention of going into business. When I came to London, though, I started thinking, "You know, there are more possibilities here".

Ged Wells:

skating and shopkeeping, Phat-style

Your designs, first stocked at Slam City Skates, got popular very quickly.

They're just bold graphics and the style comes from skateboarding. I just doodle, draw things which are around. I mean, the Hoover, the toys, the stuff in my flat. People seem to love them but, basically, I do what I like. Afterwards, I try to judge if it's good enough. The writing, too, is really important to me. I write little poems. Some of the characters I do are like illustrations of the characters in a story. Basically, I like toys, lots of what I do is toy-based.

Did you shape your work as sports couture?

The whole style of it has come from skateboarding, I have shaped it all to what skaters like. But skateboarding offers a lot of vehicles for design - from decks to windbreakers. There's a lot of creativity within skateboarding, and a lot of ingenuity. People build up strong attitudes, although sometimes it comes about through conflict. Just going out and skating, though, that's good expression. And a lot of skaters do other things. A lot of people in that scene want to be doing stuff: setting up companies, making videos, coming up with logos. It's just an energy which crosses national boundaries.

You've had Insane stickers, clothing, T-shirts, caps and hip packs. You even had your own promotional video.

Which was a showreel for two skater-directors, guys from Cambridge. Yeah, Insane also sponsored Rasmus Skousen, this real nice guy who is a Danish skater. Videos are just another thing that's big in skating, people who make boards have these teams of riders and they use cassettes to promote the team - who, in turn, will then promote their gear. I did one that was based around a story, which featured some of the characters on the boards and things.

Skating has always crossed a lot of boundaries: music, club clothes, style and advertising. I had one of my fashion shows at the Wag Club; I've had other exhibits with Alternative Arts and at Bar Vinyl - which is a place in Camden - with the Scratch Crew. One of the things which first helped Insane most was a Japanese DJ who liked this hat. He was in Dee-Lite and he wore it in their video.

When you went solo, what did you do first?

I found a space to work, which was part of Rhythm King, a record company. That was all right, because I was doing more freelance stuff. But, at the same time, I still wanted to do my own thing. So I was trying to work out a way of getting some money - getting it together so I could do that. Basically, the core problem was my ties. I couldn't actually start a whole new business, because I had to pay for some previous costs.

What enabled you to start again?

I met this guy John Deer who had the company Fat Boy. He'd been doing a couple of lines for about a year. T-shirt production, really. I had a chat with him and he wasn't totally clued up about what was going on. But I felt at the time it was a good position. John is the kind of character that's got a lot of go. And that's what I needed, just to start afresh. John had a partner, who had put some money in Fat Boy, and I licensed the Insane name to them. To do that, you need to understand what 'license' means. A license is, with design, that you have a package of ideas and you're giving them to somebody else to exploit - for money. So, what you need to make sure of is that everything will work out right. You need to think ahead, think what you want to be doing - and think out all the different problems you could get into. A license will give you security, for instance, but that kind of security's a two-way street.

But it worked with Fat Boy?

Yeah. With me, they just said, "Write down all the different points you want to make", then we drafted this thing between us, and I gave it to them. Fat Boy made the alterations they felt were needed and we just signed it. It was quite straightforward; they agreed to everything. I had an expiry date and get-out clause. And it was just for a percentage on wholesale turnover; it was purely a license for a market area. I still remained self-employed, I still did my taxes. But they had everything delineated. It all comes down to whether you're happy with their investment - and whether they're happy with your direction.

What did this license cover?

In this case it was T-shirts and clothing - for Europe. Then, because we had constant Japanese interest, that was extended to Japan as well. America is a different story, because you can't run a factory of clothing in this county. Not our kind of clothing, skatewear, and then sell it to America. It's just not possible; everything's produced out there much cheaper. We still get T-shirts that come from the States, too, so they're probably made elsewhere anyway. We did what it's easiest to do, I mean, we had control, because we were small. Of course, we too could have gotten our stuff made out in the Far East. But I didn't want to go and abuse people out there. If they made more money, it would be different.

What's the answer with financing?

I don't know about financing in this country, and where it comes from. When I've talked to other people, it's always either they're doing it off their own bat and trying to build something. Or they've been doing it and then somebody else has come in. And that's usually a contact through the work they're doing, or through friends. That's how it is with me. A friend's Dad, Bobby Gregory, has always helped me out. He's seen what I've been doing and my various problems. And he's got some money, so he's prepared to really help - because he feels it will work. I continue to actually turn over, so I can pay him back. Mind you, he's an old-style businessman; we see eye to eye on few things outside business!

Do you feel the situation for young business people is hopeful?

Well, some of it's London. If you're outside London, it's not so easy. If you come to London and work hard on an idea, at some point, somebody will pick up on it. As long as it's good, somebody will pick up on it. It's pretty rare, that you don't really see people who are very, very busy doing something with real direction where it doesn't actually happen for them. Probably the best thing for people starting out to know is you have to make sure that you've got a good product. And that there's a market which will know about it. Probably the same with music. If you do it yourself first, if you do it whatever way, if you just print a T-shirt and get some publicity for it - then you're in a strong position to find some financing. Because you know you've got a market.

What about business plans?

Business plans can't always pay for things. But if you get into doing them, you can enjoy 'em. You find out, that when you see your ideas on paper, it does make things clearer. It's a good thing to do. Apart from that, it's good for yourself, because you can actually *see* that you've moved on. You also see the things you didn't do and why you didn't.

The first business plan I did I think I was in college. But it wasn't very good. The ones that I started doing when we opened the shop are the only ones I've been really happy with. It's funny, you want to do lots of different things but you don't actually know the way to do them. It's often impossible to do a plan - because you don't know the methods. My first plans were like, "I'm going to do this and this - and this and this and *this*." I knew there was some way to do it, but I didn't know how to put it all together. Now, I can do that. Because I've learned that different things are all joined together in some way, and I can actually say why they are joined. That's very different from how I started out.

How did you happen to get the Insane shop?

In 1995, I was working with Fat Boy and things were ticking over. Boma Jaja, another skater, he'd been planning to try and do a shop for a while. We discussed this quite a lot, how best to do a shop. Boma had got some financing, but not a lot. And he didn't have a name or anything. So I said, "Look, would you want to call it Insane? Because that could be really good for me." I said, "I could put my stuff in the shop, use the basement as my studio. And, from there, we'd just see what happens." So, we looked around West London, we looked around Camden and we looked in Central London. We thought that Camden was a good place to run it, because there was a good skate scene here - and it was somewhere we knew. Plus, it was central. We found this shop in Pratt St and it was perfect. We negotiated a lease and fixed it up.

Financially, it was pretty manageable. At the beginning, though, there wasn't a lot of money for actually getting stock. But, luckily, it ticked over and it's still doing that. It started building, really, because no one took any money out of it. So it was tight, but at the same time, it kept growing. We had the core of skateboarding culture, too, because that's why we did it in the first place. Our hearts are in skating, and we wanted to do something, we both wanted that. Boma was constantly thinking about new things for skaters. When Boma moved on and started his own place, I managed it alone for awhile. Then I passed it on to a Japanese designer, Hiro. He does clothes, too - but still stocks Insane. I really wanted to concentrate on design - managing the shop as well was just too much.

Is skatewear really a viable British industry?

Look at it this way, skating in Britain is two generations on. If boards are so expensive because they're still imported from America, what that means is young kids here can't afford to keep buying boards. Not when they cost £60 a throw and they break 'em every couple of weeks! That's why we initially thought, if we sort out boards , that would be a healthy thing for skating in Europe. We started working on that early on; two years later, we were able to make them. Basically, the shop opened up at a really good time. There's another generation here; there's even now a different way of skating. The kind of philosophy of people who now do it is different. The abilities from five years ago, the abilities of kids, has just multiplied. Now, it's really brilliant.

In what way does it actually differ?

Well, I think Mark Gonzales [the Californian street skater] is quite an influence, because he's is one of those people that's become innovative. There's a few characters who have actually pushed skating in the direction it's going now, which is that it's gone to the streets. It's pushed onto the streets again, because there aren't the facilities for people who've adapted to skating there, and who are there to stay. They're not so bothered about other places - like skate parks. They're happy, really happy, to go out on the street.

The old school of skaters in London, the mid-'80s skaters, feel that the younger skaters aren't doing it "right" - but that's bullshit. They just feel threatened. You can't even compare it. These kids, they're incredible; they really are incredible. I mean, what they're doing to the body is extreme, they're hurting themselves. But their abilities are definitely more hard, more expressive. Plus, there's all these groups, all these little scenes happening.

You think it's improved?

I think it's all changed. Back in the mid-'80s, there was lots more going on. People were doing their own magazines or trying to start their own companies. They were also trying to build facilities. A lot of those are still going - like, Sony built a skatepark in Ladbroke Grove. But there are hundreds of board companies in the States. They're all young people, relatively speaking, and some are doing really well. It seems healthy and it's always changing. Plus, there's now this whole snowboarding culture.

We've got more magazines, which is good for everyone. The best thing about skate magazines is that they really make you go and want to skate. They can do it in different ways. They can show really good skaters; they can show good places to go. *Phat* magazine did that, *Big Brother* does it, *Transworld Skateboarding* does it, and *Thrasher* does it too, but not as much. Then there are the videos, video magazines, and television - skating's now seen on MTV and sports stations.

Were you a sole proprietor?

It's a little more complicated than that. Boma and I parted amicably. He now has another skate shop, called Fluid, which he started in Beak St with Sean Turpin. It's great, you know, they stock Insane products. What happened really was I started my company properly: as Insane Production & Distribution, Ltd. That meant incorporating, which is a lot of aggro. But I did it, because it was what I wanted. In the end, it was worth the trouble, but it was pretty complicated.

Obviously, running a business is different than just choosing to license your designs, or from running a shop. We did all our products, we subcontracted stuff, to printers and to makers. Plus, we bought our boards. On top of that, we were still doing the clothing. Twice a year: a summer and a winter collection. These go to other skate shops, all around the UK and a bit in Europe.

You used the shop basement as your studio; then it turned into an artists' co-operative?

That started with five of us working there: Mac operators, illustrators, painters, designers. We just wanted to have a company structure, so in 1997 we formed Flirt. Really, it's just our own design group; being represented as a group helps a lot. It totally makes sense. So many people in Britain are out there working freelance; it gets lonely and there's no support. Nowhere you can actually turn for information. We pretty much invented Flirt, it's our system. We just got together and pooled our experience: on basic invoicing, job descriptions, payment plans. Then we looked around and got advice. There are other companies who work as similar co-ops. It just took sorting out the paperwork.

Who is involved presently?

Right now, there are five of us in the studio. There's me and my old pal Pete Corry, a graffiti artist from the old Rub studio. He now works as "Etch", he's totally legal. Pete does painting and design for Sony playstations. There's Mark Abbott, a skater who designs, illustrates, and does typography. There's David Pym, who's a Mac illustrator, and David Hartley, who does graphic design. We've already done several exhibitions. We've also been doing stuff as part of a crew, part of the Scratch Crew who do a King's Cross club. When we moved from the shop basement, they became neighbours. We've done stuff to decorate their club, and some stage drops for venues like the Astoria. Having our company structure has helped a lot.

Any final words of advice?

I used to just say "get on with it and do what you can"; spend as much time on your own producing your ideas as you can. So you've got a whole package of stuff to show someone. Then, instead of you just talking about it, you've got things to show: you've done it first. But I realise it varies from person to person. I don't have great goals of what I want in the future. I can just think of things that I want to be doing. I can't imagine some overall plan of where everything's going. All you can think about when you think of the future is like power kind of things. They're the only terms you're *allowed* to think in. But I don't think they're very constructive, because that's just money. So I only think short term on what we do. I can see from there where money could be generated - and some kind of security. But, beyond that, I can't see.

Writer's camp:

Boy George on becoming an author

"Boy" George O'Dowd personified the artifice of the '80s. He was witty, daring and flamboyant - and, in London, a well-known homosexual. But, to his public world, George the pop star denied this; just as, later, he denied an addiction to heroin. By 1990, cleaning up and coming back, he assumed various career mantles: producer, record-company manager, popular DJ. He also scored a US chart hit with his version of "The Crying Game". In 1995, George unveiled a real career change. This was *Take It Like A Man* (Sidgwick & Jackson), his autobiography. It covered his career, downfall and long climb back, treating homosexuality, drugs and fame with provocative honesty. Although it led to at least one major lawsuit (from Kirk Brandon, won by O'Dowd in '97), it was unsparing, unselfserving - and often funny. Through his venture into a different field, George both reclaimed his past and revealed a special talent.

I always loved autobiographies. I've read lots of them, so I know the best are unauthorised. I made many tries and it took me years. But that really was my aim: the unauthorised book of my life! I left school with no qualifications. So, for me, that I can write is a major triumph. What surprised people most is that I was critical of myself. But I knew I was not an innocent victim - someone in the wrong place at the wrong time. Still, it wasn't easy telling the absolute truth. To the public, I always had this blaring, assumed kind of confidence. But inside, Hiroshima was going on. Only in the past seven, eight - maybe nine - years have I really felt what I flaunted. And, every day, there are still loose floorboards. Often, they come up and slap you right in the face.

Initially, I came out when I was 16. My family knew, all my friends knew, I broadcast it whenever and wherever. Then, I set foot in the studio with Culture Club, and this song I wrote about Kirk Brandon. It was called "The Eyes of Medusa", and it had these lyrics: "He loves me, he hates me, he knows me too well". We were making an early demo and the engineer stopped us and said, "'Ere, you're singing '*he*'!" I got very uptight; I said, "Well, of course I am!" But the band were like, "Er, don't you think you should be more general?" And probably, if I had stood my ground I wouldn't have been the success I was - because the world just wasn't ready. But I often wonder how it would have gone. If, from that beginning,

I had just said, "I'm gay". Instead, I became this famous, genderless doll. And I lived on a steady diet of animosity, friction and drama. That's who I was.

Now, I want to write another book. A book about homosexuality, one that deals with childhood insecurities and early preconceptions. From a humourous point of view but, still, going into it deeply. I'm gonna call it "Dicks, Dykes and Demons". One thing I want it to broach is my belief that it's not gonna be about others changing. The gay community, gay people, have to change. It's not about anyone else, it's about us. It's like the Andrew Sullivan book I read, *Virtually Normal*. He's got some brilliant things there about gay rights and issues. But it's written from a very unemotional standpoint. And the experience of homosexuals is very emotional. Explosively emotional. I felt I had to use that. But I also wanted to put my own change in a broader context. For years, I walked around with a chip on my shoulder. That was inherited from society, from the school playground. I did feel inferior, and I disguised it. Instead, I became outlandish, overly confident, and sometimes arrogant. Now I do actually feel comfortable with my sexuality - and my whole world's changed. I'm not saying I lead a boring, rosy life. But I can get on with intelligent things.

I talk a lot about heroin in my book. There were lots of questions about Kurt Cobain on my book tour. When I think of him, I feel very sad. He was one of the few, for a long time after David Bowie, who said anything to me through rock and roll. But, again, he was someone not comfortable with his own worth. That is something I tried to talk about. I'm in a good position to explain how, when you come from a dysfunctional family, it's very, very hard to re-learn what it teaches you. So, a part of you will really relish success. But a voice in your head incessantly chirps, "You don't deserve this". Growing up, dreaming of being liked and being successful, you imagine that somehow fame will fulfil every need. That somehow, suddenly, you will be made secure.

Yet nothing outside yourself can make you feel whole. Not fame, not drugs, not sex, not money. You have to come to a point where you realise that - none of those things work, nothing can fill you up. And, believe me, I know. I tried everything; in some ways, I'm like a modern-day Elvis. But, to write about it, I knew I mustn't preach. If someone reads my story and it can influence them, if they don't make my silly mistake with heroin, then I'm happy. But I'm very, very dubious about that power. There's just such a lot people want to run away from. It was worth saying and, luckily, people read it too.

CHAPTER 4

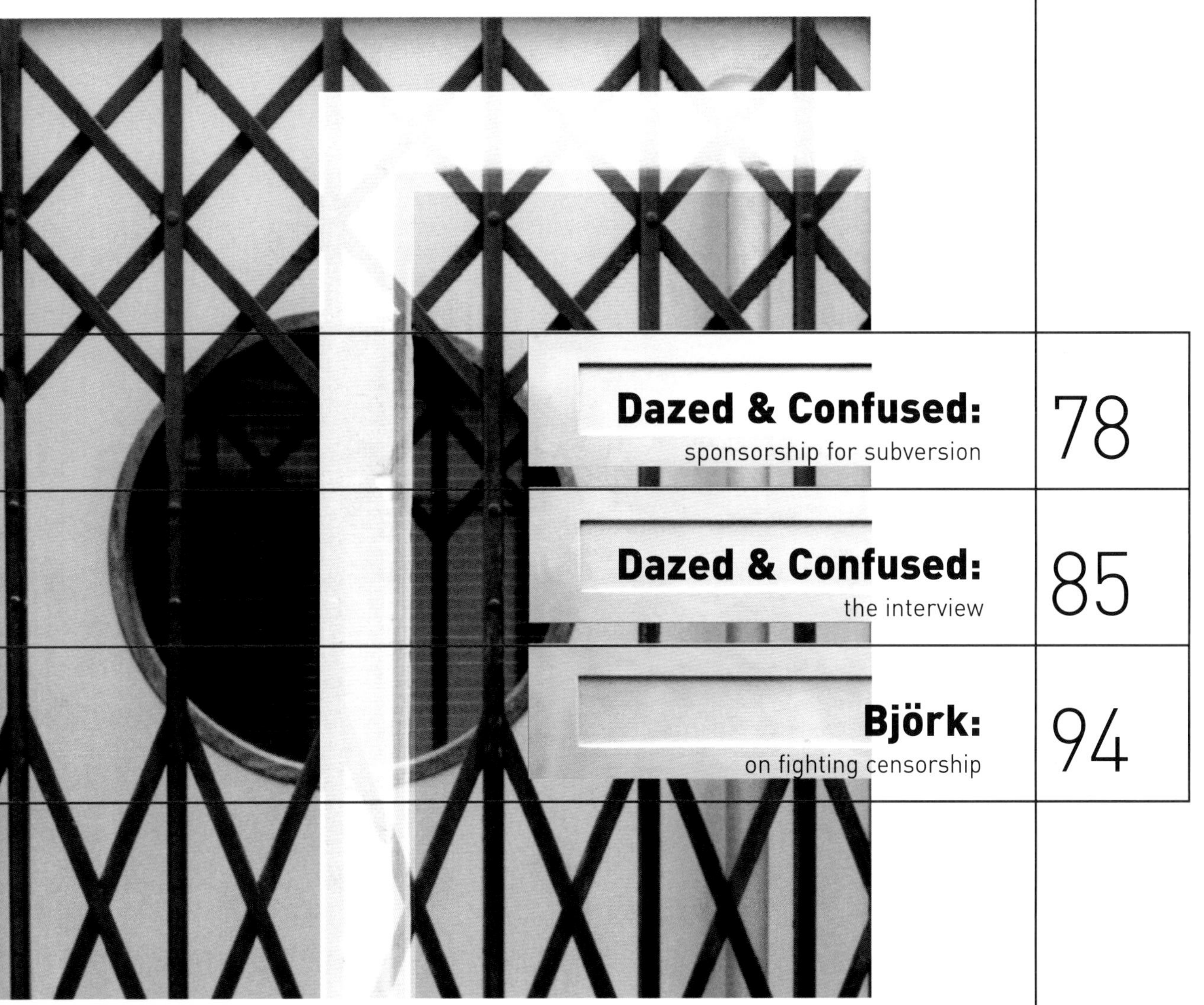

1

2

3

Dazed & Confused:

sponsorship for subversion

As Jim Heinemann wrestled to help save *Phat*, his team were handling another youth title which, at a later time, would incur similar problems. It was *Dazed & Confused*, the magazine whose two-room office was downstairs from Corinne Day's flat.

In the summer of '93, according to Heinemann, this sporadic yet interesting organ lived up to its name. Barely two years old, it was rarely punctual. Nevertheless, *Time Out* were keen to handle its distribution. Predicted Heinemann, who was seeing rivals like *G-Spot*, *Ravescene* and *Hey Tony*, "Lots of these new independent things won't survive. But *Dazed & Confused* seem to be going somewhere. Slowly, they seem to be getting their act together."

"They" were three friends from the London College of Printing: Jefferson Hack, John Rankin Waddell and Ian C. Taylor. When the trio started out, they were aged 19, 24 and 21 respectively, and their combined experience was one student magazine.

Still, they were determined to approach print differently; to, in the words of Hack, "tear down all walls between the magazine and its readers." None had any real connections inside the media, and no doors were opening because of their names or pedigrees. Therefore, they were free to try adventurous strategies - and, more often than not, they managed to make them work.

D&C was launched at a moment of expansion in entertainment, when many raves and clubs were trying 'zines of their own. But its founding trio disdained leisure coverage. They were into fashion, concept and the visual arts. But they saw all three through the eyes of a new generation. To them, *The Face* and *i-D* "took the wrong end of the stick" in even attempting to shape themselves like mainstream magazines. From the start, just like *Phat*, *D&C* aimed to be separate. They would speak only for readers of their age and temperament. Like *Phat*, however, they soon found this posed a threat.

Dazed & Confused began life as a large-scale poster, sponsored for £3,000 by Black Bush Irish Whiskey. Hack and Waddell got the money by promising Black Bush an audience, members of the new young culture known as rave. Says Hack: "We didn't bother selling lots of little ads, and we didn't go around to agencies. We just went straight to the guys who had all the money. Without that, we'd never have managed to get started."

Start they did, though, with a Thames boating launch. It was DJ'd by Paul Daley - later one half of the group Leftfield - and it featured a set from Boys' Wonder (once the '80s "positive punk band" Brigandage). For quite a while, weekly club nights would provide some funds for the enterprise, as the magazine scraped its way from issue to issue. From the first, its contributors worked for love - and their bills were footed by corporate sponsors.

For dancefloor entrepreneurs, this was an accepted practice. When it came to clubs, book launches and art galleries, the beer and liquor companies were regular backers. But, in print vehicles, they were confined to ads. Anything else, said the conventional wisdom of publishing, brought the taint - at least - of editorial tampering. But the new *D&C* trio didn't care about this caveat; having grown up with sponsors backing their clubs and raves, it seemed logical.

Ironically, their decision would result in greater freedom. For Black Bush, Levi and Stella Artois, the monies were negligible. Hack: "But, nevertheless, getting it was hard. It was just me and Rankin, sitting there at corporate tables, pleading, 'Oh, believe in us! Believe in us! We're gonna give you something back and do it cleverly!' No way were we gonna sell our souls to them."

Slowly, the tactic worked, interesting youngish folks who worked at such companies as Sony and Whitbread. By Issue Four, the one-time poster was a saddle-stitched 'zine. Issue Five, out around the time *Phat* started publishing, had a silver cover (blank, except for its strapline: "The Death of the Cover Star"). Inside, it had a "Pretty Vacant" fashion spread. But their punk models sported dreadlocks and Adidas.

It also boasted a "street snaps" jacket spread, executed with tourists serving as the models. This was an homage to the first issue of *i-D*, which had once focused on the style of readers. But there were other things which set the 'zine apart. For instance, there was an interview with an artists' agent (meaning visual art, then a rarity in the style press). Yet another piece was called "20 Things The British Discuss". For that feature, four randomly chosen Britons - all in their 20s - gave views on soap opera, sex, celebrities, money, the IRA, the cost of living, religion, holidays, their next door neighbours, politics and more.

By the time of this issue, despite a minuscule circulation, *D&C* was no longer thought of as underground. This was mainly due to a second-issue feature, "Blow Up!", which was billed as "a public

1 & 2. Hey Tony magazine
3. Dazed & Confused Pilot issue, posterzine
4. Dazed & Confused Issue 5, The Death of the Cover Star

BUYERS ON THE STREET PERCEIVE THINGS VERY WRONGLY. SMALL-CIRCULATION MAGAZINES CAN'T BE ALL THAT RADICAL.
(→PAGE 81)

4

access photo shoot". Packing just a white bedsheet, rolls of film and one camera, Hack and Waddell had set off round a range of nightclubs. With PR flyers to precede and announce their jaunt, they held an improvised photo session in each venue. The result was "a fashion shoot as styled by the people."

At clubs such as Moo, Smashing, Love Ranch, Kush, Good Enough, Glam, Ciao Baby, Fantastic, Kinky Disco, and Talkin' Loud, the pair organised more than 800 photographs. These snaps had a long and lively after-life. Sponsored by Wrangler, fifty core photos were exhibited, at The Collection. "The ones which weren't framed", adds Jefferson Hack, "we set up to project on the walls. So everyone involved got their moment's glory."

Waddell started getting steady bookings for other work, and the exhibition moved on to several venues. (As well as being shown in the Diorama, it eventually re-visited most of the clubs. Later, it was used in the "Street Style" exhibit at the Victoria and Albert Museum.)

The magazine's next encounter with notice was very different. It came courtesy of the artists Jake and Dinos Chapman, who worked in an East London studio. The magazine pictured the Chapman brothers' sculptures of children, which were clearly not quite natural, since they showed "some private parts in startling places". The ensuing uproar floored the *D&C* staffers - who had, after all, written on the pair before. (In Issue Five, they were singled out for praise by a posse of British art directors.)

1

There had been articles on the same sculptures in "quality papers". Plus the Chapmans had enjoyed a show in Cork Street. But when re-presented in a youth magazine, their works touched off a

2

Phat-style media firestorm. In the *Daily Telegraph* (writing well after the fact), Jessica Davies called the sculptures "images more depraved than anything you will ever find in Hieronymous Bosch".

More important than the censure was its aftermath, just like that imposed on *Phat* from similar quarters. Hack: "For three issues, we were totally banned from John Menzies. Which, right there, constituted a third of our whole distribution." Although it managed to weather this storm with a printed apology, *D&C* combusted once again upon re-entry.

This time, the problem was down to a whim by Hack. While he was waiting for his printer's messenger, Hack began to doodle on the issue's artwork. Over its cover barcode, he scrawled the phrase: IF YOU CAN'T AFFORD IT, STEAL IT. Unfortunately, the line was eventually printed.

It precipitated a second crisis. "This time," groans Hack, "I had every newsagent in the country phoning me personally. They gave us one more ban and threatened to shut us down."

Hack was haunted by the fate of *Phat*: "Those guys, it was terrible what happened to them; they showed us just how far things could go." So, he wrote personal answers to every fax and letter. "I think I even wrote an editorial, where I said,

'Please, don't forget to tip your newsagent'." For *D&C*, the moment was indeed crucial; they had gone monthly just the issue before.

The staff hoped it would be the magazine's final crisis. For *D&C*, says Hack, learned a critical lesson: with all print vehicles, newsagent views are critical. Says he, "They're the last people who should dictate content. But, in practice, when you're small, they certainly do." Independent magazines, he notes ruefully, lack a certain freedom - that conferred by giant sales. "Buyers on the street perceive things very wrongly. Small-circulation magazines can't be all that radical."

At the magazine, his crew plugged along. Then, a different type of problem surfaced. This time, a former model named Laraine Ashton - now the boss of her own, global agency - took very public issue with their fashion coverage. In October 1995, she complained about it, in a long piece published by the *Evening Standard*. "Girls are being exploited", Ashton claimed, "for the sake of ever-increasing sales." In addition to *D&C*, she cited a wide range of publications, which included *Cosmo*, *Company* and *Marie-Claire*.

Some of these magazines sold in major numbers: *Cosmo*, 460,000; *Company*, 305,000 and *Marie-Claire*, 455,000. *Dazed & Confused* printed only 60,000; its fashion could hardly spur "ever-increasing sales". Nevertheless, Hack was right; the harshest scrutiny fell on the smallest publication. In the subsequent debate, *D&C* were pilloried.

Ashton's views were entry-level feminism. But they were also part of an old women's-page argument, about fashion's effect on the young and suggestible. It was the same attack, in many ways, mounted against Corinne Day and Kate Moss. But, this time around, the comments held a special anxiety. Ashton, like so many others for whom fashion was a business, was finally face to face with a different generation - and a set of preferences very foreign to her.

What she presented as a monstrous change was an aesthetic which stood in opposition to Ashton's universe - one of highly monitored shifts and thoroughly airbrushed glamour. The seeming rawness of fashion's latest turf (like its fresh, unvarnished "truths") felt uncontrollable.

And from *D&C*, as from Corinne Day, it was uncontrollable. Fashion in the pages of *D&C* was a statement, but it was concept and not commodification. As with all conceptual adventures, the viewer contributed. This had the effect of cutting out the old supremos, fashion's editors and model agencies.

1. Dazed & Confused flyer: Blow Up - Class night out
2. Preservation Vamp Photo: Donna Trope '95 for Dazed & Confused
3. Press cutting: The Daily Telegraph Thurs, Oct 12, '95
4. Press cutting: The Guardian Thurs, Oct 12, '95

FEATURES

Immortal words still fail the Academie

It's not fun, it's bad taste

3

When an ex-model now running her own agency attacks the magazines that employ her girls, something is up. The industry has always excelled in exploiting beautiful women, but have demands on models' dignity grown unacceptable? Clare Longrigg reports

Dirty rotten styles

4

In addition to which, irony fuelled these fashion concepts. Gavin Hills was right: irony was the inheritance of the rave generation. Very often, those conventions it sought to milk were the sacred cows of Ashton and her cronies, a set of fashion conventions they evolved and nurtured. Whether these involved plain studio backdrops or "gentility", all the formulae were being mocked or ignored. This was not conventional glamour, but fashion as social experiment.

A good example was the issue of cover shots. In 1994, *D&C* published a fashion magazine of its own, one pointedly called *Another*. On the cover, it featured a full-bleed picture of a sheep's head. Inside, one spread - which was entitled "Livestock" - literally portrayed its models as animals.

This was just one piece in an evolving pattern; *D&C* both parodies and rejects mainstream "fashion". Notes Hack, when it comes to doing a cover: "There's a whole psychology behind the cover shot. White background, pretty smiling face, all flaws bleached out. Well, we can't base our magazine on that! We know you must make your own success story - which means you make the work appropriate to your readership."

Ashton's 1995 comments sparked a fierce debate. But it was fuelled by fear as much as outrage. Three generations were losing control of the culture - and they sensed it drifting out of their grasp. The real threat was hardly to their suggestible teens. The real threat was an audience which mystified them. But it was already present, and already massive.

It was the Ecstasy kids, the Britpoppers and techno ravers, teens who saw the world through very different lenses. Those whose one defining moment was punk (or glam, or the "romance" of the Sixties) saw things in a sequence - with their own, shifting yet personal, sense of taste at the helm. They looked at the new market's idols and saw only starvation and vacancy. Or, as The Prodigy led to Oasis, they saw little but narcissism. Yet, to the market itself, those idols looked familiar. Their celebrity was picaresque and fulfilling.

From the *Daily Mail* to television chat shows, from the *Guardian* to radio call-ins, pundits flocked to follow Ms Ashton's lead. Like her, they expressed shock and surprise - at social trends which had built up since the '80s.

The *Guardian* women's page typified the outrage: "Last year *Allure* and *Harper's Bazaar* both ran pictures of models in various states of anorexic

1

2

Facing page:
Preservation Vamp
Photo: Donna Trope '95
for Dazed & Confused

1. Dazed & Confused covers from top to bottom:
a. Issue 1
b. Issue 4
c. Issue 6
d. Issue 10
e. Issue 34
2. The Dazed & Confused gallery 112 Old St, London EC1V

WE REALLY, REALLY WANTED TO CREATE OUR OWN JOBS. TO CREATE OUR OWN EMPLOYMENT FOR OURSELVES. (→PAGE 88)

collapse with haunted eyes circled with dark rings. A story in *The Face* depicted models shot and bleeding - from the head, from the wrist, between the thighs. A recent edition of *Dazed & Confused* showed (perfectly waxed) crotch shots in close-up; one was a gusset-shot of a pair of rubber knickers straddling diamond-encrusted handcuffs. A sequence in the latest edition shows a model peering over an open cut-throat razor in a pool of red liquid; the same model, her breasts exposed, licking a red-stained axe blade and a steak stabbed with surgical scissors."

The writer saw "a combination of S&M and wasted bodies". Then, she went on to skewer *D&C*:

"*Dazed & Confused* fashion shoots show models with bruises, falling against radiators; pretty collapsing dolls. Their hunched shoulders, skinny-ribbed tops and hipsters on the tiniest of frames denote victimhood. It says: 'I abdicate responsibility. It's OK to be a victim.'"

Hack and Waddell did attempt to answer the charges. After all, they noted, just putting out their magazine took immense work from people in the "guilty" age group. "Most women's magazines", Hack maintains firmly, "are miles from the lives of our young readers. They show this whole world of perfect teeth and makeup. We deal very, very differently with such things. We don't live in that fashion-industry vacuum."

Waddell had a simpler answer: "Get real. That's what we do."

Despite the infamy gained by such press, Rankin made good on the claim. He shot spreads where women dressed as men, wore clothes inside out and back to front (title: "It's Not What You Wear, It's How You Wear It"). For "Big Girls in Blouses", he used outsize models; to showcase Isaac Mizrahi, he used Margo Dillon, a model who was then aged 89. A two-time granny, Dillon had her own strong views.

"Why should I not work?" she said. "I've already done videos for Pulp and Björk. I've been a cyber-granny and a break-dancer." *D&C*'s ideas did not shock Margo Dillon.

Others in the image business agree. Since 1995, coinciding with the uproar, Kodak have sponsored *Dazed & Confused* with film. Hack: "Having high production values for our photography, we were desperate for good film stock. At first, we went to Kodak saying, 'OK, give us lots of money; take an ad'. Only to discover, they don't do ads at all." As a compromise, Kodak gives the magazine film monthly - film which is then doled out to each photographer.

This has enabled the mag to re-emphasise the photograph, something it has done through two new initiatives. One, the magazine moved from Soho to central Hackney, where the *D&C* "shopfront" is a full-time gallery. Opened in August 1996, it is dedicated to new photographers: the likes of Mark Guthrie and his TV-lit parlours, or Tom Dunkley's year-long look at London. Once again, each exhibition is sponsored - usually, by a local printing firm. For their money, they are credited: in the magazine, at the private view, in the gallery.

D&C now also runs Special Artist's Projects. These are sections in the magazine given to outsiders. Says Hack, "It helps show more original work." We say to an artist, 'OK, you can have five pages - if you use them for an original work. Barbara Kruger did an early one that was really great. She took extant fashion images from the magazine then said, 'OK, here, have a look at yourselves.' She was speaking quite directly to our readers."

Dazed & Confused still lives up to its name, always aiming somewhat higher than it flies. A minimal Web presence is the site of many plans, and October '96 saw a "living magazine". Sponsored in a walk-in warehouse space by Nokia (a mobile phone company), it literally "tore down the walls" between the staff and their readers. The issue's text became wall projections, shown alongside blow-ups of fashion pics. Beside these were each session's out-takes. Readers could try on clothes from each fashion feature. Plus, there were lectures, films and concerts. All were by those who featured in October's issue.

It makes veterans like Phil Bicker smile. Bicker, while art directing *Hommes Vogue International*, does consultancy for *D&C* - for free. "They really are a new sort of magazine. It's because they're changing stuff themselves. At *The Face* they'll comment on the culture. But *Dazed & Confused* become part of making it."

Dazed & Confused:

the interview

In accordance with their tradition of getting artists with ties to each other's work to interview each other, *Dazed & Confused* editor Jefferson Hack and co-founder John Rankin Waddell talk between themselves about the genesis, aims and business of their magazine.

Jefferson:
How did we come up with the idea to do the magazine?

Rankin:
When we were still at college, we did their student mag, *Untitled*, and enjoyed it. Then, we were out one day and had a chat about it and decided we would like to keep on doing it. As I remember, Ian (Taylor) came up with the name.

Jefferson:
Well, I was living with Ian and I kept playing that song.

Rankin:
We all liked it. Plus, I guess we felt we weren't really gonna fit in with anyone else's idea of what magazines were about.

Jefferson:
The name's quite important, 'cause there were *Blitz*, *i-D*, *The Face*, and people were starting up magazines with names like *The Scene* and *The Hip*. There was kind of one password being used. We wanted something which set a brief.

Rankin:
I remember we started for a lot of reasons. We didn't want to do something that was just opinion,

but that was more about honest interviews. Also, one of our main agendas was "all the other magazines do this this and this"...we wanted our "this" to be different. We didn't want reviews; we didn't want hatchet jobs.

Jefferson:
We wanted to be positive. We wanted to open up a new world of creative people, because we'd already seen from dealings with other magazines that world was very closed.

Rankin:
Very.

Jefferson:
One thing I personally didn't understand was, with *i-D* and *The Face*, I never really got the reasons for their editorial. I wasn't into long journalistic diatribes. I liked *Interview* magazine, because I was much more into Q&A as a format.

Rankin:
I remember hating all those opinion pieces!

Jefferson:
In addition to which, I couldn't read *i-D*'s design. I mean, we liked *The Face*, but it was in our country yet it was always filled with what they saw as "mass" interest. Which very often meant American stuff. We weren't into mass interest anyway. But let's talk about the structure of the magazine. We had the flavour of *Untitled*. We edited that, essentially, and published it. So we dealt with all the production, all the printing and repro and getting copy in. Ian was designing it and I was writing for it.

Rankin:
But there was a wealth of students who were photographers and artists. When we left college, we didn't have that any more. We were just hungry to keep on publishing.

Jefferson:
We had contacts in the print world and we had experience. We at least knew how to put something together.

Rankin:
But we had no *real* idea how to do it, not how we would get the money and so on. But what was happening at the time, which was helpful, was that sponsorship was getting a fresh start. As a concept, an advertising concept. We knew there was a little money around. So we knew, on that level, we could do something.

Jefferson:
It was a time when big advertisers were trying to align themselves with some kind of youth culture, but they didn't really know what it was. That's why *Dazed & Confused* started as a poster, with the idea of selling just one advert to one advertiser.

Rankin:
Dazed & Confused the poster was based on a one-shot. You get three posters, you can put 'em on your wall, and they only cost something like £2.50. We thought that was a great idea at the time.

Jefferson:
Even on a low budget, we had the idea they were collectible. One side was a poster, one side was editorial. But we always hoped they'd keep the magazine. Even though it was black and white and quite...very cheap.

Rankin:
...cheap. At best, it was a cult. But, at the time, we thought we were brilliant.

Jefferson:
Part of that was just the arrogance of youth.

Rankin:
But another part is the way we'd been brought up. We'd been brought up to think if you just do it yourself, it will happen.

Jefferson:
None of us had ever had jobs in magazines, except one time I had a *Time Out* placement. That convinced me what I didn't want. To be forty-plus and clinging onto a job I didn't like.

Rankin:
None of us wanted a job in magazines!

Jefferson:
We knew no one in the industry. None of us knew another person who worked on a magazine.

Rankin:
We just knew that if we phoned 'em up, they'd have nothing to say. You know, they wouldn't meet with us. We had some experiences with those people and, quite categorically, all of them had been bad.

Jefferson:
But it gave us the sense we could achieve anything. That we had nothing to lose and everything to gain. We had no friends, we had no enemies, we were just this blank sheet. We had no agenda with the rest of the industry.

Rankin:
At the same time, we were all getting out in the world. Starting to go out to clubs, taking drugs. That was 100% what was happening. But we didn't do a magazine to get in clubs for nothing, we did the magazine because we loved the work. It's like the difference between a photographer that loves fashion and one that loves photography.

Jefferson:
That's the other thing, we didn't do it for the glory. We went out because we were young and single and wanted a laugh. When we didn't have an office, we were working out of your flat, you, me, all the other people who were working with us. There were times when we had to start the car by tweaking the spark plug - and there were times when there was snow on the floor.

Rankin:
I remember.

Jefferson:
Yeah, but we still went out and tried to make the magazine happen, tried to sell our idea, tried to get it out. It was you and me, going round, having meetings, writing letter after letter, saying, 'Come on, do this!'. Where did that ultra-mad commitment ever come from? How come we were all such workaholics?

Rankin:
I don't know. But then, now I'm married and Kate [actress Kate Hardie] and I have the baby.

Jefferson:
Now we all want to have a life as well. But we used to do four days when no one slept. Just in order to get the magazine out. We weren't actually taking any drugs either.

Rankin:

At first, it was all about the weekend. Work till the weekend, have a weekend off. Then back to work on Monday; it was really draining.

Jefferson:

But it was worth it. We really, really wanted to create our own jobs. To create our own employment for ourselves.

Rankin:

Yeah, to produce, that was exactly what we wanted.

Jefferson:

And we knew from looking round us, the only way we could ever do it was through fuckin' hard work. Nothing else, really.

Rankin:

Also what happened was, we finally started to meet people. And the people we met who were working in our field just weren't any cleverer than we were. So we realised we could do it. We could do it and make a success of it.

Jefferson:

Also we paid great attention to detail, even at the early stage, when we were doing things on a really low budget. There was still huge attention to the most minute things. I think that's been one consistent thing, we have always had sort of a perfectionist attitude. We always wanted our magazine to be better; there's no reason to put it out if it's not. We wanted to do it mainly for ourselves, to prove we could take better photos, write better articles. In a sense, it was ourselves we were testing.

Rankin:

Yeah, but we grew up in public. That's one thing for sure. We made loads of mistakes in the eyes of the media.

Jefferson:

Let's shift gears on that one. A more relevant question is: why did we choose print?

Rankin:

I still think about that one. If we'd gone into video, for instance, we'd get paid upfront. I guess the answer is we *thought* it was cheaper. Now, of course we've learnt the opposite. It's quite cumbersome, it's the most expensive format!

Jefferson:

But I actually love the smell of paper.

Rankin:

So do I. I loved it from the first, and I still do. I don't think I love any other format more.

Jefferson:

The idea that someone could hold it, and take it away, it's personal. Because when we started, we were bringing it out whenever we could. So every issue was like a special object, it had a special cover or special themes or whatnot.

Rankin:

Yeah, it really felt very one to one.

Jefferson:

We weren't part of a corporate magazine that was produced every month according to format. Companies like that just make McMagazines. There's a formula, you just fill it in. There's no growth and nothing human about it. For us, every issue always changed, each one had ideas about how we felt at the time.

Rankin:

But it hasn't changed in that way, has it? We still get excited when an issue comes back.

Jefferson:

We do. But what were we trying to prove commercially?

Rankin:

Well, we felt there was a gap in the magazine world. For one that treated young people in an honest way. A gap for something that wasn't style over content, but was style *and* content, existing hand in hand. At the time, all the media was kind of honing down, pigeonholing things into one area or another. We hated that, it was our worst fear - that we'd work in one medium and not be able to try others.

Jefferson:

Youth culture was being pigeonholed by market forces.

Rankin:

And, yet, it was diversifying madly. Far more so than in the previous decade. There was ambient, house culture, dance music, jungle stuff.

Jefferson:

It's like in my record collection, techno-rock is next to old, old John Lee Hooker. Next to hip-hop, next to old punk stuff.

Rankin:

Exactly.

Jefferson:

To pretend otherwise is patronising! It's so patronising to British youth! And that's what I felt, we'd been patronised, we knew young people had a wider set of interests, so much wider than they're credited for.

Rankin:

Like I recently photographed Billy Bragg. And he said to me, "You know, I just finished a song about Cindy Sherman." And I said, "*You're* interested in Cindy Sherman?" Which just goes to show you.

Jefferson:

That's what magazines should be about. Giving people access to information. But I think they should also carry contradictions. So you have fashion next to people on the street: you get a clash between fantasy and reality. I think also that there should be politics. 'Cause, since we started, there's been a real apathy and a lack of interest in politics. I think now that that is gonna change.

Rankin:

I think it is changing. You need to read about Sarajevo alongside Kiss.

Jefferson:

You know, though, I don't read the lifestyle titles. I'd really rather read *National Geographic*. Good photos, well researched, and well written. That's the first magazine I saw with a holographic cover. And it's the only magazine I ever subscribed to!

Rankin:

Well, what most magazines and products do is go, "OK, we know *that* is happening, so let's concentrate on just that one fragment".

Jefferson:

Our philosophy works the other way round...if we carry on, people will eventually get it. If we just carry on and do it well. When we first started, we tried to do something else, though. Something which would be unmediated.

Rankin:

Public access!

Jefferson:

We wanted something that kind of said, "We're not following what's in other mags, we want to go just totally against the grain, we want stuff here that we have a personal interest in". But to present it in a way that you felt, in some sense, you were closer to the truth. That was one reason for the Q&A format.

Rankin:

And, although that idea came from *Interview*, we decided to put our own spin on it.

Jefferson:

Yeah, we started matching up celebrities. Anita Pallenberg doing Evan Dando; Ice-T doing George Clinton; Irvine Welsh and Iggy Pop. What happens there is you get something different. It's not just one guy promoting his product, it's two people who care what each other think.

Rankin:

Was that your favourite interview like that?

Jefferson:

Thom Yorke, Radiohead, who interviewed himself. He didn't know how he was gonna do it. So I sent him a list of questions and I said, "Just hold the tape recorder, then ask the question, then play the answer." Actually, he got a bottle of wine, got really pissed, and just used two voices from in his head. It's very serious stuff, he went pretty deep. Of course, you're not as close to the truth as it may seem, because it has been edited and pre-empted.

Rankin:

We had that dilemma early on: that idea of the real public access mag. And we realised, you can't actually do that. It's not possible to do that on that level.

Jefferson:

We once got a comment: "They're like 'The Late Show' staff on Ecstasy". But it wasn't us trying to be that kind of "authority" - or the idea that we were taking Ecstasy. Our idea was to break the rules, to change the way that youth culture has to be packaged. Like, why the hell if we're really interested in music do we need a journalist to decode it for us? Someone who probably doesn't know jackshit about it, who's probably writing to make himself look good. Like when a photographer shoots a celebrity and all you get is that photographer's point of view - and not the celebrity's.

Rankin:

Well, great journalists do have egos too. They do want to place themselves in certain positions. But the good ones do that while letting the people they meet have room. And if they're scathing about someone, then there's a reason.

Jefferson:

You can make that argument both ways. But I think what actually happened with youth magazines is a lot of power went into the hands of people with less experience. Or just people who were doing it for the wrong reasons. You ended up with people who had one idea or maybe one gimmick.

Rankin:

And they made stuff which was simply...crass.

Jefferson:

OK, something else which is very important. Why do we treat visual art so seriously?

Rankin:

Well, we always wanted to. Initially, we tried but it didn't work. What I learned -myself, anyway - quite quickly was you have to really concentrate on your features. That if you are gonna cross-fertilise, you have got to know what you're on about. We're the only magazine in a style format which has regular features covering art. And the only one which gives pages over to artists. Plus, they're happy to do stuff for us - for them, it's a wider, younger audience.

Jefferson:

Maybe the thing is they saw the way we treated things as conceptual - just the way we try to present our information. The whole way we treat the magazine. They can see that work goes into the stuff, we aren't just into trying to use 'em. That our layout is clean and minimal, it showcases photographs and layouts. Because we know those things can speak for themselves.

Rankin:

That leads to our whole philosophy on photography. Which, for the first fifteen issues anyway, has been the magazine's real voice.

Jefferson:

Partly because we didn't have the ability to attract writers of a comparable level. Photography's immediate, and writing isn't. Also, a lot of writers won't work for no money. Lots of photographers will, because it's an outlet for their portfolio. There's a lot of people who can get work on a record sleeve or advertising jobs off good editorial.

Rankin:

We get very worked up about it, though, because it's harder to pick good journalists. The photographers we pick are carefully chosen, we use a process of learning what their motives are. What we've done is establish a basic ideology, to make sure they're doing it for the right reasons. Which is for the magazine or the concept. If they're just doing it to be cool or glamourous, well then, it's "Fuck off". Of course, people have now sort of sussed that, so they sometimes try to get around us - "Oh, I think what you're doing is so great!" When they really want just the fame and glamour. With photography, that's the usual story.

Jefferson:

Well, what is the motivating factor for you? What makes you different? You trained to be an accountant at one point, then you were a hospital porter. While we were at college, I know you worked in a cinema.

Rankin:

It's a massive thing to encapsulate. But it's about individuality, not about ego.

Jefferson:

OK, then, let's talk about fashion. Because we've got a very particular slant there. It's clear why we use certain photographers, and that we put concept above selling clothes, which is traditionally what fashion pictures do.

Rankin:

When the magazine started, photographers that really love photography were attempting to get involved with fashion. At the time, photography as photography - as something which excited people - made inroads in fashion. People like Corinne Day, Bruce Davidson, Glenn Luchford were doing lots of work; so were people like Juergen Teller. Of course, they loved fashion. But they also loved photography and what it can do. Add to that, we'd all been studying art. We'd all been doing art, really, and that art was conceptual.

Jefferson:

Was that the focus or the inspiration?

Rankin:

Well, conceptual art as photography was something that was a major part of my college curriculum. That was what excited me. So bringing that together with something that was exciting - on a sexy and glamourous level - was the way I wanted to go. I started to think about things in a way that was critical. I didn't like a lot of fashion, and a lot of what fashion did to people. Even though I was very fooled by that for a long time. When I got interested in it, I became less and less fooled by it.

Jefferson:

But your approach wasn't cynical. Very often you used humour.

Rankin:

I used irony.

Jefferson:

Still, what you were doing was making it accessible, yet exciting to look at, while still giving people the clothes and the information. Through that strategy, you could push your point.

Rankin:

But, when you're dealing with fashion, it becomes extremely incestuous. That's what we as a magazine try to break out of. You can't ever break entirely out of it, though. Because people who do fashion for us, even though they're thinking about concepts, it's in jokes. We've done few stories that haven't been like that, because it becomes a vicious circle. You start out on some kind of cutting edge, but you very quickly end up in the mainstream. I'm not saying that we've actually done that. I'm just saying we're still enticed by it.

Jefferson:

But you've got to give the fashion industry some payback - or you can't go forward with their help.

Rankin:

Yeah, but I'm saying here's the way I think about it: if I don't concentrate, we might make a mistake.

Jefferson:

What are some of your favourite stories from *D&C*?

Rankin:

"Big Girls in Blouses", which was about big girls, very sexy fat girls. "Hungry", which was a comment on eating, and on food. "Livestock", which was about models treated as animals. The basis of all those pieces was conceptual. "Ghost", which was about fashion being transparent; "Veneer", which was about fashion being accessible.

Jefferson:

They were all analyses of particular parts of fashion. Is there any way that can be stretched into a fashion shoot which deals with issues, things which aren't related to fashion? Is that the way you're moving?

Rankin:

That is the way I'm moving. I did that thing on children - "TV's Boring" - and that wasn't just about fashion. I try to deal with damage. I wanted to do something about suicide, something using "dead" - that Northern expression. You know: "I'm dead into it". "It's dead brilliant." "Dead good."

Jefferson:

But I guess what *I'm* trying to say is that if fashion tries to deal with, like, world issues, it's always vacuous. Because it shouldn't; it's just fashion photography. If you want to do some kind of feature on homelessness, then don't be patronising and do a fashion shoot.

Rankin:

No, you can't do that. Because fashion has to be instant, and accessible, and exciting. Sexy. In a lot of ways, I'm kind of bored with fashion. What I wanted to see for *D&C* is fashion become more of an art form, more of a commentary.

Jefferson:

More than just a way for a photographer to get an ad shoot.

Rankin:

Or shag a model. Or get in to a party. Or make some woman who happens to look at it feel uncomfortable.

Jefferson:

I suppose it's been part of our whole point, to kind of highlight that angle: *Don't Buy In*. We don't want people to aspire to some kind of lifestyle, something that the magazine has created. We want to inspire them to realise what they have, not have 'em longing for some fucking distant world. But, if you try to deal with things on an equal level, then you have to deal with the tools of the mainstream. Even if you're not really part of that mainstream. And that really can produce some headaches. Now, for instance, we have to watch our imagery. Stuff like piercing, body art, anything "erotic". Maybe we're just reporting - but people can't always see the distance.

Rankin:

You really have to work from the inside. You can't work from the outside and get anywhere. That's why we've always used marketing and sponsorship. That's why they were never really a problem.

Jefferson:

We embraced sponsorship, we never took the fanzine approach. Because, at the end of the day, then you're preaching to the converted, you've got your core of readers - which stays pretty small - and you're just giving 'em what they always wanted. Same way as bloody *Loaded*'s giving them what they want.

Rankin:

After all this time, does that make you feel tired? Do you ever question if it's really worth it?

Jefferson:

Sometimes, yeah, I do get burned out. If the critics really get on our case. Or if we have a really low month for ads. But the creative stuff is not what does that. It's the administration grind: keeping everyone paid, just the small, everyday stuff of running a business. Plus one's dealings with small-minded people.

Björk:

on fighting censorship

Schooled in music since the age of five, Björk Gudmundsdottir made a recording at the age of seven. It was called "My Little Arab Boy - How I Love Him" and, in her native Iceland, it is still played on radio. By the end of the '80s, however, Björk was a British heroine: as a singer in the Sugar Cubes. They recorded for One Little Indian, an anarchist independent record label. In the '90s, as a solo star, Björk has become the voice of a different era. She has conquered Europe and America - onstage, via record, and in video. Everywhere she's been, says Ms Gudmundsdottir, she has observed the same struggle: for a personal, individual freedom.

Freedom to express, this is a cause I agree so much with. It's like a fight I've been fighting probably since I was back in Iceland. Since the age of like, 14. Maybe even earlier, whatever, trying to challenge a lot of authority's decisions and things like that.

In a lot of things I do, you know, I have been censored. Since Day One I have been censored myself. And I think the problem is that governments and those in authority are not trusting people. Most authorities or even record companies - not to mention the media - think that people are idiots. That's where it starts. All authorities, including record companies, media, government, think people right around the world are stupid. But I think that is...unforgivable.

Because, you know, basically, this is so rude. Of course people are able to judge for themselves what they want. What is good and what is not good for them. In fact, the earlier they get to judge that for themselves, the stronger their defence systems will be in the end. The more prepared they are against the cruel things you must go through later on in life.

It becomes so humiliating when people aren't allowed to decide for themselves what will help them, what's good for them, what they wish to avoid. I really do think the earlier that people have to learn what suits them and what doesn't, the stronger their defences will be. It is important to have those mechanisms. I mean, I'm a mother, I'm speaking from that viewpoint. Because of that, I feel I know this very well.

Artists are only human. People should stop isolating themselves, putting themselves into these different groups - you know, artist, mother, secretary, all these different kinds of categories. We're all human and with that comes knowing what is good for us. Just like everyone knows what is bad for them. Besides, sometimes, we need even those bad things...even the bad things can be good for us. For a short period of time, just so we can know.

Sometimes we must just go this funny route. Because the human, the human creatures are more complicated than such a little picture. They won't just eat carrots and wake up at nine every morning. They need a little bit more complicated lives to discover about existence and their lives and all the different emotions in their bodies - and all the colours, all these things out in the world which are exciting.

I think this battle, the battle of censorship, is being fought everywhere, on every level, in all kinds of forms. It is not just pop musicians versus the system. Or a magazine or a certain person's film. In every sense, it's a completely universal battle. Of course, Europe and the USA are slightly different. But I don't think either one has gone further or is more advanced in this particular battle. In each culture, it's a matter of different things. Europe may seem to be stronger in some points, and the USA may seem stronger in others. But they are really quite similar.

In a lot of ways, it can be quite dangerous when you get a government like a load of governments we have in Europe, all of whom think they're being very culturally correct. They think they're being - well, from my point of view, they seem quite snobbish, because what they think is that they know better. That can be even more dangerous than outright censorship.

Do you know what? Really, I am an anarchist; I was brought up to be one. Both by my parents and by the punk scene. I was brought up in that, it shaped my feelings. The human being must judge for itself. People must make their own judgments and learn from them and live with it. That's it - full stop. That's what I think.

CHAPTER 5

CHAPTER FIVE

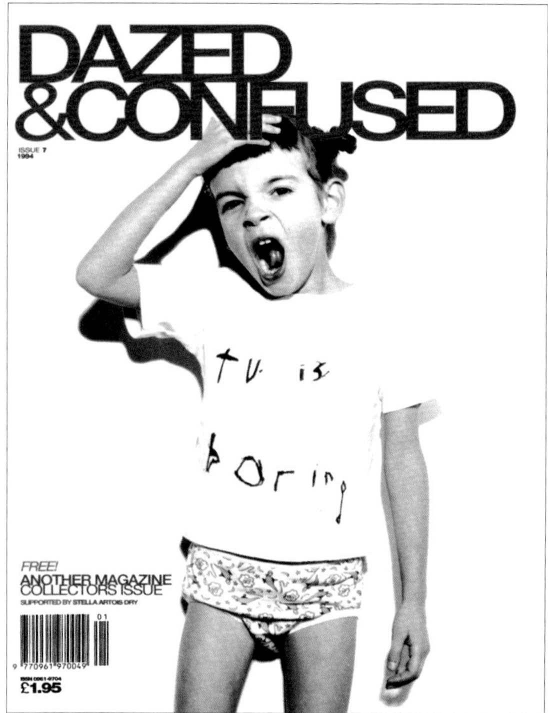

1

Trantastic changes:

fetish fashion reaches the mainstream

By 1996, Jake and Dinos Chapman had moved on from threatening the existence of *Dazed & Confused.* They were still making sculptures (according to one critic, "twistedly sexual Siamese twins", "genitally featured mutants"). But now, after an ICA exhibit, London art investor Charles Saatchi was buying them.

The Chapmans may have parlayed notoriety into sales. But this late '90s, pre-election moment had a climate of rigorous censorship. There was, for instance, special outrage over "child sex". Belgium was in the throes of a keenly followed kidnapping and pedophile scandal. In August of '96, Sweden's Queen Silvia (patron of a World Congress against child exploitation) recruited delegates from 126 countries to join her in an anti-child porn battle. And that autumn, the august Hayward Gallery altered plans for a retrospective by Robert Mapplethorpe. Among the late photographer's pictures (many of homosexual acts and bondage), they also chose to ban a portrait known as "Rosie".

The gallery dropped 50 of the 250 pictures, citing an insufficient area for display. Not all the excised works had a sexual content. But, with "Rosie", they were adamant this was the case. Press releases stated the Hayward was advised by the Metropolitan Obscene Publications Squad - and cited "a different climate of opinion about pictures of children". (All over a photo where the tiny "Rosie" is seen without underwear, skirt around her waist.) In addition to the bans, there were some landmark rules. Unaccompanied under 18-year-olds, for instance, were barred from entrance.

The portrait of Rosie was shot in County Durham; its subject was the grand-daughter of Britain's Lord Lambton. When the retrospective opened, Rosie was an adult, a waitress working in a London restaurant. She took issue with the image as pornographic. "I think it's the nicest photo of me as a child. The only reason I was half-naked was because it was taken at a party and I had just been swimming. It is so harmless."

Yet, with the passage of the Criminal Justice Act, Britain's establishment felt it could set the standards. It now aimed at controlling not just behaviour but also imagery. Only two years earlier, *Dazed & Confused* had run a cover shot of a tiny young girl, in her underwear, yawning. On her T-shirt was scrawled the slogan "TV is boring". In this new climate, that would have spelt disaster. Or as Jefferson Hack puts it, "We'd be crucified!"

Yet at the same time as sexually loaded art was pilloried, Britain was being praised for her transgressive fashion sense - one which very frankly lauded fetishism. In an article entitled "Boomtown", US fashion Bible *W* praised the "renaissance" in London style, noting "standout shops" such as Agent Provocateur ("the over-the-top Soho lingerie shop owned by Vivienne Westwood's son Joe Corré, [which] has devoted clients ranging from neighbourhood prostitutes to the world's top stylists").

The issue - the first of many to detail a new "Swinging London" - débuted just before a triple dose of stunning news. Two of Paris' most venerable couture houses suddenly ceded control to young Britons, with a third designer hiring a UK "house". Dior gave its reins to John Galliano, 36, and Givenchy to Alexander ("Lee") McQueen, 27. Even Thierry Mugler contracted with the House of Harlot.

House of Harlot are a husband and wife partnership, who specialise in stylish rubberwear. They are most famed for inventing the "pump-up bra". John Galliano is the son of a plumber. Lee McQueen's Dad was a taxi driver.

Galliano and McQueen, noted the *New York Times*, "are famously working class, wild and drawn to such provocative impulses as buttocks-baring trousers and spray-painted leather suits." The "buttocks-baring trousers" - better known as bumsters - were a Lee McQueen specialty. They were a jibe at workmen's baggy pants, which often slipped down to show the crack of the bum. Of course, his gambit was rife with gay humour. But female TV comics French and Saunders laughed at it, too.

Now, such very British jokes were out in the world. There, what they lost in wit, they made up in outrage. "Mr. Galliano", added the *New York Times*, "is known in equal parts for his fluid romantic clothes, for his club crawling, for tangled dreadlocks and for standing up Queen Elizabeth II and President Jacques Chirac of France at a recent dinner at Buckingham Palace.... Mr McQueen...is known for the mean, linear cut of his tailoring, for decorating with fake blood and for dedicating collections to Jack the Ripper and Alfred Hitchcock's lethal birds."

Such reporters were outsiders looking in; for polysexual twists and "provocation" had long fed London street style. There, sex, dress and leisure are always intertwined. Even the real-life "Rosie", who maintained the innocence of her early portrait, was the grand-daughter of a Tory involved in a sex scandal. Lord Lambton had served in Edward

1. Dazed & Confused
Issue 7, '94
2. Agent Provocateur
6 Broadwick St, London W1

HOWEVER, IT'S ACTUALLY STILL POWER DRESSING - BUT NOT BEING AFRAID TO SHOW OFF YOUR BUST.
(→PAGE 124)

2

Heath's government, but resigned over an affair with a prostitute.

UK street fashion - an energiser of Paris couture since the late '70s - had for many years walked both sides of the street. Its great trends and inspirations came from clubland, with its often druggy, polysexual climate. Graphic designers pirated imagery from call girls' kiosk cards. Lingerie shops such as Boisvert and Agent Provocateur served not only rock stars and clubbers but also hookers. From the British Fashion Week catwalk to shows by the Crafts Council, drag, kinks and bondage help define British design. Americans might describe this as "irreverent", but for Britons it marked a '90s change in attitude. It was one that challenged the Tories' status quo - with a seriousness that, later, saw Labour's election. On one election platform at that subsequent rout was a challenger who was a lavishly dressed transvestite: "Miss Moneypenny", of the "Glamourous One Party".

The emergent scene, however, had a history. In January of 1983, Londoner Tim Woodward launched a fetish club, Skin Two. It was, says one clubber with a clear memory, at that time devoid of dancefloor poseurs. "There were lots of old men hauling fat women by dog collars. Real, hardcore fetishists. Not many girls like me, interested in the look as fashion."

Ten years later, however, the tables had turned. Skin Two is still a club - but one whose Rubber Ball annually raises thousands for charity. It is also now a shop and a glossy magazine, a publication which sells around the world. Much of its dialogue with readers now takes place by e-mail and many of its sales come from a Web site. Mature folk in dog collars still form part of its readership. But fetishism has moved into the mainstream marketplace. Things which once occurred mostly in underground settings (cross-dressing, rubberwear, S&M, intimate piercing) currently shape *haute couture* and stock UK Top Shops. Says the long-time guru of erotica Tuppy Owens, deviser of the once-shocking *Sex Maniac's Bible*, "Even in south London street markets, by the mid-90s, PVC undies were hanging on the stalls."

Two men who logged this change are Vicky Lee and Caroline Egerton. During 1992, the duo founded Way Out Publishing - which, twelve months later, produced *The Transvestite's Guide to London.* This "*Time Out* for trannies" launched with a print run of 5,000. In 1994, it doubled; by 1995, it had gone international.

1

2

3

"A lot of things", says Egerton, "changed in the first two years. Our world became a source for lots of top designers: people from Westwood and Gaultier to Tim (Batman) Burton. Even high street business now thinks twice about our money. During the recession, it looked as good as anyone's." The *Guide* provides a starting-point for those who want into the market: cosmeticians, beauty outlets, dress designers and venues. But many who sought this custom misunderstand the customer.

Newcomers, says Egerton, think of this as a gay market. "And there have always been gay men who are cross-dressers, just like there have always been gay drag queens. But the fetish scene and the tranny world are mostly straight. The sexuality we address covers a broad spectrum."

To make the point, Lee and Egerton's '94 "cover girl" was Dane Goulding - a straight man who refers to himself as a "gender defector". Dane is famous as a maker of unisex fashion, fashion whose aesthetic is based in the fetish world. But by the mid-'90s, he had a lot of different outlets: a band (TVOD), a job DJ-ing for a club in Brixton (Fantastic), and a column ("Dane's World") for *Taffeta* magazine. Goulding even "created" clothes for the stars of a Japanese comic-book. None of these pursuits were curtailed by fatherhood when, in 1995, Goulding's partner Tracy gave birth to a son, Paris.

What this event did do was spur Goulding to take on a studio. "With a baby, it's really hard to work at home. But, through January '97 that's what I did. I made everything on domestic sewing machines." For his "Superstars" collection, mounted from home, Goulding pioneered holographic printing. "I used these vivid colours: pink and orange, blue and silver. For the models, I used a lot of drag queens. It was my update of the whole Warhol thing. Be your own star, without the mass acclaim."

These days, collections with titles like "3001" or "Beauty Assassins" are sold to Phyllia in Paris and, through them, to Switzerland and Scandinavia. Goulding also exports clothes to Russia, America, Germany and Australia. "The way to do it is to just get a catalogue, then send it out. The fetish fashion scene here is beyond rubberwear. I think, now, it's getting very creative."

Cognoscenti trace some of Gaultier's mid-'90s inspiration to Dane - to a presentation the latter did at Dunstable's 1994 Piercing and Tattoo Convention. The mesh tops Gaultier later printed in full-colour "tattoos" certainly echoed some of Goulding's best-known trademarks. But, lounging at home, in a T-shirt and jeans, Goulding shrugs off the critics' comparisons. "Actually, I'd met Gaultier six months earlier. I was trannied up in mesh at the time, so I expected that. It's just cross-pollination, and everyone does it." Goulding himself stole the trick of printing words (such as "JUSTICE") on sleeves from designer John Richmond. He's also made a "fetish version" of Gaultier's conical bra and "batty riders" - a ragga-style version of Lee McQueen's famous bumsters.

4

5

1. Skin Two, issue 11
2. Trantastic Comics by Simon Murphy, '93
3. The Transvestite's Guide to London '94 Published by The Way Out Publishing Company
4. Fetish wear Design: Dane Goulding Photo: Robert Chouraqui
5. Fetish wear Design: Dane Goulding Photo: Trevor Watson
6. Fetish wear Design: Dane Goulding

Following pages:
1. Video grabs from Dane Goulding's studio, '98
2. A fetish for recycling Stylists: Richard Royle and Jeanette Swift Jewellery: Michael DaNardo Photo: Davis Davis

"IF YOU WEAR IT UNDER YOUR CLOTHES," THEY WROTE IN A MANIFESTO, "YOU CAN FEEL LIKE A SEXY SUPER-HERO. YOU'LL EXUDE INNER CONFIDENCE AND SEXUALITY." (→PAGE 105)

"THE CONCEPT IS THAT SEX IS NOT SMUTTY, SEX IS ONE OF THE FEW SIMPLE PLEASURES IN LIFE AND SHOULD BE ENJOYED. THROW OFF ALL PURITAN VALUES, DRESS UP AND INDULGE YOURSELF. (→PAGE 106)

6

1

Between '92 and '94, there were four D.A.N.E. collections: *Chanel de Sade* ("I threaded a lot of black leather through gold chains"), *Gender Defectors* (which drew attention for its fetish bridal gear), *Transvestite and Justice or Revenge?*. Their mode was fetish-based; their fabrics unpredictable - ranging from denim to gold and silver leathers. Says Goulding now, "I was trying *not* to make rubberwear."

All these designs come freighted with sexual politics: a mixture of logic, tolerance and wit. Goulding: "People always mix up gender and aesthetics. Skirts, for example, are not gender-related. They're not like a bra or a codpiece. Those are made to fit actual differences in our bodies."

"If you use the term properly," he continues, "all women are transvestites. Why? All women wear trousers. We just need to lose the stigma of the term for men. But blokes really ought to work on themselves, too. Women just wear their clothes; men tend to get worn by them."

Goulding's direct approach is reflected in unisex mini-skirts. Sometimes, they boast clip-on male and female symbols. ("If you're worried about someone knowing your sex, just clip on the symbol!") Nor does it bother him when people shout slurs in the street. "They say - always loudly - *That's a transvestite!* But I'm already quite aware I'm wearing a skirt. I don't go out in my clothes to look like a girl. I go out to look like I do wearing the clothes. Those are the clothes I chose that particular night."

Although Goulding's still survives "day to day", he has a clear clientele and a regular showcase. The latter is Spitalfields' Alternative Fashion Week. "They really give you a forum. Once the press gets past that word 'alternative', they realise it's no longer only bin liners. There are some quite straight designers there who show knitwear. Then, of course, there are those of us who make mad costumes."

Goulding is proud of British fashion's new recognition. "In the '90s, we're still the best at what we do - Lee [McQueen] and John [Galliano] and Hussein Chalayan. A lot of people here still take genuine style risks. We've got a very street-based fashion look. Plus, there is a lot going on with music. And there's a much greater tolerance of eccentricity. It's a bit more to do with self-belief than in Europe."

Small, blonde Colleen Sanders shares Dane's attitude. A film and video stylist trained at Elstree Studios, she has long been immersed in this underground scene. In addition to her production and video styling, Sanders helped start Soho's Wigarama

2

(a fetish-based hair and beauty shop), worked for Paradiso and BOY, and started Bitchin' Records (London's first label for drag queens). During 1997, in addition to styling, she worked for Torture Garden: a vintage fetish club which flourishes in the '90s.

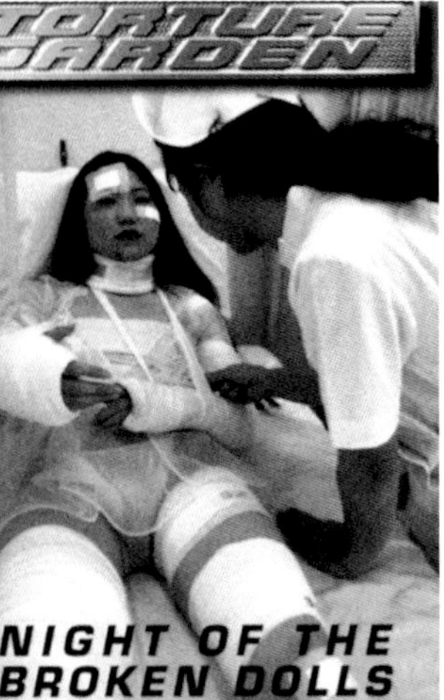

1

Wigarama's lifetime - which was 18 months - summed up central Soho's moment of change. Down the discreet stairs which led to the shop, one encountered an atmosphere of feminine comforts: pink silk, powders, nail varnish, racks of wigs. It was clearly a familial hangout, reverberating with gossip about a spectrum of clubs. These were venues with names like Submission, the Powder Room, Romper Room, The Way Out Wine Bar, Kinky Gerlinky. Many of their flyers looked identical to phone box sex cards. Yet Wigarama shoppers all called the clubs "relaxed". Inside, they noted, any aggression is consensual. None comes from narrow-minded straights or football hooligans.

This is not the sole attraction, says the stylish Sanders. "The whole scene is very much sex as play, sex as theatre, almost childish fun. That's what's altered ideas about what's sexy. In the age of AIDS, flirting and foreplay need to be ritualised. Wigs, micro-kilts, high heels, piercing, Wonderbras - all these come from that new strand of artifice." She cites enterprises such as the House of Harlot and designers like stylist Richard Royle.

UPDATE SPECIAL: **PARIS COUTURE**

MADE FOR MUGLER BY SKIN TWO!

ROBIN ARCHER works with fashion visionary THIERRY MUGLER to put rubber on the Paris catwalks. Photography by PATRICE STABLE

In November of last year, SKIN TWO Design took a call from the Paris studio of Thierry Mugler enquiring whether our manufacturing division would be interested in doing some work for the king of catwalk style. Mugler's representative wasn't sure what the work would entail, but the fact that it would be for the designer's first Couture show, in Paris in mid January, was enough to secure our co-operation.

Says SKIN TWO Design's Robin Archer: "Thierry Mugler is one of the few designers whose output I have continuously admired and been inspired by." "Constantly innovative and daring, the work is unashamedly modern in an era when fashion is constantly looking over its shoulder at the past for next season's ideas. His creations are the embodiment of fetish comic book glamour, all nipped-in waists and sashaying hips, outrageous headgear and sci-fi eyewear."

SKIN TWO began to receive sketches by fax from Paris and set about prototyping the styles, all in latex. "Before we knew it," says Robin, "Christmas had come and gone and the show itself was upon us. We boarded the Eurostar with cases bulging heavily with rubber and headed for Paris."

SKIN TWO produced several outfits for Mugler, including a scarab print latex dress (opposite page) that received rapturous applause in the opening part of the show. Our biggest honour was to have two ensembles in the finale. The cape, corset and skirt combination (main picture, this page) which glowed like a firefly on the catwalk was a collaborative effort: the transparent latex encrusted with tiny sequins was created by Jack the Rubber and assembled by us, while Mr Pearl's incredible corset sparkled gloriously. The full length black gown was hand beaded and embroidered in Paris and assembled there by us the day before the show!

The show was enthusiastically received by the world's press, and an indication of Thierry Mugler's satisfaction with our contribution is that, by the time you read this, SKIN TWO will have started on the next Mugler show – scheduled for July. ❑

UPDATE SPECIAL: **PARIS COUTURE**

THIS PAGE
Scarab print latex dress in Silver and Pewter
OPPOSITE PAGE
Main picture:
Full length cape and skirt made by SKIN TWO from sequinned transparent latex by Jack the Rubber, over beaded and sequinned corset by Pearl
Inset top:
Black latex asymmetric beaded and embroidered floor length gown
Inset centre:
Moulded rubber-trimmed wool suit made at Thierry Mugler, over Latex bra by SKIN TWO
Inset bottom:
Two piece suit in black latex by SKIN TWO, over moulded body top in glittered latex by Jack the Rubber

2

Like Goulding, Sanders spends much of her time on music. As DJ Pussycat, she spins in clubs - and has handled PR for various "fetish bands" - such as the line up on Sequential's CD "Club Fetish" or Torture Garden's "Journeys Through Cybersex". Just like Lee McQueen, Kate Moss or Goldie, Torture Garden is now known world wide. It makes tours of America, swings which move from San Antonio to San Francisco. There is now a Torture Garden book in Tower Records, a Torture Garden board game and a forthcoming CD-ROM.

Games, role-playing, ritual and dressing-up - these have also spurred Agent Provocateur, the shop which Joe Corré and Serena Rees opened in '94. *W* was right to hail it as "a standout"; ever since its opening, it has helped publicise the saucy new face of street style. Initially, the interest came from pedigree: what would the son of Vivienne Westwood and Malcolm McClaren do? Especially with a "sex shop"? Would he go all-out to just be shocking? Or would he, too, prove adept at subversion? In the end, the critics were satisfied - for, with Rees, Corré managed to update his heritage.

At first, the duo had aimed for a total environment, something more like a sensual, '90s Biba. Corré: "I liked the idea of having it to do with your whole life - not just what you were wearing beneath your everyday clothes. But your house and your surroundings and what you ate. I really wanted to offer people a spectrum of products, things that were essential, sensual and erotic."

"So our initial idea was for a larger store, one that had lots and lots of departments. From food and furniture to bathroom accessories. We tried for almost two years to finance that and we just weren't able to do it. We nearly did so on two occasions. But it always ended up falling through. After the second time, we just got pissed off. Because it's like a little jigsaw puzzle, where every little thing has to fit into place. If one thing doesn't work, then the whole thing doesn't. And you have to start all over again."

Eventually, the pair settled on lingerie - all top quality, however daring. "If you wear it under your clothes," they wrote in a manifesto, "you can feel like a sexy super-hero. You'll exude inner confidence and sexuality."

As a publicist/terrorist, Corré proved extremely apt. Early shop windows featured hanging mannequins (a London Fashion Week special was tagged "*Honi soit qui mal y pense*"). There was a dominatrix with her slave on a dog-lead, and a Christmas special - a penis-shaped tree which

3

1. Torture Garden flyers
From left to right:
a. Night of The Broken Dolls
b. Exploring The New Flesh
2. Skin Two, issue 23
Summer '97
Feature: Made For Mugler
Paris Couture
3. Cyber Collection
Design: Dane Goulding
Photo: Will Berlin
4. Agent Provocateur
6 Broadwick St, London W1

IT'S NOT SURPRISING THAT FASHION HAS TURNED TO FETISH WEAR. THERE'S A PC BACKLASH.
(→PAGE 124)

4

spurted cotton "snow". At the bottom of their jokes, though, the founders were serious. Even their Company Biography makes it clear, noting, "The concept is that sex is not smutty, sex is one of the few simple pleasures in life and should be enjoyed. Throw off all puritan values, dress up and indulge yourself."

Says Corré, "It's hard for me to answer real questions simply. Because when you start to talk about sex and liberating people, there's so many different things that come into it. I think all that you can do at the end of the day is offer people a choice and they take it or don't. But it is important to offer them the choice."

"I think", he adds, "in such a climate of 'choice' that it's important, and a little bit anarchic, to offer people a genuine alternative. To say, 'No, you don't have to have that - have this. I'm just going to present this stuff to you in a way that's my fantasy, something I like to see, something I think looks great. I'm not some marketing guy that's found a niche in the market - or someone that says 'OK, we've got 750 styles of jeans, I'm gonna do the 751st.' This is something that you haven't seen for a while, and particularly something you haven't seen in this country."

He pauses proudly. "I think that that's important. Because when you give people a choice, they can say 'I'm gonna buy my knickers at Marks and Spencers because I don't give a shit and I don't find underwear sexy'. Or they can go and get rubber things made specially. Or they can come to us and get our sort of fantasy. But the choice is theirs, which I think is the point."

The influence of Agent Provocateur was explosive. It soon launched a range of jewellery, with Erickson Beamon. Its roots, says Corré, are in "fantasy girls, Las Vegas strippers, slaves and Dominas." The pieces are made of silver, paste and crystal, and range from dog-collars and chains to handcuffs and chokers; pasties and whips to ankle and belly chains. Agent Provocateur is also an agent for Edra - an Italian furniture company whose velvet chairs serve as one of their signatures.

These are not the firm's only design commissions. There have also been costumes for a West End show (called "Voyeurz"), uniforms for a re-vamped Café de Paris, and a boutique for Milan's Fiorucci.

Many things embody the new, freer Soho aesthetic - a sampling and re-mixing of sexual signifiers. But none more so than the early work of design team Precious McBane. Behind the Russ Meyer pseudonym

1

1. **Agent Provocateur Catalogue cards**
2. **Lankie Lassie Design: Precious McBane '93/94**
3. **Weecoo Cabinet Design: Precious McBane '93/94**
4. **Display Rails Boisvert Lingerie Design: Precious McBane, '93**
5. **Bunny Chair Design: Precious McBane, '94**

THE BEST RESOURCE, HOWEVER, WAS OTHER DESIGNERS - OR THE PEOPLE WHO HELPED OTHER DESIGNERS. SMITH: "WHEN THE BANK MANAGER REALLY RIPS YOU UP AND SAYS, 'GO OFF, YOU SILLY GIRLS, GO GET REALISTIC', YOU FEEL VERY DOWN, VERY ON YOUR OWN. IT CAN ALSO MAKE YOU VERY ANGRY. YOU NEED TO KNOW THINGS HAVE WORKED FOR OTHER MAKERS."
(→PAGE 116)

YOU TRY REACHING FOR SUPPORT FROM THE STANDARD SOURCES. BUT YOU DON'T GET IT. SO YOU FIND ALTERNATIVE ROUTES.
(→PAGE 117)

lurks a pair of Scotswomen: Evlynn Smith and Meriel Scott. For three years a trio with friend Lynn Campbell-Millar, Scott and Smith make what they initially called "dysfunctional furniture". These are satin "corset chairs" with bunny-tails; pantie-clad footstools; fluffy "pom-pom" stools. All refer to women's curves or "naughty bits".

These designers have a thorough art-school training, and their first collection was backed by mainstream companies: Lochcarron of Scotland and Somerset's Fenlands Sheepskin. But the Precious McBane rationale did not come from their business plan. Like Rees and Corré's idea of a super-heroine, Precious McBane's founders also drew on a mythic female. Says Scott, "Evlynn and I were working together. Then, when Lynn joined up, we needed an identity."

"We heard about this book Precious Bane, about a father whose daughter had a harelip. So he can't marry her off. It's a cult, from the book by Mary Webb. At the time, Lynn was reading Ed McBain, and we wanted to use a heroine character. Sort of like Modesty Blaise, or something out of Russ Meyer. The 'Mc' came from us all being Scottish."

Adds Smith, "It really grabbed our imaginations. We were gonna do publicity photos brandishing drills."

One of the company's first commissions was Suzanne Boisvert's shop. Boisvert had been a model in Japan and Europe. When she married Martin Gore, of Depeche Mode, they settled down in London. After four years of marriage, and the birth of a daughter, Suzanne felt the itch to start her own business. "I always had a thing for French boudoir style. And I could tell that a market was opening up. So I decided to do lingerie with a difference: Ci-Dessous and Cadolle and Aubade from France. And some nice British and Italian lines." Married in a hand-tooled corset of ivory leather, Boisvert already had a flair for the upcoming style.

For her shop, she made "Boisvert" into a logo, then called on her old friend Meriel Scott. Suzanne gave the Precious McBane team key colours, citron and lavender. And, within three months, her boutique was finished - a rich, narrow niche out of a '50s film.

Boisvert's timing - October '93 - was impeccable. Underwear was turning into hot London clubwear, from "deconstructed corsets" by Richard Royle to outright rubberwear in traditional styles. Young shoppers loved the ambiance of tiny Boisvert: ruffled lilac moiré softening the clothing racks, a chaise and curving counter padded and customised. Plus, of course, the special "corset chair" - an elegant satin seat of distinctly female shape.

2

3

4

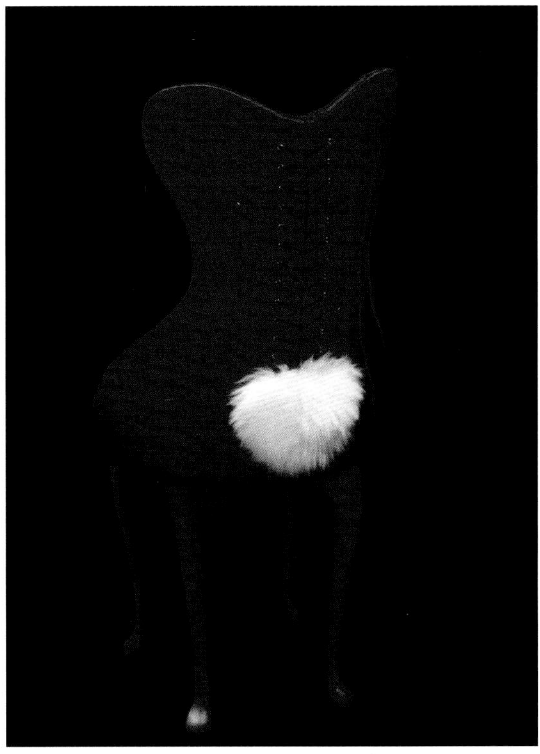

5

1

2

3

4

5

6

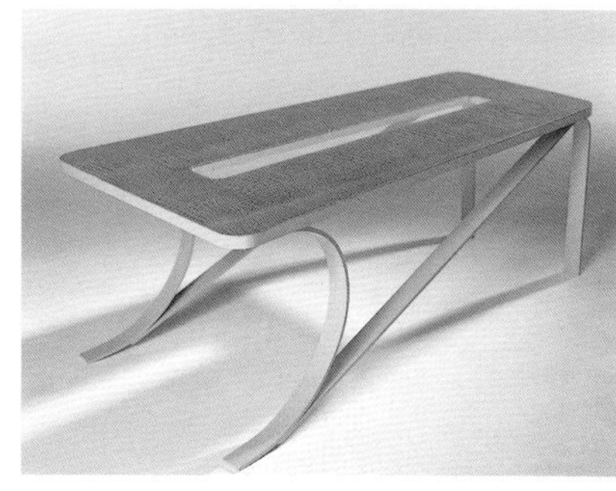

7

The corset chair was complemented by a "pantie" footstool, a combo which would become one of the team's best sellers. They were part of a look which attracted both press and celebrities. The artist formerly known as Prince ordered two chairs of his own, in shades which matched the colours of Federal Express, orange and purple. And every week brought new shoppers to Boisvert - Cher, Simply Red's Mick Hucknall, actor Tim Roth, rocker Dave Stewart. "It's amazing what people buy", said Boisvert. "Both Tim and Dave Stewart bought rubber - for their wives."

Agent Provocateur also went for boudoir style. But their version evoked Chinoiserie. Instead of lilac and lemon, they chose vibrant colours: vermilion and turquoise and hair-lacquer black. It was accessorised like an opium den, by tassled lanterns, chiffon drapes and velvet chairs.

Designers like Precious McBane took a definite interest. Says Smith, "There were no two ways about it. Suddenly, you had two lingerie shops of couture standard. Rather than just your Woolworths' garter sets. Clearly, it was more than a demand. People were realising, this marked a social change."

The first independent Precious McBane collection was "Tartan Tales", which was comprised of only a dozen pieces. Some were plays on the fetish status of the kilt. In a curvaceous "Lankie Lassie", for instance, a secret drawer shoots out from beneath a skittish rear flounce. Other pieces juxtapose fluff and fur with rougher materials. Men, say the team, like their work as much as women. Both sexes fancy a seat in the shapely, tactile furniture.

Central to Precious McBane's themes is the role of choice. All of its founders, for example, own and wear corsets. Corsets are just the sort of emblem they have played with; choosing to update the politics, but not reject them. Smith: "A corset helps you stand taller and prouder. But it also makes you think about powder-puffs, lipsticks and perfume - all those little ways you pamper yourself."

"At the same time," she adds, twisting a lock of hair, "we know their social history all too well. Corsets have always been used for restraining women. These days, pantie-girdles get hyped for the same purpose. Yet each one, in its own way, is beautiful. Sculptural."

Precious McBane's early furniture drew on tensions in sexual symbols. But its approach was bold instead of ironic. Since their transformation from trio to duo, Precious McBane have re-defined their approach to fusing fine art, fashion and

1. Pom Pom Beanbag
Design: Precious McBane
2. Lux Building, London N1
Design: Precious McBane, '97
3. Modesty Mirrored Cabinet
Design: Precious McBane, '96
4. Pom Pom Stools
As seen in Mark Whittaker's 'Soft' artwork '97/98 show
5. Faim de Cherie
(Moc-croc leather armchair)
Design: Precious McBane, '96
6. 10500 Hair Salon
Reception seats / interior
Design: Precious McBane, '95
7. Moc-croc Table
Design: Precious McBane, '96
8. Precious McBane
Photo: 44 Photography

8

design. This included re-envisioning the 'fetish object' and what, for them, it inspires in three dimensions. Says Smith, "Now we're more concerned with the notion of 'obsession', and of looking at objects beyond the purely sexual. It's an obsession with the beautiful, the sexy and the luxurious - one which likes to play with shapes and surfaces."

The partners' private corsets were eventually pushed to the back of their wardrobes. But, as a company, Precious McBane are "woman obsessed". Their seating installation at the Lux Cinema, for instance, involves luxurious "drapes" made out of etched glass. It is reminiscent of '30s cinema, with its voyeuristic overtones and secret liaisons.

Meanwhile, bras with metal tips can be found in the high street. Skin Two's Rubber Ball is part of the British calendar; it's as venerable as Glastonbury. Suzanne Boisvert has opened a second shop. Precious McBane ship to Paris, New York, Seattle. Yet those who started off the trend can feel aggrieved. "Real fetishists", says Tuppy Owens, "keep complaining to me. They say, 'The clubs are full of women in rubber. But there's nothing going on, it's only fashion'. The guy with a real fetish - he's out in the cold."

Nevertheless, Owens too has moved with the times. In 1994, her *Sex Maniac's Bible* turned into *Planet Sex*, a book about "what's happening everywhere, how the fetish scene is changing, and what are the erotic codes in other cultures." Its author was aware of the links between futurism and sexual theatre. Her first *Planet Sex Ball* was sponsored by Forbidden Planet, London's well-established comic and science-fiction store.

Thus, even in the age of techno beats and trainers, dressing-up remains a sexual matter. But its sexual edge is being re-defined. "Tranny culture" and "fetish fashion" may now be overground. But they've been there throughout English history. Whether via phone kiosk graphics or the Paris catwalk, rather than hide that fact, the '90s flaunt it.

1

1. Cybercatsuit Collection
Design: Dane Goulding
Photo: Will Berlin

I JUST THOUGHT YOU COULD TRUST PEOPLE. EVEN WITH FRIENDS, I NOW KNOW, IT'S IMPORTANT TO GET A DEPOSIT. YOU HAVE REALLY GOT TO GET YOUR STUFF UPFRONT.

(→PAGE 111)

On London's fashion scene, Dane Goulding is unique. Throughout the '90s, he designed his own collections - filtering social change and politics through fetish wear. Now, with his own label, D.A.N.E., Goulding is poised for stardom in a bigger league. Here, he talks about music, how he makes fashion, and how clothing can make new sexual statements.

So where do you hail from?

I'm from Liverpool, went to art college in Cheltenham. I think I finished there in about 1985. I had a band in Liverpool, which I was in before college. They were called Black and, when I was in them, it was a lot more punky. When I left, they had hits with "Wonderful Life" and "The Sweetest Smile". In my first year at college, I tried to transfer to Manchester so I could do both art and my band. But I didn't end up doing it.

Still, you kept up your music.

Oh yeah, but my taste changed. By the '90s, I was into liking guitar stuff. I like dance music, for instance. But the style, tracksuits and all that, I thought it sucked. For me, the music always goes with the clothes. I started DJ'ing in Cheltenham in '86; the band split up, so I started doing clubs. There's only four clubs in Cheltenham, so we had to move it round. My own band, TVOD, I started with my second collection. Now, we've got a track on Sequential's "Club Fetish" compilation.

The reason I did it was, if you go to a few fashion shows in the season, you see the same music being played for, say, three shows. I thought it would be much nicer to have your own music for your clothes. To have lyrics to get across what you were doing. We had the band just record it like a fashion track. But then it turned out well. So the other two guys decided that they'd put it out. Later we put the visual side together. When I did the band, I used to do their posters and a mate showed one of my posters to Tuppy Owens.

Cross-dressing over:

unisex couturier Dane

And she gave you work?

She gave me full-time work, which is why I moved down to London. I used to design her *Sex Maniac's Diary*, this was maybe 1990 and 1991. I also did a book called the *Sex Maniac's Bible* - designed that as well - which was tattoo-based. I was doing just drawing. But it was two dimensions, which is half the reason I got back into clothing. I do clothing 'cause I like to see it move. I still made things as I was going along; I made my friends the odd thing. But I hadn't really thought of doing fashion full time. The reason being, in between the band and the clubs, I did two collections - which I sold. I just came down to London with some samples and I got orders from shops. One in particular really bought a lot: Liberated Lady, in the Kings Rd. This was about 1985, and the collection was my first one after college. At the time, it was rubberwear.

Did that not set you up?

I made it up and I delivered it all. But when I came down to do that, the whole shop was shut; the place had simply vanished. They left me right up the creek without a paddle. So I started doing clubs and illustration. That way, all I could really lose was a drawing. If I didn't get paid, it would cost me one more pencil and my time. But, with fashion, it would cost both my time and the fabric. I did another collection, too, all the patterns and the samples. That all went off to New York - and that's the last I ever heard of it. This time it was the best friend of my business manager. I just thought you could trust people. Even with friends, I now know, it's important to get a deposit. You have really got to get your stuff upfront.

London fashion's always been ripped off, most especially clubwear.

Fetish wear is a lot more pirate-able, and it does appeal to certain couturiers. Because each piece people make is like a separate sculpture. It's not a problem, but what often annoys you is when they pick up on an idea you've had which you simply didn't have the money to see through. There are certain designers, you know, who if you see 'em in clubs, you're wise to run. I think Prince, in the Lovesexy tour, was influenced by John Richmond. I know I was when I had words down my clothes! Some of my ideas came from flyers I did for clubs. I came up with the idea for mesh back then - for printing on mesh. But it took five years to get it done.

My first "comeback" collection, *Chanel de Sade*, I did back in 1992. I just tried to imagine what Chanel herself would wear to a fetish club. I only did maybe seven pieces. But I tried to really use those Chanel chains, and to do a collection which looked rather elegant. I did also pierced nipples, and things like that. It wasn't trendy then, and it was artificial. The idea was not to have it permanent, but that you just put it on as a bra.

Do you style each model as you do it?

Yes, and I choose my models quite carefully. Two I use often, Jemima and Pauline, are in the band with me. Pauline's got lots of piercings, she looks brilliant. But I have different looks, from Chanel to Captain Nemo. For *Superstars*, I used holographic imagery, silver and Day-Glo colours: pink and bright blue, turquoise and orange. It was Warhol's basic idea, updated. My idea was "reclaim your own superstardom". You know, without mass acclaim. So, as models, I used lots of drag queens - guys from Heaven. In my case, the first show just led to the second one. At first, I just added pieces as I went. It's not so important for me to be seasonal, because it's all night wear. I don't do huge big coats or anything. But I did once do a bridal outfit! It was in the collection called *Gender Defectors*.

Did the Sex Maniac's Ball show lead to others?

Yeah. But what's really been good to me is the Alternative Fashion Week shows at Spitalfields. They also did a thing in Carnaby St, where they put designers into different empty shops, about eight different young designers. We only had the places for a month, but it was a great idea. Lots of designers in the shops got cheesed, because we got places free for a month. But we couldn't do it like retail - instead, we hung our clothes on the walls, like they were art. They've done that a few times, all in separate locations.

You put rubberwear down as a "Next Big Thing" in college, didn't you?

Yes, although then I didn't really know why! Now, however, I've changed. I still try to base my clothes on fetish wear. But I've had this whole relation to rubber. Traditionally, rubberwear was not fashion-based. So, for a long time, I tried not to use it. I tried to be as sexy or as sensual with other fabrics. When I finally got round to it, in '96, I kept as far from what it "ought to be" as possible. I made it printed and floaty.

How did the "tattooed" mesh happen?

I did the printed mesh for my band's first performance. But, then, everyone said: "Hey, make some more!" I had to find a wholesaler. I had a friend who worked for a chainstore and she knew someone and she vouched for me. Which I needed, because I could handle maybe thirty and they usually sell 100,000.

How do you work?

For a long while, I did one outfit at a time. I was working at home, with a domestic machine, having to tidy up. When we had the baby, that had to change. Around that time, a studio came up - I heard about it from friends. By then I was trying not to do just one-offs, and I was trying not to do so many club shows. Club shows are good fun - and good publicity - but the clothes get trashed. Shirts are always the easiest to sell; I can print 20 shirts in a day. But, with corsets, you'll do one a day. I branched out more with *Scandal and Corruption* in '95. I went into a whole football fetish thing; I made a Chelsea scarf dress for David Mellor [The MP whose mistress said he made love wearing just a Chelsea scarf]. That collection was to be MP-based; I had Mellor and Stephen Milligan, the MP who was found hanging in ladies' undies!

You really like details, and you find nice ones.

I like things like the quick-release buckles, which are used on rucksacks or by the Army. I just like the way they look. And they're infinitely adjustable, which is not the case when you deal with eyelets. I've done those to hold on fitted codpieces. That's another point about my clothes, I don't think they're gender-specific. I mean, I go out, I wear lipstick, makeup, high heels and so forth. And I'm supposed to live with the label transvestite. Which I don't really agree with at all. I wasn't around when they gave out the clothes. So why should I go around with someone else's definition of what I'm s'posed to look like? I do clothes I think *everyone* should wear.

What responses do you get from that?

Well, I was down in one of the Old Compton Street fetish shops. And a guy came in and said, "Do you have a copy of *The Transvestite's Guide to London*"? The salesgirl said, "Yes, and guess what: here's Dane, he's on the cover". So the guy turns to me and says, "Oh, it's not for *me*! I've got no interest in it! But I know a friend who I think would like it." Then he came out with all these theories about why someone is a transvestite - and they're all down to your mother not taking care of you! I was saying, "Have you never thought 'These are just the clothes I want to wear this evening?' Have you never just thought 'That's how I want to look'?"

People want an image they know they can recognise. They want to know if you're gay or straight. Dress comes into it as a code.

I know. But everyone's got their own reasons for doin' it. The most hassle I get is from people thinking I'm gay - because I'm going out in a dress. If they actually understood what "gay" means, it means guys that like guys. So, most of the time, they want to go out with a man who looks like some version of a man! A lot of reasons cross-dressing proliferates on the gay scene is simply gays don't have a problem with it. One of the main insults for so-called straight guys is people going, "You poof! you homo!" And we're supposed to be mortally offended and defend ourselves.

But if someone says that and you *don't* see yourself as that, then they might as well be saying, "You've got green trousers on!" When you know you haven't. I don't really see where the insult lies, you know? In this day and time, there's nothing wrong with bein' gay. But, if you're slagged for it, why should you go "Bloody hell!", "Now you're for it!" and all that kind of thing. It's odd that you could be insulted just by someone being wrong.

One theory is that people are seeking after something because they're just unhappy. If they're not unhappy, it just blows the theory.

Dream on! I remember going to a Skin Two party at the club Submission, and there was this small article about it in a daily paper. And it was just not the same thing I'd been at. It was all "these sleazy people slinking around in their rubberwear". Well, sometimes it can get kind of sleazy, but even then, it's a very stylised sleaze. I mean, that's the way it's s'posed to be. It is quite dark and people are wearing rubberwear - but it's not "rubberwear!" The way the paper framed it, they wanted it to sound really disgusting. But a lot of these fetish clubs, they're now like going to youth clubs. Everyone's dressed in rubber, yeah. But you're standing by the door with your mate, nattering on about some film you both saw. You really don't see it the way the media does.

What happens with the clothes happens because people are just totally relaxed there. They're doing exactly what they want to do. Not what they had to do to get in the club. Of course, some people put on leather trousers to get in, just because they're the voyeuristic type. That happens a fair amount; people go to fetish clubs to look "at the perverts". Because, of course, *they're* not "that kind of people". It's like perv-spotting!

But do you prefer them mainly because of the clothes?

No, what I also like is the lack of aggression. I go to any straight club - or even the Hippodrome - and, more often than not, I'll get a couple of lads who just exude aggression. I mean this feeling of "Don't even look at me" or "Don't look at my bird". Or "If you spill my pint, mate, you're dead". There's always that kind of unease in the air. Fetish clubs are one of the only places you'll go to where you might see people getting hit or spanked. But the aggression's consensual; it's not the same. If you want to be hit and someone does it, that's a different matter from being attacked. To me, that's perverted.

The fetish scene takes something from the old goth scene. A sense of drama, maybe, or a melodramatic aesthetic.

Yeah, but it depends on what club you're gonna go to. I think the Torture Garden is more music-orientated; they're really into techno and industrial music. There have always been lots of piercing-type people there. But I wouldn't really call it gothic; I think it's more like kids who missed out on that. It's reminiscent, though, and there are a lot of goth veterans. There are people who went through some of that. But, at fetish clubs, they look totally different. Except for the blackness of it all, and the elaborate makeup. Over time, there's been a range of clubs. Fantastic in Brixton - where I've DJ'd. Submission, Kinky Gerlinky, Torture Garden, The Romper Room, The Way Out Wine Bar. Some are a bit brighter; there's a cross-over from the drag thing to fetish. At Fantastic, for instance, a lot of drag queens and the girls from Madame Jo-Jos would come down. But we played music from rave right through punk. People go for all of it, this audience is broad in their tastes. They'll all have live bands and fashion shows.

Upstairs there are often photographic studios. Where you go if you want to be photographed. Because at fetish clubs, no one wanders round with cameras, they're restricted because of people who would tell the wives or husbands. They use trusted photographers to protect people's privacy. If someone goes there because they're into rubber, but they work in a bank, it's nobody else's business. They don't want to end up on a daily's Lifestyle page. Sometimes, of course, the club itself is secretive. You phone the number up and you only find out the address when you get a ticket. Some clubs, like Submission, have an older crowd. Although all these clubs, you know, have people from seventy right down to eighteen. That is probably the only time that happens. It doesn't happen at dance clubs!

But the bond is more central here.

Sure. You're all doing something which, regrettably, is still frowned upon. But Submission's very dancey, it's got a DJ who is one of London's top techno DJs. Plus, they'll play hardcore garage. Plus, they'll put on clubs in Amsterdam - lay on coaches and do all of that. They got lots of other clubs into doing that, because they had a big birthday party, in Brick Lane, and sold over a thousand tickets. And, around 11:30, the police came and shut it down. That was November 1993 and people had come over for it from Europe and America. They re-scheduled it, but they lost a lot of money. They've sometimes been done in old buildings, or under railway arches. But the parking's always a problem. Because, you know, you don't take the bus to a fetish club.

There's one taxi firm I use which is very good - really safe. But that's half the expense of doing your own thing. It's ridiculous. The only reason you must pay that price is intolerance.

People don't even *understand* why they hate you. They just think they should. I think there are lots of people who are programmed to hate, who think "Rules exist and that's how it is". You just don't break those rules! This goes into the realm of clothing and fashion. They just feel they must wear that suit and tie - always.

What about Dane's World - in *Taffeta: The Lifestyle Magazine for Transvestites and Those Who Love Them*?

Well, someone told me there was a pic of one of my shows, in this magazine which is called "Shiny". Then they said, "Oh we're doing a tranny mag." So I did an interview for them, with this woman. And I ended up doing a column. All they wanted was my daily life, but I tried to add a bit of self-help. Because there are some people who are screwed up by this, who do carry lots of guilt around. Here, they at least read that they're not alone. They've done really well with that magazine. There's a lot of tranny magazines, but some are quite porny. They show guys dressed up, then have 'em strip.

What were some details from the collection you actually called *Transvestite*?

Transvestite was just a blatant use of the word. The tranny thing is: if you're out and you're dressed up a bit, people just make a point of laughing very loudly. Of course, they haven't affected you at all. But, it's clear that you've affected them. Offence is in one's own mind, usually. I mean you're wearing a bloody skirt, a non-gendered item. Like, to me, a bra is quite gendered - it fits a body part men haven't got. Tights, shoes, trousers; none of that is gendered. If women wore a codpiece, for instance, that's the only thing which could make that kind of statement. Those are the only things that deal with the real differences in our bodies. There's only two. That's really why I don't really agree with the word, and why I decided to make it blatant. Also, because people assume you're hiding something; they assume you're trying to pass as a woman. I'm not trying to look like a girl - but me. That was the point of that one collection.

Can you see attitudes changing?

Yes, but I think blokes need to work on it. Often, when they put on a skirt, they'll adopt a different perception. Women don't do that when they decide to wear trousers. But, I do think that has also changed, not least because of bands like Nirvana. Or Stone Temple Pilots, they've all gone on stage in frocks. On the other hand, they're not bothered with makeup. People have said with the makeup thing, that I try to look like a woman. But it's a glamour thing, I'm not changing my body. It's just a cosmetic thing, you take it off again.

What came next for you?

The mesh body thing, which is difficult to print, it's messy. The collection after I called *Justice or Revenge*. All my clothes, they are fetish-based. But the messages in them are broader. They're almost...ethereal. Maybe just because they have to do with perception. To me, "justice" and "revenge" are points of view. The reference point there was our double standard, people who just see a load of perverts - as opposed to seeing you and your friends, looking good and feeling happy. *Scandal and Corruption* was the next collection; then *Superstars*; *3001*; *Beauty Assassins* and so on. *3001* was subtitled *Daddy, When Was the Future?* Because, since the '50s, there's been a very clear-cut idea of the future and what it would look like. I was imagining my son at 15, trying to look at "now" as a moment in time. It was also a completely new collection, because in January '96 I got my studio. So I really had a place to work, and I started completely from scratch. I designed 70 pieces, could only afford to make 30.

How have you managed?

For a long time, I managed because of the dole. But I always wanted to be street legal, which of course was very, very difficult. But, I now have a studio. I export to Russia, America, Australia, Germany. And to someone in Atlanta, someone in Seattle, someone in Texas. The way to do it, of course, is to get a catalogue and send that out. But I'm taking it one step at a time. I just learned about making business plans; I did a three-week course at Portobello Business Centre. My next step is to get some sponsorship. There's a lot of very big companies who can see how either the right image or a bit of controversy will help their product. A little bit of glamour goes a long way; so does any kind of link with nightclubbing. It gets a product into magazines where it wouldn't be seen otherwise. Ten thousand pounds can make a whole collection. But, for the benefit to a sponsor, that's not a lot.

Meanwhile, I've bought my own printing stuff. I'm making more long dresses and jackets and things like that. Last year, I was doing what I could make most easily. Now, I'm try to think, "Do I want to make another one?" Because I'll be doing a lot of them.

Precious McBane:

on building a company

"Couture furniture" company Precious McBane started in 1993. Initially, there were three partners; now, there are two. In the four years it took to build up a business, Precious McBane have been adventurous, canny and foolhardy. Here, they talk about their highs and lows - plus the importance of both imagination and pragmatism.

Precious McBane started in September of '93, with a commission for the interior of Boisvert. Suzanne Boisvert, who owned the lingerie shop, was acquainted with Meriel Scott. She also knew Meriel's work with Evlynn Smith - from a show called "Domestic Kitsch" she had seen in '92. In October '93, Meriel and Evlynn were joined by Lynn Campbell-Millar, who presented a proposal for working together. The Scotswomen called their company Precious McBane and set a target: two collections a year. They began with "Tartan Tales: Roamin' In the Gloamin'", for which they made nine pieces - and got sponsorship from several Scottish companies. One was Locharron, maker of tartans for Vivienne Westwood.

From the beginning, Precious McBane had a lively image. They wooed sponsors and the press with up-to-date themes and professional info and media packs. They sought to marry sculpture and functional furniture; they got out and about and found "who knew who". Said Meriel Scott, two years into the business, "There's a large gap in some people's eyes between fine art and furniture. But for us, it was a logical crossover. You can't market sculpture and we want to make a living."

Added Smith, "All of us have an interest in fashion. We're all 'tag hags'. That would be lost, if we stuck with fine art. In Precious McBane, it's central."

Within eight months, Precious sold three-quarters of "Tartan Tales". They also scored a hit with the "Corset Chair" designed for Boisvert. Initially, it was pictured in *Time Out* magazine, then the *Scottish Sunday Mail*, then BBC Bristol used it as a prop. It led MTV Europe's fashion show *The Pulse* into doing a piece on

Precious McBane, as it did Carlton TV. Later, the chair appeared in *Vogue*, *Casa Vogue*, Italian *Vogue*, *GQ*, *Homes & Gardens*, Germany's *Bunte* and *Elle Decoration*, the *Evening Standard*, and America's *Allure* magazine. The artist formerly known as Prince ordered a pair of chairs for his Paisley Park studio.

Along the way, the team struggled to find useful advisors. While each held another part-time job, she did research into a separate area: sponsorship, sub-contracting, insurance, copyrights, tax. Says Smith: "You have to plunge in and do it yourself. The government says there are all these agencies to help small business. Well, we've tried them all. Most of them are pretty clueless."

Added Scott, "If we were a newsagent, it might be different. Our first real support came from the Crafts Council. We applied for their setting-up grant and we got it. It gave us money towards equipment, money for maintenance." On the weekend course required by the grant, the makers found they garnered few new tips. Says Smith: "They said things like 'Get in touch with your local paper'. No one said, 'OK, shoot for the *top*'. To me, it just reeked of the Britain I hate. Which is 'Oh, you don't want to get out of your league. So, please! Remember! Start small!'" In November 1994, however, they were featured by *Crafts* magazine.

When a company in Japan wanted some furniture, the trio contacted the Department of Trade and Industry. Although Campbell-Millar found it "a bit like the Kremlin", the DTI held a wealth of information. Smith: "I got in touch with the guy who dealt with trade in Japan; Lynn and I went to meet him and we got on very well. We found out a huge amount of stuff: tariffs, demarcations, outreach set-ups. Any time he has anything helpful for us, he will still either telephone or fax us."

"There was stuff no one advertises", she adds. "Like these Japanese reps who come over, who'll be sent applications from UK makers. Plus, the DTI will rep your work *in* Japan. And they have these things called Outward Missions where they pay your fares and fees." Precious nurtured such relationships - sending their contacts letters, clips and reports on progress.

Along the way, they learned more by trial and error. Sub-contractors let them down and caused delays. They lost a studio and were forced to work from one bedsit. Says Scott, "You learn: *get everything in writing*. What you expect of clients, that 50% is upfront, and what the final delivery date will be. Because you'll have a lot of conversations, where you think, 'Oh, this person's nice' - but you're wrong."

Precious learned about DACS (the Design and Artists Copyright Society); about ways to insure against lost profit; about going "to the top" with investors and sponsors. Campbell-Millar: "Never be afraid to do that. Never be afraid to talk to the boss."

The best resource, however, was other designers - or the people who helped other designers. Smith: "When the bank manager really rips you up and says, 'Go off, you silly girls, go get realistic', you feel very down, very on your own. It can also make you very angry. You need to know things have worked for other makers."

Adds Scott, "Especially on your third business plan. Things looked up for us when we met Kaspaar de Graaf, who's a corporate designer and consultant. He gave us much better advice than the economists. Because when we went to banks with our business plans, it wasn't us having done them by ourselves. They came about because we *had* advisors. So we'd end up thinking, 'How could they say no?'"

By 1996, Precious was well established. They had completed numerous private commissions; as well as designing Portobello's 10,500 Hair Salon, the London Film-maker's Co-op and a second Boisvert shop. They had a Semi-Precious range of accessories, and the corset chair was still going strong, featured in a UK show called "Unlaced Grace". They launched an ambitious, Western-themed collection - one they titled "Raunch at the Ranch".

"It was a watershed for us", says Smith. "We showed it at a gallery off Edgware Road, and the whole thing there was very disorganised. We'd come up with the ideas two years earlier. So, by the time we got round to them, we were bored. Yet we were obliged to see them through." They were also obliged to pay £300 towards the private view party and £200 just to show in the gallery.

After "Raunch", they went through two more studios - and Campbell-Millar decided to leave the company. Smith: "We were just going in different directions. Lynn felt compromised and she wasn't happy. So we parted. Then, we went on holidays - having authorised our lawyer to close on the studio. While we were in Greece, our landlady sold the building. The rent doubled and, if we didn't like it, we had 24 hours to get out."

Through friends at a party, Scott and Smith found another space. Artist-run and artist-friendly, it has the support of Southwark & Lambeth Council. Traumatised, they settled in to re-think their purpose. Smith: "We went to see a business consultant and we talked about all our dreams for the company, because we set up to pay for us to do sculpture. But it was so insatiable, we couldn't do that. We needed to merge our sensibilities - with relation to sculpture - and our furniture."

The result has been a change in direction: towards more classical and sophisticated products. "It's less referential", says Smith. "It's no longer always theme-based. But we hope there's still a sense of humour."

Precious McBane the company still retains its double structure. It is split into Precious Products (interiors, one-off designs and private commissions) and Semi-Precious (small runs of objects or accessories priced £50-£250). The latter includes mirrors and "pom-pom stools" - with plates, glasses and cushions in the wings.

By 1997, re-thinking had paid off; sales were up by 35%. In 1996, the turnover was £32,000, with only £16,000 in sales. Halfway through '97, sales alone were £32,000. For the first time, Precious McBane took a stall at The London Contemporary Design Show. They were pleased by the results, which included a plug in *The New York Times*. Says Smith, "It was our largest ever mainstream exposure, and we fitted in with the moment: with its colours and the very clean lines. But what was consistently said was how 'different' we were."

It was salve to a certain wound: the criticism for "going mainstream". But Scott and Smith remain unrepentant. Says the former, "Nothing's changed all that much. We just had to get more practical. We still stick with what we learned so early: that other artists are your best advisors. You know, they know, you're more than a name and a product. All these years, we played with image, language, concepts - just to keep people's attention on us. We controlled our company extremely carefully. And, at the end of the day, we're very glad."

Adds Smith, "You try reaching for support from the standard sources. But you don't get it. So you find alternative routes."

Corsets & kilts '95

Tartan had been one of punk's initial signatures. At the beginning of the '90s, gay street youth in London brought it back - with a twist. Suddenly, it was everywhere: from Alexander McQueen's "Highland Rape" collection to Nina Ricci, Romeo Gigli, John Galliano. Tartan appeared on record sleeves by Britain's Cornershop, Germany's Rausch, New York's Salt-N-Pepa. "Kilts have been hip," wrote one fashion critic in '94, "since Madonna wore hers over leather jeans, Axl Rose slung his under a T-shirt and Jean-Paul Gaultier made his a personal trademark." Kilts and tartan would appear again and again - a new fetish object, just like the corset. In late '95, as the trend peaked in London, Precious McBane's Scottish founders considered the kilt and the corset.

Lynn:

The social history of the corset parallels things like footbinding; both of them have been a way of confining women. But corsets are lovely objects! People like Vivienne Westwood make them more wearable. It's an update, because she's aware of the politics and the history of the corset.

Meriel:

She amplifies the whole goddess thing. She knows if you take the feminist thing to an extreme, you repress yourself. There are now too many layers to things like corsets and kilts, to them crossing over from their past to our present. People have become very aware of it.

Evlynn:

We've certainly used tartans, used both kilts and corsets. In the "Kiltie Cabinet" from our very first collection, where there's a drawer which comes out through the sporran, we wanted that to look politely obscene. Or, at the very least, cheeky.

Lynn:

It was there because of what sporrans are there to protect. A man wears a sporran to protect himself when he puts on a kilt.

Meriel:

We were raising the kilts of Scotland, uncovering Scotland's bum! Talking about fetishism, kilts were totally a fetish when we did that. They're still having quite a successful run.

Lynn:

It was a very staid image to subvert. More than people know who aren't Scottish. Because, traditionally, kilts are just for a certain context: weddings, Burns night suppers, the Scotland-England football match. You won't see a working-class brickie walking around of a Saturday night with a kilt on.

Evlynn:

Now, they're being combined with things like piercing and "body décor". There's one guy who's got a silver bone through his nose, a shaved head and all these piercings - and wears a kilt, heavy boots and stockings. Kilts are used a lot for showing your wares, so to speak.

Lynn:

There's also a lot of places for hiding things, which is something we tried to use in our pieces. Lots of secret little drawers and pouches - like a condom pocket in your knickers!

Meriel:

Most men we've met seem to find 'em liberating; just to have the air blowing around the tops of their legs. It's the equivalent of women wearing the Wonderbra: getting your wares out. It's the straight man's opportunity to look crooked.

Lynn:

It's very much like men jumping in a pool together after a football match. We tried to do with tartan what gay men have done for the kilt - that is, find a way to modernise it. So many *haute couture* designers have used it, tartan's now become a modern fabric.

Evlynn:

But it's not like we're making it into a female fetish object. Men are just as receptive to everything we do. We've had a lot of male interest in the corset chair. Pieces like the "Corset Chair" may seem quite feminine. But others, like the "Sleepyhead Bed", are quite masculine.

Meriel:

In the '90s, there's been a huge change in attitudes. Over the past five years, underwear became outerwear. Corsets, bras - it's been de-mystified. Look what Vivienne Westwood did for the Liberty bodice. We've all got corsets. I've got one made to fit. I remember when one time I borrowed Lynn's - which is this really proper showgirl corset. I thought I was going to faint. But, after a couple of drinks, I got into it and it was nice.

Lynn:

What's important is: choice makes the difference. What's disturbing is commercial restraining clothing, like the relaunch of the pantie-girdle.

Evlynn:

I hate the political history of those things. But, their structure can be beautiful - and I like the way I feel when I wear one.

Meriel:

But a pantie-girdle meant for you to wear each day, to control your figure, that's something different. It's a matter of context. Like, I've got a large bust. So if I wear a corset to a "normal" club, I get lots of nasty hassles. So my ideal place to wear one is a gay club, a fetish club or a girls' night out. With clothes, the politics of choice just goes so far.

Joe Corré's parents are two of England's most original characters: designer Vivienne Westwood and entrepreneur Malcolm Maclaren. In the '90s, co-founding his own shop, Corré has continued their punk legacy - self-reliance, provocation and sexual honesty. He talks about how and why he launched his enterprise and about its special kind of social ramifications.

Why did it occur to you to start a shop?

My whole family background and upbringing was surrounded by this sort of shop mentality. Plus, you've got that saying from Napoleon or whoever, "Britain is a nation of shopkeepers". There is that mentality here; it's fairly easy for young people to get a shop and open up, much more easy than in, say, Paris or Milan - or even America. There is that kind of culture where people feel they can start their own business - you just need a good idea and a bit of capital. All the systems are sort of set up for that. It's fairly easy to get a lease, to start turning over money. That's one thing. The other thing, of course, is my family background, always being around shops and fashion.

How did you formulate your business strategy?

If you've got a shop you're not only selling to sell a product, you've got to actually put forward an idea about something. My parents when I was a young kid were a lot to do with that. They were interested in whatever political thing of the time or of music, and they pushed those via their shop. As a result, you had other people that were also interested in those ideas hanging around that shop. It became a focal point - perhaps there wasn't anywhere else to go, or maybe they could buy the things there that got them into that whole lifestyle. That's something that I grew up with; I had the know-how to be able to do that.

Shopkeeper Joe Corré:

on marketing female fantasy

But did you have hands-on experience?

Yes, I worked with my mother for nine years in shops and fashion. Initially, myself and my partner - Serena Rees - had a much larger idea. We felt that nobody had really represented a sort of sexual or erotic or sensual lifestyle as an entirety. If you wanted sexy underwear, you might go to some funny little place. But there weren't many places in this country. Most people were giving their friends orders when they went overseas. Unless you were into the fetish scene, into rubber and that. Britain's quite good for that; there's a lot of small people who will make up special stuff for you, small enterprises doing their own little thing. But, on a more mainstream basis, it didn't really exist.

But you had to pare down the idea to make it feasible?

We decided to take the one idea that we knew we could do, which was lingerie, but create the environment in the store around the first idea. Make it glamorous, comfortable, sensual - all of those things that we felt the products deserved. So it wasn't like going into Ann Summers, it wasn't cheap and nasty. Not a sort of Soho sex shop kind of thing - though there's nothing wrong with that. But not boring, either, like a department store sort of environment. So, we started from the point of view of creating the space first and then filling it with the things we liked. Rather than, let's say, being a small designer and having a little collection and selling it to a few people - then opening up our own shop. We thought of opening the shop, making the shop look how we wanted, *then* filling it up with stuff.

How does it work now?

The two of us do the buying, designing and manufacturing. We design our own range. A lot of things have been around for years - corsets, say. But some of the stuff is quite original and we're starting to do more of that. We've been open two years now and every year we've gotten more and more on our own label. So we're building it up. But I like the idea that you've got a mix, between our own label and other people's. So it always keeps the stock interesting; you can always have new things in all the time. And if you find something that you really like, it doesn't mean you rip it off and do it yourself. You just buy theirs - that's much better and more honest.

What about the shop's ambience?

Certainly it has that whole sort of Frenchy boudoir feeling. But, then, I think the whole issue about British sexuality is fucking confused. The French as a nation seem to think that the British as a nation are very sexually open and tolerant. But we think, "Oh no, we're not really tolerant, we're really backward and the *French* are really tolerant - and they are sexy." Everyone has these impressions of one another. In reality, I don't know what the truth is. So we just mixed in that sort of Chinoiserie, Chinese style, which came about in the 18th century - both in France and in the UK. All over Europe at that time it was fashionable. We felt that was kind of boudoir-looking and we wanted some strong colours. So it's sort of a mixture between French, Chinese, British and everything really, just an idea of sexiness. It's a little bit '50s-looking but not a lot. It's all to do with glamour.

How do you feel if people say, "Oh, you're running a sex shop"?

When we opened, I remember going into Ann Summers and seeing this thing called "Lager-Flavoured Nipple Drops". And I was so shocked - I mean if I'd seen a harness with dildos up the arse and tits cut out, I wouldn't have been shocked. I would have thought "alright". But, somehow, "Lager-Flavoured Nipple Drops" summed up the whole of this funny, ha-ha perverse attitude of scared men towards sexuality. What they thought was sexy, you know? Go down the pub, get pissed out of your head, have a curry, go home and put the lager-flavoured nipple drops on the missus! I thought that was so disgusting and so unsexy that I really wanted to do something which was a challenge to it, to display underwear and lingerie in a way that was obvious and screamed out at you.

I mean, we've made our window look very provocative but in a way that is very normal. "This is great looking, you don't have to look like the whole Ann Summers thing, you don't *have* to look like that." And it's not a joke, it's something that's gorgeous, it's something special. It's not alright to go and spend £1.99 on your girlfriend and think that it's a joke. It's not a joke. It's one of the few simple pleasures in life, so let's give it a bit more respect and attention.

But you're going against quite entrenched British values.

That sort of Carry On mentality, when it comes to sexuality, has a lot to do with the so-called Victorian values. The fact that on the face of things they were very highly moralised, they had very clear rules about what was OK and what wasn't, about how you were supposed to behave. Yet, at the same time, you had things going on you wouldn't believe now, and it was very well known. It was a tourist attraction for international paedophiles - you know, child prostitution, babies for sale, everything a pervert wanted was available. In London at that time, you had the most brothels per square mile than anywhere else in the world. You had two different things co-existing. It's the same about Victorian architecture; the house looks great from the front but it's all a facade.

The Carry On thing slightly comes out of that - in that it says if you can't be OK about sex and you can't be open-minded, then the best medicine is to laugh about it. Joke about it and say that it's something funny. I like Carry On films. But they've become something that's sort of a cult, because it's looking back and saying, "God how prudish these people were, isn't it funny!" It gives men - and women too, to an extent - the excuse that they don't really have to look far for the answers. They don't have to look at themselves at all; they can just laugh it off. And if you don't get the joke you're a bit stuck up. Of course, it isn't true. But now you've got these magazines like *Loaded* - you've got millions of them because they're all trying to be like *Loaded* as it's the most popular - and it's the same kind of reaction. When people feel a bit worried, or don't know how to deal with something, then they go the other way.

Why have you concentrated on the female market?

In the last six or seven years, you had a lot of companies trying to make men's underwear sexier, making it more pouchy, trying to make your packet stick out more. Or that whole Calvin Klein look thing. Gay guys saw that and said, "This is great, I don't have to wear these Y-fronts any more. I don't have to just go to that one gay shop that has the funny little pouch things. There's a whole new load of stuff to wear." As a result, when straight guys get those things, they then feel gay - they think this is what gay guys wear.

It's not really a shame - I mean good luck to gay guys, they said, "We're going to wear it and here comes my cash." But, meanwhile, the straight guys were, "Ooh, I'm not sure; I think I'll hold on to me boxer shorts a bit" - and they missed the boat. Now that whole thing with *men's* underwear has become sectioned off as being "a gay thing". I don't know what will happen in the future, but it's sort of stumped me, really. Besides, I really like to see women dressed up - much more than men. When it comes to their bodies and what you can do with it.

What helped you out the most, other than your background?

When we started doing the things that we sell, looking for our product, we sort of went back to the '50s. Not because we're retro maniacs, but because that was the last time when craftsmen and designers really looked at creating garments in mainstream lingerie. I'm not talking about rubberwear and that. But it was the last era when people really looked at doing garments that had an effect in changing the shape or form of a woman's body. You know, waist cinches that nipped you in, things that curved you up. The Wonderbra really comes from that period, and they're still sort of living off of it.

Because after that time, towards the '60s and during the '70s, women were much more interested in being perceived as equal to men. They didn't want to look like Marilyn Monroe, they felt that having that sort of form or look or silhouette or even bothering to dress up for men in that way, somehow kept them in this lower bracket. Where they weren't taken seriously, they were just dressed up and put on a plate. Then there was the thing of women burning their bras and all that, which in reality wasn't widespread. But it made an impact in people's minds, people started to think about it a little bit more. In reality, it became less about being equal, and more about being better than a man. You know, "I can beat you at your own game; I can wear this suit with the big shoulder pads and I can be the head of a corporation". They started to lose sight about what real power and delight there is in the feminine form. I think we're now trying to rediscover that; our customers are saying, "We don't have to be like men - we've got our own thing which is much more interesting."

Certainly, you've made the shop both famous and successful.

Well, lingerie has become very fashionable. Though I don't like to ring my own bell too much, I think that we had an effect in creating this. From the amount of press and publicity that we've had - and what we've pushed, presenting it quite fashionably. Now, suddenly, it's OK for the woman that reads *Marie Claire* to go out and buy crotchless knickers - because they're actually in *Marie Claire.* When, before, they were in *Ritual* or *Skin Two* or some funny, topshelf porn mag, it wasn't the done thing, but now it's totally cool. In fact, if you don't do it, you're a little bit off track, you're not quite where it's at. I think that's fantastic. Because I think dressing up really does have a major role to play in sexuality, and in people's fantasies. So I think it's totally great that it's happening.

House of Harlot:

on fashionable fetishwear

Robin:

House of Harlot started as a concept before it was called that. I was making dresses for Michelle and other people started saying, "Oh, that's a nice dress, can I have one?" Eventually, we decided we'd better sort them out. Michelle came up with the name early in 1992. We worked out a graphic for the label, got labels printed and started making stuff.

Michelle:

I just quite liked the sound of the name - and it is couture clothing. It's very much a house style, a definite look. So we wanted something to reflect that. We've both worked in mainstream retail and high street fashion. So, although it was just a hobby, we had the knowledge to make it work.

Robin:

We had the know-how to make it cost-effective, make it financially feasible without becoming a nightmare. When we first started we worked in anything, almost any kind of material. It was like, "Ooh let's try this, let's try that". Michelle works in leather in her day job. So we always had access to non-rubber fetish fabrics - like leather, PVC and patent leather.

But rubberwear is nice to specialise in. We're not the only people specialising in glued rubber, but it gives us pattern-cutting potential stitched materials don't have. The construction technique means that you can have bizarrely shaped things, cut edges with contrast colours, which you could never put together in a stitched garment. It allows other types of specialist construction, too, which is what interested me about it. Inflation, for instance, lets you de-form the shape in a unique way. You get a very smooth surface - completely unfeasible in any other fabric.

People come to us because what they actually want cannot be found elsewhere. We offer diversity; the fetish market is oriented towards people with particular fantasies. We do work for film, videos, stuff like that which isn't fetish, but still in the fetish style. Advertising companies approach us because they want something which is fantastic, but in a fetishistic way. The music industry is especially hip to fetish style. So are a lot of advertising ideas people.

Michelle:

Robin's very good at making things happen. Someone can have an impossible drawing and no one else is going to make it up. But Robin will actually draw something and that will be an outfit.

Robin:

Harlot is also for research and development. I use it as a way of constantly honing my pattern skills, shaping my tailoring skills by trying things out. Some of them eventually end up - in a simplified version - in the *Skin Two* line I do, which is useful for *Skin Two* and, at the same time, helps maintain my interest in the whole phenomenon.

Michelle:

It's not surprising that fashion has turned to fetish wear. There's a PC backlash, it's a question of women wanting to be women. In a way, however, it's actually still power-dressing - but not being afraid to show off your bust. In itself, that is power-dressing.

Robin:

We may be entering a time when women can actually be feminine and goddess-like. In a way which is not ashamed of the female physique, the female form. In the '80s, power-dressing was like men with tits in business suits. Now, the fetish fashion industry, such as it is, has got a leading-edge aspect to it; it enables women to be entirely feminine and powerful in a way that's powerful over men, because it is sexually expressive as opposed to repressive. Myself and Harlot and all the other design I'm involved with is largely staying within the fetish industry.

Michelle:

We're not actually out there trying to convert anyone, however. We're not pushing for a concession in Top Shop. At the moment, we're not even aiming for an off-the-peg range.

Robin:

One thing that does attract me about the fetish industry is that there are certain stable parameters within it. There are certain requirements - unwritten, unspoken ground rules, especially as we now work exclusively in rubber. I mean, rubber is a fetish fabric. It's not mainstream. It means design has a foundation and stipulations. What interests me about fetishism is its requirements - and the fact it has a sexual content, one which is still involved with social and moral perspectives.

When we came into the scene, it was very po-faced and serious. And the lion's share of the market is still suburban swingers. The fashion element can also be extremely serious - and the sexual, domination-and-submission side can be dull. They are desperate to be taken seriously; they want to be recognised, but also left alone. We came to it very much to add an extra element, which is an element of humour and of colour.

Michelle:

It's an extension of our personalities; it's the way we are, the way we wanted to look. It's basically dressing up. It's a totally gorgeous thing, but not too serious. We don't spend our weekends in rubber, we're not really fetishists in the truest sense of the word.

Robin:

Fetish, for me, is making something extraordinary and glamorous, rather than just being for the sake of being in rubber. There are plenty of people for whom rubber is enough. It doesn't matter whether it's good, or very bad; well made or badly made. But those things are important to me: styling, colour, cleverness - they're all important.

Michelle:

Personality is important, too: the people that wear it. There's a lot of input from our buyers. Someone will come here and say, "I want to wear this, I want to look like this, this is my idea". It's just a matter of realising their fantasy - then they *can* look like that. So it's not just down to us. Harlot is a collective of interesting people, interesting ideas made to happen.

CHAPTER 6

CHAPTER SIX

1

The baby Bransons:

British music's mini-moguls

Corporate fashion - from style magazines to actual makers - around the world are quick to co-opt British style. But can corporate ears from abroad detect the best in our brands of music? In the case of massive export campaigns like Oasis or Blur, it's simply a question of marketing, touring and media flackery. But what of the UK's true indie scenes, everything from junglist to "trip-hop" or bhangra? Whose ears can hear the hits from Stevenage or Bury St Edmunds?

Since the advent of land-based pirate radio and rave culture, the answer to that question has encased a fascinating development. A new kind of entrepreneur has evolved - the twentysomething mini-mogul who shapes a personal label. Scornful of working slowly up through the corporate ranks, these fans find and market what they want to hear. In doing so, they have plugged a gap in the music business. But, in the '90s, their sort of hobbyist labels made a huge transition. Suddenly, they have became desirable, viable companies, capable of cutting meaningful deals with major labels.

Those behind this *coup* began as pushy, cheeky and irreverent, the children of rare groove hustling and pirate knowledge. But there are sure reasons for their sense of self. Each began with a roster of artists - or friends - a clear sense of purpose, and ambitions. Though some of their labels handle records by non-Britons, all pride themselves on showcasing a British identity. Like their inventive predecessor Richard Branson, such rogue moguls keep an eye on their global clout. This time, it is digital and image-based. But, in many ways, they are the country's new Bransons.

When he began at the age of 19, James Lavelle was one of the youngest. Known on the British dance-floor circuit as "The Holygoof", Lavelle had already been part of the business for seven years. Before making his début as label-owner of Mo' Wax, he had worked as a shop assistant, journalist and a tireless DJ. Until his own business was quite successful, he still managed to hold all four jobs at once.

Holygoof now has a posh office in west London; one he purchased from his own manager, then a neighbour of rock video company Oil Factory. Lavelle has a staff in London and one in New York; he has a smart home and a new family; he now dines on Thai food instead of Burger Kings. Although known for keeping close friendships few and private, he remains out and about and he still DJs.

James Lavelle also buys art and stages exhibitions. (His deal with A&M Records hinged on a rider which specified the purchase of a Basquiat painting. He has also helped revive appreciation of graffiti's Futura 2000.) But Holygoof still displays small regard for a life outside "beats". Music is what he walks, talks, eats, shops and - when he *does* sleep - sleeps. It's a single-minded passion which produces big business.

By the spring of 1994, Lavelle's record label Mo' Wax was two years old, and was launching its eighteenth release. It had just recently moved into West End offices. Its records were being sold in America, Europe and Japan. Asian marketing was helped by a partnership deal with Major Force, a Japanese label Lavelle had long admired. He was embarking on more and bigger negotiations - with Virgin and the entertainment conglomerate Polygram. At the time, each hoped to back his first big-league label. But, before the meetings even came about, he had a sexy name for the venture. James hoped to call it SFT, for "Smoke-Filled Thoughts".

Putting image first is characteristic of '90s moguls. Their labels favour catchy names, striking slogans, memorably quirky graphics - or the opposite: total mystery. Some have debuted under the guise of imports; others have been "compilations" down to a single maker. Behind every artifact, however, are hard workers - not trend-hoppers or fashion victims. Lavelle's original flat showcased the toll of their lifestyles: overflowing ashtrays, unsteady stacks of vinyl, stacks of magazines left to moulder in corners.

3

4

5

1. Video grabs
Honest Jon's, '98
2. RPM
2000
Mo' Wax '94, MW 018
3. Repercussions
Promise
Mo' Wax '92, MW 001
4. Major Force - Love T.K.O.
Tongue In Your Ear / Season Of The Witch
Mo' Wax, MW MF001
5. Major Force - from box set
The Original Art Form
Mo' Wax '97, MW 082 CD
6. Mo' Wax HQ
James Lavelle's office, '98

IT'S LIKE - YOU EARN FIFTY QUID WHEN YOU DJ, THEN YOU SPEND ALL THE DAMN MONEY ON NEW RECORDS. (→PAGE 131)

ALL I'D WANTED TO DO WAS WORK FOR A RECORD COMPANY. BUT THERE WAS NO SPACE TO DO THAT, I HAD TO CREATE IT. TO CREATE A PRODUCT SOMEONE WOULD WANT. (→PAGE 147)

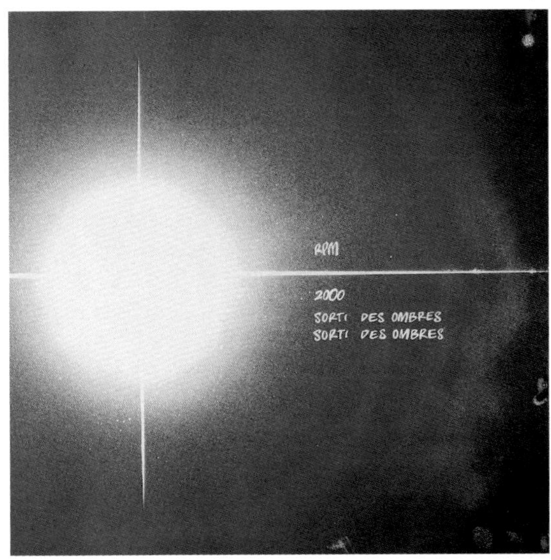

2

6

BLONDIE
PRESENT
HAMMERSMITH ODEON
LAUGHING CLOWNS
BLACK FLAG
SYMPOSIUM
MASSIVE ATTACK
EPIC SOUNDTRACKS
BUTTHOLE SURFERS
WARNING
ASIAN BEATS
ELECTRO
LONDON ACID TECHNO

1

Everywhere one could see the souvenirs of airlines: British Airways socks, Air India eyemasks, little red zipper-bags stamped with the logo "Virgin".

But, then, James Lavelle was always a man in motion. "I started at 13", he says, "in a rural sound system. Actually, I wasn't even aiming to DJ. I wanted some real job in the music industry." Throughout his school days, Lavelle worked in record shops and, most nights, he DJ'd in some club.

The hours he put in on many different dancefloors are entirely typical of young label proprietors. There, whether nodding to beats or raving with jungle, they learn what compatriots want to hear, what trends are being born, and how to sell. They also forge many international connections. But, says Lavelle, "It can really be quite manic. Probably my toughest experience was going to LA for three days, getting to London at 10 am, flying to Germany at noon, then driving to Lyons. There, I DJd for 10 hours straight, then drove back and flew right home to London."

"Still," he shrugs, "I've done a lot of that. Because, to get things out, you put things in. I've spent money to become what I have. It's like - you earn fifty quid when you DJ, then you spend all the damn money on new records. Early on, people said, 'You get to go to America'. Well, the first time I went, I certainly *paid* to go. If you want to crack New York - no one's gonna bring you there. No one'll help you do it. You just get yourself there, meet people, do some gigs."

1. Video grabs
Top 4 rows:
Rough Trade Record Shop
Notting Hill, London, '98
Bottom 3 rows:
Mo' Wax HQ, '98
2. James Lavelle's column in
Straight No Chaser magazine
Issue 17, summer '92

1. "HAVE A GOOD IDEA, IT HELPS!"
2. "THE SHIT'S GOT TO BE ORIGINAL, SOMETHING THAT PEOPLE WANT BUT HAVEN'T GOT."
3. "YOU'VE GOT TO DELIVER A PACKAGE, NOT JUST MUSIC BUT A WHOLE LIFESTYLE."
4. "BE TOTALLY OPEN MINDED. LOOK AROUND AND USE WHAT YOU NEED."

(→PAGE 132)

James 'HolyGoof' Lavelle can be found spinin' a bag of goodies at Talkin Summer, The Fridge and trading in wax at Honest Jons, Portobello Rd, W10

JAMES 'THE HOLYGOOF' LAVELLE - THE KING OF THE ECLECTRO ONES 'N' TWOS GOES IN SEARCH OF THE GROOVES OF TOMORROW

REPERCUSSIONS PROMISE / FIELD TRIPPIN' *(MO'WAX RECORDS)*
D-Day! The launch of Mo'wax Records, coming atcha with NYC's ,the Repercussions massive. Straight outta Brooklyn 'n' lettin' off the vocal 70's funk influenced 'Promise' and 'Field Trippin' - a the native tongues new wave hip hop summer groove. Massive music droppin' live 'n' sample free.

it definitely adds the flavour. The BNH massive kick to the rhymes of the most respected rhymeologists - Blacksheep, Puba, Mainsource, Masta-Ace etc). Dig tha phunky pheel thang.

GROOVE GARDEN YOU'RE NOT COMING HOME *(TOMMY BOY RECORDS)*
N.Y.C. Japanese new wave hip hop vibes. Tommy Boy brings it forth. Female rap, meets from hip hop to the ultimate in fusion beats. What an ode to the creator. R.I. PEACE

JAMIROQUA WHEN YOU GONNA LEARN *(ACID JAZZ)*
The sound of young Ealing. Massive and classic music slightly on the Gil Scott Heron tip. Positive lyrics, and what a backing track, reminding you of real music. Damn it, sends a tingle down my spine.

2

Early on, Lavelle also garnered a column in *Straight No Chaser*, a music mag for jazz, "world beats", and hip-hop. He called the column "Mo' Wax", after his club in Oxford. The Holygoof's work schedule expanded exponentially: in addition to London clubs and self-financed trips, he was invited to DJ in California and Tokyo. "Delicious Vinyl in LA brought me out, and I played some clubs. There were major scary gang types there, but I didn't know enough to even see that. How should I know? Eighteen hours later, I'm back behind an English shop counter."

But Lavelle did know he was engaged in serious business; he was "creating a vibe" around the words Mo' Wax. At one point, Island Records asked him to start a label. Holygoof knew what he wanted, and when negotiations failed, he refused to give up. He borrowed £1,000, pressed up a track, and launched Mo' Wax as his very own label.

Over the next 18 months, it issued 16 records. Lavelle publicised them via *Straight No Chaser*, spun them at his gigs and sold them via his job in Honest Jon's Record Shop. It was the perfect system: a grass-roots monopoly. Through it he ascended, too, as a personality. In *Phat* #3, he appeared as the subject of their "Career Guide for Losers".

It cited the first Mo' Wax forays into lifestyle - merchandising T-shirts and record bags. "Not content with this," read the article, "he also wants to produce totally collectible items such as plastic candy novelties like bubble bleepers and Star Trek tribbles." Mocking his then residence, a west London council flat, *Phat* zeroed in on Lavelle's recipe for success: 1. "Have a good idea, it helps!" 2. "The shit's got to be original, something that people want but haven't got." 3. "You've got to deliver a package, not just music but a whole lifestyle." 4. "Be totally open minded. Look around and use what you need."

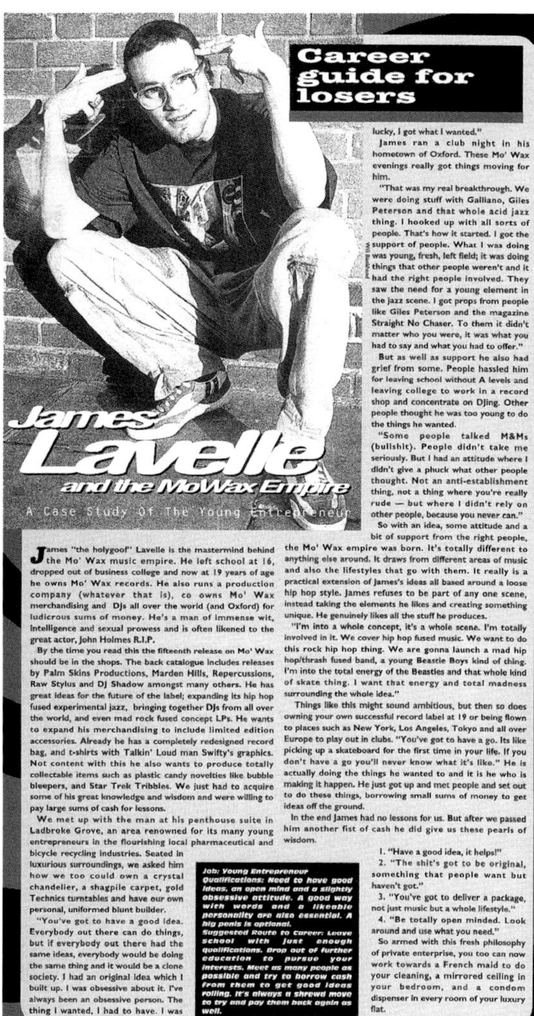

Career guide for losers

James Lavelle and the MoWax Empire

A Case Study Of The Young Entrepreneur

James "the holygoof" Lavelle is the mastermind behind the Mo' Wax music empire. He left school at 16, dropped out of business college and now at 19 years of age he owns Mo' Wax records. He also runs a production company (whatever that is), co owns Mo' Wax merchandising and DJs all over the world (and Oxford) for ludicrous sums of money. He's a man of immense wit, intelligence and sexual prowess and is often likened to the great actor, John Holmes R.I.P.

By the time you read this the fifteenth release on Mo' Wax should be in the shops. The back catalogue includes releases by Palm Skins Productions, Marden Hills, Repercussions, Raw Stylus and DJ Shadow amongst many others. He has great ideas for the future of the label; expanding its hip hop fused experimental jazz, bringing together DJs from all over the world, and even mad rock fused concept LPs. He wants to expand his merchandising to include limited edition accessories. Already he has a completely redesigned record bag, and t-shirts with Talkin' Loud man Swifty's graphics. Not content with this he also wants to produce totally collectable items such as plastic candy novelties like bubble bleepers, and Star Trek Tribbles. We just had to acquire some of his great knowledge and wisdom and were willing to pay large sums of cash for lessons.

We met up with the man at his penthouse suite in Ladbroke Grove, an area renowned for its many young entrepreneurs in the flourishing local pharmaceutical and bicycle recycling industries. Seated in luxurious surroundings, we asked him how we too could own a crystal chandelier, a shagpile carpet, gold Technics turntables and have our own personal, uniformed blunt builder.

"You've got to have a good idea. Everybody out there can do things, but if everybody out there had the same ideas, everybody would be doing the same thing and it would be a clone society. I had an original idea which I built up. I was obsessive about it. I've always been an obsessive person. The thing I wanted, I had to have. I was lucky, I got what I wanted."

James ran a club night in his hometown of Oxford. These Mo' Wax evenings really got things moving for him.

"That was my real breakthrough. We were doing stuff with Galliano, Giles Peterson and that whole acid jazz thing. I hooked up with all sorts of people. That's how it started. I got the support of people. What I was doing was young, fresh, left field; it was doing things that other people weren't and it had the right people involved. They saw the need for a young element in the jazz scene. I got props from people like Giles Peterson and the magazine Straight No Chaser. To them it didn't matter who you were, it was what you had to say and what you had to offer."

But as well as support he also had grief from some. People hassled him for leaving school without A levels and leaving college to work in a record shop and concentrate on DJing. Other people thought he was too young to do the things he wanted.

"Some people talked M&Ms (bullshit). People didn't take me seriously. But I had an attitude where I didn't give a phuck what other people thought. Not an anti-establishment thing, not a thing where you're really rude — but where I didn't rely on other people, because you never can."

So with an idea, some attitude and a bit of support from the right people, the Mo' Wax empire was born. It's totally different to anything else around. It draws from different areas of music and also the lifestyles that go with them. It really is a practical extension of James's ideas all based around a loose hip hop style. James refuses to be part of any one scene, instead taking the elements he likes and creating something unique. He genuinely likes all the stuff he produces.

"I'm into a whole concept, it's a whole scene. I'm totally involved in it. We cover hip hop fused music. We want to do this rock hip hop thing. We are gonna launch a mad hip hop/thrash fused band, a young Beastie Boys kind of thing. I'm into the total energy of the Beasties and that whole kind of skate thing. I want that energy and total madness surrounding the whole idea."

Things like this might sound ambitious, but then so does owning your own successful record label at 19 or being flown to places such as New York, Los Angeles, Tokyo and all over Europe to play out in clubs. "You've got to have a go. Its like picking up a skateboard for the first time in your life. If you don't have a go you'll never know what it's like." He is actually doing the things he wanted to and it is he who is making it happen. He just got up and met people and set out to do these things, borrowing small sums of money to get ideas off the ground.

In the end James had no lessons for us. But after we passed him another fist of cash he did give us these pearls of wisdom.

1. "Have a good idea, it helps!"
2. "The shit's got to be original, something that people want but haven't got."
3. "You've got to deliver a package, not just music but a whole lifestyle."
4. "Be totally open minded. Look around and use what you need."

So armed with this fresh philosophy of private enterprise, you too can now work towards a French maid to do your cleaning, a mirrored ceiling in your bedroom, and a condom dispenser in every room of your luxury flat.

Job: Young Entrepreneur
Qualifications: Need to have good ideas, an open mind and a slightly obsessive attitude. A good way with words and a likeable personality are also essential. A big penis is optional.
Suggested Route to Career: Leave school with just enough qualifications. Drop out of further education to pursue your interests. Meet as many people as possible and try to borrow cash from them to get good ideas rolling. It's always a shrewd move to try and pay them back again as well.

2

By 1996, these words from Lavelle were enshrined on the World Wide Web. And, thanks to his US deal, he was also popping up on "enhanced CDs" - like Om Records' "Mushroom Jazz" or Planet E's "Header". Here, when slipped into a fast computer, James would surface in a video clip, once more detailing his label's aims - through Quiktime soundbites.

Mo' Wax even made it into *Rolling Stone*, that most corporate of music magazines. The occasion was the ascendancy of "trip-hop", publicised in the mid-'90s by artists such as Tricky and Portishead. Trip-hop was descended from a whole line of Bristol artists: Massive Attack, the Wild Bunch, Smith & Mighty. Although Lavelle was a big fan of Massive Attack and had once attempted to sign Portishead, he had few other connections with it. Nevertheless *Rolling Stone* decreed his label trip-hop's founder.

1

Rolling Stone critic Peter Margasak called Mo' Wax: "the label which gave birth to the hip-hop hybrid that has been dubbed trip-hop. Produced outside the usual American urban centers [*sic*], trip-hop replaces rapping with a head-tripping spaciness, creating a sound in which hip-hop, experimental rock, jazz, ambient and techno vibrantly co-exist." From the magazine's July, '96 perspective, the "Mo' Wax sound" had not been fully established until '93 - with the release of "In/Flux"

3

4

1. Mo' Wax sleeves Design: Swifty
2. James Lavelle 'Career Guide for Losers' Feature in Phat magazine Issue 3, Oct '93
3. DJ Shadow and The Groove Robbers - In / Flux picture disc - Mo' Wax MW 014
4. Major Force - Love T.K.O. Tongue In Your Ear / Season Of The Witch - Mo' Wax MWMF 001
5. Mo' Wax clothing Label from T-Shirt Design: Swifty Typographics

IF YOU WANT TO FORM AN 'INDEPENDENT RECORD COMPANY', FORM IT TO MAKE MONEY, THEN THERE'S NO POINT DOING IT. BUT IF YOU WANT TO DO IT 'CAUSE YOU'VE GOT A PASSION FOR THE MUSIC, THEN GO AHEAD AND JUST DO IT. AND GOOD LUCK. (→PAGE 141)

by DJ Shadow. This was in fact the label's 14th release. It came well after Repercussions had departed for Warner Music; after the huge success of record #2 (Raw Stylus' "Many Ways") and the UK-wide "buzz" of Palmskin Productions (whose first EP was already deleted by '96).

Mo' Wax tunes - which are often fusions of jazz and hip-hop - come from America, Europe, England and Japan. But they are united by a strong label identity. In the beginning, this was the (unpaid) work of Ian Swift, also *Straight No Chaser*'s graphic mainstay. Says Lavelle, "Mo' Wax was mixing up a lot of things, at a crucial time. From the time when I was 13 to 19, British music split in a big, big way... When I started DJing, we played house, hip-hop, jazz, soul, funk, reggae, we had a graffiti artist, it was all one thing. I didn't hear Soul II Soul at the Africa Centre, I never got to go. But I know they had visuals and I know guys who would go and play a load of house and a load of dub, and everybody would dance; then you'd have someone else play a load of hip-hop, then a load of funk, then spin some rare grooves. Now, for people who care, it's very hard to do that."

5

1 
U.N.K.L.E.
LIMITED EDITION

 2
Mo Wax
Lost and Found (S.F.L.)
Kemuri

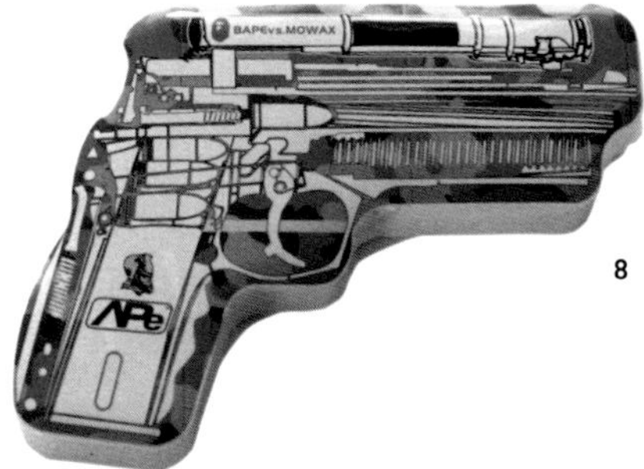 8
BAPE vs. MOWAX

3 

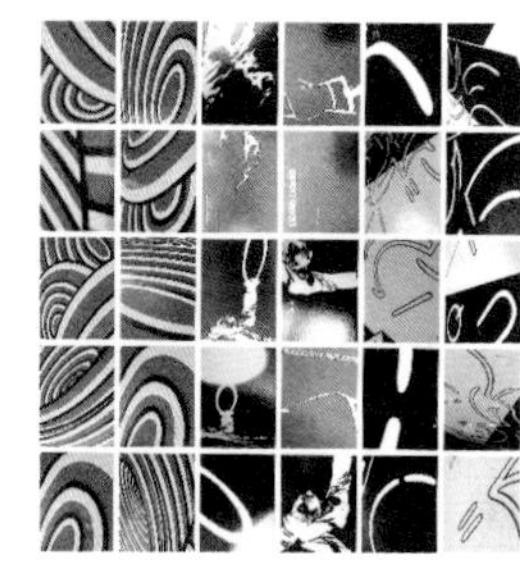 4

5 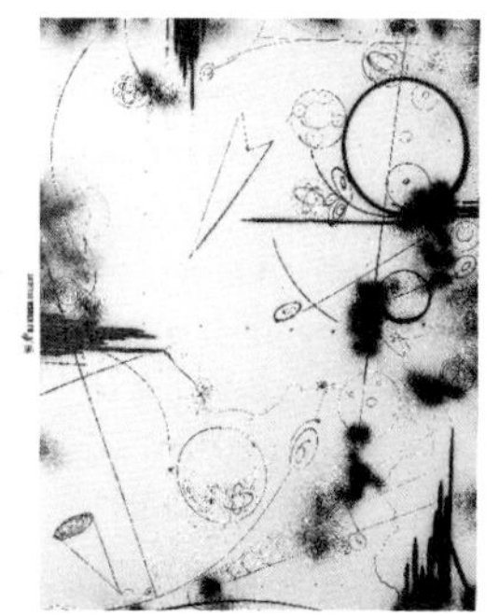

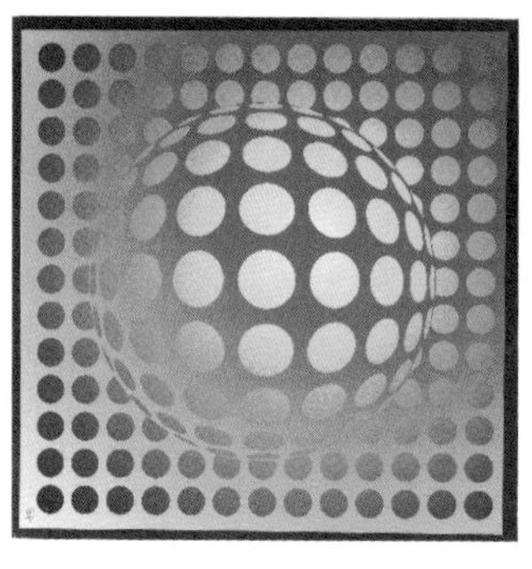 6

DUSTED
SAT 13TH JAN

DUSTED
SAT 16TH DEC
PURE
ALL BEEF
WORLD FAMOUS
SAT 13TH APR

DUSTED
SATURDAY 23RD SEPTEMBER

DUSTED
SATURDAY 26th AUGUST

DUSTED
SAT 11TH MAY

9

7 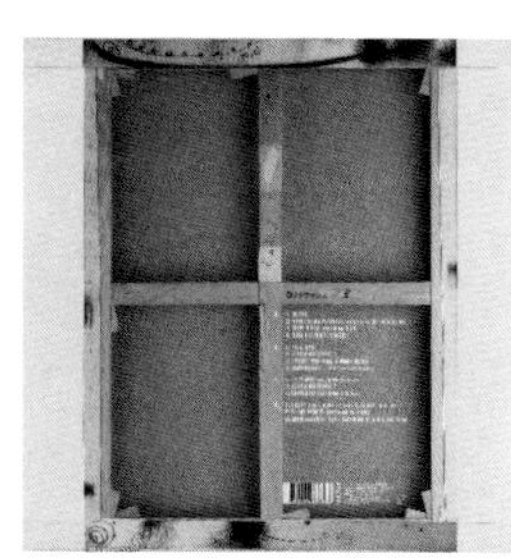

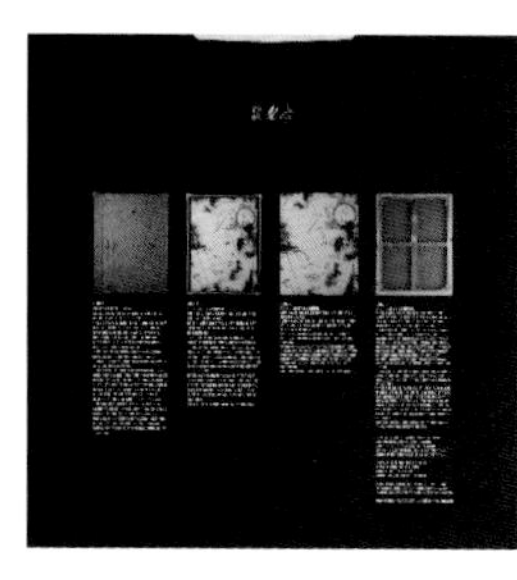

10

14

11

12

13

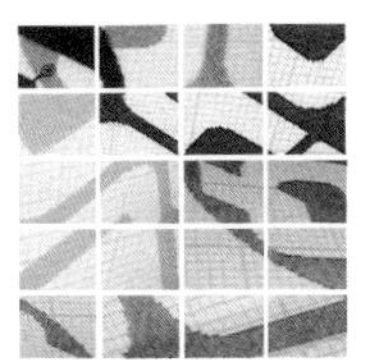
15

1. Major Force - U.N.K.L.E. The Time Has Come E.P Picture disc - Mo' Wax MW028
2. DJ Shadow / DJ Krush Lost and Found (S.F.1) "Kemuri" - Mo' Wax MW024
3. Liquid Liquid (back cover) - Mo' Wax, '97 MW 078LP
4. Liquid Liquid (front cover) - Mo' Wax, '97 MW 078LP
5. DJ Krush - MiLight Mo' Wax, '97 MW 078LP
6. As One - Planetary Folklore Mo' Wax, '97 MW083
7. DJ Krush - MiLight (inner sleeves) - Mo' Wax, '97 MW077LP
8. Bape vs Mo' Wax T-Shirt packaged in the shape of a gun
9. Mo' Wax - Dusted flyers
10. DJ Krush - Holonic The Self Megamix - Mo' Wax MW088LP
11. Promotional Mo' Wax vinyl stickers - MWA002P
12. Dusted 2 flyer The Bounty Hunter Sessions
13. Cavern - Lets Hear It For The B-boy Remix Mo' Wax '97 MW078LP
14. Attica Blues Mo' Wax MW080LP
15. Cavern - The Cut Chemist Rocks a Rave in a Missile Silo Remix - Mo' Wax MW091

IT ALL COMES DOWN TO ONE THING: MY AGE IS THE AGE OF MIXING. I MIX FASHION AND DIFFERENT SOUNDS AND LIVES - AND I'M MIXING CONTINENTS AS WELL AS BEATS. SEPARATE MODES OF EXPRESSION, THAT'S WHAT MO' WAX IS ABOUT. IT'S NOT JUST MUSIC, (→PAGE 147)

1

"That's why, for me, the jazz scene has been so cool. Because, at this time, it's quite eclectic. It's a scene where, if you like a house record you go and play it. If you like jungle beats, airport records - play 'em. Play Boogie Down Productions, play a soul classic, then play Masters at Work. You can't do that at many other gigs."

If Mo' Wax represents the young Briton as globalist, Bite It! is a label for streetwise UK homeboys. It is the brainchild of graphic designer Trevor Jackson, from north London. Jackson, who was 26 when he started it, named the label after his one-man art studio. But it provides an outlet for his love of hardcore hip-hop beats, tough design and rough edges. Bite It!'s first release was an EP by The Brotherhood, a set of Jewish rappers Jackson had discovered near home.

Bite It! also emphasises British style as international - its logo crosses the Suzuki rhino with a bull terrier. Selling UK rap, however, means fighting US dominance. "Hip-hop has remained very American", says Jackson. "We're always in that shadow unless we manage a breakthrough. Which means more than just putting out good music. It means selling British looks and British attitude."

In the progress of Bite It! (the words are hip-hop slang for "steal it", in reference to others' work), "attitude" became perhaps the key ingredient. In the end, it led Jackson to establish a second label. He calls it Output and has framed it as his rap label's opposite. "I want Output to be eclectic, but not thought of as 'eclectic'", he says firmly. "I want it to sell attitude." His first Output issues bear this out: they range from instrumentals he himself composed to a singer-songwriter of Chinese heritage.

His initial label's packaging has an aggressive character. Each record's cover is composed of a full-bleed photograph: black and white, stark and grainy. All type and credits are relegated to the back side. This was a reaction, says Jackson, to his career in commercial graphics. "That whole industry formula is so tired: image here, type on top. That's the size of it."

Both Bite It! and Output mirror Jackson's character, that of a single-minded entrepreneur. But the labels depend on a network of friends. The photographs on the hip-hop covers, for instance, were taken by Jackson's mate Donald Christie. Demo-tapes that lead to releases come from a range of clubbing pals. Music production, however, he does himself. For Jackson has a second role, as "The Underdog".

"Underdog", for some time also known as "Pete Bull", is Jackson's *nom du studio* for remixes. As these gained him fame in hip-hop circles, he strove to keep a trio of careers separate: he was, at once, a graphic designer, a label head and a studio spin doctor.

At times, his determination could be comic. Jackson set up his graphic business in Clerkenwell premises. But, quite soon, clients rarely found him there; frequently, they faced only his apologetic colleagues. If they do discover Jackson, he is behind his Apple Mac, a portable phone beside it, the computer covered in Post-Its. These notes detail exactly the progression of each remix, each design and personal project. Almost all in-the-flesh conversations are severed by phone calls, and a visitor will hear tirades like the following:

"Hey! Yeah. Look, this Gang Starr tape, it's great, really great. Yeah, yeah, yeah - but - why - what I don't understand is this...why have they made that one track the single? Yeah, yeah. 'Cause, look, they say 'mother-fucker' twice and also 'shit'. I know they're listening to the music, yeah, yeah. And the music's great. But why choose a track where they're fuckin' cursing? Man?! On the other side, yeah? The second track? It's a better single, way better. Uh...yeah, maybe, yeah. But if I remix it, if I come to do it? I'm gonna INHERIT THE PROBLEM! Words, man, *words*...words are half the story."

Jackson's savvy made him a second reputation; his remixes have genuine industry clout. But he is not one to follow industry dictates. "My label", he said in *The Face* about Bite It!, "is a reaction against Talkin' Loud and its sound - the smooth production thing. We're looking for a dirtier, funky sound that doesn't smell of record label money."

And, although he stays friends with early clubbing mates (such as Lavelle, whose label debuted after Bite It!), Jackson has no problem speaking his mind about their products. "James is a friend of mine, but he's hi-jacked hip-hop language. I'd say it to his face. He's just young and what he does is very trendy. But Bite It! and Output aren't trendy labels. I don't want that; I'd like to believe they're for people who think a little."

2

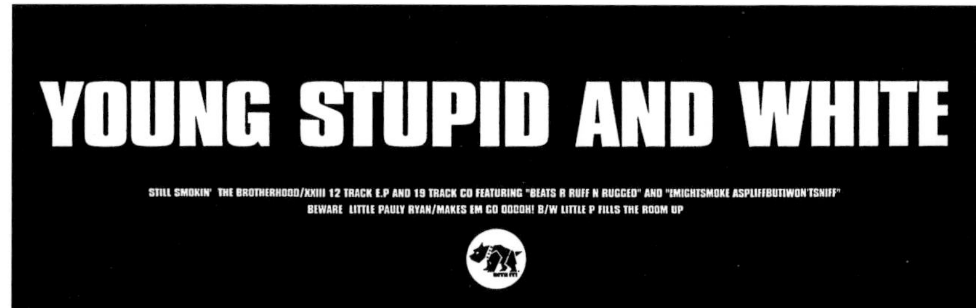

3

4

5

1. Money Mark limited edition action figure Mo' Wax Toy Division
2. Bite It logo Design: Trevor Jackson
3. to 6. Bite It labels Design: Trevor Jackson

THE DEATH OF MINDLESS HOUSE MUSIC IS APPROACHING VERY RAPIDLY, AS FAR AS I'M CONCERNED... AND I WANT TO BE THERE TO CHOP ITS HEAD OFF. I WANT TO SHOVEL THE LAST BIT OF DIRT ON ITS GRAVE. THERE'S A NEW WAVE COMING THROUGH AND IT'S GOING TO BE POWERFUL.
(→PAGE 140)

THE MOST INTERESTING ARTISTIC WORK COMES OUT OF LIMITATIONS. IT ALWAYS HAS.
(→PAGE 150)

He has always sought his own, special audience. "Bite It! was aimed at your street rap fans. The majority of rap fans are narrow-minded - mainly because I don't think they're offered much alternative. Nothing which is true and which is real. Most of the alternatives they're offered are both marketed and

6

BITE 8

1

2

3

4

5

1. Little Pauly Ryan
   Make Em Go Ooooh!
   Bite It
   Bite - 8
2. Scientists of Sound E.P.
   Bite It
   Bite - 5
3. Scientists of Sound
   Bad Boy Swing
   Aybee's Remix
   Step On Stage
   Bite It
   Bite - 9
4. The Brotherhood / XX111
   Bite It
   Bite - 7
5. 100% Proof
   Different Neighbourhood
   Bite It
   Bite - 4
6. The Brotherhood
   Wayz of The Wize
   Bite It
   Bite - 6
7. The Brotherhood
   Alphabetical Response
   BHOODD2

6

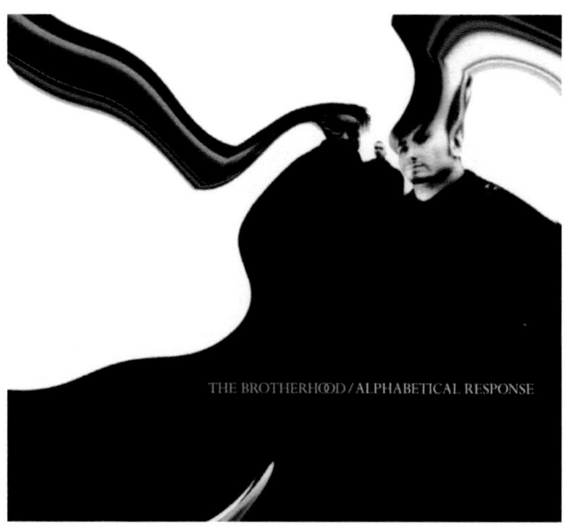

7

manufactured. Someone will create a hybrid of rap and just use it to sell records, right? Lots of trip-hop - I mean the knockoff stuff, not the Trickys or the Portisheads. That's just rap for people who hate hip-hop."

Equally, he has little time for the posse of labels whose début eras paralleled his: from ambient's Soma, Limbo, Cowboy and Good Boy to the techno variants audible on Cake and Sugar Sweet, or the would-be funk of Party Rockin', Somethin' Else and Soul Jazz. Jackson's views on house and jungle are frankly judgmental; he can like a "real artist", but he tends to despise a "movement". In 1993, in *DJ* magazine, Jackson even predicted - with some relish - the end of house music:

"The death of mindless house music is approaching very rapidly, as far as I'm concerned... And I want to be there to chop its head off. I want to shovel the last bit of dirt on its grave. There's a new wave coming through and it's going to be powerful."

Around the same time, in another magazine, he wrote an editorial which aired his views on hip-hop's down side. It pre-dated by three years conservatives Bill Bennett and C. Delores Tucker in their censorship attack on American rap. But Jackson emphasised hip-hop's potential for good, even as he noted the problems with its influence:

"Celluloid has never been as influential as rap. Guns are now becoming a fashion accessory on rap album covers, which can only reinforce the idea to kids that it is cool to carry one. My main dilemma is that as much as I can criticise the current state of rap, I find it very hard not to enjoy 'Deep Cover', '6 Million Ways to Die', 'Pass the Gat' or 'Now I'm Gonna Wet'cha'. Does rap have to concentrate on this kind of subject matter to be powerful? Can anger not be interpreted in another way? If not I feel rap can only deteriorate into a form of entertainment more interested in using shock tactics to make bucks than excelling as an art form able to make serious social changes."

"...I'm fed up trying to justify to intelligent people why I love my music so much, when it's currently so open to criticism for its lyrical content. Because rap's biggest-selling artists are its NWAs, its Dr Drés, and its Geto Boys, rap is still going to be considered by most as an immature, pornographic and violent fad, instead of the most creative, innovative and prolific music of our era."

"Most people will never get to read the praises of Diamond D or a Tribe Called Quest because the media will be trying too hard to criticise Ice Cube.

1

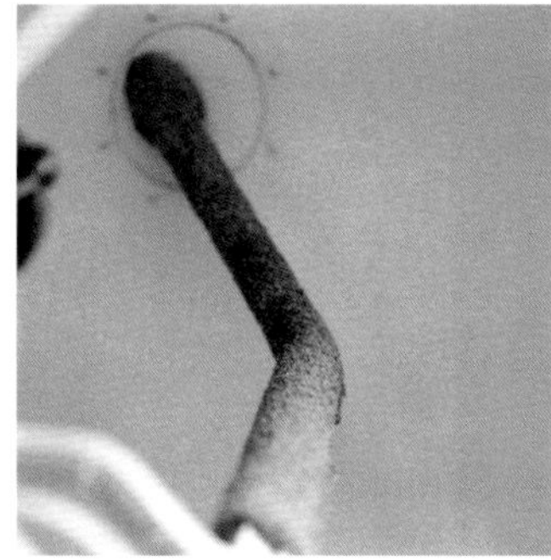

2

People will not know about Paris or Pete Rock, because the press will be too busy counting the number of 'fucks' on a 2 Live Crew record or the number of deaths on a Geto Boys LP...and I'm fucking sick to death of people trying to support these current trends in rap, claiming them to be reflections of society. As long as there are rap records using sensationalist sex, drugs and violence lyrics, rap and its true message will be ignored or dismissed."

"...Rap creates and reinforces attitudes, most of which we could do without. Rap does focus on the gaping faults in today's society and yes, the faults existed long before rap existed but things are getting worse. Rap's intentions at showing reality may be honourable but there are too many out there willing to turn their problems into controversial products and marketing campaigns at the expense of the very society that hip-hop should be helping."

Although he is "stubborn and opinionated", Jackson always repays the loyalty of his friends. When, early on, he clinched a major-label deal for The Brotherhood, he threw a private warehouse party for 800 people. It set him back a cool £1,200. But he shrugs at the suggestion that it was anything special - or much different to the parties he used to throw in his old, shared graphics studio. "The party was a celebration. It did cost a fortune, but I didn't do it for money. I did it for my friends to enjoy themselves, and for them to hear the music."

"I'm stupid in a way, because if I worked things better, I *could* make a lot of money out of it. But, for me, that's just not what it's about. I'd rather do what I love and make a little money than do something I don't enjoy for a lot. Maybe when I was younger I saw it otherwise. Now, I really just don't see the point. Because it just doesn't give you any satisfaction."

Initially, Jackson funded Bite It! from his own design work. Then, he shifted more and more towards remixing. But, by taking things slowly, he learnt how to break even. Now, he can spend and recoup £2,000 a record. "What it really costs", he says, "is *time*. You can do it, you can do it easy. What you spend is time, time and lots of running around, that's it. The actual money side is you don't need that much cash. It depends a lot more on just what you're into."

He leans forward, over his note-papered Macintosh. "If you want to form an 'independent record company', form it to make money, then there's no point doing it. But if you want to do it 'cause you've got a passion for the music, then go ahead and just do it. And good luck."

3

4

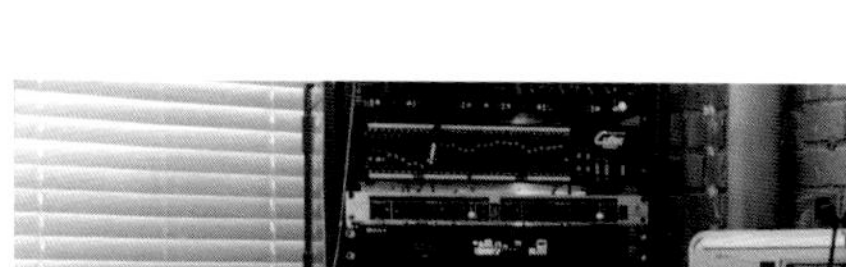

5

1. Fridge - Lign
Output
2. Fridge - Lign 0.18
Output
3. The Brotherhood
Elementalz
CD BHOOD1
Design: Dave Mckean
4. Fridge / Semaphore
OPRCD12
5. Trevor Jackson's studio, '98

OTHER PEOPLE MAKE GOOD MUSIC, BUT NOBODY ELSE CAN GET THE WHOLE PACKAGE RIGHT. TO ME, THE WHOLE THING IS REALLY, REALLY IMPORTANT. (→PAGE 151)

WALT DISNEY DIDN'T MAKE SNOW WHITE TO SELL FUCKING DUVET COVERS! HE MADE IT FROM HIS HEART, AND THE HEARTS OF HIS ARTISTS. (→PAGE 152)

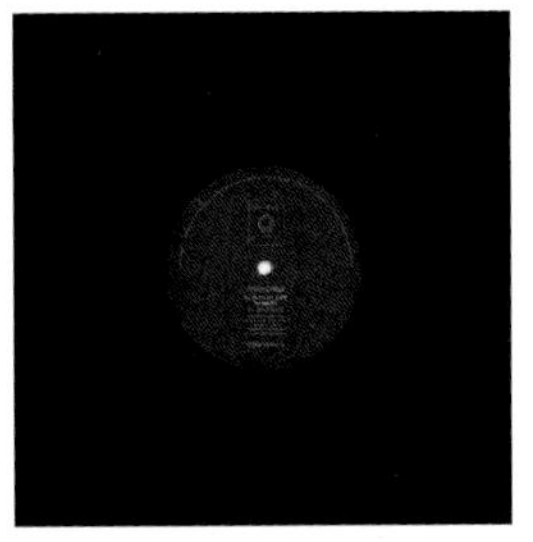
1

2

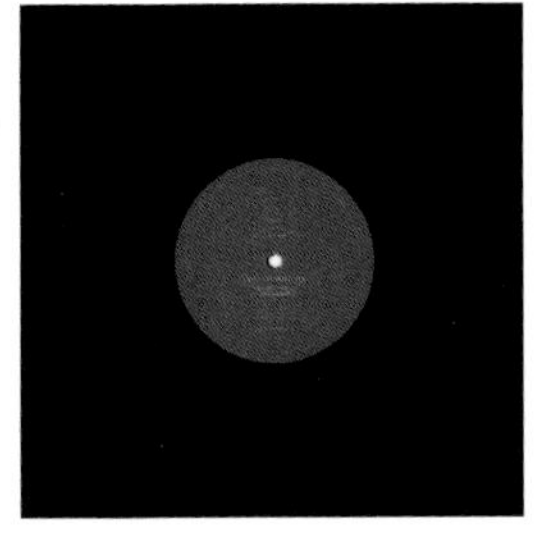
3

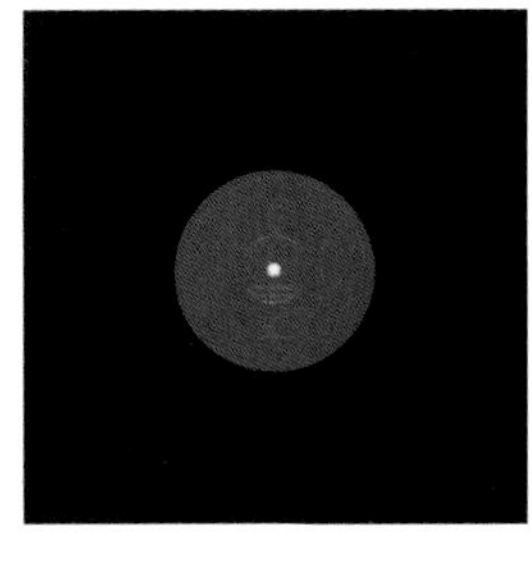
4

Wiiija Records' Gary Walker agrees. But Walker sells a very different product: UK indie pop. This home-grown genre revolves around perennial themes: teen lust, teen angst and teen rebellion. Self-started indie labels have been popular here since the days of punk, but Wiiija's roster reveals a changing Britain. Currently, it releases the likes of Cornershop (initially hyped as the "Asian Sex Pistols"), chart-toppers Bis (a three-piece from Glasgow), Jacob's Mouse from Bury St Edmunds, Oxford's Comet Gain, Skinned Teen (three "punk-rapping" schoolgirls from south London) and UK popsters Velocette - plus one-offs such as 12" techno platters from the Essex-based Mucho Macho (offshoots of a club called Monk On Fire and its subsidiary label, Monk on Vinyl).

Walker has a history of felicitous partnerships with American indies: Olympia's Kill Rock Stars, North Carolina's Merge, Chicago's Touch and Go, Thurston Moore's Ecstatic Peace and the Beastie Boys' influential Grand Royal. Many of his artists have been cult bands, from the (now defunct) "feminist insurrectionists" Huggy Bear to Seattle's Action Suits (a band which includes Peter Bagge, creator of the comic HATE).

London's Rough Trade Shop started Wiiija Records in 1988, from tapes various wanna-bes brought into their shop. Its first artists were Thule, Terminal Cheesecake and Bastard Kestrel, and the name Wiiija came from Rough Trade's postal code (W11 1JA). However, it was Walker, then their mail-order clerk, who really took the label on and made it happen. He began with two auspicious signings, both of whom he lost to major labels. One was Silverfish, who went on to Creation; the other was Therapy?, who went to A&M Records.

After losing his first signings to bigger labels ("people who could afford ads and sent journalists out with the bands"), Walker lowered his sights financially. His next signings, Huggy Bear and

5

6

Cornershop, gave the little label a new jump-start. Each, under Walker's tireless management, generated press, played gigs and garnered sales. Soon, Rough Trade had Walker managing A&R, as well as masterminding a broader Wiiija strategy. He worked hard to shape and project an identity, and to assemble a solid business team.

By 1994, Team Wiiija had exploded: it had five members plus the Rough Trade accountant. Such tight organisation, the work of much networking, left Gary Walker free to liaise with bands. It's a task that still keeps him running: from Belfast to Birmingham; from Austin, Texas, to Tokyo.

Walker also set up Wiiija as a publishing company. Because of this, income which would otherwise go to a publisher now comes to him. "That helps to maximise earnings", he notes. "But money really starts coming in through licensing deals. If you've recouped on a record, you go for new advances from outside labels. Anything you can bring in there is pure profit." Walker began sharing profits 50-50 with his bands, even though different groups had different costs and rates of sale.

He has always used his pivotal ties in America but, early on, decided not to focus on sales there. "The States", he said in 1994, "is still just too much of a lottery for us. There's just no guarantee about what will succeed there. Instead of gambling our time and money on that, I work at getting my bands into lots of territories."

In May 1995, Cornershop signed a US deal with David Byrne's label Luaka Bop. The Talking Head's independent project is handled by Warners which, says Walker, has helped everyone. "Luaka Bop is basically a small New York office, with a slender staff. But Warners handles all the distribution. They're set up for the States so, really, it's brought us the best of both worlds. It's the same as Grand Royal - they are handled by Capitol."

Wiiija's first headquarters was a spartan affair: two tables in the basement of Rough Trade's shop, two staffers, two phones, a fax and some crowded shelves. By 1995, Walker had his own home office. It housed posters from around the world, his American collection of Pete Bagge comics, and a constant stream of telephone calls, FedEx packets and faxes. At the heart of all the action was selling records, something Walker is eager to demystify: "It's not some mystical thing. Anyone can learn it. At the very bottom level, any indie band can produce a 7" single. And if they're any good, it will sell 1,000 copies. Just that one thing can establish a fan base."

"Seven-inch records cost 30p per unit. A proper sleeve adds maybe 10p or 15p. So it's really cheap. Sell them to the shops for £1.25 each. Then, if you made the music cheaply, you at least break even." Walker knows what he's talking about. Wiiija stars Cornershop, who have topped the indie charts, made their début on 7" vinyl.

Walker feels Wiiija has a "user-friendly" image, and he has always striven to keep it that way. He will often go on tour with bands, just to check out action in the provinces. In the early '90s, with fellow indies Clawfist and Too Pure, he united to create a newsletter they called *Plug*. (The labels also held regular meetings with their mutual distributor.)

Walker credits part of "the Wiiija vibe" to the company logo. This was created by his friend Ged Wells, the skateboarding retailer. Wells saw Wiiija as a metal screw sprouting petals, a "marriage of soft and hard" that Walker knew was perfect. "Because all our bands had separate agendas: they were Asian; feminist; hardcore; European. We needed one symbol that could pull them all together."

Walker has never been afraid of new ideas. He was quick to use e-mail, build international bridges, launch a World Wide Web page - even start a second label. Entitled Whole Car Records, this was for "less experienced" bands: groups like Fabric, Chicken Bone Choked, Des Man Deablo.

If these names sound colourful, Walker's personality matches them. When it comes to plugging,

7

8

1. **Brainchild**
   Output, '96
   OPR - 1
2. **Open Music**
   Output, '96
   OPR - 3
3. **No Exit**
   Kingsize Just a Moment
   Output
   OPR - 4
4. **Open Music**
   What If? Realtime
   Output, '96
   OPR - 3
5. **4T Recordings**
   Double Density
   Output
   OPR - 7
6. **Gramme - Mine**
   Output
   OPR - 10
7. **Gary Walker**
8. **Plug 3 - Posterzine**

YOU THINK, "I'M NOT DOING THIS BECAUSE I WANT TO DO A BUSINESS PLAN AND RUN A BUSINESS. I'M DOING IT BECAUSE I LOVE WORKING WITH BANDS, AND PUTTING OUT RECORDS AND SPREADING THE WORD." BUT TO BE A SUCCESSFUL INDIE, YOU NEED BUSINESS SENSE. (→PAGE 156)

1

2

3

4

5

6

7

8

9

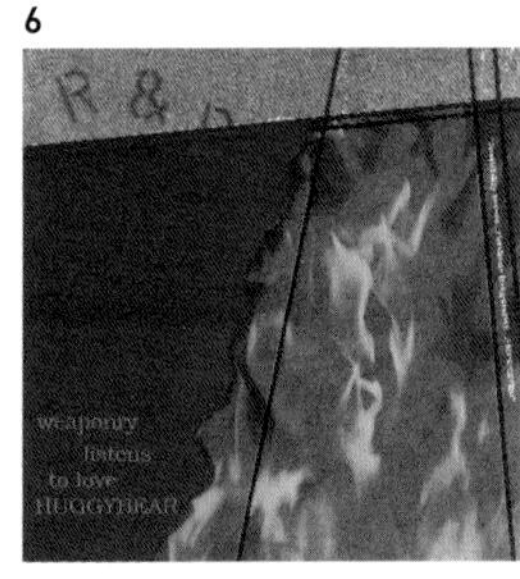

10

ligging, cosseting and championing, he is a match for any honcho from the industry. He is even a popular speaker at music-biz conferences. At an early '90s Umbrella seminar, a gathering of indies and distributors, Walker gave the key-note speech - although he had never joined the organisation. His words noted a sea-change in musical tastes, and anticipated the second half of the '90s:

"I'm an outsider to the dance scene or scenes, but it appears to me that you have [in those] a great way of getting the kids to hear new records within their own social environments, that labels like myself can only dream about."

"Despite the whole grunge fashion explosion, dance has more mainstream cultural significance. With the association of drugs, illegal parties and raves, dance culture now has the 'stigma' of danger and rebellion which guitar-based music no longer has. In an age when it's so easy to blame computer games for the decline of our music, we should be looking at that kind of inspiration. Because we have only ourselves to blame if our music is culturally insignificant, unattractive and uninventive."

Walker informed the professionals about his strategies: the joint fanzine (to produce "interaction"); the regular talks between Wiiija, Clawfist and Too

Pure; the joint meetings with Revolver/APT. All, he noted, aimed at "raising label awareness". This desire distinguishes all the baby moguls.

Like Mo' Wax and Bite It!, Wiiija's success and strong image made it highly desirable to major companies. Walker, like Jackson and Lavelle, had plenty of offers. But, by then, he was cautious. In late '94, he was debating "three good offers" - but he still remained unconvinced. "I'm just not sure it's the right thing for us. East West, for instance, came to me and said, 'Would you like to do a licensing deal, an international thing, and feed into the Atlantic group of records?' And I was like, 'Yeah, that's a pretty good set-up'."

He grimaces. "Then they said, 'We actually want to be involved with you in the UK, too.' So, it was suddenly like, 'Uh-uh, hands off there.' At our *third* meeting they moved the goalpost again. And said, 'Look Gary, we don't actually like your bands. But we like you, so come and work for us'."

In summer '95, Walker found the perfect match: he got a funding deal with Britain's Beggars Banquet. Beggars is owned by Martin Mills, who bought the majority share in Wiiija. Gary Walker is now the other owner - as well as the legal head of the label. When the deal went through, he gave up Whole Car Records. "I had to make decisions about my workload. So, of course, I wanted to concentrate on Wiiija." In February 1996, he astounded the industry by signing Bis - a band who were being courted by every major.

If it came as a surprise to the business world, it did not to many British musicians. The new labels have what many look for: clear identities, "good ears" and flexible strategies - not to mention very good connections. Those talents that won the mini-moguls clout are the qualities often absent from mainstream management. Ask James Lavelle why and he becomes heated: "If you started a record label the way you're really supposed to, take it from me - you'd never manage to do it. I know that is why Mo' Wax has worked. 'Cause I went in *not* working the way you're meant to. And I know I pissed off quite a few people."

"You just have to jump in and take the consequences. You'll have some headaches later. But that's cool, you know? Because then your empire is spreading and building."

11

1. Bis
Wiiija
WIJ69X
2. Cornershop
Wiiija
WIJ29V
3. Blood Sausage
Wiiija
WIJ20V
4. Velocette
Wiiija
WIJ68
5. Comet Gain
Wiiija
WIJ46V
6. Guv'ner
Wiiija
WIJ39CD
7. Terry Edwards
And The Scapegoats
Wiiija
WIJ51
8. Recline
Laidback 01
9. Jacobs Mouse
Wryly Smilers
JCOB 001V
10. Huggybear - Weaponry
Listens to Love
Wiiija
WIJ037
11. Wiiija logo
Design: Ged Wells
12. Wiiija direct order
comic strip

12

James Lavelle served a musical apprenticeship behind shop counters and club turntables. When he founded the label Mo' Wax, he married dancefloor sounds to street marketing savvy. The result? By the time he was 23, his label was wildly successful, thanks to a major-label deal with A&M Records. He talks about what helped him learn and why it works.

How did this really start for you?

I went to Paul Bradshaw at *Straight No Chaser* magazine, and had an interview about doing a column. We did the column and it's become a culty thing. I was 17 when I started - and they needed somebody young. They really needed a column about new music. Plus, it had to be written for no payment. Of course...I can't write to save my life.

But you had experience with music?

Yeah, and I'd met everybody before: all the DJs and the writers, because I'd worked at Bluebird Records in West London. I started there at 14, on a work experience program. I'd served names like Norman Jay, Gilles Peterson, Jeremy Healey - and some posses like the Stussy skateboard boys. I started DJing, though, in my home town of Oxford, at the age of 13, with a local sound system. We were called Underground Movement and there were half a dozen of us.

Bluebird was the dance thing; rare groove was happening. I was at school and working there on Saturdays. Then that finished and I went to this sixth-form business college, the Oxford College of Further Education, to do business studies. I really loathed it but my attitude was, "You've gotta do something". It was either stick at business studies and go to university - or get a job that had to do with music. By then, I was working three days a week, commuting from Oxford to London. I worked for Jon Clare at Honest Jon's in Portobello.

So I decided I'd beg Jon to let me work full-time. Because his shop was about more than the music. It meant being mixed up with amazing people, which to me, at 16, was a real experience. We had gay people, anarchists, reggae experts, Canadians, jazz buffs, plus this totally mad boss - Jon. He was studying to be a psychiatrist.

James Lavelle:

from clerk to CEO

I remember the first day I went in there, I was asked something like "Have you ever fancied your father?" Well: get through that, you can get through anything! Plus, the whole work atmosphere is amazing. You get hardcore raggas and these Ladbroke Grove kids. And your worst kind of pretentious trust-fund types. But you can build up a real street following. It was just the best experience for learning. It was totally unique, this amalgamation. One of the hardest things I ever did was leave; I had worked in record stores five straight years.

The opportunity you found at Honest Jon's was special?

Yeah. The first year was spent kind of doing my thing, building up the stock, selling soul and hip-hop and acid jazz. The second year was building my DJing. Then the third year was getting Mo' Wax started. Honest Jon's is how I started to get known, I was building up my reputation. Of course, also I filled up a hole; they had no hip-hop, no music like that. I built on that, then I did the label. I was just lucky I was accepted there. A lot of kids would have known about hip-hop. But they didn't have the attitude those guys were looking for. You had to be, like, exceptionally open-minded. Plus, they really put you through the hoops. But we got on. And there's no place in London like it. I could not have asked for anything more.

What did you bring to them?

Well, my lucky thing is I've always been on a street tip, able to mix all these different scenes together. I think it's the thing which everyone lacks; people who are part of one thing don't want to look anywhere else. I like to keep in the middle of things, try and get to know as many people on as many different sides as possible. I know the old school and I know the 19-year-olds. But I'm also down with Slam City Skates. Or the clothing guys at Fuct and Xtra Large and Pervert. Streetwear, skatewear, I've been into that.

Mo' Wax does reflect the clothing thing, though I've kept away from focusing on style as much as Talkin' Loud and Acid Jazz. I didn't want that whole "Cinzano Bianco" flavour, I wanted something just a little more rough. The Acid Jazz label borders on an indie thing. Talkin' Loud borders on sophisticated London jazz - but with an angle; kind of elitist. Mo' Wax, it's younger, a bit more out of order. Like we did this Japanese ad with a picture of David (Kung Fu) Carradine. And the slogan read, "Kicks more funk than a Shaolin monk". "Kicks more flavours than a pair of old-school Rod Lavers." That sort of thing, it's a different generation. I mean, I grew up with *Star Wars*.

There's another thing which was good for me: I'm not from London. I don't have those London strings attached, I always DJ'd a lot out of town. That's what my real thing was, working out of town and in Europe. Even when I did my US deal, I was still not a London jock, not really part of that scene. A lot of those people, you know, went to school together. In the late '80s, the deep club scene was very exclusive. Then, with raves and that, it became more open.

Let's hear how you actually got the label started.

Well, me and all the guys at Honest Jon's, we were acquainted with the Groove Keller in New York. They had this band called Repercussions. At the time, I was talking to Island Records about a job. I was really hoping to work at their offshoot, Antilles - and start a label. And sign Repercussions. But - so typical! - it never happened. One of the guys in the band said, "Look, just give us a grand; you can put it out anyway."

So I thought, "OK, fine, I'll start the label myself." I went off to the New Music Seminar in New York, and I hooked up with Repercussions. Mark Ainley - who was then one of Honest Jon's managers - he lent me the £1,000 I needed. I did the track, I sold a couple of thousand. And there was my label on the way. Originally, Mo' Wax was a club, I used to do it with Tim Goldsworthy. Then it turned into my *Straight No Chaser* column. Then I couldn't think of another name for a label! But "Mo' Wax" works well; it's short and quirky and *there*.

All I'd wanted to do was work for a record company. But there was no space to do that, I had to create it. To create a product someone would want. All along, people constantly tell me, "Christ, you're so lucky!" Well, it's not about luck. It's about finding something people want which they haven't got. That is how you make successful products, whether they are washing-up liquid or records. I mean, I was doing it for the love of it. Only slowly did it turn into a career, a life. It was started out as a laugh.

But you had a vision behind the label?

Oh yeah. As much as I love jazz, I've always been into hip-hop. I came from hip-hop, that's my biggest influence. Then came Soul II Soul, who merged hip-hop with soul music and created a special, British thing. Smith & Mighty, Massive Attack, Wild Bunch, Soul II Soul: they're my *ultimates.* A British sound with an American element: phat beats, but with vocals on the top. When I started out, that was very important. Then the acid jazz thing came along, which was merging old records with new ones. That was a British thing as well, because it could be instrumental. It didn't need rap.

Really, it all comes down to one thing: my age is the age of mixing. I mix fashion and different sounds and lives - and I'm mixing continents as well as beats. Separate modes of expression, that's what Mo' Wax is about. It's not just music, but everything around music. That's why it's done all right. It's got a whole identity, it's got a vibe. My whole thing as a DJ, as a person, within the music, was to be more transatlantic than other people.

What about your deal with A&M Records?

I came to a point where Mo' Wax couldn't really go on the way it was. It had to go to the next level or stay the same. You want to move forward and I desperately wanted to move forward. Be able to sign different people and get bigger production. And be able to do what I want to. Plus, I was never interested in the business side and I wanted that taken care of. I didn't want to have to think about it.

When you're a small label, you constantly get things taken away from you. Or you're creative and you build something, then you lose it. The major label's view of the independent has always been that you're a good way to build bands up so they can poach 'em. Sign them for bigger money because the major acts as a bank and they've got the resources.

Is that why you did the A&M deal, to get resources?

Originally, I was going to do a label with London Records - just as a sub-label. I was gonna call it "Smoke-Filled Thoughts", run it, get paid for it. Then I met Steve Finan. He began managing me on an artist level. But not on a business level, I was always afraid of that, because you always want to be in control of your own destiny. But, I got a bit scared with the London thing. So I showed him the deal - and he just laughed. He said, "You know, this is ridiculous. If you split the label up and do different labels, you're not really benefiting Mo' Wax as a label. You're detracting from what it is. If you have Smoke-Filled Thoughts *and* your own label, it detracts the emphasis from what you spent three years building." Then he said, "Just let me introduce you to three people."

You took him up on it?

Yeah. He introduced me to three people he felt were really exciting people in the industry, who would want to work with me. One ran Deconstruction Records; one was chief head of A&R for Virgin, who signed Massive Attack and Neneh Cherry. One was the Managing Director of A&M Records and was on the Board of Directors of Polygram. I met all these labels and I really liked Virgin, actually, because of their history in music, and because of Massive Attack. All of them made me offers and I thought about each of them. But I was all ready to do a deal with Virgin. Then Steve told he was going to A&M, and it freaked me out, because I realised - it wasn't really about any of these three labels. It was actually about my and Steve's relationship. That was the most important thing. So, I changed my mind and went to A&M.

A business relationship kept you away from Virgin?

Yeah. It was all to do with Steve, completely to do with him. And if I hadn't gone with him, Mo' Wax would be fucked. I knew that within four months; you know, I spoke to him twenty times a day. Also, Virgin's idea of Mo' Wax was really about a logo within Virgin. Whereas, with A&M, it's about building a company. Essentially, we are a joint venture with A&M. We are not a subsidiary, but a joint venture. Mo' Wax is a proper record company: one day, we could be viewed in the same way that A&M is within Polygram.

But it has less cachet than Virgin.

With A&M, they've got eight domestic acts over here; Virgin have got a hundred and fifty. So it's pretty small, really. They're very boring in a sense, which is another thing. Virgin's all about trend and fashion - and that's cool. But, ultimately, you've got to build that within your own company.

Mo' Wax, it's got that to a certain extent, so we might be better off with a company that's going to spend more time building us as a company, rather than building you as a fashion item. Especially where we've already attained some of that, and we can continue to do so on our own. From a record company, here's what I need: support, faith, money, and distribution. But we also don't even go through A&M. We're independently distributed. We have our own rules and regulations, so we're unique there. We can basically do whatever we want.

Is there some special pressure you think young Britons feel?

In a way. Here, we always think America's a better place to be successful because "Over there, that's what it's all about". That's sort of the American culture: money and power. As a basic thing, it's like the more successful you are, the more you're accepted. Whereas here, the more successful you are, the more people dislike you. The harder it is to convince them you did the right thing. A bigger consideration is that there are lots of successful people in both the British and American music industries. Very clever people. So if you don't rise to certain standards, you're never gonna compete. Because they are creating the stakes, and you can only change that by attaining their level.

There are lots of people out there who constantly repeat, "I do this for the music", and blah blah blah. Well, I do it for the music, too. But at the end of the day, I want to be here for twenty or thirty years. This is my career. I don't want to be selling two thousand records when I could sell half a million, because people want to hear the music. What is music about anyway? It's about getting what you do out to people.

There are people out there that have worked to make it harder than I have and *haven't* been paid. But it's all about the way things are presented. And the thing with Mo' Wax was: I never marketed myself to make money. I marketed myself to give back a bit more to people, to those people who were buying the record. I made more expensive covers. I did different formats, different-coloured vinyls. Things people just got into. So they felt you weren't trying to rip them off, but that you were trying to give them a little bit more. In a certain way, that is why we're successful.

Because it wasn't just about the music?

Yeah. It was also about the people behind the records, what they would think and what they might want. Basically, I just put everything about my childhood into a little box and gave it to people. It said "I like *Star Wars*, I like graffiti, I like pop-orientated records. But I like it when it's a little bit different. Like this."

It's all about marketing, whether you like it or not. A group like the Beastie Boys, they wear the clothes, they break different styles, they add a bit more to the records. They give a bit more away, they look good - and they still come out and do a great show. Life's fickle like that. What girlfriend does everybody want? If you're a guy, is it the brains or is it the body? Eight men out of ten say it's going to be the body, it's the look, because you're geared towards that. A guy's not going to walk into a club and say, "I'm going to go out with the girl that I get on with the best." The first thing a guy's doing when he walks in a club is looking which is the dopest girl - that he's attracted to.

It's the same way with records. People look at the artist they're most attracted to, or the labels that they think give the best overall value. At first, they're not going to care so much about little things because it's an overall package. It's like the guy in the club: "All right. I might not be able to talk philosophy with her. But I'll go out, that's what my life's about." It's like why are people into Björk - and not some other girl that writes great songs? Why are people into the Beastie Boys, not Lords of Brooklyn? Or why aren't they into House of Pain? Why are people so into Massive Attack - and not another band with hip-hop beats on an indie label? Because they're what people want to be a part of.

Doesn't that become a little elitist?

Yeah and, sadly, you piss off lots of people. But, as with anything, either you are going to be there or somebody else is. You just be as constructive and nice about it as possible. I had a hard time, because a lot of people think "he's this" and "he's that" - or "he doesn't deserve this". But, if I wasn't here, somebody else would be.

And I am here. It is me. So I have to do it, and I try to do it in the best way possible. I'm not a Don King; I'm not trying to take away people's creativity for my personal benefit. But I am the person that's had to sit here for nine hours a day, talking to twenty people, trying to get them to do one thing.

I'll probably make more money than my artists will. But not because I'm trying to rip my artists off. It's because I've got twenty artists to make money out of. They've only got one label. That's not me being evil! I've got to sacrifice things that a lot of people wouldn't know what it's like to sacrifice. So, I just do my thing, and try and be the best person I can be.

Has your age made things harder?

Let's say when you're my age, you know there's a lot to learn. A lot about growing up. People that are around me who are older are never going to accept me as they would someone their age. I just get an instant look-down. It's as if a twelve-year-old came up to me. I'm not going to accept him in the same way that another twelve-year-old accepts him. If I'm dealing with a 30-year-old, on some level, they're gonna talk down to me. That's human nature; it's the way things are. I just have to deal with it. But, in a certain way, maybe it makes me stronger. In what's coming out now, lots of much younger kids have positions of power. So they're going through stuff which others didn't go through. Because those people, they were 25 or 26 when they got that power. I think there's a great difference between being 18 and being 24.

What advice would you give to that generation?

I just think living day to day is an experience. My biggest thing is I don't think going to university or college is always beneficial. Within both media and entertainment, lots of people who are successful on the business level are just people who slog at it for years. Everybody thinks success is given to you on a silver platter. But it just isn't. I started my work from a thousand pounds I borrowed, and support from my mum - who had no money. Then I worked in a record shop for £130 a week. Now, I have my own record label. I'm very, very lucky but, by the end of the day, I know I fuckin' well worked for it, too. It's a more American view, but it's spreading. You just get up and do things. You don't just fuck off and hope you'll be rewarded. Here in the UK, we've got an elite. If you're not aristocratic, you're never going to be a part of that. Because you can't be.

What can help young Britons most?

It's just down to the way people grow up. Here, you're led to believe that you can't *be* as successful as everyone else; that reaching such a pedestal is impossible. In America, everybody knows that they can do it, because they show that everybody can. Here, nobody's shown they can do anything. I remember when I left Oxford; everybody said, "Man, you're mad. You're not gonna to make it. Why even bother?" That's the English attitude: "Don't bother because you ain't going to make it". But, to me, it's more like, "You haven't even tried. Why don't you try?"

I'm not a happy person all the time, because you're always struggling to be something else, to try and attain a thing which is never quite there. I'm totally guilty of that. Before I had any ounce of success or money, I just enjoyed things. When everybody's attaining, there's a constant pull. You're constantly trying to be the person people pay attention to. The other hardest thing in this business is change, learning to deal with change. One reason people don't like successful people is because those people have to remove themselves so much. My whole thing has always been built on friendships. But there comes a point when shit changes. If you get too close to people and things change, it can be horrible. It's happened a lot to me, people that I know just changing. But it's change, that's life, so what do you do? You owe everybody, all the time, all your life. You're always gonna owe somebody. You just get on with it.

By 1988, Trevor Jackson had established a one-man graphic design studio. He called the firm Bite It!, a phrase from hip-hop slang. Jackson loved hip-hop and as his design and record production work flourished, he decided to found a label. Also called Bite It!, it is dedicated to British hip-hop. Six years later, he started Output - a second record label for a different selection of musics.

How did Bite It! start?

Well, I was playing around with music at home anyway. And a friend of mine came to see me with tapes and stuff, one of which was a rap tape by The Brotherhood. I thought it was really good, so I wanted to put it out. The record which resulted, "Descendants of the Holocaust", went really well.

How did you pay for the mechanicals that were involved?

Well, because I'm a designer, I have another living. I've always designed for the music industry so I've always had an interest in music. I was just using money from the company - also called Bite It! - to put our records out. The main idea of the record arm has never been to make money. It was just to put good music out and clear my costs. I don't want to *lose* anything by doing it. But if I can be involved in putting out good music, that's cool.

When I started, there was hardly any decent British rap. So I thought it was about time someone came through and put some out. At that time, I couldn't really afford to put covers on the sleeves. So I designed this logo, this doggie Bite It! logo. After that, I started taking it more seriously. Realising, OK, it is a hobby, *but*... And by the fourth release - the Scientists of Sound - I thought I'd better start doing this properly. Because I had achieved a standard where I thought the music and the concepts were solid, but they weren't being packaged well enough. So, I got Donald Christie, who's a friend of mine, to start taking photographs for me. I'd worked on loads of graphic stuff with him, things for the Jungle Brothers and stuff for Gee Street Records.

Trevor Jackson:

on personal labels and packaging

We decided I would use the label to showcase Donald's work, but also I wouldn't put any type on the sleeves. I thought, "Fuck it, I'll just put it on the back - people won't even know what the record is!" A rack full of records, where all you see is photos on the front, I thought people might find that exciting. It's a strong image. We did the Scientists of Sound like that, and it was fine, it did OK. It sold pretty well, and got lots of support on the radio from Westwood and from Max and Dave and Richie Rich.

I can't afford to, and I don't want to, put out too many records a year. There are too many rap records that are put out. It floods the market and most of it's shit. Also, most British rap bands don't have an identity. The labels putting out rap in this country when I started? I felt most of 'em didn't have any identity; most of their music was really rubbish. It didn't do British rap as a whole any justice. When I tried to sell records to America, they'd already heard all these crap British rap records. And they thought, "We don't wanna touch it". So, I wanna put out good-quality records. I thought, "I can wait a whole year and put out two records. The year after, three. After that, maybe ten." Because I want to pay more attention to what I do.

Name some of your earliest artists.

The Brotherhood; Scientists of Sound; 100% Proof; Little Paulie Ryan. Originally, I was keeping exactly the same design format on the back for each one. Then, I decided I wanted to start changing it - and I started doing picture backs as well. But we still kept everything black and white. It's what's relevant to hip-hop but, also, I couldn't afford to do a full-colour sleeve. I still think it's got impact, and strength and power. The most interesting artistic work comes out of limitations. It always has. Black and white to me is somehow quite political. And it's strengthened my label's identity. At the time, I wasn't doing all that much design work. Record-sleeve design work had gotten frustrating. I'd taken what I was doing - that whole logo/illustration/computer graphic thing - about as far as I could imagine taking it. It's gone up it's own ass, all that kind of work. But, by stripping the graphics away from the sleeve, and just having the strength of photography, I still managed to get something I like.

I was always absolutely influenced by the music. That always kept me away from the photograph with just a bit of type on it. Also, I'd much rather be designing sleeves for myself than for someone else. I can't really relate to a lot of the music going on now - so I don't really feel I have a place designing sleeves in the music industry. Unless it's just the odd project which comes up, that I really like working on. I used to design loads of sleeves for dodgy house records, but I just couldn't do that anymore. I'm in this position where it doesn't interest me. And there's no point if I can't get really excited. Obviously, the music I'm involved in, and the kind of music I remix excite me.

You've been critical of other British indies.

Other people make good music, but nobody else can get the whole package right. To me, the whole thing is really, really important. With Bite It!, I want to have a British Def Jam or a Tommy Boy. Not, of course, in size. But symbolic of the essence of what made *me* start collecting hip-hop records. I want a good roster and a good-looking logo. I'd like people to see the Bite It! logo and know it means a quality release. I might not have more than twenty records a year - I just want them all to be exciting.

Also, it's a word-of-mouth thing. I don't spend a fortune advertising. And hip-hop today is a multi-million pound industry. But I've slowly gotten interest. I spent five years doing it before I felt it was working properly. The Brotherhood signed to Virgin in 1994, Bite It! through Virgin. Actually that's a production deal; they signed The Brotherhood through me. So I can produce and do all the graphics, and so on. It means a bit more money for videos, fly-posters, all that sort of thing. Basically, for me it's just a passion.

You don't seem to see any downside, though.

The only thing that's a pity is I've really fulfilled that stereotype of the Jewish rap company businessman. Like, Tommy Boy was run by a Jew and Rick Rubin ran Def Jam. You may laugh, but think about it! All the rap labels, in the beginning, they were run by Jews! I mean, to me, I receive a lot of - not intimidation; that's not the word, but there is a lot of resentment from people. The amount of rumours that go round that I'm some fucking little Jewish rich kid who's running this label from his Dad's money is incredible. And the point is I've done this label off my own back. I ain't got no one helping; no one funded me! But: I'm fulfilling that role. It's just a pity there isn't a black-owned, black-run rap label in this country. That would be a bit of a balance.

With Bite It!, the aim of the label was to make British rap that people could be proud of. Because I'm not the only person who slags off British rap. But, things are never stable. In 1994, I heard more good British rap than I'd heard in my life. Hopefully, my label gives some others a kick up the ass. Because it isn't just about me and my ears, it's about the whole British rap community.

Did you still see Bite It! as underground, even after the Virgin deal?

It ain't aimed at your *Telegraph* reader, your *Face* reader. It's aimed at the kid who sits there in the small hours tuned into Tim Westwood. I'm flattered that other people have gotten interested in what I've done, but it's not essentially being done for them. Just because they've read about Snoop Doggy Dogg or Tupac Shakur in the *Independent*. From the essence of rare grooves and Soul II Soul to how things are covered now, it makes me sick. People don't find out about things now, they don't discover them. It's shoved right in their faces. Everyone writes it up. It used to be exciting to hunt out things. I'd rather build something up slowly than be just taken up and dropped soon after. When I'm 40, I can still be putting out records. If you want to go places and do things and buy things and read things and see things that you want you've gotta do it yourself. Know what I mean? You don't need money. Words don't cost any money whatsoever. And there are so many ways to communicate nowadays.

There's no excuse - outside extreme cases of utter poverty - for not doing something if you want to do it. I do my sleeves in one colour, right? Other people might do a full-colour label for their record and not bother putting a sleeve on it, which might cost more than the sleeve. It all depends on your way of thinking. You've got to work things out properly.

How do you fund the mechanicals now?

Depends on the sort of music you're doing. The music I was putting out, in the early '90s, there ain't a chance in hell you could do it and make a penny. You can make your money back, but you couldn't make money off British rap till now. So, not many people have passion enough to do it properly - because they weren't going to make money and didn't want to lose money. But in the years ahead, things are gonna change. And when British rap blows out, I want to have been at the forefront. Have been involved in the best. But I'm also lucky, because I've got other options. I could always fund what I do from other sources.

Still, it doesn't cost a fortune. If you want to do a white label, you need a thousand pounds to do a thousand records, basically. But to put a good sleeve on it, to get your promos out there, to do it properly, costs about £2,000 a single. Plus there's no reason why, if you're making good music, you can't just put it out on tapes. It doesn't have to be vinyl. I've always felt - why don't I just do a cassette of something? Why not just sell cassettes of recordings, because it's a lot cheaper and kids can afford them? Yeah! But, unfortunately, the market for rap is 12" vinyl; it's the radio. Still, there's no fixed reason why - if you got good music - you can't give it to radio DJs and get it heard that way. I mean, it doesn't even have to be released! I do my record labels so people can hear the music and get really excited about the whole package.

But, Trevor, you could have been the new Neville Brody.

Yeah, but that's a whole scene - what's happened in graphics and everything. The Apple Mac has destroyed a lot of people. To me, the logo is now redundant. Because the concept of logos and stuff like them has just been fed to people *ad infinitum*. It's great that people can do stuff for themselves. But 99% of that stuff is shit. And, often, it's because the music is crap. Because house music and a lot of what followed it is disposable rubbish. It doesn't matter, there's no longevity.

Don't get me wrong, though. It's great that people want to be designers and that a kid can now sit at a computer. But no one's been especially exciting with it, everybody's followed on each other. What is exciting is the combination of visuals and music - the whole multimedia trip. That is what is exciting. I dunno, though, because there's been pretty bad taste for most of the '90s. It's not even kitsch bad taste, just *bad taste*. Some time around '96 that started changing.

What keeps you going - most of all?

I just think of myself and my friends, we sort out good records, we sort out good clothes. Not because it was told to us by some magazine. But because we went out and we actually found it exciting. We were just on the same level. It's so easy to grow up now, looking in a magazine which will tell you what to buy. Most of today's youth are being led around by the nose. Who is to say those people leading them are in any way doing the right thing? Most movements are made up of music, fashion, design, and attitude. I certainly think that hip-hop has got all those. I mean, hip-hop is a culture - worldwide. Worldwide. Hip-hop is an American culture which has now been adopted worldwide. And it's being changed worldwide. The essence of it was art and graffiti, music as in mixing and rapping, clothing as in sportswear. House music, techno, those to me are kind of cultureless musics. There isn't any kind of design to them.

Compared to what kinds of music, besides hip-hop?

Well, you could compare it to hippy-type, tripped-out, progressive jazz-rock. At least that was poetry, art, visions, dress, dance - some kind of a whole. House and rave has been this hollow nothingness. Nothing around you, just wallpaper. Of course, it's disco and some disco's good. I mean, there is some good house and techno. Something's gonna come out of that. A kid can now sit down at a keyboard and generate what he calls good design. But he hasn't really had the background to pull it off. You need a knowledge of the past to create something great. And people don't have that knowledge at the moment. It's so in and out, so fast, such a quick turnaround. Nothing has staying power, so nothing's classic. Even things in magazines are so *topical*. I'm sure when I read mags as a kid, it wasn't all just what's happening now. It was all different things. I buy every magazine; I'm a magazine maniac. And when you buy the *NME*, *The Face*, *i-D*, there will be the same face on every cover, the same person giving the same interview inside. It wasn't always like that.

Now, an interview has got to be selling a record. You know what really sickened me? In 1994, I went to see *Aladdin*. And there were these two adverts before the film, before the film was even shown on the screen. One was "Buy the new Mattel *Aladdin* doll", and the one after that was "Buy the new *Aladdin* soundtrack". I was so... *This is absolutely crap.* It ruined the whole thing for me. Because I realised Walt Disney didn't make *Snow White* to sell fucking duvet covers! He made it from his heart, and the hearts of his artists. *Aladdin*, as beautiful a film as it was, was just one great big marketing enterprise. And it sickened me. My record labels are not a marketing exercise. They exist for the love of it. To me, in ways, *Aladdin* summarises the '90s. And I find that unbelievably sad.

It really upset me. What if I was there with my kids? My kids would walk out of there wanting a fucking doll, wanting a duvet! *Star Wars* must have started it, but this was sad. It was great that Robin Williams sued them, because he didn't want his voice in their advertising.

But what's your response?

I buy things for what they stand for - that's what you should do. Say I'm wearing a Phillies Blunts T-shirt, that's not because I saw it in *The Face*. I bought it because of what a Phillie Blunt is about. A lot of people don't understand that. It's like music. I buy music because I like it. I don't like the Dr Dré album, I don't like Snoop Doggy Dogg. I don't care how many people tell me it's good; I don't like it. I'm like the only person that I even know that didn't like Dr Dré's album, but that's too bad. I'm not gonna like things just because that's "what's happening" in rap music. It's not just to be obstinate or awkward.

Like I never took Ecstasy in my life, right? By the mid-'90s, everyone had stopped taking it; now they're all taking God knows what. But I find I'm quite interested in it. For the right reason - which is I'm simply curious. It's because some of the music I'm getting into is all music and visuals and design. It's a whole thing from the '60s and '70s. I think that was possibly the most exciting time, in the music, in the art, in attitudes. To be quite honest, it seems more exciting than punk. I wasn't there, but from what I read of them, it seems more progressive and exciting. It was experimenting, the whole thing was experiments. I like that.

There must have been something in the air or in the water. Because the sound on records is just so great. I think maybe it was naiveté; naive people suddenly getting into other things. When you think about the whole of youth culture, how old is it? Thirty-five years old in 2,000 years! Something like that, it's really such a short time! I mean, 1995 was the biggest amount of teenagers in history or something. Even the image of a kid at a computer is archaic. I mean, it's gotta be a kid sitting at home with Nintendo.

So, what do you think of that?

It's great, because the doors have opened now. People have this massive communication. They can tell each other things. People can see the most amazing things. But it's also been warped by the making of money. It's gone a step too far. Today you can make money out of almost anything. Sometimes, I just want to live on a desert island with nobody else and my record collection! Just play records. But you know what would happen? Some bastard would come out and write a film about it. Someone else would write a book, make a film, do a T-shirt. And base a computer game around it. But I never lose heart. What will happen is people won't have to put up with it. Because they can do it for themselves.

Once they were signed to Virgin, The Brotherhood ate up time.

Yeah, I spent a year on that album. But what happened was that a good friend of mine died, died of a brain haemorrhage. He was also managing the band, so it affected everything. There was a period when I just did virtually nothing. We made the record in January 1994 and it came out in January 1997. Basically, in that time, I did loads and loads of remixes. It all started when I was very first in the studio with The Brotherhood, and they were on the same label as House of Pain. I heard this track "Top of the Morning to You", by House of Pain, and I really wanted to remix it. Then, because that remix did well in the charts, I began to get more work from it. Most of my remixes followed a pattern, which is a hip-hop thing. But I'm now more interested in the melodic side.

Like this quintet from Newcastle, who are called The Emperor's New Clothes. I've been working with them for the Acid Jazz label, it's been almost a year. First I did their remixes. Now, I'm doing the album. I've spent that year because I care about them, because they're closer to the stuff I now listen to. Which is, basically, really old stuff, progressive jazz-rock from the '60s and '70s. Their sound's a bit outside of the London thing. It's east coast of England. Sort of a rock-punk-funk-disco-dub.

Is the change in interest why you founded Output, your second label?

Well, a lot of rap stuff, a lot of the people who are involved with hip-hop, they can be pretty narrow-minded. They don't like much else. I'm much more wide-ranging in my interests. Plus, I was never 100% happy with Bite It! I mean, it was fine, but I wanted another avenue. So I started Output. The first few things I put out were just mine; they were instrumentals. But I knew there was all this new stuff I wanted to work with.

For instance, I've got this group called Fridge, three Londoners. Seventeen-year-olds. We're recording everything live in their home. Another group's called Gangsters on the Strand, and they're like punk-disco dance music. Live with attitude. What I want for Output is *attitude*. I've even got a group called Suspect Packages. But I've also got this female singer, Moni. Moni I had met through my friend who died, and we've started writing stuff together. She's a Londoner, but she's also Chinese. Her music is semi-warped hip-hop pop stuff. It's classic singer-songwriter material. In a way it's all very early '80s. Just not so contrived.

But you can work with the majors. You're no longer limited to re-mixes.

Sure. I could have made house music until I dropped. Now, I could be making endless trip-hop records. That's what everyone is doing now that jungle's finally going over in America. And I do love Tricky, don't get me wrong. I think he's incredible; I love Portishead and Massive Attack, too. But the sound has become this crappy formula. You just get a semi-hip-hop beat and a very slow female vocalist. Go for a weird, slow-sounding hip-hop vibe. I could do it easy; but I really don't want to.

I have a philosophy on all this that's very simple. Like everyone else, I want to make a living. But I'd rather make a reasonable amount and be proud of my work. The things I'm interested in aren't what other people are interested in. So I'd rather step out in another direction. If I don't want to do the things other people are doing, then I can be very obstinate. But I think being different makes you special - and that makes people interested in your work.

But do you feel "anyone can do it"?

It's not hard in quite the way people think. I mean, in the business sense, it's not so hard. But it's not as simple as "anyone can do it". Because not everyone has the right instincts. Basically, if you got it, you've got it and you exploit it. If you don't have it, you can still succeed. But you're always gonna have to work a great deal harder. Ever since I started, work has landed in my lap. Almost none of it was work I solicited. One thing has led to another - or one thing I pursued took me somewhere else. There are always times you think you'll never work again, just like there are times you wind up skint. And, just when you're at your lowest, that next job will happen.

But I'm not saying you don't need to work bloody hard. You need to work bloody hard all the time. I take what I'm doing very passionately, very seriously. Take the Emperor's New Clothes album, for instance, I've now spent an entire year on it. The amount of money I made on that, I could've earned in a *week* - from doing a single remix. But my life is about achievement, it's about what I do. What I can be proud of. It's not at all about making loads of money. I'm not saying that will never change. I don't have a wife; I don't have kids to feed. But money's not important as a *goal*. In itself, more than anything, you want to be proud of your work. Of course the more you earn, the greater your expenditure. But you don't have to earn a lot to start something. You don't really need money; money's got nothing to do with it. You need ideas - which are absolutely free. On the other hand, you can't go out and buy them.

You also need connections; you must have those. In that sense, I was lucky. I've been in the right places at the right points in time. I was part of a scene as it grew, from something very small, into something that's now a mainstream culture. I mean, from Soul II Soul right through rave and jungle. With Bite It!, I thought, "Hey! Here's the music I love - hip-hop - happening in Britain. And nobody's doing anything. I gotta get in there *now*!"

What do you feel about the change you lived, from underground to mainstream?

I feel that I'm suffering from media overkill. It's become a DJ culture, DJs are like supermodels. It's pushed me towards instrumental music and live music. Initially, I wasn't into those. I like space rock, right now - groove-based rock music. So, I'm back buying records from Rough Trade in Portobello: imports like Tortoise, Directions In Music, and Designer. Their sales guy Darryl also has a label I like, called Soul Static Sound. That thing is fucking wicked!

What about the thing which started you off - design?

Right now, I don't do so much of that. I do it for myself and I do it for friends. And, of course, I do design for Output. But the idea there is to be sort of under-designed. I want it to be minimal but not look "minimal". I don't want it looking like anyone else, like Ian Swift or Tomato. Basically, I'm suffering from serious overload. I'm fed up with most of the stuff I see. I'm bored by it. Don't get me wrong, though; I think Tomato are brilliant. I'm very jealous, I wish I could do stuff like that. They're basically using high art in a commercial aesthetic. You'll see a Lilets ad, it's like a piece of abstract film. It's amazing that, at last, people have actually got some taste.

Have you seen change make things more global; hook people up across continents and cultures?

Yeah, I have. Most important, it's made black music available. There's always been so much great black music, and now people are more able to get it. Even in America, which is really racist, hip-hop and computers have just made it available. Hip-hop stars can have a number one record. When you really think about it, that's fucking amazing. Rap is now one of the biggest-selling forms of music. It's just a crazy, crazy situation. But it really shows an amalgamation of cultures. Look at the massive exchanges that happen just through licensing! Like, Japan talks to Newcastle talks to Germany. Like, the Beastie Boys licensed Alex Empire - for four 7"s on Grand Royal. Things are slowly, slowly coming together.

I think they will do so even more. Take me, I still want to try film or video. I can do it, because I'll be able to use my computer. I use a Mac for music, I use it for design, I use it for communication. Why not centralise? Why not use the Mac for everything? There's no reason why, with computers, you can't pull it all together. It's gonna be mad whenever it actually happens. But I'm happy to sit tight and wait.

Gary Walker didn't start his Wiiija label. But he took it from obscurity to global renown. Not only did he sign a watershed deal - one which protects his project's hard-won identity. He has even had an act choose him over the majors. It's all down, he says here, to hard work and friendships.

How did you get to London?

I came to London in 1986, went to college for three years at The West London Institute of Higher Education. I got a degree in modern drama, then spent a year working in the Community Department of Sadler's Wells Theatre, doing videos of their projects. Then I got offered a job at the Rough Trade shop, which was a cool place to work but, also, I needed the money.

How did Wiiija start?

Basically, Rough Trade shop started the label. The three people that worked in the shop - Nigel House, Pete Donne and Judith Davis - decided they wanted to have another go at putting out records, which they had tried once before. But they wanted to avoid some of the pitfalls that they had seen their previous employer go through. Meaning Geoff Travis, who started Rough Trade the label, which was stocked in the original Rough Trade shop. That was all an outgrowth of the first punk thing. They did three bands, all of which were very late '80s. But the fourth band they put out was Silverfish. I was working in the shop and I knew Silverfish. They were my mates and we hung out. Then, when I helped out with the Silverfish thing, they started selling more records than any band had. So Pete, Nige and Jude said, "It seems logical, you take it over".

What was your first signing?

My next signing was a band called Therapy? from Belfast, in the fall of 1990. They gave a tape to Leslie of Silverfish up in Glasgow. She never got around to giving me that tape, but I got another. And I got their single from Southern Studios, who were Wiiija's distributor at the time. I went over, saw them play - they were really exciting. They weren't just noise, they actually had songs. I think the thing that struck me the most was their lyrics, lyrics that I knew their potential fan base would relate to. *"Every day I've been the same, every day drags into the next."* Teen angst stuff. They were really tight, they put loads of energy into the gig, and they already had a really big following in Ireland.

Gary Walker:

independent label strategist

What did signing involve then?

We didn't have enough money to fund the Therapy? project on our own as Wiiija. So we approached the guy who ran their company about giving us an advance on potential royalties. He said no: "I don't do that sort of thing. If I do I want to invest and be a part of it." Then it all got very complicated. The band signed a contract with Southern Studios which said, essentially, "all records will come out on Wiiija through Southern Studios". Out came the first mini-album and, of course, they got big very quickly. I was suddenly sort of frozen out of the picture; it was like, "Well, you're doing one of our bands on your label". But Therapy? didn't want to work directly with Southern. Then there were things they didn't want to do; the whole situation just degenerated. Finally, the band said, "We can't work under these circumstances. Sorry, Gary, it's not you. But we've been offered a deal by A&M and we're gonna take it."

Everyone seems to need one of those to learn.

Yeah, well, straightaway I got myself a solicitor: James Wiley. Our accountant at the shop, his girlfriend's sister worked for him. So I asked if she might just put a word in. Basically, James Wiley managed Shakespeare's Sister, helped on Anxious Records with Dave Stewart from the Eurythmics, and was also a partner in Beggar's Banquet and Momentum. He had a lot of experience of all sides of the industry. It was the most incredible help. James was always there when I needed him; he also helped me set up a publishing deal with Momentum Publishing. So it became Wiiija Music/Momentum.

That means that you get money back for your publishing?

Yeah, I'm getting a cut of it. What people really don't understand about the business, is that to get record contracts just means an advance. And then the band have to earn out that money. A lot of expenses can be tacked onto that. So, unless they own the publishing, they don't really make much income. The major labels often say to a band, "You've got to record from your advance as well". Then they've gotta pay for the equipment; they've gotta pay for the recording; they've gotta pay for everything - from their advance. The way we've worked is that we very rarely give the bands big advances. Because we just can't do it. And when I say big, I mean a couple of thousand pounds between four or five people. What we tend to do is say, "We'll pay for your recording, we'll give you some tour support, we'll help out as we go along". Because whilst the records are coming out, you're recouping money as you're spending it, like from the sales. So you can advance the band a little bit more.

You regard it more as a long-term relationship?

Definitely. But different labels do it differently. Wiiija does a lot of what is sort of management stuff. Our first bands, none of 'em had a manager. Cornershop had someone who helped organise stuff but was by no means a manger. Jacob's Mouse, the drummer's Dad helped them organise stuff. But he's no manager in the same way that PJ Harvey has a manager. Most of them were friends or relatives. So, I ended up doing a lot of that.

You're talking about a lot of administration: booking hotels, booking tickets, getting visas.

Yeah, that's right. I do a lot of that. For example, when Huggy Bear went to Japan. Whilst there was an agent out there, sorting out certificates of eligibility, I had to go through all those forms with the band - then send them to the Japanese Embassy, with instructions. But I don't mind, because one reason we're successful is my close working relationship with the bands. I was determined not to give that up. Every minute I've spent doing accounts, or other general administration, I'd rather be with the bands. I would never say to a band "You can't put that out", because I like to believe they know what they're doing. At the same time, I probably give more advice, and work more closely with the bands than many indies.

You were your own A&R person, right?

Yeah, but that came about in a funny way. After Therapy?, I did two London bands, Love Blobs and Sun Carriage. Both of them happened to split up as Therapy? left. So I started again from scratch. I signed Jacob's Mouse, who had put out stuff on their own label I really liked. I saw Huggy Bear play and they gave me a tape and I liked them. So, we started working together. Then came Cornershop. Cornershop I met through Mark, this legendary Northeast indie character - someone who's been around the Manchester, Blackpool and Liverpool scenes for years. He offered to give 'em a hand because he really liked them. He rang me one day and said, "D'you want to come and see 'em?" I went up and I liked them straightaway. So, I said, "Let's do something together".

Put it this way - after the Therapy? thing, it took eighteen months to build a roster. You have to invest a lot of money in that time. Luckily, my bands were able to record fairly cheaply. So I was able to recoup what I spent quite quickly. Even by mid-'95, I was spending maybe four and a half thousand to record.

Did Wiiija depend on Rough Trade the store, or did it turn over by itself?

It nearly did, but not quite. We wouldn't have slipped by without that support. Plus, we got a really good distributor after Therapy? We went with Revolver/APT. They could advance me money when I needed it. See, once bands get to certain stage, more money starts coming in for the label. Because they start to get licensing deals, they start to tour in other territories. For example, all my stuff is actually distributed in Europe, so going out to continental Europe and playing there will always help generate sales. All the bands on Wiiija finally broke out of the UK. It's also quite liberating to go out of the UK, because it's easy to become obsessed with the UK market.

Is the turnover in the UK enough to keep anything going?

Well, in small indie terms, our stuff's done well. But, if you break even on a project, you are really still losing money on it - because you're paying wages, you're paying your bills: your telephone, your electricity. So a UK turnover does have to be kind of vast, really. I've been lucky, because for years I had rent-free work space, a store where there's a fax line and a photo-copier and all that kind of stuff.

Hearing you, one feels it's not as daunting as it seems.

Well, I didn't even have a business plan. My solicitor is still saying to me, "You've got to get a business plan for next year!" But you think, "I'm not doing this because I want to do a business plan and run a business. I'm doing it because I love working with bands, and putting out records and spreading the word." But to be a successful indie, you need business sense. I was lucky with the first team around me; I could never have run a label if they weren't there. Not only was there everybody at the shop, there's also Charlie Inskip, who always did national press. Charlie's based out of a company called Real Time, he's done press for labels like SubPop, Mammoth, Matador. Except for Cornershop and Bis, he still handles overall press for me.

There is a guy at another branch of Real Time called David Whitehead. He began my European distribution, helped get my worldwide licensing deals. Sean Newsham, who was based at Too Pure, he did all my radio work. When he formed Mutante, he kept on - he now does everything but Bis. Sarah Lowe worked at my office, she did all the regional press and retail marketing. After she left to join Mute Records, I worked on my own for a year. In September of '95, Shelley Austin joined as my personal assistant. I also had a great relationship with my label manager, Peter Thompson, while we were at Revolver/ATP. All these people have had quite pivotal roles. Besides, Wiiija had bands all over the place: Bury St Edmonds, Leicester, Essex, Oxford, London. So we really needed our central team.

People get obsessed with getting press, but how important is it?

It's a very small part of being a successful label or a successful act. Yes, it is the most important and most basic starting point. Yes, you have to get a certain amount of coverage. But that isn't the be-all and end-all, it's not automatically gonna sell records. But, if you *get* that press, you're going to get gigs out of London because the promoters will have heard about you. It also means you'll get national radio play and, particularly, play outside of London. Whilst the papers are seen as very London-based, they are good at helping bands get bases outside of here. Then, once you start getting into Europe and breaking *those* markets, you realise how many sales there are to be gained - in Germany and so on.

But people do go crazy trying to get on the radio. Is crossing over the only way to make real money?

It depends. For us, the money really only starts coming when we license stuff. Because if you've recouped on a record, and you get an advance from an outside label, then that's all profit. A lot of indie labels move it away from that, once they get to a certain stage - because the label could end up spending on very stupid things. Some friends of mine recently had a problem with a label because £900 was allotted for photocopies and taxi fares. Now, £90 perhaps would be reasonable, but not £900, not if you're on 50-50 profit share. A lot of labels moved away from that; they pay the bands 12% of dealer price for every record sold. But I think my relationship with my bands is very trusting. They know I'm not going to spend absurd amounts on things - I'm not going to say I spent monies I haven't.

It's also good for the record label in terms of licensing. For example, say Huggy Bear had signed for a deal where they had to receive 12% of dealer price, usually that means you have to pay 12% of dealer price for the licensed stuff as well, unless you get a contract that says you only get a reduced percentage of the dealer price for a foreign licensed product. Let's say I had a deal with Huggy Bear at 12% of dealer price - and I was only getting 14% of dealer price from Japan's Time Bomb, I'd only be getting 2% for myself. Which would be great for the band, but not for me, because we're still sharing profit 50-50.

An example: what deal did you get with Time Bomb?

They are actually giving me 12% of dealer price of each copy sold as a sales royalty: just a royalty for every copy sold, as opposed to a mechanical royalty. That's publishing money. Mechanical money's actually the legal percentage a record company label has to pay a songwriter for every copy of that song pressed up. Whether the band wrote the song or not, whoever wrote that song is legally entitled to that mechanical royalty. In the UK, it's 8.5% of dealer price - which is the price shops buy it at. That's the legally established thing. I mean, you can negotiate your own publishing deals, but that means you have to bypass M.C.P.S. (Mechanical Copyright Protection Society). So, for example, on a record with a dealer price of £3.50, 30p of every copy sold has to go to the songwriter, which goes back to me having published songs I put out. It means I'm getting a percentage of that 30p for each copy sold.

The 30p on each copy sold goes where first?

If the band have a publishing deal, it goes to the publisher. If the band have a publishing deal that isn't very friendly with the label, it goes through M.C.P.S. first. The label has to pay M.C.P.S. Basically, you can pay the publisher direct. I did that with Rough Trade Publishing, who did publishing for Huggy Bear; I paid them direct. If a band don't have a publishing deal, you can actually pay them the mechanicals direct. But if a band is looking for a publishing deal, and you sort that out, it can affect their deal. Because, obviously, the publisher has less to recoup if you have already paid it direct to the band.

Do you try a different deal for each band you sign?

Not really. Almost all the bands have the same deal, with the exceptions - now - of Cornershop and of Bis. Different bands have different needs, though, which always has to be taken into account. Plus, different bands sell different amounts of records. But the basic deal, there's no reason for it to differ. At this level, you're only talking about a difference in hundreds of pounds - not tens of thousands.

Can you parlay UK status into American sales; does it really work?

You can't really say, "This band is going to be massive in America." You can think they will be, but there's just no pattern. I'm talking about what the US public go for. Who'd have thought someone like Radiohead would have a Top Ten American single hit with "Creep"? Whilst someone like Teenage Fanclub, who do well there, were by no means huge, even with Geffen's help. But you always have to think about American majors - just as a means of being able to survive.

In the States, I began with side projects: the Blood Sausage single, then an album with Bikini Kill. That was licensed from Kill Rock Stars in Olympia - Washington state, near Seattle. It was an excellent album and it did really well. But, when I started doing various acts from America, I also did a double 7" pack, in which I put a band on each side - four new, really exciting, English bands. It was like: "World, please have a look at them!" That came out in the UK, of course, but it sold a lot in export to Japan and America.

What about the perennial indie problem: losing the acts you built to a major?

I've never wanted to lose anyone - although Huggy Bear, for example, did break up. Therapy?'s circumstances were sort of different; they didn't really leave me. But when Silverfish went to sign with Creation, they said, "Look, we need money you can't give us". Remember, until 1995, only one of our bands was financially self-sufficient. That was Jacob's Mouse because they got a publishing deal early on - and they had a song used in an American commercial. They earned so much money for it that they signed off, but that wasn't money from me and the record company. All of my other bands were still on the dole, and what money they did get was spent on touring. Another problem I had as my label progressed is the stage of life that people were into. They all had jobs - as social workers and things. Fabric, for instance, the drummer had a full-time job and he's got kids. I didn't have one band who could afford to just be a band.

By the mid-'90s, did that bring dilemmas?

Yeah. By '95, we were a full-on label, which wanted our acts to sell as well as possible. But our bands just couldn't be full-time bands, unless they wanted to rely on the dole for their money. Then, those guys who *were* on the dole were bored. People would start asking, "OK, Gary, what are you doing for us?" And I'd have to I say, "I can't do anything, because the album's out, but you haven't promoted it. I want you to get in that van for at least four weeks - and play the shit out of the country! But you're telling me you can't do that. Because you've got a job, everyone's got a job." That was just a very difficult situation. It led to a really crucial, transitional stage in the label. Because what do I do? Do I go to my box of demo tapes and pick out a couple of bands who aren't that special, but who are at least able to give it a serious shot? For a while, it was very hard. I just didn't want Wiiija to be standing still, to be saying, "Oh we've got our own little audience, we're in our own little ghetto, it's our own exclusive club".

Often, Britain's indies lack that kind of ambition.

Really, I think you have to be ambitious. Like, I'm going to try to reach new audiences and I'm going to get the widest possible exposure for bands. But without saying to anyone, "You know, you've got to write a song that sounds like a Top Thirty hit". It came down to one thing: I know how to sell records. I know the mechanisms for selling records. It's not that it's hard to do, but I had been doing it for seven years. It's very easy but you need that experience. Bands like Comet Gain and Skinned Teen haven't got that experience. So I say, "Get on with your music. There's no point in you worrying about the business and the actual mechanics of selling. You do the music, I'll do the rest." I mean, I fully support doing it for yourself! I support it for *anyone.*

How did you really start getting places?

Once again, Huggy Bear was a good example. Before I took on Huggy Bear, for instance, I'd never done a 7" record on Wiiija. This was the mid-'90s when, partly due to recession, the 7" market suddenly grew incredibly. Gallup introduced what they called the Breakers Chart and mainstream stores were saying, "OK, we'll stock that chart". Well, in the first-ever Breakers Chart there was, we had a Cornershop 7" only, and another by Huggy Bear. All these kids were hearing about new bands, reading about these bands. They'd go, "We haven't heard 'em yet! But it sounds interesting." They weren't gonna spend £4, £4.50 on a CD single. But they would spend £2 on a 7" record. It was a little bit like a punk revival; lots of bands were just doing it for themselves. There's a list of Wiiija bands who had a first 7" which they did themselves. Obviously, the label spends more money on cutting our records. We insist on being there when they are cut, being involved in the EQing and so forth. Also, we insist on a certain level of artwork.

So what is it that stops people from making their own records?

Nothing, really. Most of the bands that I would deal with haven't even actually got that few hundred quid. But most distributors are also sympathetic. So, there's two options. One: a distributor can arrange credit, on behalf of bands at a manufacturers. Then, they can pay the manufacturers back from record sales. Or, a distributor can give a band a manufacturing deal where they manufacture on the band's behalf, for 10% of the total cost. Say the cut cost £200, they'll add on 10% and take the credit risk. They'll pay for everything, on behalf of the band.

Do you see yourself as having a British identity?

Oh yes! We're *very* English - although what we do has parallels with smaller American indies. Plus, a lot of Wiiija's bands have agendas, things they really feel they've got to say. I want to give them the opportunity to do that. It's contributed to the image of Wiiija - as a label that supports artistic freedom and freedom of speech. Another thing we have achieved is a breakdown of categories. I think there's very few labels that have a scene around them. But if one kid who likes Wiiija records goes to see a new Wiiija band, they're 90% certain to like it, even if the whole musical style is different. Because what I see in that new band, what has interested me, they will see it too.

Basically, I try to present a whole entity. It goes back to how I myself moved down to London. All I wanted to do then was meet people who were into the music I liked. I wanted to belong to a gang, belong to something. All the kids who now write to me, come up and speak with me, that's what they want too - something to belong to. Another thing is that kids who are into music don't usually get a chance to be into a band before that band is big. That's still a very charming part of music; to be into a band before they get huge, discover a band.

How did the sale to Beggars Banquet come about?

Well, by mid-'95, the label was making more money, and that was great. It was also good for Rough Trade, because they didn't want to put in as much money as they had been having to. But, we both started to realise that we were in a period where the label needed an injection of money. To move Wiiija up to the next level. To solve some of those problems I talked about. But Rough Trade just hadn't got that money.

The label, being at break-even stage, wasn't gonna have that money, either. It was a difficult point; I was getting job offers and the label was getting offers. There was something appealing to me about doing A&R for a major. You work with bands; you're on a wage; you've got no other headaches. But, at a major, I also knew I wouldn't be able to sign who I wanted. And what I *really* worried about was the label changing. I wanted to be a bigger label, I wanted to solve my dilemmas, I wanted all my bands to sell more copies. But I still wanted to be Wiiija - that seemed impossible.

But, in the end, it happened.

Yes, it did happen. That summer, I got a funding deal from Beggars Banquet - giving me 24% ownership and them 76%. They're a very solid, reputable company who have both the Charlatans and The Prodigy - which, for America, are licensed to Madonna's label, Maverick. Wiiija is now part of the Beggars Banquet Group. I got a 50% wage rise and I'm the label head. Momentum Music still does our publishing. Things had already started to happen; at first, just little things. Like, Brian Eno used a Cornershop track for his "War Child" fashion show and Richard Norris did a Punjabi re-mix of one of their singles. Then, in May of '95, David Byrne's label - Luaka Bop - licensed Cornershop for America.

In February '96, I also signed Bis, which was another thing I could not have predicted! They had already been on "Top of the Pops" without being signed; every major label was offering them massive deals. I really didn't think we had a look-in, but I still sent them a package of Wiiija stuff. As it happened, they had it all because they were fans! Then, in the end, they confounded the music business - signing with us and with Grand Royal for America. All in all, things could not have gone better. We've been able to find what we needed: a company which realises why Wiiija is successful. Because we've been allowed to do our own thing, in our own way, without interference. Plus, we found a company that knew what it was getting. Something you can't really buy, because you can't ever buy credibility. You can't buy contacts and networking, years of it.

Has success brought out a lot of envy?

Yeah, there are lots of people who want me to fail. People in bands, or people in certain scenes. I've had a lot of anger at my success. Journalists as well, often they don't like the idea of Wiiija achieving my goal. This goes all the way back to Huggy Bear. People just wanted them to fail so much; they didn't want the message to get across. They didn't want the Huggies to sell those records. They didn't want them to become good musicians, which they did become. People just want you to fail, they totally do.

But, anybody can do it?

Anybody can do it, but it's a particular grind. On my days off, I get calls from all the bands. To call the US - on the far West Coast - they're eight hours behind. So you're constantly losing your relaxation, your "I'm watching TV time" by going, "Oh shit, I've gotta call six places in America!" All that really does kind of get in the way; it just has to be a full-time thing. Still, I'm really grateful to be doing it.

CHAPTER 7

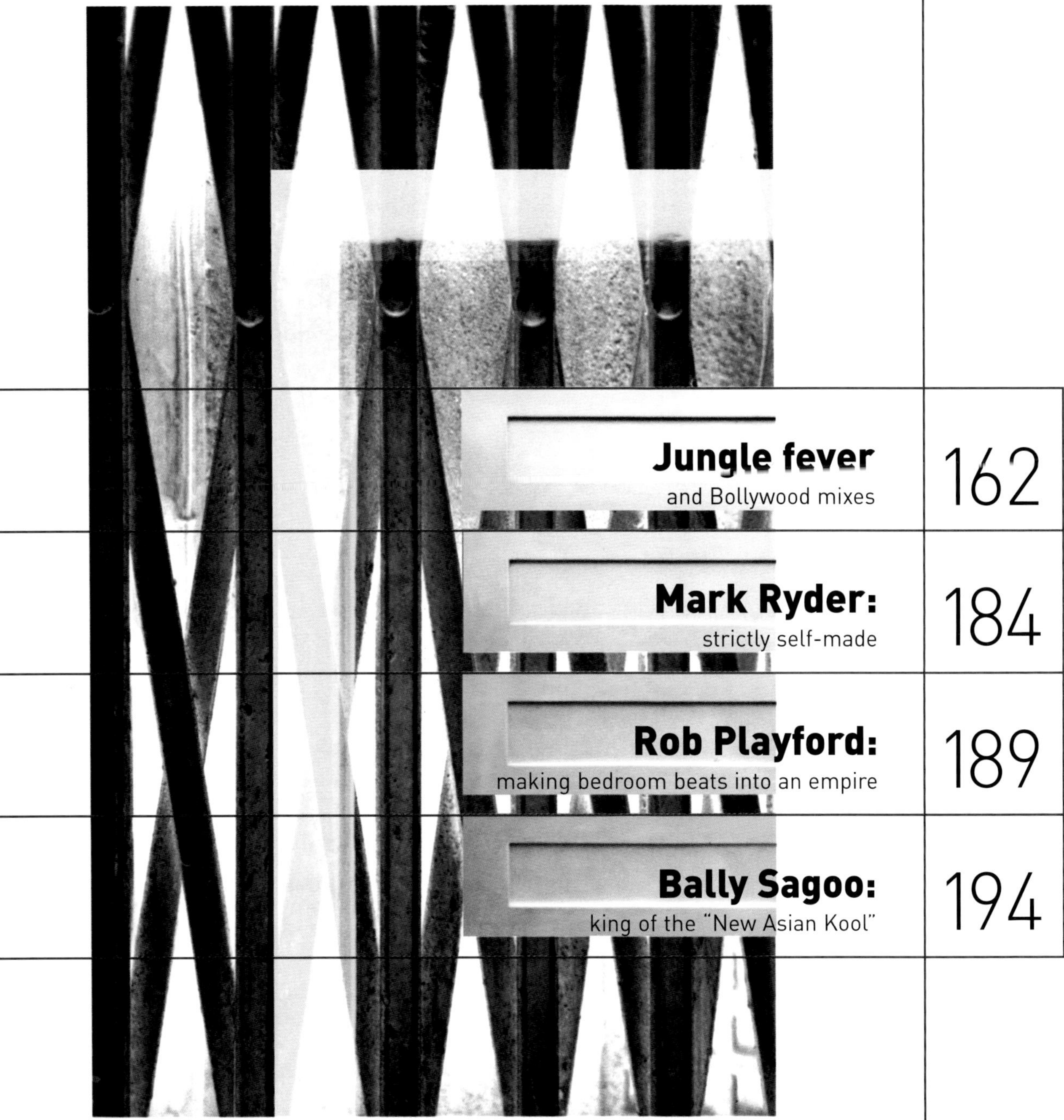

CHAPTER SEVEN

1

Jungle fever

and Bollywood mixes

Passion for music was part of another, parallel, story. But it was one which involved a different sound. "Jungle" surfaced from the mutating techno underground, entering mainstream UK consciousness circa 1994. It had begun to coalesce three years earlier, when aficionados started to dub it "junglist". Press reservations soon made that name an issue. Nevertheless, "jungle music" it would remain, a speeding juggernaut of revved-up techno beats, flogged to devotees and DJs on white labels and - from the first - framed as a rugged "outlaw" music. Despite its reputation as ultra-underground, by 1994 jungle had a mainstream star: the graffiti artist and hip-hop veteran Goldie.

For the first few years of "junglist rave"'s existence, there were non-stop rumours which concerned its provenance. As with the whole expansion of UK raving, the emergence of jungle spawned a tabloid frenzy. At its centre was young Britain's booming drug use. Raves, claimed many critics, were merely organised drug markets. Jungle records, claimed these voices, were investments by dealers. Never mind that ever since the '80s - and the cry of "aciiiiiiieeeeed!" - drugs had been completely intertwined with clubs and raving.

As far back as January, '89, the fanzine *Soul Underground* produced a "Top Ten of 1988", giving their nod to Spectrum, as "The first club to pull 1,600 people every Monday, the first club to receive 'Ecstasy' media attention, and the first club with a handout good enough to exhibit at the Tate Gallery." It was a combination of music, euphoriants and style that would run and run.

The Ecstasy-driven "Summers of Love" in '88, '89 and '90 garnered constant coverage. There was head-shaking from both "inkies" and "quality papers", with hippy-dippy praise from most style magazines. In *The Face* issue of July 1990, with an unknown Kate Moss on its cover, the inside front editorial read thus: "Most [ravers]...are pointing to the festivals, the gigs, the bands who came up in the past two years, bringing an energy perhaps unseen in rock since punk... The sun is shining, the attitude is there and the summer starts here." In the attached "A to Z" of upcoming bands, there were plenty of drug references, from LSD to "draw". Yet the performers lauded by *The Face* were just that - performance lineups in traditional band form: the Stone Roses, Flowered Up, the Happy Mondays.

There, DJs and sound systems received no name check. Yet this was the same year an ex-DMC mixing finalist named Mark Ryder started a rave label - under the apt name Strictly Underground. Now a player on the techno-jungle scene, capable of throwing a rave which fills Wembley Arena, he was then an ex-clerk from a chain record store. On the compilation records he put out, Ryder posed as a whole Rolodex of "bands". Each had some slice of the scene to offer: acid, techno, "Happy Hardcore", rave, junglist.

Says the neatly dressed, fast-talking Ryder: "In 1990, I decided to open a market - giving young kids what I deemed credible rave music. So that they would be our next generation of ravers. That year, I put out what I think was the first proper rave compilation." Initially, however, Ryder was told by the Our Price chain that they wouldn't stock it; to them, rave music "was not a viable market".

Although labelled as tracks by different acts, Ryder's "compilation" had been made completely by him: "Since I couldn't afford to license tracks, it was just me. But no one knew that, everyone thought it was compiled. The only way I could get it into chains was to sell it to them - on CD - for the price of a 12" on vinyl. To the best of my memory, that was about three pounds. Then, they retailed each one for £12.99. So those stores were making a serious profit."

Ryder soon disproved the "unviable market" claim, with four albums he released sequentially: "Illegal Rave I", "Illegal Rave II", "Illegal Pirate Radio I" and "Illegal Pirate Radio II". "They all went out at that silly price and sold 15,000! Plus, the bottom started falling out of the 12" market. So, before you know it, the people who were financially stable, lots of them started getting into those compilations. Telstar jumped on it with 'Hardcore Ecstasy '89'. And on it went, all commercially targeted Top 40."

At the same time, Goldie's eventual partner Rob Playford was moving from the DJ scene into making music. Says the blonde, soft-spoken godfather of drum'n'bass, "I started out as part of a sound system too. But when acid house came along, I was DJing. This was at a lot of illegal parties and raves, the ones in the late '80s and the early '90s. But the law started clamping down on that quite strongly. I had a good job, so I couldn't risk continuing."

Playford, then employed as an engineer, had "too much to go and throw away." Instead, he decided on a change of course: "I became more 'big behind the scenes'. A whole new industry was coming alive then. Something which was based on rave culture, not on trendy clubs."

2

3

4

1. Goldie - at Speed
Photo: Pav Modelski
2. Strictly Hardcore
Illegal Rave I
The Compilation, '91-'92
Strictly Hardcore Records
STHC CD1
3. Illegal Rave II
Back To The Underground Scene, '92-'93
Strictly Hardcore Records
STHC CD2
4. Illegal Rave III
Keeping The Vibe Alive, '94
Strictly Hardcore Records
STHC CD 5

THAT? OH, IT'S NOTHING, YOU JUST INVENT A NAME. ONCE YOU KNOW THE MANUFACTURING SIDE, AND YOU'VE GOT A DISTRIBUTOR, YOU'VE GOT A LABEL.
(→PAGE 184)

Ever since the warehouse parties of the late '80s, listeners knew musics like "garage", "hip-hop", "house" and "techno". Jungle, however, brought with it more of an attitude. Like old-style reggae and new-style dancehall, it had an overlay of audible blackness charging the issue. Plus, it was the music of a new generation. Its biggest fans were not Britain's rare groovers, Rastas or raggas. Those fans were their much younger nieces and nephews.

A shop like Honest Jon's in Portobello Road, which was a mainstay for rare grooves and jazz, was perplexed as well as fascinated - even though artists like Goldie were long-time customers. Says the shop's current co-owner Alan Schofield, "From the first, it was such a London hybrid. With just a few key people who helped to make it. I remember some time in '91, hearing jungle music spring up everywhere. I thought, 'This music is the end of the world! I hope I never have to sell it and deal with it!'"

Schofield laughs. "Now, it's so mainstream, it's past discussion. Most of the jungle we sell sounds like gentle fusion. It's just become airport music with that weird beat."

Listeners found the first jungle mixes just where Schofield did: on a stream of pirate radio stations, some of which started out playing house and techno. These had newly minted, volatile titles, such as "Eruption FM", "Rush FM", "Pulse FM". Pirates still publicised clubs run by their own DJs, such as the Astoria's crowded Sunday Roast. But they also hyped raves with evocative names: AWOL, Jungle Fever, Voodoo Magic, Thunder and Joy. Most were run by promoters with similar monikers: Dreamscape, Desert Storm, Eclipse, Ravelation. More and more, their music of choice was jungle. Even at large, traditional raves (like "Tribal Gathering"), jungle won its place. It became a genre.

Musically, its transformation was slower. Just a year after the term "jungle music" went public, journalist Alex Spillius described it thus in the *Guardian*: "Jungle is weird music. Typically, there are no melodies, no lyrics - unless provided by toasters that have moved over from the reggae and ragga scenes. It is often furious, always loud, a lawless soundfield that inverts drum patterns and rewinds basslines. Many people who have been into all sorts of dance music still can't handle it." Just like Schofield, he could hear little in it.

It was up to that few to feed the "London hybrid". Like Goldie, Rob Playford saw it as really new. Jungle, to him, was more than a music. Jungle was Britain's whole leisure culture changing. Even when

1

2

3

4

1. Illegal Pirate Radio, '94
Strictly Hardcore Records
STHC CD3
2. Illegal Pirate Radio II, '94
Strictly Hardcore Records
STHC CD4
3. LTJ Bukem
Photo: Pav Modelski
4. A Guy Called Gerald
Photo: Pav Modelski
June '94
5. Joi Sound System
Photo: Gavin Ferrnandes

I KNEW A LONG TIME AGO THAT NOT ONE PERSON CAN MAKE THIS SCENE SURVIVE. IT TAKES EVERYONE IN IT, WHETHER YOU'RE NEW AT IT OR YOU'RE LONG IN THE TOOTH. AT THE END OF THE DAY, DIVERSITY MAKES THINGS WORK.
(→PAGE 186)

that change involved old faces, it was aimed at open ears with fresh opinions. Says Playford, "The party organisers, the DJs, the movers - that whole culture of people had a different attitude. On the one hand, it was quite easygoing: don't care much about the law, let's all have a good time. But on the other, to engineer things, they had a lot of discipline and precision. It drew on what came before, but it was different."

In the middle of 1989, with a bedroom set-up, following the guidelines he read in a D-I-Y book, Playford made a record as The Orbital Project. He sold 1,600 copies himself - and discovered it was certainly a "viable market".

At Christmas in 1990, he incorporated a company. Playford adopted the underground moniker Moving Shadow. He also had a crew, which he dubbed Two Bad Mice - even though, including himself, it had three members. One of the seminal antecedents of "drum'n'bass" was the Two Bad Mice track "Bombscare".

At first, many hipsters from the West End hated jungle. It was seen as the province of a younger crowd - and one with very different class roots and references. But, with experiments by artists such as Goldie and LTJ Bukem, 4-Hero and Gerald Simpson, jungle soon mutated. Its wide acceptance then became unstoppable. It turned into a music akin to jazz, able to incorporate ambient moments, breaks, improvisations, and vocal flights of fancy.

Plus, it gained an elite West End night - Speed - which was held at the tiny, venerable Milk Bar. At

5

1

2

3

Speed, old-school jazzers mixed with junglists: leading to some works which soon pushed the envelope. Two names in particular had great resonance: sax player Steve Williamson and vocalist Cleveland Watkiss.

Both had been part of an English jazz renaissance which took place in the late '80s. Before that, Cleveland Watkiss had played in funk bands (like La Famille, with Soul II Soul star Caron Wheeler). Along with names like Julian Joseph, Orphy Robinson, Courtney Pine - and Trevor Watkiss, Cleveland's brother, a pianist - they had earlier re-shaped London leisure. Now, they brought that history into jungle.

Watkiss became the freestyling MC at Metalheadz, a club evening held by Goldie at Hackney's Blue Note. He also developed a relationship with Dorado, an acid jazz label, and formed a project he dubbed "23". Now, he calls it "futuristic fusion".

When it comes to jungle's jazz proclivities, Steve Williamson - always outspoken - is also explicit. When the saxophonist released a 1995 album, "Journey to Truth", he laid out his vision of a new music: "In hip-hop, you've got one sample of a certain length and another of a different length. It's compulsive...maybe they never meet! That's the whole beauty of it. You're always on the edge, waiting for something to happen. My music's just like that...making it work with real instruments. That's the direction we're moving in."

Much of Williamson's LP, said critic Paul Bennun, was made in what the writer dubbed "junglist bedroom style". Williamson saw nothing new in co-opting the form: "I'll take it [jungle] and mix it with jazz. That'll move jungle a step forward, jazz a step forward."

For four full years, musicians and producers saw jungle as the future - whilst the press continued to ignore it. A contributing factor was the class bias; this music came from techno-savvy males in Essex and Hackney, Bristol and Birmingham. Another fact was that its lyrics did matter. As Trevor Jackson noted in a hip-hop context, "words are half the story" - even at this kind of fresh and feverish pace.

Jungle music also spun a story of payback. It would end up by revising an old catch-phrase, the expression "the sound of the drum and the bass". In the late '80s, pirate stations such as Solar, LWR, Confident, City, Time, Kiss, Faze 1, Rock II Rock and Vibes-FM were playing reggae, dub, "rare grooves", hip-hop and house music. Some shows billed themselves as "the sound of the drum and the bass" - meaning a range of black musics (especially reggae-influenced sounds) which could not be heard commercially. In this context, the phrase bore a wide meaning: it embraced the roots of all such genres. Those roots reached around the black diaspora, yet emphasised the UK's Afro-Caribbean blackness.

With jungle, the hit-and-run patter of raggamuffin MCs finally gained a hearing inside the mainstream. Reggae artist-commentators such as Macka B had long made their acidic observations. But they circulated to a closed society. This - a society made up of black, West Indian Britons - certainly chuckled at their top-speed, topical barbs (spearing non-"conscious" hairstyles in tunes like "Wet-Look Crazy", or bashing Edwina Currie with the hilarious "Food Scandal"). But, despite late '80s rock-steady "ragga raps" by Longsy D, Double Trouble and Rebel MC, the old-style MCs never tried to "cross over". Theirs was exclusively humour and news for their community. It took their raggamuffin grandsons and granddaughters to meld their spoken arts with a different beat. The result was a special vindication: of black leadership in humour, music - and technology .

This being Britain, however, it was also collaborative. Hand in hand with "the sound of the drum and the bass" went a "theory" from the sound systems. Such collectives - mobile disco units - were very hierarchical business outfits. They had been born in the West Indies. There, as in Britain, they played anniversaries and birthdays as well as parties and "raves". Even the term "rave" came out of those systems' orbit; initially, to "rave" meant simply to party.

British sound systems spawned many star DJs, from Norman Jay and Jazzie B to successors such as Goldie, Grooverider, DJ Randall, Fabio, Peshay. Even James Lavelle of Mo' Wax spent time in one. Working sound systems taught one to handle business, to assess a dancefloor crowd, and to delegate duties. But, above everything else, this was its heritage: to know your music; to have a full command of grooves, breaks, loops, vocals and - most especially - what they all do on a dancefloor. An old-style sound system was a group which worked together, clearly conscious of what such unity meant. Jazzie B describes it thus:

"Drum and bass, it's the old reggae thing. It's deep roots and I think it's very spiritual. It's like having one plate of food, knowing that if you share that plate with everyone, then you all have strength to go on. That's sound system theory: and when you strip that down and knock it back, it ain't nothing but someone knockin' on a door, goin', 'Excuse me - can I come in?' And they open the door, as opposed to kickin' it down. That is totally the idea which came

1. 2 Bad Mice - No Respect
Moving Shadow, '91
Shadow 3
2. 2 Bad Mice - Hold It Down
Moving Shadow, '91
Shadow 14
3. 2 Bad Mice - 4 Bad Remixes
Moving Shadow, '92
Shadow 14R
4. Fabio - at Speed
Photo: Pav Modelski

YOU'VE GOTTA HAVE THAT LITTLE GUY IN HIS BEDROOM, WHO DOES HIS WHITE LABELS.
(→PAGE 187)

IT'S NOT HOW GOOD YOUR TRACKS ARE, IT'S NOT WHOSE PALM YOU GREASE, IT REALLY IS HOW GOOD YOU ARE TO OTHER PEOPLE. IF YOU LOOK AFTER PEOPLE, THEY'LL LOOK AFTER YOU.
(→PAGE 187)

4

1

2

3

4

from sound systems: trying to develop something in terms of our own community."

Having the pirates' on-air forum for "the drum and the bass" made a watershed difference for young black Britons. Yet, between the '80s and '90s, those words shifted meanings; they became another media tag for post-"junglist" music. "Drum'n'bass" is now just the dancefloor title of a genre, one which serves not just those whose roots are West Indian - but a wider, younger, broader community.

Jungle's first mainstream notice came courtesy of "Incredible", an overground collaboration between reggae's General Levy and M-Beat. M-Beat would then make it onto Radio One with "Sweet Love" - a "jungle" version of the tune by Anita Baker. But, by October 1994, the music-as-phenomenon even made it into *Billboard*. This recognition by a top trade journal was thanks to Goldie's deal with London Records (for two LPs, his advance was seven figures) and the US licensing of a two-year-old hit. That track was "Bombscare", from "Hold It Down" by Two Bad Mice.

By this time, Rob Playford was no longer an underground figure. His Moving Shadow imprint had become home to Goldie - when the latter took his oeuvre off Reinforced Records. Goldie was now a genuine media star, famed for his work with Rufige Kru and Metalheadz. His posse of sidekicks ranged from Watkiss to DJ Peshay (eventually also wooed by Lavelle's Mo' Wax). They were seen shaking hands and working the room at Speed, then holding court two nights a week at the Blue Note.

After the release of his début CD, "Timeless", the flamboyant Goldie would take jungle global. This was not least via a stint as Björk's boyfriend and another presenting MTV awards. (Taped at the Alexandra Palace in London, MTV Europe's lavish '96 award ceremonies were re-broadcast in America. There, they were eagerly scanned by Anglophile musos, keen to catch the latest on jungle and "trip-hop".)

Jungle had come out of hardcore, the techno-rave sound which preferred to emphasise breakbeats. Hardcore was a staple of the expanded rave scene and, from the late '80s to the mid-'90s, was heard in London clubs such as Rage. But its junglist step-child also drew from ragga, using MCs who chatted over racing beats to the muse of a heavy, booming bassline. Jungle mixed many traits, but its matrix was febrile speed and ragga craziness. Samples - and sometimes live, recorded drums - were pushed and then stretched in the studio. Sometimes, they exceeded 170 beats per minute. At first, it sounded like real anarchy in the UK: rough and chaotic, dense and sinister.

Yet jungle was primarily the product of veterans, DJs and producers who had worked rare groove and raves. Spinners like Fabio, Grooverider and DJ Randall were names familiar from the late '80s. Jungle's LTJ Bukem (who would bring strings to the mix) worked the clubs in '91, when he played garage tunes. "Happy hardcore" tracks by names like N-Joi pleased young ravers, but they were made by characters like Mark Ryder - formerly a star of the DMC mixing finals.

Similarly, jungle producers like Nookie (a former ragga mixer) made hardcore music "happier". They did it with a timely addition of synths and piano. Reinforced Records, an "old school" hardcore label, came out of London's history of breaking and hip-hop. Three Reinforced members, Mark, Dego and Ian, went on to form the influential 4-Hero, who had a '91 hit with "Mr Kirk's Nightmare". One year later, with "Journey Into the Light", 4-Hero became the first to studio "time-stretch" breakbeats. This gave hardcore and techno a reggae "dread". Said one member to *i-D* two years later:

"Hardcore to us meant hip-hop, aggressive music. In 1990, we started playing around with hip house, speeding up house, putting breaks underneath, giving the music...as much of an edge as we could."

1. to 3. Conrad at Speed
Photo: Pav Modelski
4. Mark Ryder at The Strictly Underground HQ. Essex, July '98
5. 4 Hero - June '97
Photo: Pav Modelski

Following pages:
1. Savinder
(The Face magazine, no. 44 May '92)
Photo: Corinne Day
2. Video grabs
Brick Lane, London E1, '98

5

At the time, they called the sound they were making "freestyle". But the emerging jungle formula was ferocious. Soon, it was gobbling up everything it could: soul, jazz, hip-hop, ambient music, Asian pop, dub, ragga, reggae, techno, spoken-word. In 1988, the Mancunian Gerald Simpson, an original member of 808 State, produced a seminal techno track called "Voodoo Ray". By 1990, Simpson signed to CBS, but big-league success somehow eluded him. By 1992, he was back producing - for Juice Box, his personal jungle label. In 1994, he had another hit with "Finley's Rainbow", a very different sort of "tune".

There were reasons such veterans were attracted to jungle. Jungle is not, as *Billboard* once put it, the "UK's first indigenous form of black dance music." (That title had already been given out, first to UK reggae, then to lover's rock, then to Soul II Soul, then to the "Bristol sound".) But it was a form with plenty of room for anyone. Especially important was a booming market in Asian-based "junglist". This mutation began to mix ragga patois and bhangra beats (from the Punjabi) with centrepiece female vocalists.

It was a trend which had started over a decade earlier. The moment UK hip-hop and graffiti emerged, young Asian Britons made their aesthetic felt - with many of the most stylish tags and the toughest beats. Says DJ Tim Westwood, who staged many an early "throwdown": "From the very beginning, in every part of hip-hop, young Asian Britons made this huge contribution. But, except for articles on the emergence of bhangra - which is a different thing - the media passed them over." For over two million Asian Britons, however, social and musical trends flourished by word of mouth.

With rave culture, and its split to incorporate ragga, young Asian-language musics gained a new focus. Its first indicators came in the late '80s, when bhangra beats began to fuse with house, in re-mixes of tunes like "Pump Up the Volume". Following the bhangra-house and bhangra-techno scenes which sprang up in Manchester, Birmingham and London, there came the stardom of Apache Indian.

Apache Indian was the first Asian Briton to achieve true crossover star status. He did it in 1993 with a string of hits: "Fe Real" (with the reggae stalwart Maxi Priest), "Chock There", "Arranged Marriage" and "Boom-Shak-A-Lak". His début album, "No Reservations", sold over 160,000 units worldwide - and he was rewarded with a Radio One show. His blend of rap and ragga musics, however, led to awkward terms such as "bhangramuffin".

1

Apache Indian's stardom was symptomatic. It showed Asian Britons were well up with the beats. In fact, they were marrying junglist themes with Hindi and Punjabi sounds. Cutting percussive break-beats together so fast the sound stuttered, they added samples from lavish Indian film tracks.

"Here! we're gonna get wicked!" intones a child's voice on Mangal Singh's "Aja Pind Di", from the 1994 Multitone compilation "Deep Into Jungle Territory". The track's sinewy beats then soar off into cultural density: both "chatting" and raging Asian-language vocals, undercut by a ragga MC who intones - among other sentiments - "Indian jungle a-come". In mid-song, two DJs banter ("hear the bassline drop", notes the West Indian commentator). The black influence is undeniable. But it's clear the song is shaped and coloured by Asian elements.

"Deep"'s tracks were in fact already club hits. Were one to look on Multitone's World Wide Web site, one would find the following rundown: "Indian percussion, such as the tabla and the dhol, take on the furious beats-per-minute of jungle; bhangra vocals and sitars weave around massive grooves. Ten already-massive tracks have been radically

SANGEETA
BALTI HOUSE
RESTAURANT
STANDARD BALTI HOUSE
TANDOORI RESTAURANT
OPEN
HAFIZ GENTS
HAIR STYLES
MODERN SAREE CENTRE

2

1

2

re-mixed and re-shaped, including 'Challa', where the classic vocals of Reshma ride on a jungle groove overlaid with ambient dubs, 'Aya', a classic track from bhangra star Premi re-worked by DMF into a furious jungle stomp; 'Doabe Dia Jatta', where Pammi's vocals (from the 'Balle Balle' album) weave together with sitars and new instrumentation, and 'Nastik', a furious, ravey jungle track with a massive groove and ethereal vocals from Bindu."

Besides "ethereal" singing, there were also what Rob Playford calls "chipmunk vocals": on a "Speedy Gonzalez Mix" of "Apna Sangeet sings Apna Sangeet" (with Sardara Gill). As well as Asian-language chatting and vocals, this also features a looped English-language cry "Uncon*ceiv*able! Unbel*iev*able!"

Yet, after all this time, it was conceivable. In fact, it was as much of an epidemic as jungle proper. Bhangra-influenced jungle records and remixes were flogged on many of the 150 plus pirate stations which, by 1994, were all over Britain. These stations were the heirs to LWR and Solar. They too advertised raves, records, club evenings. But, most of all, they showcased new mixologies: cut-ups from Brick Lane juxtaposed with Tottenham patois; "Smells Like Teen Spirit" turned into a dubwise anthem. It was a reprise, in ultra-British terms, of the techniques used to invent hip-hop.

Christmas Day '94 saw a watershed for the jungle-bhangra crossover: the London release of a tape called "Bollywood Mix". Soon, it was blaring out of shops in London's Brick Lane, long the East End centre of Asian shopkeeping. Billed as "PRODUCED + MIXED BY MR SMITH... DON'T WORRY ABOUT IT!!!", "Bollywood Mix" was on a cassette tape. It had a colour-xerox cover and six cuts, with titles such as "Ek Larki Dekha To (Junglist Massive)".

The shops which stocked it shifted 1,000 copies a week, leading of course to "Bollywood Mix 2". This installment also bore liner notes from "Mr. Smith": "DJ BOOKINGS: DON'T WORRY ABOUT IT. TEL: DON'T CALL US, WE WILL CALL YOU."

Mr Smith's direct precursors were artists like Raga Kaka Winston, whose tapes - like "Bhangra Inna Me Yard (Coconut Mix)" - proved sonically provocative beyond expectations. Ragga Winston, who is Jamaican, alternates between Hindi, ragga and Punjabi. He is a pioneer of multicultural mixology. But the Goldie of the Asian movement, its breakout star, is a Northern-based Briton by the name of Bally Sagoo.

Now 32, Bally Sagoo was born in Delhi. But when he was six months old, his family moved near Birmingham, to Basall Heath. There, his father

1. and 2. Bally Sagoo
Higher Ground
Sculpture, design and art
Direction: Intro
Photo: Merton Ganster
3. Bally Sagoo
Turn Bin Jiya
Sony Music, '96
Higher Ground
Columbia Records

ALWAYS MOVING ON: THAT'S WHAT IT'S ALL ABOUT.
(→PAGE 193)

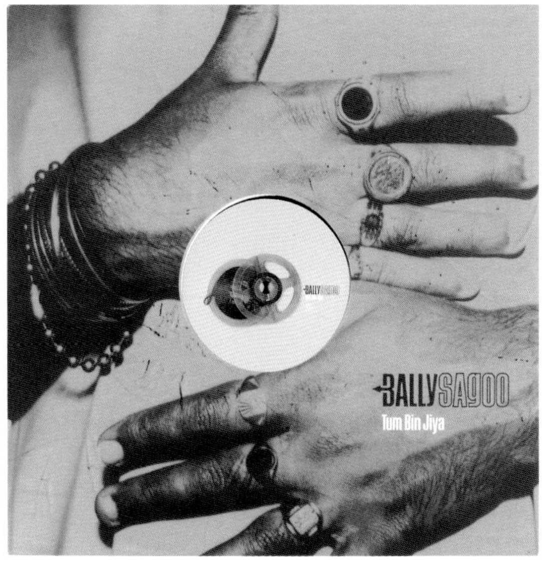

3

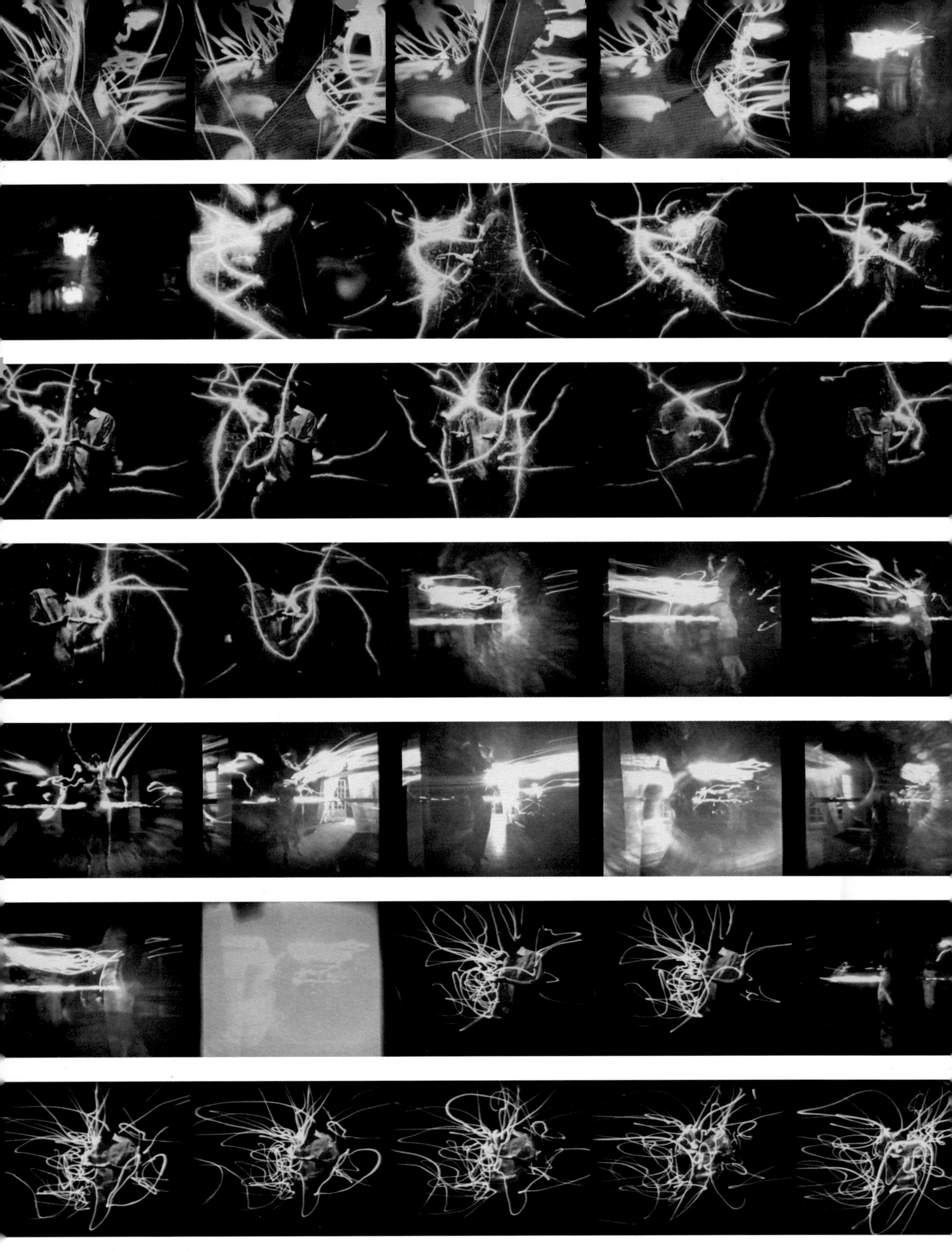

1

started a specialty record shop, which imported Indian music for the locals. By adolescence, Bally - like so many Britons - had a "bedroom studio" of his own construction. There, he played 7" singles and made up mix tapes. Until he finished college, he claims his parents' taste - their music, his own heritage - embarrassed him. "I just could not relate", he remembers. "There didn't seem to be anything funky about it."

At college, however, Bally Sagoo broadened his views. He started to hear funk as pioneers such as Afrika Bambaataa heard it: a constituent of every culture's music. He started experimenting, fusing Indian music with beats. After graduation, he took a job selling stereos, but he still indulged his aural alchemy.

Bally's Dad had connections with Oriental Star, an established label for a range of Indian musics. He played them one demo remix from their back catalogue. Offered a chance to remix for real, Bally came up with "Hey Jamalo" - and a contract for further work, which he had to do by night.

In 1990, while jungle was being born, Bally Sagoo played a part parallel to Rob Playford's. While still selling electronics at Comet by day, he finished up "Wham Bam", his début album. Its title, which came from a love of Batman movies, was a token of his prominence on the scene. Like so many other young UK movers and shakers, Bally Sagoo had a whole new world in his head. It had no boundaries around what it meant to be British.

If a Two Blind Mice track could draw on Beatrix Potter, Bally could make reference to a Hollywood blockbuster. With Asian listeners, there was even a special resonance. For in south Asia - India, Pakistan, Bangladesh, Nepal, Bhutan and Sri Lanka - pop had a long-standing and strong relationship with cinema. As world music authority Peter Manuel wrote in '88, "In south Asia...film music constitutes a majority of all the popular music dissemination. The weakness of the print-based media in India has contributed to the vastness of the Indian cinema industry, which, generating over 700 feature films yearly, is the world's second largest."

By 1994, those figures had climbed to 1,000. But the Indian film industry now faces possible change - as, increasingly, its patrons look towards the West. By 1994, the barons of Bollywood were feeling the effects of a law passed the preceding year. It allowed Western films to be dubbed into Hindi and, effectively, shattered the barons' monopoly. Steven Spielberg was among the first to exploit this market, with his foreign-language "Jurassic Tumbi" ("Jurassic

1. Video grabs
Bally Sagoo video - Dil Cheez
Director: Tim McMillan
Courtesy of Paul Ayre,
MTV Europe
2. Nusrat Fateh Ali Khan
Mustt Mustt
Remixed by Massive Attack
Realworld, '90
RWST 1

IT IS FOR US TO EDUCATE THEM: US, THE WESTERN ASIAN YOUTH WHO GREW UP WITH TWO CULTURES. OUR PARENTS WANTED TO LISTEN TO RAFI, WHEN WE WANTED TO LISTEN TO SHABBA RANKS. (→PAGE 194)

2

Park"). His budget for the blockbuster had topped £50,000,000 - far outclassing most of Bollywood's traditional budgets.

Despite the interest in Western stars and genres, many Indian film pundits retain faith in the native recipe - a fusion of glamour, action, music, dancing and singing. Some Western staple, they add, have no Indian market. In 1995, former film producer Rajkumar Bajaj told the *Sunday Times* that there was little market for a Western staple like science fiction. Says Bajaj, "If you come from a village without electricity or running water, science fiction is seeing a house with lights that work and water coming out of taps."

Indian film music, it seems, will continue to be intertwined with artificiality, escapism and glamour. The rabid film fans of the subcontinent love mixologies, combinations (however improbable) of locations, costumes, emotions, songs and movement. If they feature Western touches, so much the better. What seems enduring are their own film traditions.

When he became a house producer at Oriental Star, Bally Sagoo became exposed to another important Asian tradition. For the late, great Pakistani singer Nusrat Fateh Ali Khan, he ended up producing "Magic Touch". It was a milestone musical work in many ways, one of which was Nusrat's unique religious stature.

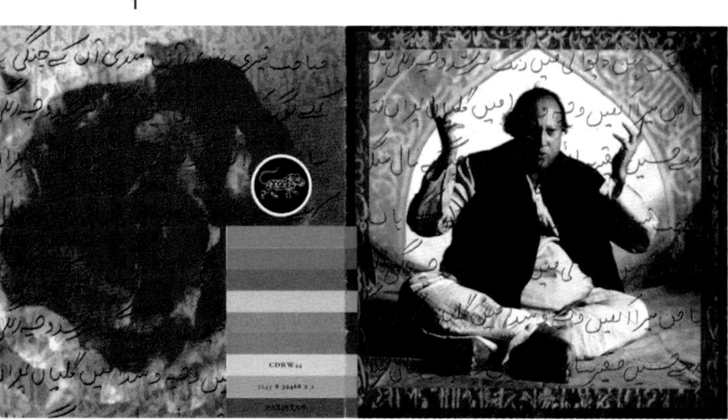

1

2

Nusrat was born on October 13, 1948, in Faisalabad (later, he was based in Lahore). For him, music was a family vocation - one handed down through many generations. Both his father and his uncle were renowned musicians, and Nusrat trained with them from the age of nine. But, after 1971, he displayed a personal genius. Just as importantly, he started transforming his genre - which was qawwali, a Muslim devotional music. In the Arabic, literally, qawwali means "utterance".

The words Nusrat sang may tell of Sufis and saints, but they attracted fans from Peter Gabriel and Mick Jagger to Eddie Vedder. Their singer became a leader in the "world music" boom. Then, in '91, Canadian Michael Brooks oversaw Nusrat's Real World Record album "Mustt Mustt". Given the nature of this task, as well as the genre, Nusrat's moves on it were extraordinary. For one thing, he eschewed his qawwali "party" (those classical music masters who form the music with him). Instead, he added multinational players: from New Zealand, the West Indies, and New Orleans.

Thanks in large part to its title track (remixed by Massive Attack and now one of the most-sampled soundbites in Asian music's entire cassette culture), "Mustt Mustt" became both a world music smash and a landmark. As late as 1997, Coca-Cola used it in a global advertisement. Yet, "Mustt Mustt" is a Nusrat improvisation - on Urdu lyrics dedicated to a saint. Says UK educator Parminder Chadha, "Mustt Mustt Kulunder means lost in joy or drunk as in intoxicated with joy from the saint. With my every breath, it means, I give joyful devotion."

"Taken away from a directly devotional context," she adds, "it becomes almost like a hypnotic chant. Which is probably why the Massive remix works so well." The ritualised roles of repetition in qawwali emphasise the release of energy and a pleasure beyond rationality. Or, as it is expressed in Nusrat's liner notes to Real World's "Shahen-Shah": "Both performer and listener are drawn into this heightened experience - words are repeated until all meaning is exhausted and only the purity of the form remains - a universal understanding transcending even linguistic barriers."

It is something all black musics understand perfectly; they, too, specialise in the uses of repetition. Their route has similarities to Nusrat's - African-

Americans, too, took a sacred music out of its formal home. Now, whether it be James Brown and "Please Please Please" or a jungle DJ with his "wicked, wicked, wicked", they bring repetition into the everyday world. There, its circularity can be both inclusive and ecstatic. But, with qawwali, says Parminder Chadha, sampling and remixing are still controversial.

Still, another set of Nusrat re-mixes - entitled "House of Shah" - was commissioned from the British producer Mick St. Clair. Together with Bally Sagoo's remix of Nusrat's "Jewel", these consolidated the holy singer's global standing. In addition, in November of 1995, UNESCO crowned Nusrat the Best Musician in the World. In 1996, he collaborated with Eddie Vedder, on a track that was used in the film *Dead Man Walking*. (Nusrat's tunes had already been heard on Western soundtracks, from films such as *The Last Temptation of Christ* to *Natural Born Killers*.)

Nusrat Fateh Ali Khan died in London's Cromwell Hospital on August 16, 1997. (A diabetic, he was taken ill en route to the US for a kidney transplant.) He was just 49, yet had become a global boundary-breaker. Nusrat's music may have derived from a sacred form. But Bally Sagoo's work is helping shape a new Britain. In 1994, he signed a deal with Columbia Records, for whom he cut the LP "Bollywood Flashback". He used it to take listeners on a personal journey, from his bedroom workshop (which he dubbed Currywood Studios) through his ragga, hip-hop and soul experiences. In tribute, those fans bootlegged tracks in record numbers; Bally's bio lists 41 different pirate versions which can be found just in India.

Back home in England, "Bollywood Flashback" sold 50,000. Its single - "Chura Liya" - became the first Indian-language record heard on Radio One. But it was Bally's own remix of "Chura Liya" (in 1994) which really raised the ante, as well as propelling him to a new level. This remix typically shifted 400 units per shop leading, first, to appearances on VH-1 Europe (at that time, a brand-new broadcaster), then to Bally's own show on MTV Asia.

Meanwhile the music was exploding everywhere, going from strength to strength - and place to place. It gave a fresh clout to Britons like Talvin Singh, a tabla player who left Leytonstone at the age of 15 to study in the Punjab. Like Bally, Singh is fully part of the dance-floor culture - as a musician, he's worked with Courtney Pine, Björk, Massive Attack and Sun Ra. As a DJ, he runs his own club, Anokha. And, in 1997, as a label head, he produced "Anokha: Sounds of the Asian

3

1. **Nusrat Fateh Ali Khan and Michael Brook Night Song Real World, '96 CDRW50**
2. **Nusrat Fateh Ali Khan The Last Prophet A Womad production for Real World, '94**
3. **Bally Sagoo - Chura Liya Columbia Records Sony Music Entertainment**
4. **MTV - Asia logo**

YOU HAVE TO SELL SOMETHING MORE THAN JUST THE MUSIC. YOU'VE GOTTA GIVE PEOPLE SOMETHING THEY THINK THEY WANT. (→PAGE 185)

4

1

2

1. Talvin Singh - at The Blue Note
   Photo: Gavin Ferrnandes
2. and 3. Talvin Singh
   Photo: Gavin Ferrnandes
4. Video grabs
   Talvin Singh
   Blue Note projections
   Design and art direction: Intro

Following pages:
1. Sangeeta Shop
   Brick Lane, London E1, '98
2. Video grabs
   Sangeeta Shop - interior
   Brick Lane, London E1, '98

3

4

1

Underground". It featured names like vocalist Amar, State of Bengal, and Future Sounds of India.

Singh has long been well acquainted with Britain's new mixologies. ("As people," he told one critic, "we're already fused!") But he knows they signify a worldwide shift. They are not just novelty and fashion. Fusions of bhangra with beats and crazy samples can be found in US grocery stores, on Dutch compilations like "Jungle Fever", or from the Panjabi MCs on Nachural Records. (Here, one finds a perfect sample of scrambled cultures: the Panjabis' use of the US TV theme song from "Murder She Wrote".)

In London's Brick Lane, stores like Sangeeta handle it all: tapes, CDs and Indian films on video. Says one of their young salesmen, Foyzal Islam, "There are five people on the staff here. Except for me, they've all been in the trade a decade. Though I'm the youngest, I know my music well. I've got over 600 tapes at home. Six hundred tapes and three hundred videos."

Sangeeta stays open "366 days a year" - including Christmas Day, 9 a.m. to 9 p.m. It stocks books, watches, wedding gifts and food items. But it also houses a range of sounds. Islam: "We have Punjabi, Pakastani, bhangra, Hindi, Bengali." But he dates the '90s explosion of younger musics to the initial Hindi remix of "Chura Liya". "Kids had always been making up tapes at home. That was what got something going overground."

"As Asians," he grins, "some of us are getting sick of it. I myself am sick of so many remixes! By mid-'95, there were 50 titles called 'Bollywood'; everything from 'Bollywood Fever' to 'Bollywood Jungle'. In terms of beats, then jungle started taking over. But they all remain incredibly popular."

So does the novelty of such cultural thievery - what James Lavelle refers to as "word bootlegging". A Sangeeta tape by The Unknown DJs starts with a CNN "streets of London" update. Then, it offers

2

"shout-outs" to many compatriots - in places like New York, San Diego and Chicago.

To listeners, these mixes export something especially British: the central importance of a female vocalist. It is a feature in lover's rock, in Soul II Soul-era classics and in modern trip-hop. Now, it's a feature of Asian-based mixes, too. Take The Unknown DJs' "E-Eagle Mix" - or a more traditional Hindi tape like "Lover's Magic". "Lover's Magic", produced by the West Midlands-based Saint Records, features Deepa Singh as its vocal centre. In '91, she was Britain's Hindi Female Singer of the Year. "Lover's Magic" ends with a track called "Saxual Healing", plus its very own brand of "Junglee Remix". But there are other ties which seem explicit. For instance, the Saint logo on these cassettes clearly echoes the "Funki Dred" of Soul II Soul.

1

Female voices command the heart of lover's rock. They have mutated into their genre's pop successors: from Smith & Mighty's early, rough-edged vinyl through hits by Soul II Soul, Massive Attack, Portishead, Tricky. In Asian musics, the female voice has always been pivotal - but for somewhat different reasons. Indian films use a method called "playback", where a few professional vocalists "sing for" all the stars. Among the most famous of such playback singers are sisters Lata Mangeshkar and Ashle Bosle. Mangeshkar is considered the world's most recorded voice - having sung central parts in, literally, thousands of films.

Such Indian movie music has natural affinities with the formats of reggae and hip-hop. Each one deals in topicality and allusion, making in-jokes while using cultural referents. Each mixes past and present, levity and seriousness. So, in its way, does the Indian cinema - which has contributed so much to the new Asian mixers.

Writes the critic Peter Manuel, "film music, like Indian cinema in general, can be said to reflect in its own way the dialectic interaction of tradition and modernity, city and countryside, and national identity and the West. Most film songs combine Western and indigenous elements. Imported instruments like congas, synthesisers, horns and, especially, violins are used alongside tabla and dholak drums and melodic instruments like sitar and sarod."

Lata Mangeshkar's female vocal style, heard over and over in such movies, typifies the female role in such Indian favourites. Her shrill, ultra-girlish vocals have become, according to critic Raghava Menon, "the ultimate measure of sweetness in a woman's voice". This is exported wherever Indians emigrate, most especially to Britain and Canada. It may also have played a background role in bhangra's pop renaissance - centred in Britain, in '84, with the success of groups such as Alaap and Heera.

The development of bhangra pop in Asia was equally syncretic, yet more lyrical. Many songs in both canons deal with Eastern culture and its unavoidable collision with the West. Take a tune like Dilshad Ahktar's "Desi bandri vilayati cheehan" ("Native girl, foreign style"). It tells of a local Indian girl returning from England, speaking a monstrous mix of Hindi, English and Punjabi. She is fancied by local men, admired by the girls. Yet she finds her Indian life most frustrating.

Asian-made bhangra tunes tend towards the meaningful. But their British counterparts often mirror the "Dance, dance/Wicked, wicked" themes of disco and techno. When Asian Britons entered the mixer's market, they were brilliant at collage, but less adept at lyrical subtlety. The catchiest hit from Bollywood Mix One was eventually issued in English. But, as "Hey! Girl in Mini Skirt", it suffered from translation.

Nevertheless, the new bhangra-driven beats are booming. Their production encompasses a huge diaspora, one that stretches from Toronto's Boys' Club to London personalities like DJ Gora Gora ("gora" being slang for "white boy" or "honky"). London may have club nights like Anokha or Bombay Jungle (started by Shakir of Outcast Records and DJ Ritu). But the World Wide Web has innumerable sites - such as Desi Arts, Connect and The Bhangra Dimension. Their correspondents link the "First" and "Third" worlds by e-mail. And they send tapes whizzing around the globe. If the new music's popularity (and its syncretism) thrive at this rate, it will provide revenge on colonialism.

2

Certainly, it proves DJ culture's astounding reach. Not to mention validating a new kind of career path: from the sound system and the demo tape to the full-fledged, techno-merger of cultures. It's no accident that Bally Sagoo, like so many of his era, started with remixes. England, after all, is remixing everything; her global status, as well as her politics and identity.

Bally Sagoo calls his music a vibe and an aura. He refers to "funky riffs", hip-hop beats, uptempo techno. "I am Asian, loud and proud", he says. "But I am also British. My music represents bringing different worlds together."

1. Humse Hai Muqabala
Kadalan
Venus Records
2. Hey! Girl in Mini Skirt
Cassette cover
Venus Records
VCB - 3007

IF YOU WANT TO DO IT FOR YOURSELF, HAVE A GO! I NEVER THOUGHT ABOUT GETTING ANYONE ELSE TO DO IT. THE FIRST PIECE OF VINYL, I DIDN'T THINK ABOUT SENDING IT TO RECORD COMPANIES. NEVER, EVER THOUGHT OF SENDING THEM A TAPE. JUST HAD MY OWN TUNES AND THOUGHT "THAT'LL BE FUN." ONCE I KNEW ABOUT IT, FOUND OUT ABOUT THINGS LIKE PUBLISHING, I LEARNED YOU HAVE TO BE ELIGIBLE UNDER THE SOCIETY'S RULES TO BE A PUBLISHER. BUT YOU FIND THINGS OUT AS YOU GO ALONG. SAMPLES, FOR INSTANCE, CAN GET VERY TRICKY. IN THE EARLY DAYS, WHEN YOU'RE SMALL, YOU DON'T REALISE WHAT YOU'RE DOING. PLUS, AT THAT LOW LEVEL, PEOPLE AREN'T SO BOTHERED.
(→PAGE 192)

Mark Ryder came to the music business trained by computer games. He's written software, entered mixing contests, and pretended to be numerous, different bands. Out of '90s rave and techno culture, Ryder has built an empire: records, radio stations, tapes and club nights. His close friends remain his "production house". And when Ryder wins, he sees that they do, too.

How did it all start? It started just like everyone dreams of starting. I was unemployed and I was DJing, just for friends at house parties, to top up the dole. Like most kids, I was being kicked to get a job. I had a very strong interest in computer games. Although, at school, I was totally ignorant, on a computer I could do anything. My father bought a ZX81, because he wanted me to get into them. It must have cost him £100 and it didn't even have keys. It had 1K of memory; now it would just be a piece of junk. But, before you knew it, I was writing games. I was fascinated; I was like a brain surgeon.

My father saw that, so he got me another, a Commodore 64. Playing games made me want to know how they worked. So I used to take the games apart, crack into 'em, then learn what the programmers had written. Learn the sub-routines, then re-create 'em to do better things. Before I knew it, I was writing from scratch. Dad sort of pushed me into college and I went on this course, for idiots who didn't know computers. This was in East Ham. I spent only three weeks for a year and I passed it. Top of my class; I knew more than the teachers!

What happened next? I got a job in London writing the software for Boustead Commodities, which used to be this firm in Liverpool St. I was on a pager in case something went down. Bear in mind, I was still only 17. I'd be there in the day then, at 3 a.m., in bed, I'd get a page. So I'd have to go in again, so they could carry on in-putting all their data. I was dreaming in numbers, but I was getting paid excellent. Still, I wanted to work with people and I still loved music. So, at 17, I left my £22,000 job to work at Romford's Our Price Records. I think I took a drop of about £17,000! My girlfriend, who I've been with about 16 years - she's my wife now - she thought I had gone koo-koo. But I just couldn't hack it any more.

Mark Ryder:

strictly self-made

It must have been a shock. Yeah. I was on like four grand. I started working up my little ladder there. Then I started DJing, trying to get into clubs. I knew absolutely no one. Then, I used to go to Hastings, to be by the sea. One day I was in a club there and, as you do, I started bugging their DJ. You know, "Look mate, I can do better". He let me try and I literally burnt up the decks. Once again, it was a game and I'd learnt it. I could scratch with my feet, my elbows, everything. Before I knew it, I had a job at Flamingo's in Hastings. So I moved to Hastings. This was right before I started the label. I got better and better, too. I entered the DMC competition. One year, I came third and the next year I came second. I think this was '88 and '89.

You were still living in Hastings? Well, I still didn't know what I wanted to do. I mean, I'd worked in Our Price and I didn't like the system. Of course I should've been in a specialist shop; I just didn't know how things were done then. But, finally, I got offered a job in London, at the megastore in Marble Arch. There I met Dave Lee, who then headed up the dance department. We hit it off immediately; we were mad vinyl junkies. We brought truckloads of records, the full-on stuff. Dave and I started looking at what we were buying, all the Trax Records and stuff - before it was "house". We thought, "Hey, this is really simple. It's just a kick drum and a set of sounds. We can do this! We know we can sell music. So why don't we make some of it ourselves?"

We decided we would try doing it. But there was this bloke at work, highly strung. Him and me didn't get on, and he managed to get me out. Six months later, then I got a call from Dave. He had found this guy in with a studio and wangled some time - for a percentage of the would-be profits. That's where we cut our first record. It was "Get Down", by MDM. By then, Dave was running D-Mix, he was selling dance records. So we got a deal with them, we got it pressed up, we really started crackin' on, getting all this MDM stuff done. We set up a label called Republic Records.

How hard was it to set up a label? That? Oh, it's nothing, you just invent a name. Once you know the manufacturing side, and you've got a distributor, you've got a label. Owning a label is really owning a name. But, then, Dave got offered a job with 'em; where he'd be on wages. He came to me, and said, "What should we do?" And I said, "Well, I'd take it." But they wouldn't take me on as an employee. So I didn't even get a job with Republic! It was ironic, because I did lots of work for them. All the Shy Boy remixes, all the Phase II remixes. And soon it came home: "Hey, I'm not getting paid!"

Out of that, Strictly Underground was born. There was some stuff we didn't want out on Republic. So, we put it out under the name Masters of the Universe - and we called the label Strictly Underground. The name was a combination of Strictly Rhythm and underground music. Which, of course, was what we wanted to make.

Did you change your style for the label?

Dave's like me; he's not a frontman, either. But he also realises that you have to sell something more than just the music. You've gotta give people something they think they want. And, at that point, people wanted garage music. But, to sell garage music and be British, that was unheard of. So we had to have the knack of making it sound American. That was our scam; that was what set us up as these unknown artists. We had all this stuff coming out and people bought it "on import". "Together Forever", for instance, was a massive hit. It went into the Top 100 as an import. If we'd put it out as a UK thing, it would have sold nothing.

So we realised, this industry has two faces. One is people who love music. And one is those who love the scene. In reality, those things are pretty separate. Because the people who like the scene can get off to most things, irrespective of what is played. It's about what they wear, what they think is new, all those kind of factors which make the industry. But, we only wanted to be involved with the music. I didn't want to run around kissing anyone's ass. All that stuff, we both hated it. Guys who run majors, even the dance divisions, they're totally cliquey. We could have maybe got in there; maybe not. But we really just hated the business scene.

So how did the label grow?

Over time, Strictly Underground just grew. It became hip to be associated with. I mean, people knew this "Mark Ryder" was involved. But they assumed that Undercover Movement was a band and that MDM was a band, that Hackney Hardcore was a band, that Sonic Experience was a band. Of course, they weren't. They was just me or me and one person.

See, I could put myself in the picture of MDM and say "As MDM, I'm a happy uplifting vibe with a housey beat, get the hands in the air, really feel free." Then, when I'd do a Hackney Hardcore track, I'd think, "I'm a really bad attitude, gangland sort of Hackney force and I wanna make a statement with my music. So I'm gonna call this one 'Dancehall Dangerous'." If somebody had said, "MDM is the same bloke as Hackney Hardcore", people would've replied, "No way in a million years." But they were. I was proving the music could cross boundaries the trending and the attitude couldn't. But I lost out from it, because people do want face and people want image and people want the hype. That's why lots of people want to buy the music. So, in one sense, I really sell to purists.

So you are deliberately underground.

I set myself up so I *had* to be; there was no escaping it. A lot of people now know Mark Ryder is behind a lot of things. But they don't, say, know how much involvement I had with N-Joi. We had a No 1 hit in the early '90s. There was three of us doing it; there were the two guys in the band. But they denied my involvement, and there were quite a lot of bad vibes at the time because I sold N-Joi to Deconstruction. I was clear, though, they were too big for my label. I didn't have the power to get them where they deserved. Still, my name didn't turn up on anything. It was omitted on the writing credits; it was omitted as a producer. On "Anthem", you'd need a magnifying glass to find it.

I've never had any help from any label, or anyone outside my own small circle. I hit as many walls as anyone can hit. But, rather than stop, I went around them. There are loads of walls, too. Like the press - you don't get it, because you don't know the people. I wasn't in with the right record shops, so that didn't get me a chart position. I didn't give a free box of records away, so no one would sort my record out. In nine years, I never back-handed anyone. The records I had in the charts got there because they were good records.

People say you can't do that.

But you can. And I've probably pulled it off better than anyone else. I'm doing what I love, I've got a big house, I own four properties, I've got a flash car, a really pukka studio. And everything I've got, I got from working hard. I don't have a thing about being "underground". I just hate kissing anybody's arse. Also, I truly do believe two things. One, what goes around comes around. Two, if you really keep your head down, you'll succeed. I've got four dedicated friends who work with me now. We've become like a production house. They're best friends and we've all grown together. I've set 'em up with their own studios. The really detailed stuff, we do at my place. I'm trying to get house music to a state which, I think, there's just a few people aiming for.

People like Gus and Goldie and Dego and Rob Playford - those guys are unparalleled, they really changed things. They got on a breakbeat thing and got into the computer; looked at its brain and jigged it around. Played with the break, and said, "Hey, hold on, we can take that sound and put it *there*!" They actually went right into the workings and thought, "Look, this gear can move the snare." Then the chopping of the breaks came up, and the breaks became more important than the music. It had a funkiness that can draw you into it. Out of everyone I know, I credit them - for structurally making this music different. Because, to be innovative, you must understand equipment. Anyone and everyone says they can make music.

But stick 'em in the studio and just see what they do. The bottom line is engineers know how things work and they're the people who can make things happen.

How do you feel about the jungle phenomenon?

The problem with the jungle scene is that there's two strands to it: there's reggae jungle and there's rave jungle. And rave jungle is breakbeat orientated. It has a reggae influence, but it's a rave transition. It's like a bug, it's like a computer virus; it's forever growing, changing and mutating. The problem with the jungle thing is, as it was being born, reggae artists realised they were being taxed. They were being caned for *their* vocals on our music. And they wanted a slice of that - which is totally fair. But they also saw it from their own perspective, that this was their reggae being translated. So you had this really strong, heavy reggae music called "jungle". But you also had this breakbeat music called "jungle". That confused an awful lot of people.

You had "Jungle Hits", which is a reggae album with breakbeats. Then you had my album "Junglistic Fever", which is a rave album. Some reggae guy buys that one and he goes, "What's all this then, what's all these beats flyin' around? And this MC - goin' *Hold it down! Hold it down!*" You know, he's used to the MC goin', "Rewind, Selecter", plus he can't hear the bassline like he wants to. Then, of course, you get the British media - who had not a clue what jungle was.

What about your pirate radio stations?

Even when I set up my first one, it was really for fun. First off, we ran it weekends, 24 hours. It was funny how we did it too. I went out and bought loads of cheap personal stereos, all of which had auto-return, and called this mate of mine who was an electronics geezer. He put contacts on the top of the "play", so when it was finished playing it would pop up and hit that. That contact was connected to the next power input. So, we had ten of these players, all with contacts on the "Plays", all of the "Plays" pushed down. So, when the first one finished playing both sides, it would pop up, switch the contact on and send the power to the next one which was already on "Play" mode. So it would start playing that one - then *that* one would pop up!

Since there was ten of 'em and we had 90-minute tapes, we used to cut the leaders so there was no blank gap, just a funny sound as it started over. Then, we'd cover the blip when it switched by saying, "Ooops, there's a bit of transmission problem on the airwaves." We'd have the clock set hours ahead and try to approximate the time. And we'd always complain the studio clock was just never right. Everyone really thought we were broadcasting live!

How long did that last?

We must have done it for three months like that, all on tapes. I had all these tape machines buried up at a certain location, in a box, with a wire going to these big lorry batteries. I changed 'em every twelve hours. A wire went up a tree and the aerial was up there. It was hard running a pirate station in those days. You couldn't mess about so, if someone crossed me, I was vicious.

Some guys came round looking for us, but they never managed to figure it out. They tracked us to this park, looked for the source of electric - and it was this farmer's house! So they smashed the door in and beat the poor guy up. This was not the D.T.I. [Department of Trade & Industry], by the way; it was other pirates. We were on our way down to change the batteries and, when we got there, we saw police. So, man, we were gone. But the next day, in the papers, there was a story about it. All about this pirate farmer! It was all incredibly inflated. Within a week, I mean, this was headline news. Pirate radio tracked down! Underground in a field! Housed in this huge, bunker-like ammunitions box! When the box the tapes were *actually* in was one used for soft-scoop ice cream from Tesco's! Ice cream! When they were biggin' out with all this crap.

How did you react?

We quickly put it back on, one more time. One more weekend. We said there was gonna be a big Christmas party, and the tickets would be £5. Well, so many people turned up at this party, I think I cleared something like £4,000. It made me realise just how big the pirates were, how many people were into our kind of music. I'm not so nasty anymore, I don't need to be. But thereafter, I was hooked on radio. I've pretty much always kept my pirates going. And I will until there's a station playing music which stops people wanting those pirates. Whatever it takes, I'll help keep 'em going, whether it be a station like Kool FM or Eruption.

What's the basic way of running a pirate station?

First, the logistics of running a pirate is: find a tower block, put an aerial up as high as you can, try and link by microwave from another point which is in visual sight of the block, so as to protect the studio. But the long and short of it is, now they can always track you down. You just make it a bit harder with your microwave. But they can track you, that's how it is. They're not silly, the D.T.I. aren't silly people. Sometimes I question the way they work, but they have their job. But, again, they've never caught me. Quite frankly, a long time ago, I was resigned to a court case - and to being fined £2,000, £4,000. It won't hurt me.

I help other stations run who do nothing for me. But I ask nothing, either, except to stay on the air. I knew a long time ago that not one person can make this scene survive. It takes everyone in it, whether you're new at it or you're long in the tooth. At the end of the day, diversity makes things work. If there's only me, Reinforced, Moving Shadow, if there's only three or four key labels putting out music - well, that's not enough to sustain a scene. You've gotta have that little guy in his bedroom, who does his white labels. You gotta have the ones who are trying to get it together and what they do is sometimes good and sometimes not. You have to have everyone and all their experiences - from where they live to the holidays they have - to make the industry really diverse and big.

You think competition is healthy.

Yeah, and my company stays competitive. When one rave organiser threatens me, I think: you are just one person. I have more hands in more pies. That's why I do all those things, because I know they're all important. Running pirates is important, running raves is important. It's not just one thing anymore. I'll do whatever it takes to promote my music, and to promote everyone else's.

There's no rule on my stations that you must play all my records. They're not overkilling what I do. OK, you will hear my ads on loads of pirates. But it helps them and that's just good business. The whole underground is about helping each other. It's not about kissing arse, but scratching backs. To me, those two things are worlds apart. If you give something out, you'll get it back times ten. You just might not get it back when expected. I've been helped out when I least expect it.

Is that a rule you'd advise others to follow?

Starting in this business, that is your key to success. It's not how good your tracks are, it's not whose palm you grease, it really is how good you are to other people. If you look after people, they'll look after you. The people who work for me, they make money. We don't rip anyone off to make our profits. No one gets conned and everyone does well. I don't know how long it will last but, as long as it does, we'll all be happy. Then, when it all comes crashing down, no one's bitter. No one is under contract; they stay because they want to. And you pay them 50%. All the records I co-wrote were 50-50. My view is: I've no need to screw anyone, because I can always make music on my own. That's not true of all other companies. Some of the guys who run those can't make music. They need to squeeze every penny out of their artists. Most of the music industry is like that.

When you're running your own operations, you don't need Kiss-FM to play your music. You don't need to give big-name DJs dub plates. It takes too much time, I want to be making music. I'm not a promo company, I'm not a plugger, I'm not any of those things everyone thinks you need. But you don't need them, in my experience.

That's not the usual viewpoint.

Well, it all depends what you're in the business for. I never got into this business to make money. And, OK, now I make a lot, but I spend it, too. That goes back into the industry which makes me the money. I don't compromise in my studio; I don't compromise with my stations; I take my DJs on two trips a year. Last year, I took my DJs - pirate DJs, this is - on a big coach up to Alton Towers. At Christmas time, I took them all to France. That comes out of profits generated by the station. So, if we put on a rave and that makes money, it doesn't all go back into my own pocket.

It can't go to people individually, because being on a pirate isn't about getting paid. It's about playing the music you love. But if a station does make money, that should go back to who makes it work. Once I month I run this Hellraisers club in Romford. And it's rammed, 300 capacity, it's full-up to the ceiling. We also do Jungle Buzz, which is a separate night. That money all goes back to the people who generate it. Because I don't need to take that money; I'm making money on my albums and my singles. My friends are my friends - and, if we all grow together, we stay together.

Where does that philosophy come from?

It comes from when you don't know anything. You don't know how the business works, so you rely on friends. You should also realise that that can't be free forever. That your friends have to win when you win. Plus, they have to understand the process - so they know they're not bein' ripped off. I sit down with people and I tell 'em, tell 'em when I have a financial problem. At any time, anyone can see my books. So they know I can make £50,000 - but they also know how much they can make. It doesn't work on percentages or things like that. But we have deals where we're all happy, mainly because we talked it through from the first. They know I'm gonna make more money than them, because I'm the key figure in the story. But they also know they will make more money with me. If you clear £3,500 a week off me, you know that is serious money.

We don't work on a record-company basis, we work on established friendships. I should get 75% if I write a track, but I'm happy with 50%. Then, later on, maybe that guy who worked on it with me will do me a remix. And he won't be charging me to do it. We don't quantify the pounds, shillings and pence. But, I tell you, it works bloody well. Someone told me once I had the ideals of Islam. Well, I'm not religious. But my philosophy's friendship - I think friendship's worth much more than money.

But when you become successful, problems arise.

Well, of course, you should maybe be contractual. Because that's the true test of a friendship. If it's all upfront, well, write it down. There is some of that. But they all know the inner workings of the company. Plus, who knows what will happen in the future. We might fall out over somebody's girlfriend! But there's definitely an illusion that, if you're successful, you're rippin' people off. People see me, they see my flash car, they know I own property and that I'm running pirates. So they assume I must be doing that. They don't realise everybody can win - and we'd all work harder if we were all earning.

We're used to clearing serious, serious money. I was clearing over £100,000 at one point. But I've got 20 tracks which have gotta be cut. And I've also got 20 singles ready to go. But I've also got 20 I can't release - and I've given out big money for those. So, that's my money tied up for the moment. If I get too deep into that scenario, and album sales start dropping due to the competition, then I might have to slow down on the income. I explain that out to everybody and they just buckle in and Boom! We get the singles out and we're up and running. We do go through slight hard patches, as with anything it goes up and down.

Does your success worry you?

Yeah. There's people out there I feel threatened by. But that keeps my business on its toes. Like the people you help who then backstab you, I try to just laugh at it. Because we are doing well here, we're all having it major. All my artists bought new cars and every one of 'em's earned it. They deserve it; they're working bloody hard.

How do you feel mainstream people perceive your music?

For a person who don't know anything, music is like a running stream. It's always going somewhere and it's always changing, and every so often a fish will jump out. Well, the outside person only sees that one fish - that's all they will discuss. It doesn't really matter if they jump on "jungle" and misunderstand it and say "You know, General Levy made it happen." It all depends on how deep the reader will scratch - or the writer who's addressing that reader.

Really, we're all part of a global industry. It's reality, whatever the papers say. You just can't ignore it. For a long time, for instance, I didn't want to do merchandising because I was a music company. Then I realised that you have to play the game to a certain degree, or you can be physically excluded from things. You can be edged out if you're not noticed. So I found out, yes, I have to do it. Yes, it has helped me to sell my music. But I still want people to know the music's credible. If you wear our jacket, you're wearing the logo of a company that's really popular. Image is important. But I don't want that personality thing. It's better to walk down the street as just another person than walk down the street as some star that was. Realising that helps me keep a lower profile. Otherwise, you get stamped and dated like you're on a passport. Whatever happens to you is only as good or less good as it was on that date. I see people like Goldie and I think, good on 'em. But I don't want that sort of profile.

If most well-known drum'n'bass practitioners have one thing in common, it's likely to be label head Rob Playford, who started Moving Shadow Records from his bedroom. His roster has reached from Two Bad Mice (himself and two mates) through EZ Rollers, Foul Play, Omni Trio and, of course, Goldie - much of whose work Playford co-produced. In 1995, he moved from Stevenage to Soho, released Moving Shadow's 100th record, and signed his first non-UK artists (from Florida and Germany). Here, he talks about his label's origins, how the pre-Criminal Justice Act police clamp-downs inspired him, and how he managed to learn about the record business.

How did you start out?

I was a DJ part-time, I used to work in Leeds in the electronic industry. I was an engineer for a company that made television broadcast equipment. From that I got into the software side so I've always had a natural inclination towards technology. Knowing about technology has always helped me, it's second nature. Get a new piece of studio equipment, I can work it. Get a new piece of software, I can work that, too. I wrote software for the company where I worked, but I was also a DJ part-time with another guy there. We used to have a mobile disco, doing stuff like weddings, parties, birthdays. There were actually four of us in the outfit, which was called Charisma. That's how I really got into that side of it. Charisma was a dance outfit, so it was black music-orientated. I was the only white boy out of the four. At the time that was before house music came along. So it was mainly soul and hip-hop and any old funk, those kind of things. Each of us had our own forte within that.

What changed it, made it more personal?

When house music came along, because it was a bit faster, it appealed to me more than anyone else. So that was an area I picked up on and that became my forte. I was attracted just because it was different. At that time, I didn't know how it was made. It was actually very, very simple stuff, the early sort of house. I had no idea it was really closely related to my kind of engineering background. It was just something I naturally felt happy with.

That was the biggest buzz of all, the warehouse parties and the old-style raves. Once you've got in a warehouse, got thousands of people in there and the party's set up, you know you've beaten quite a few members of the law. Sometimes, they just didn't care. Or they didn't have the manpower to do anything about it. Sooner or later, though, they had to start making stands. That was when I decided to back off a little.

Rob Playford:

making bedroom beats into an empire

How did that affect your future?

Yeah, because just before it happened, I'd bought myself a sampler. I had a computer I could sequence on as well and I had a keyboard. With the pocket money I got from DJing, I was quite OK when it came to equipment. I'd got all the stuff in a two to three-week period. What changed things was actually one rave event, about a week after I got that sampler. It was in a place called March in Cambridgeshire. It was very bad, there were police just truncheoning the party-goers and setting dogs on 'em. Spotlights all across the fields. So, it was just like, "OK, that's it. That's not the point of going out." It kind of got the message across to me. Rather than just forget it completely, though, I went to the other side - which was making the records.

How did you start that?

The first thing I did wasn't really part of the music at the time - because that was still very techno and acid-orientated. Because I've just always liked the bass elements of music, it was just sequencing a bass loop. The most simplest thing. I had a really nice system in my car and I just went out with that bit looping round and round. It sounded really nice. I literally test-drove it! Then I added some beats to it. We'd be going out on weekends, to the legal clubs which were still going, like at the Astoria. And it was good testing it on the people I was going out with at the time. They really loved it and they knew I got upfront stuff all the time, from DJing. But I told 'em I'd done it and they were quite shocked. So that was good, I thought. You know, at least it's working. After that, I made another three tracks and I decided to find out where I could get records pressed up.

Where did you go to find out?

Foyle's Bookstore, actually, in the centre of London. It was from a "How To" book I heard about on Radio One. Something like "The Town and Country Guide to Making Your Own Records". I was just down there one day, thought "there's a bookstore", went inside and found it. I was quite pleased with that and - it was superb, it had everything in it that you'd want to know. Because of the Town and Country Club connection, it was more of an indie record company thing, but, after all, pressing a record's pressing a record, regardless of the style. It had loads of manufacturers' addresses, all the rough costs and things. I had a good job and money from DJing, so I had enough money to think, "Right I can get these made". Thought it would be a bit of a buzz to make your record, get it pressed.

I've always liked the company idea, always had it in my mind that I'd really like my own company. I'm sure all that came from working with the sound system. So, once I actually had all these contacts, I rang around 'em all, getting the best prices, finding out who was the cheapest, how long they'd take to do it. And it's absolutely amazing, but for five years of my pressing records, I still used the people I chose on that date. So many people choose the wrong people or just waste their time trying to find someone. I was so lucky! I stayed with the same pressing plant. They're just so good, they'll bend over backwards. I could phone 'em now and, in three hours, if I needed it, they'd have something done.

How did you start distributing your stuff?

I did it all myself. There were six or so shops in the West End I used to buy records from. I'd pop in those to see if they had stuff, when I was DJing. So I knew the people in there. Three of them were pretty much my main shops; there were three more I knew well. So I went in to each one and took a test pressing - of which I'd had 100 made. I just said, "OK, what do you think of this?" And they said, "Excellent, we'll have some of 'em off you." Went back the next week and they wanted more. So I got another 500 done. This was The Orbital Project, which was about the rave clamp-down.

They went really quickly. Went out to some other shops on the edge of London, round the perimeter and they were also, "Yeah, we'll have a box". So I got another 1,000 pressed and they went as well. By now, I'd done 1,600 units. It was played on pirate radio, too. But I hadn't done any promotion. I'd just go in a shop and say, "Here's one of my tunes, they're £2.50 each, how many do you want?" The price didn't change for five years either, funnily enough. And they were in plain sleeves; I'd stick 'em together myself, with no made-up labels. Instead, I just printed labels out at work, said what the things were called, and stuck 'em on the sleeves.

Dead easy; 36p pence per pressing; 9p for a sleeve, then just driving around London with 'em in my car. That's the best way to make a profit because you are doing everything yourself. It was good fun, so I decided: let's do another one. I did a 5-track EP for the second one. I was taking around the test pressing, trying to get some orders from the stockists, look ahead a bit. Then I realised, I was getting a bit fed up just driving round. Taking days off work, in order to visit five shops. Because that's what it takes, that's all you can do in a day - you need to go in and have a bit of a chat. By the time you finish, all you've managed is five shops. So I thought, hey, I'd better expand it a bit.

How did you manage to do that?

I started asking round at all the shops, "Who's a good distributor? Who's done well at carrying this kind of thing?" Again, I was lucky there, because everyone I was warned against went bust a year later. When I was in Music Power Records in Green Lanes, this guy come in with a box of records - and he was the actual distributor. I'd seen him come in before, and plump a box of records down on a counter. I started talking to the guy behind the counter and he said, "Yeah, you know, they're starting to do your kind of thing. They might be worth you going to talk with."

So I went and saw them, SRD, Southern Record Distributors. And they have distributed me from Day One. This was one of the arms of Southern Records, who are separate but they have stuff like a Web site - on which we now have a mention. I was really lucky again there, because they were excellent. But they really were just beginning to do our sort of stuff. That October, I sent 'em down a copy of my new track and The Orbital Project - and they rang me. They said, "Your first one you had out, we've heard that on the pirates every day, all summer. So, definitely, we'll distribute your next one". I was like, "Oh, well, *that* was easy." At the time, they were small as well - which I liked. Full of crusty, indie people. But they had good attitude and, since I joined 'em, there have been lots of companies similar to my own which have come along and come on board.

When did you incorporate yourself as a company?

I founded Moving Shadow at Christmas of 1990, because I started having reliable financial comeback. I had my third EP out, which was "Charley Says" - the one The Prodigy clearly later listened to. I thought I'd do something different, so it was all done on white vinyl. I mean, there were the obvious connections with "charlie". Again, I did a lot of the distributing myself, taking the initial ones around to create the hype. I wasn't convinced at that time that Southern were capable of doing exactly what I wanted, so I created the demand first and actually sold about 2,000 of 'em for myself. It was so big and so hot, however, I eventually thought "OK, I'll hand this on to Southern."

Around that same time, I was once more starting to do some DJing. For myself, just in clubs and pubs. So there was me with a sound system, promoting it as well - this was outside London, in Hertfordshire. We did the first four months of '91 in the pub which was great! Because of going out, I met some guest DJs, people I brought in to join in on things. As it turns out, one of those guys is still with me - Sean O'Keefe, he's my graphic designer. And he's one of Two Bad Mice as well.

So you started working with other people?

That was kind of the time I started to do things so it wasn't just me. People knew that I'd made a record, they knew I had some gear at my house. It was just like, "OK, can I pop round?" We'd all sit round, with a bag of records to sample, and come up with ideas. That was when we started getting into Two Bad Mice - which was a name that came from one of the samples in our very first track. There was a bit in there out of a Wendy Craig narration, of a Beatrix Potter record. At the time, that was the kind of funny, cartoony things you'd try and sample. But the way she said it! I just thought, "That'll do!" Of course, there weren't two of us, there were three.

So, that was really the start. There were other people I was working with as well. The other guy I DJed with at the pub, we did three EPs together as Cosmo and Dibs. At the time, this music was called rave or techno. It was mixed or sampled and it was faster than house, 135 beats per minute which isn't fast at all. I remember doing one at 142, and we were going, "Oh, that's gettin' ridiculously fast!" But in them days a 128 track *was* really fast, just because the norm was 120-125.

Was this the moment techno went supersonic?

Well, it was the moment lots of people started to do things. That was when the speed increased dramatically. It went through a barrier and, suddenly, we were all doing stuff at 150, even 155. People did stuff at 165 and it was like, "Oh God!" It's like a guy thing, it was guys in a race. But the trick is, you *can* really make something sound good - really good - by just speeding it up. That's where all the chipmunk vocals and sounds like that come in. Because it's all energy, you don't even need drugs to feel it. It's just like, "Whoa! That's fast!" and it sets you up. So, that was all part of totally speeding it up.

Because of the style of the vocals, being that chipmunk style, you didn't really know how fast it was. All you knew was it is fast. I mean, it wasn't until 1995 that we went half-speed - because it had got a bit childish. A 160 or 165 track became the equivalent of 80 or 82 and a half.

What about the ragga influence?

Well, around 1991, 1992, it stopped being so chipmunky, then it went more ragga. That was the first time the ragga stuff started to come through. Those sort of high-energy samples fell off. And they were replaced by the more normal ragga and hip-hop samples, which are normally 80, 90 b.p.m. So you doubled the speed and they fitted, at 160-165. But it sounded different and the bassline started to change. It was not so techno-influenced. There was a lot of differences, like we started to use breakbeats. With those, again, we were right in the thick of it - with the early Two Bad Mice stuff. Straight breakbeats, all the way.

Had you wanted to use breakbeats?

Not particularly. At the time it was just something different. It wasn't like we were getting fed up. We were just looking for something different to use, rather than a 909 kick-drum and a hi-hat and that's it. We just wanted something with a bit more shuffle in it. So, a breakbeat off a hip-hop track, it was, "Let's put that in." And put that right at the end of these four-four kick drums. Then it was slowly taking over and the kick-drum was still there - all the way through - but, at the same time, you had a breakbeat rolling with it. Things were getting denser. For us, the bleepiness of techno was dying.

This was just us, of course. We were always trying something. But other people were taking an interest in us. We'd had about six or seven releases then. I started to get tapes, from people thinking we were this big label. Which, of course, we weren't. When people don't know who you are, they think you're Sony! The very first tape we ever got was Blame, a very early version of "Music Takes You". Which had a very big Seal sample in it, which got bootlegged as well, it was so popular. I tried to get permission to use it, which was the very first time we ever tried to get permission for a sample.

The only thing I got back from ZTT, who owned the rights, was that Seal's manager didn't want it to happen. But they wanted to put it out themselves, they were offering me £1,000. Like, "Hey Rob! Here's £1,000!" I was, like, "So?" Because I knew from the interest and from the records I'd already had out, pretty exactly what I was likely to make on it. I did offer it to 'em at a price, and they still weren't having it - even though, with their backing, it could have made the Top 40. So, we took the Seal sample out and we put it out, different mixes of it. We got remixes done and they were done by us, Two Bad Mice and Counts of Chemistry. We're both acts from Two Bad Mice - just different names.

What was the next step?

The next step only came, really, in late '94 and '95. All the other time, we had plenty of remixes to do for other people, we were trendy, we were underground. So a lot of people asked us to do remixes. Did plenty of them and it was nice, easy money. But it got in the way, because every new idea we had for a track would end up in a remix. We did 12 remixes over that period, and it really drained all our resources. The more business-orientated it's got, the more it's been, in a way, bad for me. Because, although it's fun doing this, it does take me further and further from making music. I just started off as a record company. But because of the natural progression and the level I was reaching, that led to my own publishing company. Then came merchandising, because we have a saleable, merchandisable item there, with credibility.

What advice would you have for others?

If you want to do it for yourself, have a go! I never thought about getting anyone else to do it. The first piece of vinyl, I didn't think about sending it to record companies. Never, ever thought of sending them a tape. Just had my own tunes and thought, "That'll be fun." Once I knew about it, found out about things like publishing, I learned you have to be eligible under the society's rules to be a publisher. But you find things out as you go along. Samples, for instance, can get very tricky. In the early days, when you're small, you don't realise what you're doing. Plus, at that low level, people aren't so bothered.

I found that out when we sampled big chunks of certain tunes and we had releases set. All of a sudden, we'd get a phone call from BMG saying, "Hold on, you've got a sample from X" and it wasn't a sample, it was a whole *capella*. But all we were selling of that was 3,000-4,000 units. Great for us, you know, lovely pocket money. But they had it in their minds it was gonna chart. So they were, "How high do you think it's gonna go?" And we were saying "High? Go? Go where?" Because we'd had nothing in the charts, not yet, not even in the Top 75. So they were saying, "OK, you can use it but we'd like to see what promotion you put behind it." Once they realised we just didn't do that, they were like, "Three thousand units? Three *thousand*? Uh, well, *Bye, then*." Which kind of gave us one more year's rope to hang ourselves with.

But, as time goes by, all these samples build up. And you do think, "Well, we really shouldn't be doing it." One, the whole style of sampling's becoming unfashionable. That's the way things go; everything will become live again. That's what we were up to by the mid-'90s. Two, the thing about samples is - we couldn't dream of getting away with it now. Not at the level we're at, not even if our sales were still only 3,000. We just know too many major labels now; we couldn't do it to 'em. We're like their dodgy cousin down from the country. We kind of play it by the book now. We're in the real world.

How did you meet Goldie?

Well, he was a graffiti artist - he still is. But he got into the music by hearing various records. And the one which made him want to have a go at the music, made him want to go out and meet some of these people so he could start doing it, was "Where Mouse", which is one of the first Two Bad Mice tracks. I'd met him out at Rage and at other places - and he made a point of hunting me down. He's the sort of guy who'll do that, hunt you down, congratulate you. He even tried to interview me for a film; he's got all this footage of people from that time. He made a ten- or twelve-minute pilot of it, just before he got his London Records deal. And it was great, too! It really was great to see all those people, shot around the middle of the '90s.

But he'd been doing his own stuff and that had been going out through Reinforced Records or Synthetic, which was kind of a hyped-up company, meant to pick up only on certain things. I think it was owned by EMI. He got a deal with them to do his early Metalheadz stuff. Which was selling loads but it wasn't loads to them, so they basically decided to stop doing it. He was also not getting on so well with Reinforced. Since he knew me, and we were going so many places together, we just planned to do some stuff. The first thing was a series that we were doing on Moving Shadow, which was the 201 series. There, the idea was to get a guest artist on one side of your vinyl and a Moving Shadow artist on the other. Just to bring through people we respected, whether they had their own labels or had just brought out white labels. Just people we could see were really gonna be an influence - or people who had already done that. We really wanted to pull them along as well, to show everyone, everyone does work together.

Did it work out like that?

Well, on the first one, I thought I'd put Goldie on one side and Cloud 9, which was one of my acts, on the other side. But I co-wrote and engineered and produced that track with Goldie, so it wasn't totally a stranger on the other side. But it was a good one to start with, and it was our first time working together. As I say, he was then falling out with Reinforced; he couldn't do any more with Synthetic. So he was looking at me to put out the new Metalheadz stuff. Therefore, we started working on the track "Timeless". Which got far beyond anything I wanted to put out - it ended up as a 22-minute track. I didn't want to hold it back, because there were now plenty of big people interested in it. Hence the story of Goldie and London Records. That's all I did for the whole of '95, I just worked with him on the Metalheadz album.

How would you yourself describe the sound you forged together?

On that album? There's a lot of - well, you can't even call it jungle, because after the media hype of 1994, that has such a *meaning*. But the sound is definitely aimed towards the drum'n'bass. Still, there's one track on it which doesn't have a breakbeat. It's just a total ballad: strings, atmospherics, eight whole minutes of vocals. I've never listened to an ambient track in my life, so I don't know a lot about ambient music. The style of it - I don't know where it comes from. But, with our stuff, I know the "ambient" side. It comes from all the sort of things we would sample, soul tracks, things like that, which you stretch and put effects on, to make them blend in and sound totally new within our tracks. That's what I would call the ambient side of jungle.

Writers use terms like ambient, techno and jungle; but do you really see the music as genres?

It's like, at one point, everyone was going along doing a similar thing. Then they start branching out. Because they're individuals, and they've all got their tastes and feelings. So they're parallel, but they're getting further apart. It's always changing, too, because as soon as we realise we've come up with something, we've already moved on. Which is not necessarily the best thing when it comes to making money. But you don't want to be a factory, either.

Doing remixes is both helpful and interesting. Because you might completely change a track, or you might use what's there. Either way, often it will be something you wouldn't have gone out and listened to. So to have to work like that gives you new ideas, helps you broaden out. Always moving on: that's what it's all about.

Bally Sagoo is the first music producer of Indian origin to cross over into the global mainstream. Yet another British-based DJ who started out with remixes, he ended up a solo star breaking barriers on Radio One and Top of the Pops. Bally's hit albums "Bollywood Flashback" and "Rising From the East" awakened folk around the world to an Asian Britain - and the unique role it plays in modern culture. Here, he talks with Nyan Bushan, another pioneer. Bushan is Editor of India's *CONNECT* magazine. *CONNECT*, which was born in 1990, covers international entertainment - but from a new, evolving Asian perspective. In 1995, it became the first Indian magazine to publish online (at http://www.netropolis.org/connect).

Nyan: How did the Bally Sagoo sound come about?

Bally: When we moved to England from Delhi, I was about seven months old. My parents are very traditional and so they should be. I went through a struggle in the early years, being brought up in a black area, not having too many Asian friends, losing my identity as a British citizen really, not knowing what India was all about. I mean, I was one hundred per cent kala (black). This was when I was probably 15, I was listening to what was called "electro" in those days, the early '80s.

I got into remixing with my friends in my bedroom. I always dreamt of having a pair of Technics turntables, because it was the Rolls Royce of mixers. I couldn't afford them, though, so we were using turntables with no kind of pitch control where you could speed up or slow down a record. That's really how I got my experience. I was getting so much into remixing, that every time I heard a record, I was instantly doing something different with it. And I was getting so much credit from the black crowd because I was beating the black guys at their own game. It was a compliment.

Nyan: What about the Indian music around you?

Bally: The music scene was very traditional - Indian music was Indian music, Hindi music was Hindi music, bhangra music was very, very Alaap: that band were the pioneers. I did not go to the Indian parties; I did not hang out with Indian people; I didn't like Asian girls, to be honest. I was too much into the hip-hop side of things. I think, as the years went on, it worked to my advantage, because then I realised, "Listen, I am Asian when I look in the mirror. My parents are speaking Punjabi, I eat with my hands and not with a knife and fork. Yet, when I walk out the door, I am walking with a little bounce."

Bally Sagoo:

king of the "New Asian Kool"

By the mid-80s, my parents could see what I was doing. While other guys were doing things like studying hard in their bedroom, I was remixing. I was not good at studies, I got kicked out of college, kicked out of school, I got no education - I was so into my music. But then, with all the groundwork I built in the early '80s, I adopted that feel to Asian music. By 1987-88, I started remixing Punjabi by making the sound more beefy. By turbo-charging the backing track, and giving them a whole new injection.

Then I would rotate those tapes at shows where the crowd was freaking out to Western music and then they would just go ape. When they heard an Asian song sounding so beefy, because Indian songs don't have basslines. And, now, it is a trend. What started out a demo turned out to be a road to changing the whole world music scene. I feel like I am a trend-setter worldwide, giving influence to a lot of DJs and mixers. And now, people respect DJs more for what they do. People always thought that DJs just stand there and play records one by one. They don't realise how much of an art it is.

Nyan: You're now signed to Columbia as an artist/producer. Can you be specific about the deal?

Bally: It's a five year deal and all I've got to do is what I've been doing in the past five years. Give them albums with good material and good production, my kind of music. Which they will release in the Western market. They are focusing on me as a Jazzie B for the Asian market. I have artistic freedom to pick up new talent and produce material with them. Every week, I am looking for new singers.

The gora (white) market doesn't know the Asian side of things; we are educating them. In all their interviews, Columbia was quoted as saying the best signing they ever did is Bally Sagoo - simply because they feel that they have been part of breaking world music mainstream. They want part of the struggle to break Asian music into the Western world. Because they can see how the Enigmas and the Youssou N'Dours have broken into the charts and created major mayhem all over. It's just because there are not so many Asian people in the business that, in the Western market, we get brushed aside. They think we all wear salwars and pajamas.

It is for us to educate them: us, the Western Asian youth who grew up with two cultures. Our parents wanted to listen to Rafi, when we wanted to listen to Shabba Ranks. This is where people like me come along and throw them both into the arena and, Pow! It comes across as a major hit and now it's the in thing. So everybody wants to jump on the bandwagon.

Nyan: Your famous track "Mera Lwang Gwacha" mixed traditional Punjabi vocals with the reggae vocals of Birmingham's white rapper Cheshire Cat. How did you meet?

Bally: Cheshire Cat is the baddest white DJ in the world; he is bigger than Snow. He has a huge fan base in England through "Mera Lwang Gwacha". Everybody who hears his voice says, "This guy is not a gora", and they have a major culture shock when they see his face. It is the same with me - people hear my work and think it is the work of a white guy. I met Cheshire through a friend when I was working on "Mera".

I needed a rapper and a friend who knew Cheshire brought him over. I said, "What the hell, why did you bring him for?" Because Cheshire looks like a Status Quo, Bon Jovi kind of guy. But when he got on the mike, I was amazed. So I put him on the song and everybody went mad. Then I put him on "Chura Liya". You've seen the magic between him and Malkit Singh (when they performed live at Delhi's Fireball nightclub). Two different guys, one with locks singing ragga and the other with ear-rings singing desi. They go together, beautifully, like roti and dal.

Nyan: What DJs or producers have influenced you?

Bally: People I have always looked up to are David Morales, Jimmy Jam and Terry Lewis (early Prince associates and producers for Janet Jackson) and Teddy Riley (the "New Jack Swing" king who produced Michael Jackson's "Dangerous"). I would like to portray myself as one of them, in being Asian, making beats very funky and heavy. If you listen to a song like "Wada Na Tod" (off "Bollywood Flashback"), that's a typical Jam and Lewis production. No one would believe that a Mr Singh produced that track! That's what the black magazines have said. Because I have lived my life amongst black people in Birmingham and that's the kind of music I grew up to.

I think we will see a change in the music scene worldwide. Indian Asian music is going to explode on the map, just like raggamuffin came on the scene from Jamaica. That is what is going to happen with New Asian Kool - which is more than simply bhangra.

Nyan: Yes, but how much of the New Asian Kool will come from India? You have said you haven't heard the music of any of the new Indian singers. But is that because they haven't crossed over into your scene?

Bally: Indian stars haven't crossed over so far because they just go up the street and come back round the other side. They never make it to the airport. The other thing is - no disrespect to anybody - those kinds of songs are not up to world standards. When you deal with the UB40s, the U2s and the Enigmas, you are dealing with experts. If you want to go mainstream, those are the people you are competing with.

I'm not saying the Indian sound can never be part of the New Asian Kool. I just think at the moment it is not of that standard - simply because the knowledge, the experience, the production does not stand up to the Western market's. But it also works the other way around. There is no way somebody like me can make a pure Hindi song the way the guys do it here because India is the master of making a Hindi track. But, when India wants to make a Western track, in the Western style, it doesn't stand up. This "I am too sexy for my T-shirt" influence in Indian films does not stand up internationally.

I am working on some Hindi film songs but they will be in my own style. I can only do what I am good at doing - which is making Western Asian music. I have been making my kind of music for over 15 years; India has been making its own for hundreds of years. It's like, where is the best place in the world to make rock music? It's America. That's why, when it came to looking for tracks for "Bollywood Flashback", we had to go to Bombay.

Nyan: How do you compare the audiences in India to the Asians in Britain?

Bally: The crowd in London is more desi and wild. I found the nightclubs in India more tame and very Western. I can't have a long session of bhangra music there, because they want to listen to more international music. It sounds very funny, how India is more modern than the Indians in England. But I can tell you that, because I have played in nightclubs across the world. The crowds in India are so modern, you could be in New York, you could be in a club in Paris. The beauty is it's a good feeling that they are Asians.

Nyan: Your first release after "Bollywood Flashback" was "Aby Baby" with Amitabh Bachchan (the Indian film superstar). How did you approach it?

Bally: I wanted to give him a Barry White sort of feel, with his deep baritone voice-over as part of "Kabhie Kabhie" - which was the first single. Gregorian chants give it a gospel monk feel, an Enigma vibe. "Kabhie Kabhie", it's such a beautiful production - and the saxophone instrumental version is a beautiful mix. It features a serious black American saxophonist called Najee. He is like a Kenny G, and all the serious black guys worldwide rate him big time. I have been a big fan of his since I was a kid; to get him to play the sax on one of my tracks was a big honour. Of course, the video for the song is fantastic. Everybody is shocked! This is Amitabh like they had never seen before. You don't watch the song, you just drift on a blue cloud. You relax; you unwind; you chill. And that's what the song is about. I have given it a slow jam feel.

Nyan: What was the major difference between "Bollywood Flashback" and "Aby Baby"?

Bally: "Flashback" was more Stateside and "Aby" was what Amitabh wanted. "Flashback" was my show, my call on everything. "Aby" - it's totally an Amitabh project; I was employed as music director. But "Rising From the East" is me - my inner skills. Leaving "Flashback" far behind, introducing new material. Now, I am not just a remixer, I am a trendy Asian music producer with the flag on my head. In 1992, I did "Magic Touch" new material featuring Nusrat (superstar Nusrat Fateh Ali Khan). But people still called me a remixer. With "Rising From the East", I went to India - and recorded vocals for new songs. I also went to Pakistan for the Punjabi songs. They are rendered by famous film singers, like Shabnam Majid, Sham Shaq Anwar and a big qawwali singer called Ali Khan - who looks and sings like Nusrat. I used big, dramatic sounds.

Nyan: You said "Bollywood Flashback" had a mission, and it was going to tell the world something. Did that happen?

Bally: It achieved more - international status worldwide. I didn't realise it was going to become an anthem. "Flashback" crossed over simply because of my name, because I had previous underground albums. Word of mouth got out; the first single, "Chura Liya", became the talk of town, the talk of two countries: the UK and India. Everybody was buying it; blacks, Asians, whites - the old and the young. I know what the Asian people like to hear. I was interested to know what people wanted worldwide. I hit the key right on the head and the proof was in the pudding. That album was available in chart retail shops, like Our Price. And it was filed under "B", next to Bruce Springsteen. It was not hidden under any crappy section. Right this second, three years down the road, people are still talking about it.

Nyan: On "Rising From The East", what was the agenda?

Bally: It's a culture clash. It's coming from the East and rising in the West. So the title says it all. It's a statement by Asian people: where we are coming from, what I am about, what the album's about, what my music is about, and what I am trying to achieve. It's brand-new music, powerful lyrics and very, very serious musical production. The first single, "Dil Cheez", is a slow song by a girl called Shabnam Majid. It's got some beautiful Arabic vibes to it. The B side features "Teri Ankhiyan", a Punjabi dance track - but very Western, i.e. house beats with a heavy organ sound. There is also a girl rapping; very much like a housey song and a bit like the girl in 2 Unlimited.

Nyan: What were your expectations from that album?

Bally: For "Rising" to be marked as an album that linked people together all over the world. Musically, it's far superior to everything I had done. I got big phat sounds like mandolins and instruments from other countries - tablas drifting in the background and great vocals. It is a cry from the East, from the Arabian side and Egyptian side of things. It's not just India, India; it's something from those Sinbad, Ali Baba days. I think everybody will get into it. I hope "Rising" will answer for the Asian success story: speak to the Macarenas, the Youssou N'Dours, the Deep Forests.

Now is the best time we have ever had, simply because Asian music is sounding great. So many great videos, so many great tracks. There is some genuine talent coming out, not just from the UK but also from India. Now, it's like the whole world wants to be part of India. It's like if you are Asian, you are lucky - because you have the best of both worlds. Others have only got one world; we have the West *and* East.

Nyan: You are also in demand in the Japanese market. How did that come about?

Bally: Sony/Epic in Tokyo got a big demand for my material, as in past hits like "Chura Liya". Japanese DJs play my tracks - I have been told by them that my songs like "Gur Nalon Ishq Mitha" (the Malkit Singh bhangra hit) are played in Tokyo nightclubs. So they gave me vocals by a singer called Sandy, who is a sort of Japanese Madonna. She sells millions of records in Japan, and I did a remix for her called "Hi Hi", which became such a hit, it outsold the original. From there onwards, I was bombarded with Japanese remixes. But I do a lot of world music - just because it shows you that a Punjabi boy like me, coming from India, I can do most things, man.

Nyan: After the success of "Flashback", how close are you to working with the major international stars?

Bally: I have got no problems doing remixes for major stars, since I have access to them through Sony. But I want to concentrate on doing my stuff; I don't want to be seen only as a remixer. I want to show my skills and my own music. In the future, I will probably do some remixes for your Mariah Careys, your Jackos and your Springsteens. But, at the moment, my goal is to put an Asian song in the Western market - right alongside your Madonnas and your Jackos. Because if the Macarenas and them people can do it, why can't we? An Asian song hasn't gone to number one yet, but I'm not going to give up!

Nyan: One of the highlights in your career has been your collaboration with Nusrat Fateh Ali Khan. With "Magic Touch 2" did people still say Nusrat was selling out? Or was that debate now outdated?

Bally: People's tastes change with the times. As long as you keep giving them the goods, you are fine. Nusrat had done Western things, "Kinha Sohna" and "Mera Piya" are played in every nightclub in the world. His traditional songs are played in every house in the world. He appeared in Hollywood with Madonna and all these other people were falling on their feet. They couldn't take it! People were so fascinated with his voice. Look at Nusrat's collaboration with Pearl Jam's Eddie Vedder (on the movie soundtrack to *Dead Man Walking*). Again, it shows you, there is no limit to what can be done.

When I did "Magic Touch", people didn't think it could be done in a Western way. But that didn't stop me. Then, Nusrat himself was doing Western songs. You know, he had it in his blood same as Amitabh. Amitabh is going to J49's (the Birmingham nightclub);

and he sees everyone rocking away and he thinks, "I want to be blasting out of their sound system". Once, "Kabhie Kabhie" couldn't get blasted in a nightclub. Now it can.

Nyan: Let's go back to your bhangra roots. Today, the British bhangra sound seems to have been sidelined by the overkill of Bollywood remixes and Indian pop. Is that unfair for bhangra?

Bally: My last big bhangra production was "Gur Nalon Ishq Mitha". That was a long time ago. It is true to say that Hindi fusion is in and, in fact, it's sad because everybody is jumping on the bandwagon and it's taking the piss. Bhangra is still there but, at the moment, more attention is being paid to the Hindi side. But I will be doing traditional Punjabi productions for my Punjabi brothers and sisters all over the world who like that kind of music. People ask me when am I going to do another "Jugnee"; my answer is that it will be coming soon.

But I don't want to be governed. From 1992 to 1996, all my albums were Punjabi remixes. A couple of years ago, I had demand from people saying, "Try something Hindi". So I said "OK, I'll try it because you told me" - and "Bollywood Flashback" was born. Because of the language barrier, it may be bhangra can't sell to a bigger audience. It's a strong dialect. And, obviously, the bottom line is that all over the world, more people are tuned in to Hindi songs so they have a bigger audience. You've got to do what everybody wants to hear as well. However, I want to do both Punjabi and Hindi. I was the king of bhangra remixes. Now I am the king of *Asian* remixes.

Nyan: What do you have to say about upcoming British Asian artists?

Bally: There is now this whole army of DJs, producers and remixers and there are a lot of copycats. I don't really look at what they are doing; I lock myself up in my studio and I do my own thing. That's what it's all about. I have got a tremendous amount of pressure on my shoulders because everybody listens to my work and regards me as the icon, the originator. There are a lot of imitators, but there's good talent. I still admire Indian music film directors who are doing well - like A. R. Rahman. I do listen when I can. The only man I have always admired from day one is S. R. D. Burman (the late, legendary Bollywood music director). You can listen to his tunes any time, any place, and they are funky. If you listen to "Dum Maaro Dum" (a '70s classic), it still sounds like it came out last week.

Nyan: The basslines on your songs are a test for any system.

Bally: Of course they are! I have been known as the Bass Doctor. I do severe damage to people's speaker systems. Guaranteed, or your money back! My studio is a bass surgery, I always push the limits. People all over the world have flipped on my bass. They ask me how I get it; I'm never going to tell them!

Nyan: One last question. Do you always have some idea of what's going to work?

Bally: I have an idea, but I never know. I just pray to God, please, Babajee, make this big for me. I don't know what the public is going to like. I have nine big albums behind me, so I am very fortunate. But you can always tell a Bally Sagoo tune. I don't know what it is - maybe the way I work. I like to make an intro to a song and flirt with it, before the vocals come in. I like to have the mid-eight and that makes your head start swinging. When it sounds good in the studio, then I know it's going to sound terrific out there. I have a terrific sound system in my studio, and in my car, and in my home. When I hear the song with my friends and their heads are shaking, then I know: it's road tested! It's working; I know, it's having the effect.

CHAPTER 8

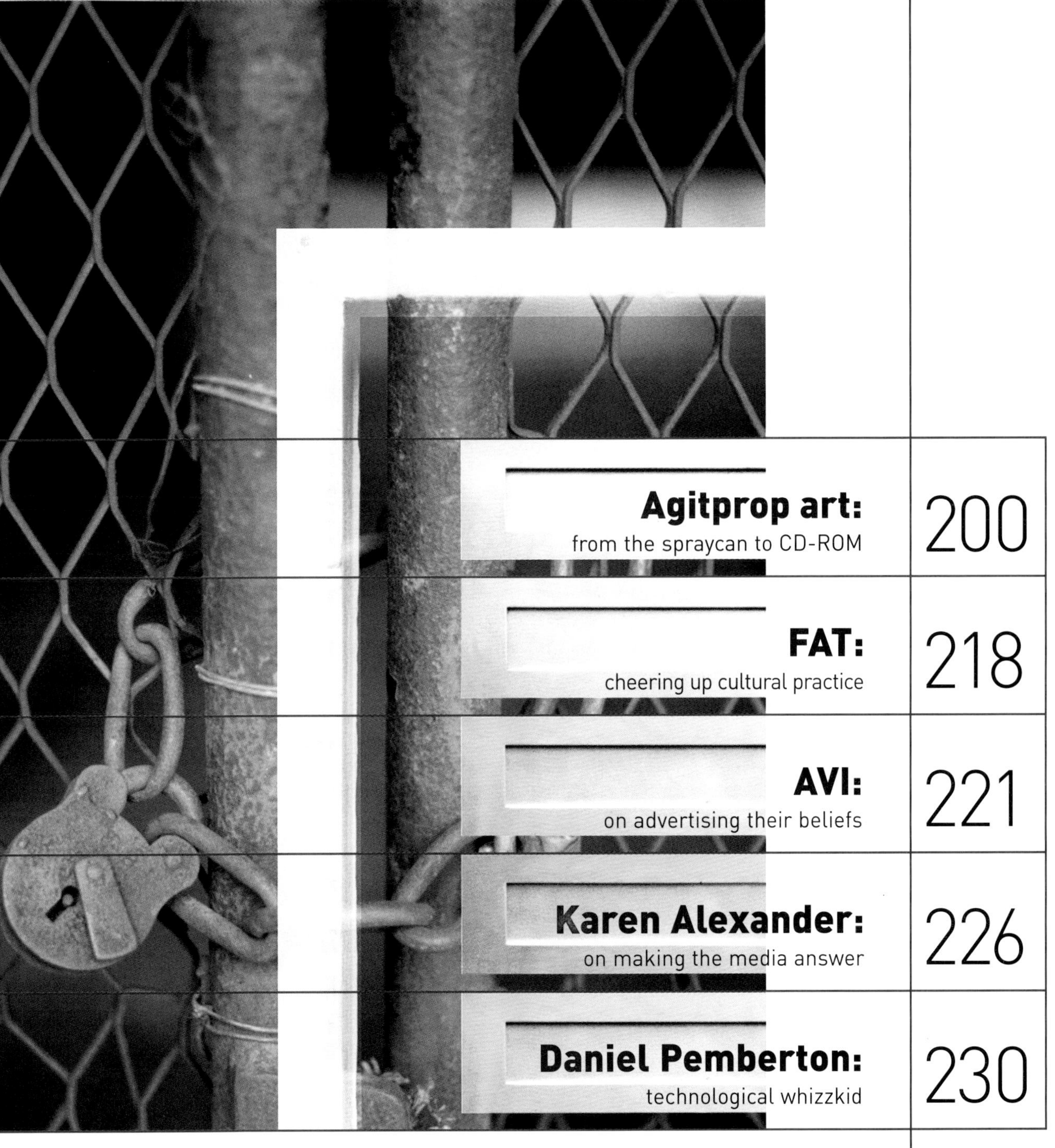

CHAPTER EIGHT

1

2

Agitprop art:
from the spraycan to CD-ROM

Mixology - the fusing and juxtaposing of different worlds - now has no more pervasive arena than Britain's daily life. Merely in the course of living, travelling and working, we are barraged by countless electronic symbols, printed slogans and visual icons. These range from the seductions of advertisements to the faces (on television and in the flesh) of the homeless.

Most of us now take such strange disparities for granted; we expect to see real beggars under the ads for *Les Miserables*. But, for some Britons, this becomes art's raw material. Theirs is an agitprop art, a reaction to surreal circumstance - but a reaction which seeks to assert morality.

Agitprop art has had a long British history. Like much of UK fashion, like much modern music, it often finds a way to use "found materials". Billboards become the subject of its alterations; promotional flyers carry its political parodies; art's market and its awards become its targets - rather than the ways it seeks approbation. From the simplest of tools, the graffiti spraycan, to the grandest - the annual Turner Prize - '90s agitprop artists have displayed a taste for intervention.

Increasingly, they have also drawn on a global audience, and its emerging, international youth consciousness. This is the same consciousness exploited by those advertisers who aim to sell Levis, Pepsi and MTV. But the guerrilla practitioner views both the products and the process differently. In the late '80s, the KLF ("Kopyright Liberation Front") subverted both pop songs and the national charts. In '94, they disrupted the annual Turner Prize - and went on to continue questioning the role of money.

Groups like "AVI" do the same for billboard adverts, which they change to question the whole idea of slogans and context. "Who is enfranchised?" they seek to ask. Collectives such as Fat (Fashion, Architecture, Taste) take on yet another range of targets: from traditional architecture to the Royal Academy - or the way a London nightclub is designed. Pop tunes, nightspots, the logos of trendiness; all of these can play a role in agitprop art.

This was always a practice which could bridge cultures, resulting in Graffiti Summits and world-wide word-of-mouth publicity. Now, agitprop art can also bridge economics. One doesn't have to be poor to work as an agitprop artist. But, with both

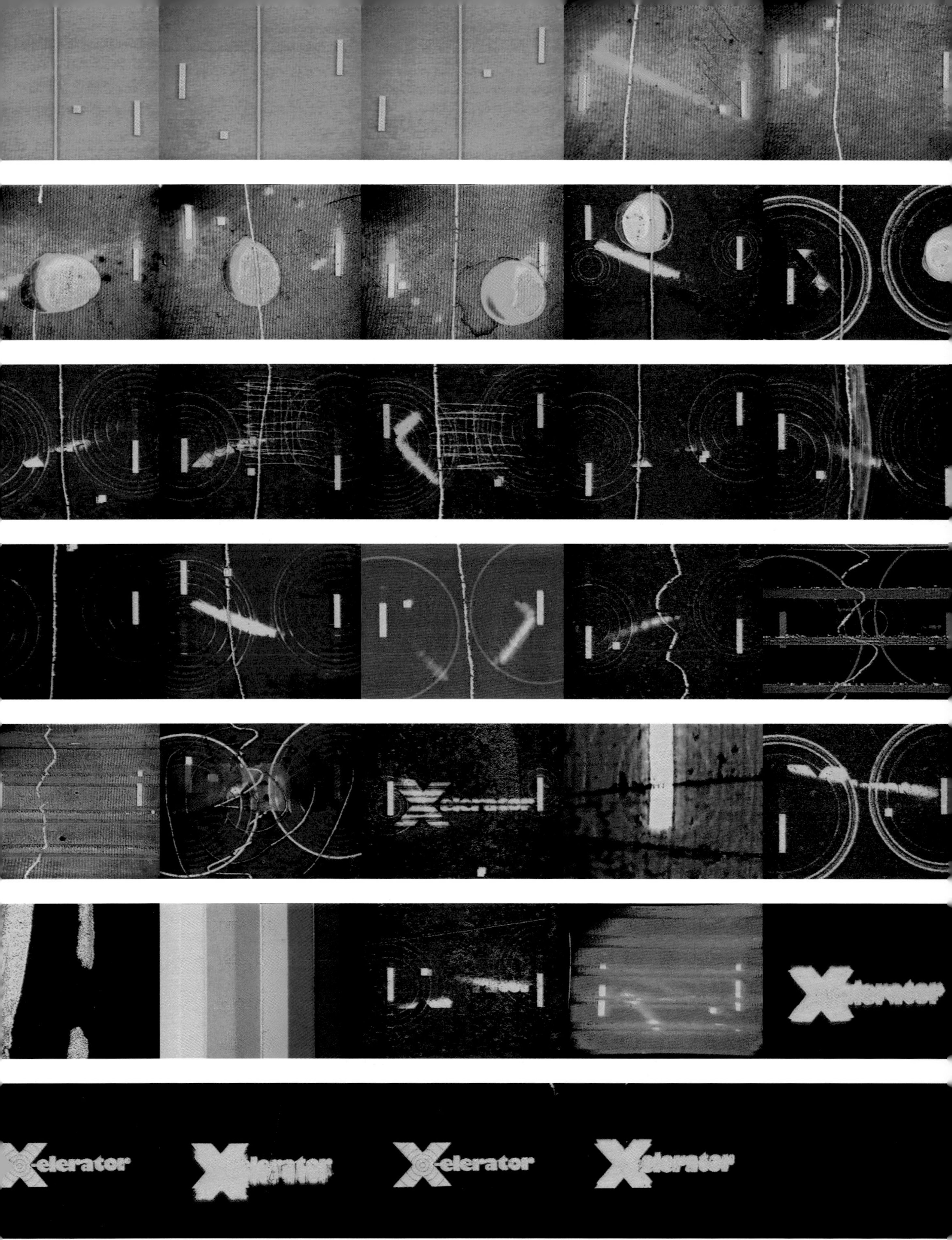

3

adverts *and* the art world supplying the targets, anyone can function in this role. All one has to do is frame the questions.

It may seem like a David and Goliath scenario. But British wit and ingenuity prime the slingshot. Plus, even if they do make separate demands, the *status quo* and its opposition now share their tools. Agitprop art mirrors struggle and dissatisfaction. But, just as clearly, it mirrors progress. This can be seen in the use of new technologies - for sampling, bootlegging, graphic theft and parody.

Critics speak of "radical art" as a discrete genre, an *oeuvre* fit to be academically logged and studied. This has led to the celebration of certain works as icons, artefacts like Jamie Reid's cover for "God Save the Queen"; 1979's *Labour Isn't Working* Tory billboard; 1984's *Gone with the Wind* poster (with Thatcher and Reagan); the KLF's hijacking of Rachel Whiteread's Turner Prize. These images are enshrined as the bearers of potent memories. Yet many practitioners see such nostalgia as worthless. Others go further and contend it is downright dangerous.

Conrad Atkinson, now in his fifties, is one of Britain's best-known and canniest political artists. He speaks, teaches and collaborates around the world. ("Every time I do a show in Britain," he likes to say, "I then have to leave the country for a while.") The soft-spoken Atkinson went to art school with John Lennon; he was born in Cleator Moor, part of Wordsworth's scenic West Cumbria. He credits that romantic heritage with his ideals. But he also cites its less famous realities: the illness and dangers of life in mine and mill. These, he notes, helped give him a politics. "I try to render visible", Atkinson says firmly, "the invisible things which control how we see."

Atkinson's very first exhibit, 25 years ago, resulted in the unionising of a factory. His most notorious, *A Children's Story: For H.M.*, was censored by the Arts Council before it could open. (The piece questioned why the Royal Warrant was held by Distillers - the corporation accused of negligence with Thalidomide.) Atkinson has been taken to court, banned, cancelled and hounded. Yet he retains great enthusiasm, excitement and humour. "Oh, I've been through some really Kafka-esque stuff. But then, some people probably told Goya, 'Lighten up!'"

For a quarter of a century, Atkinson has produced paintings, sculpture, prints, and constructions which have been seen in Britain, the States, Russia, and Europe. His work is shown in trade union halls, in Underground stations and on the sides of buses - as well as galleries, universities and museums. For the younger generation of agitprop artists, his work has perhaps been the defining influence. It is not so much that they know his name, but that, in Britain's art world, he pioneered their tools. Atkinson is deft at interventions; he made it feasible for "low" art to comment on "culture".

At the very end of the '80s, Atkinson was working with posters, huge fake versions of pages from the *Financial Times*, *Wall Street Journal* and *Le Figaro*. He would "intervene" in their versions of the news, replacing "official" commentators with art-world pundits - speakers such as Fra Angelico or Leonardo da Vinci. In addition to appearing in

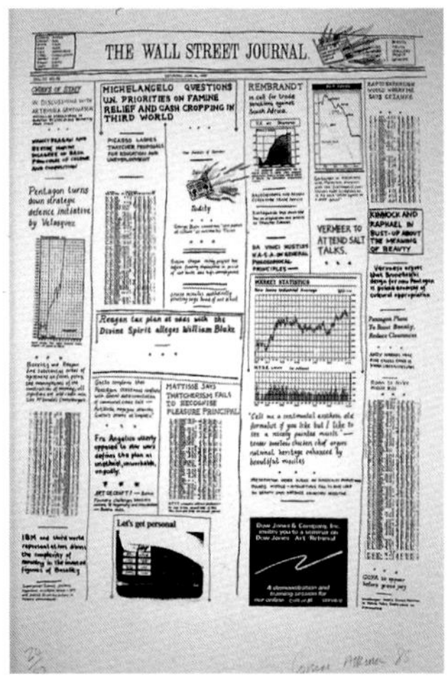

1

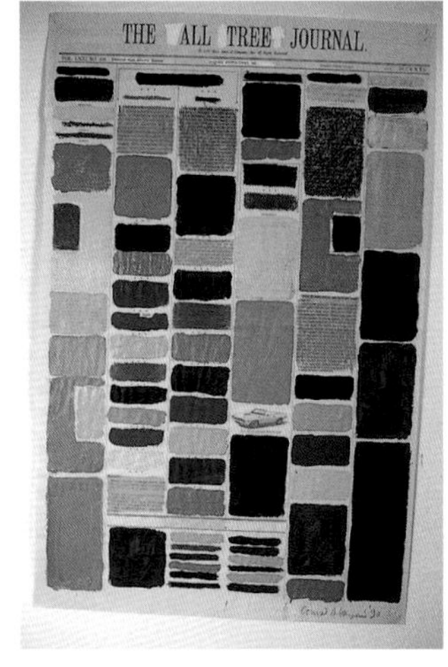

2

3

galleries and on television, these pages were also made up as giant posters. They were then mounted as "ads" in two central Underground stations.

Atkinson has never liked playing the "elder statesman". He stays in constant touch with young artists and with new music, trends and sounds. "You can hear the Third World in Western music", he likes to say. At the beginning of the '90s, Atkinson took on new metaphors. He designed a set of banners for Glasgow's Sports Stadium, which depicted a typical set of footballers. This time, each wore a jersey with a provocative slogan (such as "*Bizarre Politics Disguised as Actions*"; "*Artists Safely Back in Galleries Says Police Chief*" or "*Competing Ideologies Often Take Bizarre Life Forms*").

In '92, he mounted *For Emily*: a two-part installation based on *Wuthering Heights* and sited near Halifax. With it, Atkinson reinstated the novel's centre: how race and class can destroy, as well as shape, destiny. He zeroed in on the race of Emily Brontë's Heathcliff (whose origins, in the novel, are kept mysterious). For Atkinson's purposes, he became an Asian Briton.

The one-time factory where he worked gave him the central idea: to design and make a pair of large carpets. These Atkinson produced in collaboration with Asian locals. The finished pieces contained 15 colours and were patterned with text, knives and animal figures. Wrote one critic, Nima Poovaya-Smith, "The motifs link them with Islamic carpets, particularly prayer mats which are woven with calligraphic designs. The calligraphy usually embodies passages from the Koran and serves a talismanic purpose."

For Emily and its companion, *Zones of Gold*, told their story in a series of installations. The carpets were supported by a pantheon of "Welcome" signs, which alluded to the "welcome" symbols of the subcontinent: writings in rice flour; strings of mango leaves; and mats made out of coir. There was also a wall of windows - an allusion to Brontë's symbol for seeing while excluded. (Heathcliff and Cathy, joined, look in on a richer family - one whose status will soon part them; later, Cathy's ghost hammers at another window, in her desperate search for redemption.) Atkinson filled his windows with different hands. *Their* palms were painted with henna, and contained Emily Brontë's words - in Urdu.

If the Urdu, the calligraphy and the text invoked Islam, a cross-shaped installation of freezers invoked the Christian world. These contained gilded shoes, gilded books and golden trophies - parodies

Previous pages:
1. Billboard by AVI
Conform / Consume
2. Home Ideals
An inter-disciplinary project located in three London sites, supported by the Arts Council. Aug '94 - June '95
Fat
3. Video grabs
MTV title sequence
X-elerator
Design: Paul Ayre

1. The Wall Street Journal
Watercolour - 24" X 28"
Conrad Atkinson, '89
2. The All Tree Journal
Acrylic on newspaper
Conrad Atkinson, '89
3. Le Monde
Silkscreen - 24" X 28"
Conrad Atkinson, '89
4. Madonna with St John
From Mining Culture, '96
Glaze transfer with hand painting on biscuitware
9" X 5" X 5.5"
Conrad Atkinson
5. The K.L.F.
Photo: Ralph Perou

SO MANY ARTISTS ARE BEING ASKED TO DO PUBLIC WORK, AS IF ART CAN EXTEND ITS HAND EVERYWHERE. I DON'T THINK YOU CAN EFFECTIVELY DO THAT EVERYWHERE. THINGS CAN BE DONE, BUT THEY'RE BETTER NOT CALLED ART.
(→PAGE 222)

4

5

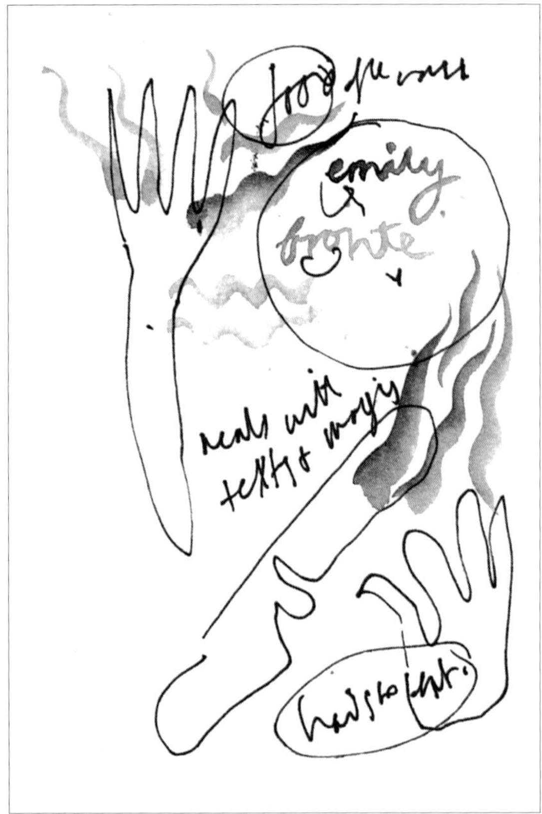

1

THE Sun
EXCLUSIVE
JACKSON POLLOCK EDITION
FRONT PAGE ABSTRACT EXPRESH STYLE RIDDLE
BREAKFAST AT THE WHITEHOUSE
thanX jackson

2

3

STATE
OF READINESS
welcome

4

5

transient
transient

6

7

8

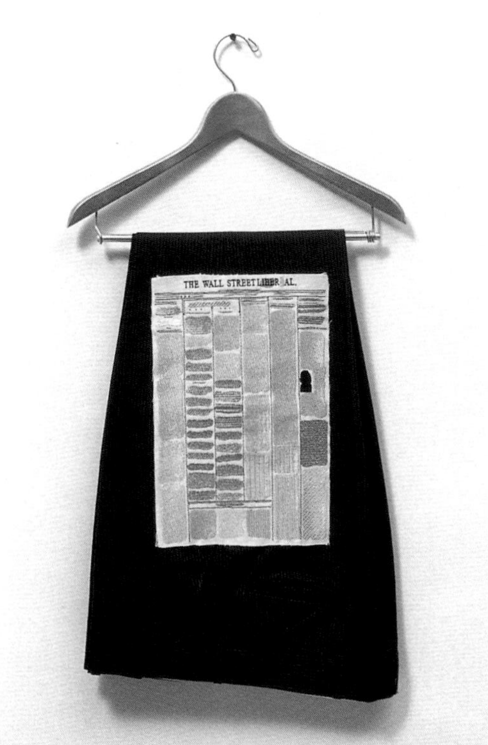

9

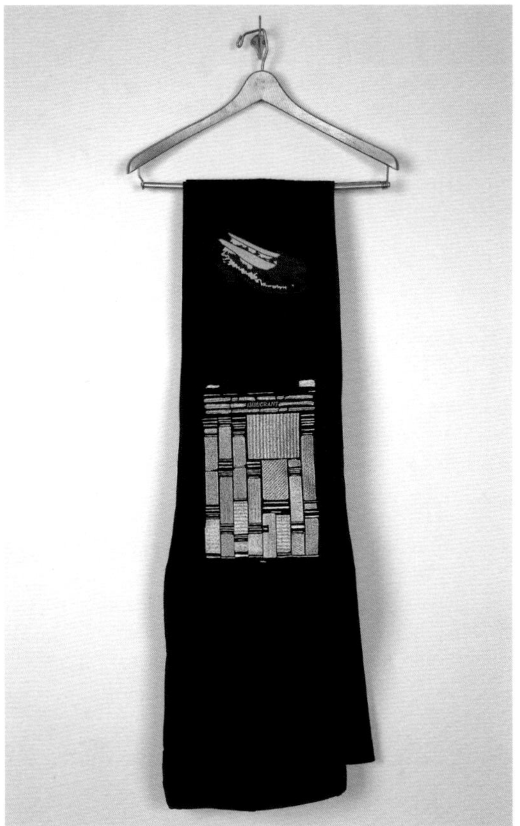

10

1. Page from the book:
   For Emily
   Conrad Atkinson - '92
2. Thanx Jackson
   The Sun
   Front Page Abstract Expresh
   Style Riddle - oil on canvas
   40" X 30" - collection of Mr
   and Mrs Syd Banks
   Photo: D. James Dee
   Conrad Atkinson - '88
3. The Seductiveness of The End
   of The World
   coir mat, 60" X 40"
   Photo: D. James Dee
   Conrad Atkinson - '86 - '87
4. State of Readiness
   coir mat, 30" X 40"
   Conrad Atkinson - '86 - '87
5. State of Decay
   coir mat, 30" X 40"
   Conrad Atkinson - '86 - '87
6. Ruby Slippers
   From the exhibition
   'Transient' (Visual Arts UK)
   at Tullie House Museum
   Photo: Guy Pawle
   Conrad Atkinson - '96
7. The Wicked Proposition of
   the World - installation with
   glitter shoes and boots and
   embroidered labels -
   14' diameter
   Photo: Zindman/Fremont
   Conrad Atkinson - '95
8. A Dying and Minority Art
   Form
   Canvas, thread, trousers,
   acrylic, hanger - 38" X 17"
   Photo: D. James Dee
   Conrad Atkinson - '95
9. Silver, Gold, Ruby
   Canvas, thread, trousers,
   acrylic, hanger - 38" X 17"
   Photo: Zindman / Fremont
   Conrad Atkinson - '97
10. Conrad Atkinson
    Photo: P. K. Gill

WE'RE INTERESTED IN THE CITY AS A GALLERY, BUT ALSO IN THE NOTION OF AUTHORSHIP. (→PAGE 218)

WE NEED A SITUATION WHERE A SMALL AMOUNT OF TEXT CAN TRANSFORM THE WHOLE BILLBOARD BECAUSE OUR RESOURCES ARE LIMITED. (→PAGE 221) of awards from the British sporting world. On them appeared speech familiar from everyday life (*"I don't understand men"*), side by side with phrases taken from *Wuthering Heights* (*"Shall my heart quarrel with my pulse?"*).

Critics saw here Britain's best agitprop art: inventive and imaginative; modern yet historical. It was mixology with a political purpose - but one which was both considered and inclusive. By contrast, two years later, couturier Karl Lagerfeld made front pages, with his own allusion to Islam. Muslims were outraged when, on model Claudia Schiffer, Lagerfeld launched a strapless, sexy ballgown. Its bodice was embroidered with words from the Koran.

To Lagerfeld, the script had offered merely a novel pattern. As a story in the *Evening Standard* revealed, "Lagerfeld said he was 'terribly sorry' and that he didn't know the passage was from the Moslem holy book. He said he was told it was a love poem in memory of a *maharani*, or Indian princess."

Conrad Atkinson believes agitprop must be accessible. But he knows that such work is never simple. Most recently, he has worked with issues such as the banning of land mines and the global problems of immigration. His tools - as well as his targets - include e-mail, multimedia formats and the World Wide Web. They connect the world, he knows, but may not confer unity. Or, as he puts it now, "We have to recognise that truth is obscured, it's not easy to recognise. And that its use as a weapon is shot through with contradictions."

All UK agitprop artists know that the world is shrinking: thanks to fax machines, modems and satellite broadcasts. Yet separate cultures will continue to differ, even as they rapidly adopt each other's symbols, broadcasts and causes. One of Atkinson's favourite stories concerns an ad-man from Coca-Cola, charged with introducing that US totem to China. Carefully, his team chose a very respectful slogan: "Coke Adds Life". But, laughs Atkinson, "In *Chinese*, that translates as 'Coke revives your dead ancestors'!"

Agitprop art has ever-changing heroes and pin-ups. Often, they deliberately decide to remain anonymous. In the mid-'90s, cheap street posters "outed" John Major. Not as a homosexual, but as "mediocre". *"Under nice Mr Major,"* read one example, *"1,000 families in London become homeless every month"*. The piece was one of many issued under the logo "Direct Faction". Conrad Atkinson has no idea who they may be. But he is an admirer. "That is the real thing; that is agitprop art. It's not something you go and look up in an art-school library. It's an integral reflection of your daily life."

AVI (sometimes billed as "Active Visual Intervention") also admire the modesty of those flyers. They themselves exploit the huge budgets and vast reach of adverts, because their primary canvas is the billboard. Using typefaces they can generate on a computer, AVI act as "hitpersons" who change the billboards' slogans - and politicise their large, lavish ads. A slogan for water privatisation, for instance, may read *It's not2 late2 apply for shares*. Clearly, it invokes the "class" of ads for Perrier water. AVI alter it to supply their own rejoinder: *You already eaun it*.

AVI's work has been extensively reviewed in the media. But AVI - "Gavin" and "David" named it for three shared initials - have "fairly negative" feelings when it comes to mainstream media. Still, they are animated about the issues involved. They talk of sampling, imitation, replication and appropriation. What's more, like Atkinson, they see it all historically. Says Gavin, "Just take a walk through the National Gallery. They were doing all this stuff in 1500."

Adds David, "The questions which matter in agitprop art are very basic. 'Who's really talking?' and 'Who's *dis*empowered?'" He rather hopes their

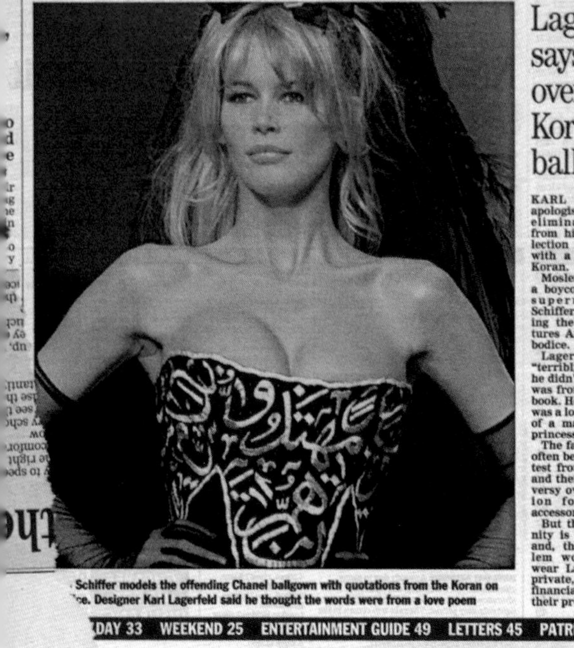

Lagerfeld says sorry over Koran ballgown

KARL LAGERFELD has apologised to Moslems and eliminated a ballgown from his new Chanel collection which was printed with a passage from the Koran.

Moslem clerics called for a boycott of Chanel after supermodel Claudia Schiffer was pictured wearing the dress, which features Arabic script on the bodice.

Lagerfeld said he was "terribly sorry" and that he didn't know the passage was from the Moslem holy book. He said he was told it was a love poem in memory of a maharani, or Indian princess.

The fashion industry has often been the focus of protest from religious groups and there has been controversy over the recent fashion for crucifixes as accessories.

But the Moslem community is the most sensitive and, though devout Moslem women would only wear Lagerfeld's work in private, they still have the financial muscle to make their protest hit home.

Schiffer models the offending Chanel ballgown with quotations from the Koran on ...ce. Designer Karl Lagerfeld said he thought the words were from a love poem

...DAY 33 WEEKEND 25 ENTERTAINMENT GUIDE 49 LETTERS 45 PATRIC WALKER 44

1

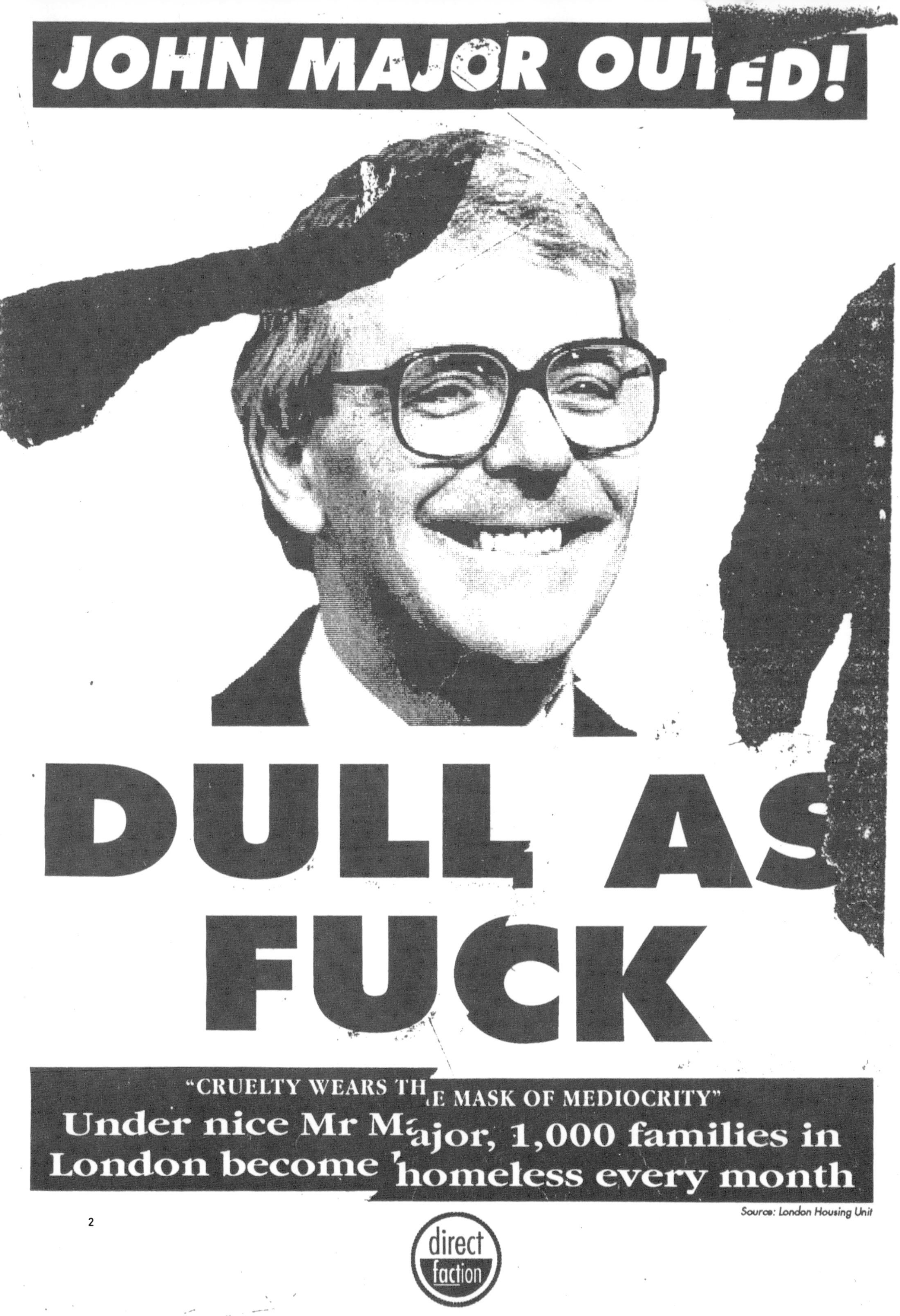

JOHN MAJOR OUTED!

DULL AS FUCK

"CRUELTY WEARS THE MASK OF MEDIOCRITY"

Under nice Mr Major, 1,000 families in London become homeless every month

Source: London Housing Unit

2

1

billboards aren't classed as art. "When we first got noticed, AVI were perceived as vandals. No one ever, ever used a word like 'art'."

But *Campaign* magazine remarked on the changes, and media personnel started to speculate. "The industry", says David, "thought we were bored copywriters." Soon, the press was calling them "art terrorists". Advertising conventions, however, make their work easy. Says Gavin, "They use imagery in a very loose, very sensational way, with just a single line of copy used to anchor the thing. All we need is a small amount of text to transform it."

AVI place their faith in confusion rather than labels; they treasure those double-takes "unauthored" work produces. Gavin: "Of course we deal with specific political things. But we also try and make people think about power. About advertising, and questions of control."

David feels agitprop art comes with a sell-by date. "That's why it isn't potent if it's made into icons. When we did some billboards which dealt with the poll tax, they existed in a context of public debate. If you try to enshrine something, you strip that away."

One word this pair often use is "gatekeepers": meaning cultural mediators such as curators, critics, reporters. "You have to bypass them", maintains David sternly. "Get your own audience and answer to one another. Because the gatekeepers survey art work less than the public. Much, much, much less. That's why the street comes first."

A group which agrees is Fashion Architecture Taste (Fat), who began existence in October '93. Their aim is an "interaction between different disciplines in the visual arts". Fat operates from a five-part mission statement. But the most important goals they have are populist:

"Specific projects might pursue questions of how the possibilities of fine art practice might be extended beyond their present scope but the superimposition of an understanding of another

2

3

4

Previous pages:

1. Press cutting from the Evening Standard 21 January, '94 "Lagerfeld Says Sorry Over Koran Ballgown"

2. John Major Outed! Dull as Fuck Fly poster Direct Faction Thanks to Clifford. Where are you!

1. There Is No Longer Such a Thing as Society Sandwich board, Piccadilly Circus, London

2. Customised billboard H and M Hennes fashion advertisement, before / after AVI

3. Customised billboard Volvo Estate advertisement before / after AVI

4. Customised billboard Water Privatisation, advertisement, before / after AVI

LIKE, IF YOU STUCK 500 RED DOTS ON ONE PIECE, IT WOULD SUDDENLY GAIN THIS HUGE CRITICAL CURRENCY. (→PAGE 218)

1

3

4

5

6

2

7

8

9

10

1. Fat members
2. Roadworks project
Audio-visual art installations which utilized 10 bus shelters in central London as a site for public art
Tottenham Court Rd site
Design: Beaconsfield / Squarepusher
28 Oct '96 - 9 Nov '96
Fat
3. New Oxford St site
Design: Nigel Coates / Rad Rice / Peter Lazonby / Full Circle for Fat
4. Tottenham Court Rd site 2
Design: Sue Webster / Tim Noble / Bowling Green for Fat
5. Russell Square site
Design: Rankin / Billy Bragg for Fat
6. High Holborn site
Design: John Isaacs / Pusherman / Speedway for Fat
7. Built project for The Leisure Lounge night club, London
Fat
8. Built project for The Brunel Rooms - leisure development (1st phase) Swindon
Fat
9. and 10. Conversion of office space for Kessels Kramer advertising agency - Amsterdam Holland, '97
Fat

WE'LL SET UP AN OBJECT, THEN SEE HOW IT FUNCTIONS. WHETHER IT'S FIXED OR NOMADIC, WHAT WE DO IS ALWAYS POLITICAL. (→PAGE 218)

THAT WORK, ONCE IT'S FINISHED, GOES ON A "FOR SALE" SIGN - WHICH IS POSTED OUTSIDE THEIR HOUSE. SO, ESSENTIALLY, THEIR STREET BECOMES A GALLERY. AND, WHEN YOU DO THIS IN HACKNEY AS OPPOSED TO HAMPSTEAD, WHAT'S REVEALED IS OF COURSE VERY DIFFERENT. (→PAGE 220)

NO ONE USED THE WORD ART. THEN, PEOPLE STARTED INTERVIEWING US IN AN ART CONTEXT AND WE GOT LABELLED AS ART TERRORISTS. (→PAGE 221)

The Guardian
NEWSPAPER OF THE YEAR
WEEKEND EDITION
The estate agent as artist

1

media (eg how an understanding of electronic media might be brought to bear on sculpture), thus broadening the scope of established disciplines beyond their present boundaries."

"Most importantly, Fat exposes these ideas to the widest possible cross-sections of the community by circumnavigating the established institutions of cultural discourse such as the gallery, buyer/client and curator. This is achieved by utilising mediums of mass dissemination such as the business/calling card and the advertising site. This form of engagement also extends to interventions within institutions that already have an identifiable condition or ideology."

Fat is currently composed of nine members: Maria Beddows, Emma Davis, Sean Griffiths, Sam Jacob, Paul Khera, Clive Sall, Thomas Tatum, Cordula Weisser and Geoff Ward. This core includes artists, architects, film-makers and graphic designers. They have implemented their objectives in numerous ways: through public installations and open projects; pickets of "official" events; even applications to competitions. Fat has always tried to question "the rules".

Fat's first project was entitled Adsite. It involved mounting 6' x 4' original artworks on 250 public bus shelter signs. These sites were rented by the organisation, who also helped to subsidise some of the artist-contributors. Says member Clive Sall, "We knew that if we used a sponsor, that sponsor would dictate the terms of our engagement. The whole point was to challenge the notion of what differentiates a piece of art from advertising. If the means of presentation is the same, how do you define which territory each lies in?"

The primary aspect of this - and many Fat projects - is the exploration of an urban condition. Normally art is hermetic and site-specific; like Atkinson, Direct Faction and AVI, Fat are seeking to see art spring up everywhere. Says Sall, "We ask an architectural question: what happens when the city itself becomes a gallery?"

For another sort of artist, who produces graffiti, the city has always been a gallery. But, in 1994, three West Londoners changed that. Tim, Pete and Ricky founded a shop they called The Rub - a design and

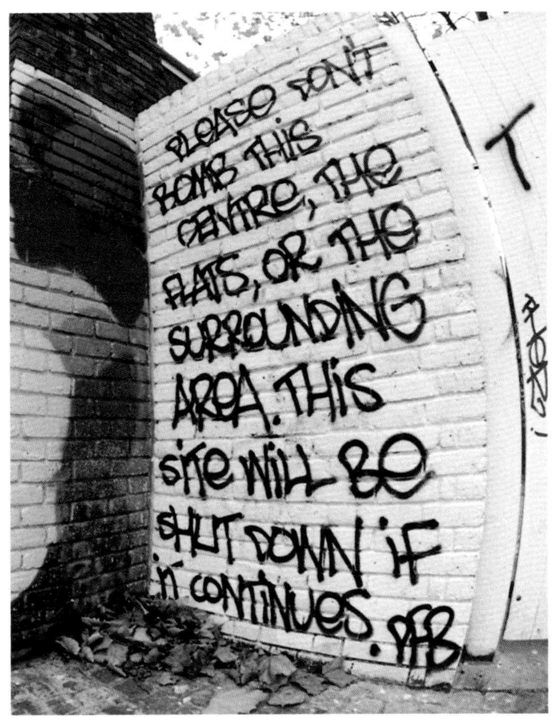

2

ANDREW NEIL:
Minister for Propaganda

STOP IRVING
BOYCOTT THE SUNDAY TIMES

direct faction

3

4

T-shirt firm using graffiti forms. The proprietors were spraycan veterans, who had opted to "go legal". And, for eighteen months, their business flourished. Most of its custom came from ad-men or TV folk, all of them desperate to purchase street credibility. Says Pete, who is now a part of the Flirt studio, "We did banners, murals, homes, stage sets, offices." Most of their earnings bankrolled a line of T-shirts: agitprop items whose slogans ranged from "Life Is What You Make It" to "We Know Where You Live".

Skateboarder Ricky Plante is proud to hear The Rub's work called graffiti. Although adamant that his work be "legal" (in a former incarnation, Plante was busted for it), he feels the genre will never lose its politics. "Nothing about those has to do with being illegal. Graff is just *gesture*. It's the style and sentiments of real people, moving outwards. Wherever people have something to say, you find graffiti. So when I say 'graffiti', I *mean* political art."

Plante and his crew have now split for separate jobs as artists. But, on southwest London's Bayonne Estate, similar, illegal, art remains impressive. There in '95, in a sunken netball court, graffiti teams from all over London held *Unity 2*. It was the second year of a special, competitive "throwdown" - with the single theme of peace. As with every *Unity*, the walls were covered in imagery, and the premises were piled with empty spraycans.

1. Press cutting from The Guardian newspaper Sat June 14, '97 "The Estate Agent as Artist" Fat project: Home Ideals
2. Warning, seen next to Unity 2 graffiti site, '95 Photo: Tim Leighton-Boyce
3. Direct Faction Flyposter
4. Street handout creator unknown

Following pages:
Peace on Earth Part of Unity 2 - graffiti site Design: Prime - '95 Photo: Tim Leighton-Boyce

YEAH, LIKE WHEN I WAS PHOTOGRAPHED FROM AFAR FALLING DOWN IN THE ROAD. THE PEOPLE WHO ACTUALLY "RESCUED" ME AND TOOK ME TO THE SIDE OF THE ROAD, THERE WAS NO WAY I COULD LET THEM KNOW WHAT I WAS DOING.
(→PAGE 222)

REFERENCE BECOMES A SMOKESCREEN FOR LACK OF HARD-HITTING CONTEXT. DO IT TOO MUCH, IT'S LIKE A PETER GREENAWAY FILM.
(→PAGE 222)

YOU USE SOMETHING VERY SMALL, NOT ONLY TO KNOCK OUT AN EXISTING MEANING, BUT TO PUT ANOTHER MEANING IN ITS PLACE. BUT THE MOMENT IT COLLAPSES, YOU ARE THE GOLIATH.
(→PAGE 224)

Every year, "graff" becomes more global and more popular. It has led to books such as *Spraycan Art*, *R.I.P.* and *Graffito*. Now, it's also the subject of numerous World Wide Web pages, with titles like *Art Crimes*:
(http://www.graffiti.org/index/phatlist.htm)
L'Art Urbain:
(http://www.mygale.org/03/rap2/graf_11.hm)
and *La Galeria del Graffitti*:
(http://catalunya.net/Expressions/comic/comic.html). Such sites preserve vast archives of an ephemeral art. But *Unity 2* marked a resonant moment for Britain. All its completed pieces, as usual, were dazzling - and tagged with resonant names like New Angelz, Transcendental, and The Pure Language Crew. But the champ who emerged, the symbol of a new '90s, was "Prime", with his epic work "Peace On Earth".

Prime was already a well-loved artist, one who works by day in a very legal studio. His "Peace On Earth", however, was done in a special mode, one the artist termed "Islamic wildstyle". Like Conrad Atkinson's re-vision of *Wuthering Heights*, "Peace" interwove Eastern styles and calligraphies: things which, in life, might literally fight one another. His work was a huge, formally complex accomplishment - with a 3-D presence which stopped onlookers cold. Yet it was not didactic. Like Israel's Rabin shaking hands with Yasser Arafat, "Peace On Earth" didn't posture. It *embodied.*

The works which surrounded and succeeded it are impressive. But "Peace On Earth", now vanished, remains exceptional. Its creator is a shy man of colour. But he is quite aware of those issues he handles. Says Prime, "If I were in a Britain where I felt represented, I might not feel the need to do graffiti."

"My graffiti", he adds, "went through three stages. First, I was saying 'I'm here; I'm alive.' Then, 'I'm here, I'm alive and creating something beautiful.' Then, 'I'm here, I'm alive and I'm creating something beautiful. Something beautiful that can make you think'."

With the powerful emergence of the Internet, and the growing power of computer-aided work, the stakes of making such art are changing rapidly. The projects now evolving from new technologies tend to derive from existing paradigms: movies, television and computer games. But it's only a matter of time until this changes.

Many of the young Britons who succeed in film, music and graphics are skilled with computers. But the parameters of what they can use are exploding. It is more profound than the Royals finally going online, hackers altering Tony Blair's image on a Web site, even Peter Gabriel's landmark Real World CD-ROMs. All the change, however, has to hinge on code - on the instructions which tell computers what to do.

Code creates structures such as "multi-media"; code spurs every re-appraisal of what computers can do. And writing code is an art like sculpting or painting. Says Philip Crewsden of East London's interactive firm Oscar Music, "Programmers work with a language, just like writers or poets. It happens to be a math symbol language. But it's still very much a means of self-expression." Just as artists use lines to create a picture, or writers use words to construct a poem, programmers use code to make computers do things.

For Britons, as for the rest of the world, many of the things they will do still lie in the future. But the current work on tools such as CD-ROM (exemplified in Britain by Peter Gabriel's "Eve") or "enhanced" CDs (such as the funky "header" created by Mark Ainley, Luke Pendrill, Neil and Martin Aberdeen) are symbolic of changes in creative syntax. One's art and what drives it have always been inseparable. As the former Microsoft exec Tom Corddry puts it, "Throughout history, artists have been technologists. They've always needed techniques and had to master tools."

What's different in the '90s is the speed of change; for digital technologies make unheard-of jumps. As each new generation surfaces, existing code bases can be rendered obsolete. They might still run on the newest computer chip, but they are not in any way optimised for that. Corddry puts it much more simply, "That seems quite hard to picture. But just think of it this way. What would have happened during the Renaissance if the available tools had just kept doubling and doubling?"

Often, agitprop art has led the way with new technologies. Its irreverence and initiative help us see beyond our current models, and can lead the way to revelations. (Hip-hop music is one now-established example; its mix of "high" and "low" technologies is a worldwide business.) For, unlike movies or print, the way these new entertainments are made is intertwined with their structure. Says 21-year-old Mitch Veerson, who writes gaming software, "The main thing is that narratives are no longer linear. When you watch a movie or read a book, you enter into it. Then you come out the other end. Now, that's different."

Games, online sites and CD-ROMs are already different. People dip into them, go where they please, stay as long as they want or they feel they need to. As Veerson notes, this creates new questions. "Like,

1

1. and 2. Images from interactive CD - Drum
Producer: Karen Alexander
Real World

how do you hold the user's attention? What kind of content will become most valuable? How do you start to re-evaluate a structure?"

Although he lives in suburban London, Mitchell Veerson is paid from Japan. He has few anxieties about his future. "Young English people like me know we can't see what's coming. But what we do know is we can adjust when it comes." He concedes that, "not everyone can be a programmer. But we all need ways to work together. That's what's going to produce the real innovations."

Not to mention the ultimate in trade secrets. For most young Britons who make their art into business, certain aspects of the punk ethos still persist. Their multi-faceted ingenuity still proves you can, somehow, "do it yourself". For them, too, the street still maintains its prominence. In its widening, cosmopolitan whirl, creative energies gain important renewal and all viewpoints are effectively challenged.

Moreover, in this changing urban universe, the real "high tech" hardware is individual: it is your body, your politics, your perceptions. The software, technologies and tools are just "peripherals". David from AVI sums it up when he says, "Art and advertising may be closer than ever before. But a lot of current work isn't about either one. It's about the kind of things we care about. Like: does this actually *work*? Does it manage to mobilise people? Does it *really* help to forge a kind of consensus?"

2

WHEN YOU HAVE AN ANTI-ESTABLISHMENT PRACTICE. IF YOUR VIEWS REALLY DO BECOME POPULAR AND THE POLITICAL PENDULUM SWINGS, THEN YOU'RE ACTUALLY LEFT WITH NO MATERIAL.
(→PAGE 225)

BEING AROUND AND WORKING WITH PEOPLE WHO CAN ENGAGE WITH PROGRESSIVE IDEAS HAS BEEN IMPORTANT TO ME EVER SINCE, NO MATTER WHAT MEDIUM THEY ARE WORKING IN.
(→PAGE 226)

NOTHING CAN REALLY PREPARE YOU FOR THE MAGIC, CHAOS AND SHEER WILL-POWER YOU ARE GOING TO NEED TO MAKE A FINISHED FILM.
(→PAGE 227)

Fat (Fashion Architecture Taste, Ltd) is a group of architects, fine artists and graphic designers. They united to re-define and enliven the urban experience. All Fat's projects invite viewers' participation - and all symbolise a cross-pollination of various disciplines. Here, Fat's Clive Sall discusses their projects and philosophies.

In 1993, you created Adsite, 200 works shown in bus shelters all over London. You mounted artists' work in the poster boxes. What motivated that?

We're interested in the city as a gallery, but also in the notion of authorship. If you aren't familiar with the graphic signature on a piece - like the ones in our bus shelters - then how do you negotiate its value? Its critical value or its economic value? Some of the pieces were by artists like Helen Chadwick; in other words, they were worth a bit of money. Some were stolen, and the stolen works were the ones with that value. Still, none of the works were signed. So, either you had to be familiar with an artist, or you had to like the piece enough to steal it!

Using a familiar place, like a bus shelter, lets viewers be more familiar with the gesture we're making. For example, with that Adsite project, people questioned those works very differently - in a much more critical way. Because they saw this territory as a place they actually own. In a way, they clearly felt *they* had a right to decide whether that piece of art should be there or not.

For four years now, Fat has mounted a project called Outpost. Outpost has taken place at the Edinburgh Festival, the Venice Biennale and, in 1997, in Münster, Germany. Each contributing artist had to supply 100 image cards and 100 signature cards - in a standard business-card format. All these exhibitions, they were open to anyone?

Yes. We publicised those in a lot of ways: on the Internet; sending posters all around Europe; and, in the UK, through educational institutions, libraries and bookshops. The work wasn't at all edited or curated. Whoever submitted work, that work was included. So it was very interesting because people think if a show is not curated, it will always suffer in terms of quality. But, if you look at the requirements in our brief, they are extremely complex. Especially for Outpost Münster, where the cards were digital. So, as far as we're concerned, any artist who participates is "worthy". Because to produce 100 image cards, 100 signature cards, off your own back, paying for all that production yourself? You're not gonna do that badly.

Fat:

cheering up cultural practice

In 1994, you did several guerrilla projects. Red Dot placed red dots - indicators of purchased work - against a random selection of works in the Royal Academy Summer Show.

That came out of the nature of such presentations. It's kind of a strange thing to stick a red dot next to an artwork. It confers a certain kind of economic status, a certain kind of cultural status, on the piece. But it's a status which lies outside your immediate critical engagement - it makes you look at it in a different way. You see it differently to a piece without the dot. Just looking at the Royal Academy show, I thought, "Here's an exhibition which pretends to be democratic and inclusive, but of course it isn't." Because 10,000 people submit their work; they pay their £10 fee and - in 1994 - only 1,325 were selected. Then you come along as a spectator and *you* pay £5, and the Academy stays open three months and makes a killing. They sell £3,000,000 of work and keep 33%.

What's even more disturbing is, once you walk in the gallery, you realise there's no enjoyable way to consume it. It's a bit like a giant shopping experience, like an end-of-the-year sale. So we at Fat thought, "Well, one way to rectify it would be to stick red dots on all the work, or maybe preference some works over others." Like, if you stuck 500 red dots on one piece, it would suddenly gain this huge critical currency. We went to the gallery on a certain day and handed out posters to everyone in the queue. Those posters detailed certain notions of consumption. Then, in teams of four, we went into all the rooms and started placing red dots on various works. I actually lost my teaching job at the time because of it. But then things like that always are kind of predictable.

Fat refers to projects like Red Dot as "nomadic". That same year, you held another nomadic event - one called Work - outside the Turner Prize award at the Tate Gallery.

We got 300 people to come and hold their works up on sticks outside the gallery. Plus we had fireworks and projections onto the Tate. This was not just aimed at the Turner Prize. It was a reaction to the Criminal Justice Bill, which had just become legislation that week. More than 19 people meeting without the prior consent of the police had become a breach of criminal law. So we thought, "OK, what is going to happen if 300 predominantly white, middle-class people meet like that? Are we gonna get arrested? No." Nor did we.

Fat also designs nightclubs. In 1994, you did the Leisure Lounge; in 1995, the Brunel Rooms; in 1997, the Scala Cinema. What are the aims for those projects?

We treat those as installation opportunities. We try to learn how the occupant of a space reacts to that space. Then we make assumptions based on those observations. We'll set up an object, then see how it functions. Whether it's fixed or nomadic, what we do is always political. With the Leisure Lounge, Sean McLusky, the DJ and promoter, came to us. He'd seen some stuff we did and he wanted to find out if we'd find a design solution for this club - one which would help him to secure the job of running it. But there wasn't a lot to start with. If you imagine an underground pub with a snooker hall, that was the basic space. Panelling, the usual suspended ceilings and so on. Lots of really cheap partitioning and built-in furniture. It was a really tacky spot, where lonely middle-aged men go to drink their beer and play snooker. Also, the budget was small.

So the idea was, basically, to strip the whole place out - then prioritise certain elements. We threw as much money as we could at things like the bar. The cloakroom and the bar act as central elements in dividing it up - into a chill-out area, bar area and a dancefloor. Along the dancefloor, we put a 54'-long projection screen. There, we tried to incorporate computer aesthetics. We used that concept to decide how to do the colours, how to place objects and how to deal with them spatially. It helped us to create illusions of depth.

Did you consider any musical genres?

Yeah, at that stage everyone was very into techno, so the design we decided on was quite hard. It wasn't at all like other clubs - in terms of a Café de Paris or something like that, where you have soft furnishings, velvet and cushions. This was much more underground and bunker-like. Again, our designs try to let the occupants of an environment take control of it. So, the long projection screen, its images change continuously. Plus, if you watch the screen, with people dancing in front of it, it becomes a very theatrical moment. When you go to a club, a part of that experience is watching others dance - as much as dancing yourself. The Lounge led to further projects, like the old Scala Cinema in King's Cross. We're also designing that, for Sean. There the basic idea is converting the building into a restaurant, a cinema, a club and - if possible - also an art gallery. The highest priority is the club, then the restaurant, then the cinema. Those will happen in the first phase.

The Brunel Rooms, which you did in 1995 in Swindon, was a different kind of nightclub design.

We used that one to collide certain aesthetics. For example, airports and allotments; running tracks and swimming pools. Essentially, each became a two-and-a-half metre wide strip - which ran the length of the entire nightclub. Each strip had its different aesthetic: one was a running track, one was tarmac, and so on. In a sense, when you look across those strips, you see the relationship between a municipal landscape and a commercial one: aesthetics which, in actuality, fight each other. We tried to compress a whole world of utopias into a single moment. Just to see what happens.

What about your '95 exhibition at the Architecture Foundation - the one which was called Success?

Basically, that one was a laugh at ourselves. Fat is always excluded from being asked to exhibit because the nature of our interventions always seems to be against institutions. So institutions are fearful of letting us in. But we decided to have this exhibition. And, after many proposals they didn't accept, the one they finally accepted was one where we would produce all our work up to that point. Only we transferred it onto popular commodities: plates and tablecloths and umbrellas and things like that. Rather than placing the work on the walls, we made the work impure and commercialised. We made it into artefacts and souvenirs. So the question became, "How does the content shift?" Which it does, because the same work will not be taken seriously if you do something like this with it. On opening night, we had most of it auctioned off.

The same year, you did a project you called Portrait, which was filmed and broadcast for the BBC's Art Marathon.

We had just staged an event called Picnic. It occupied Hyde Park, as when people have raves, and it was another response to the Criminal Justice Act. I mean, essentially, the Criminal Justice Bill was brought forth to confront that exact sort of activity. So we thought, "OK, we'll occupy a park." We commissioned 100 artists, from various disciplines, to place their work on a 10-metre grid. The Criminal Justice Act, of course, stipulates that more then 20 people within 10 metres of one another constitutes an illegal gathering. Picnic included lots of disciplines, from performance artists to musicians and sculptors, and - yes - it was filmed by the BBC.

From that project, people who came down from Northern Ireland wanted the same project to go back to Derry. But we changed it, to a new project we called Portrait. As you know, in Northern Ireland, there are Catholics and there are Protestants. So we thought, "OK, let's work with that." So, we put Power PCs with digital cameras linked to them in two shopping centres: one in a Protestant and one in a Catholic area. Then, we invited anyone who was shopping there to sit down and have their portrait taken. It was fed into the computer and came right up on the screen, so they could sit down and help construct their portrait.

What were the results?

Obviously they were dealing with notions of identity, of masculinity and of beauty. But rather than being passive - as the sitter usually is in portraiture - these sitters became active. They were able to re-invent, enhance and alter their images. We downloaded these as photographic prints, which went into Derry's Orchard Gallery. But we also had them printed up on T-shirts. Each sitter kept their T-shirt and, eventually, they got the actual print.

The question then became: which one is more authentic? The one on the T-shirt, worn by the producer? Or the one in the gallery, presented by a curator? The other phenomenon was that, on opening night, the people involved invaded the gallery - with all their kiddies and their grannies and aunties. And the images in there were about *them*. It was quite revealing, their actual faces walking around in front of all their altered selves. It kind of gave you clues to their personalities.

What is Fat involved in at the moment?

We're in the middle of a project called Home Ideals. It's a two-part project; part one we did in Hackney; part two we're doing in Islington. There, it's sponsored by Holden Matthews Estate Agents, and it's part of the Islington International Festival. Basically, we have the work of 50 artists, which we've produced as a catalogue of images. We knock on each resident's door in a specific street, and we invite them to choose an image from among those. So they become a critic.

The artist who produced the image they chose then collaborates with them on another artwork. That work, once it's finished, goes on a "For Sale" sign - which is posted outside their house. So, essentially, their street becomes a gallery. And, when you do this in Hackney as opposed to Hampstead, what's revealed is of course very different. It's a bit like the BMW parked outside as opposed to the battered Metro. Again, though, it's Fat trying to make external what is normally hidden away inside. But also what it does, like some other projects, is allow local residents to be the critics. Because they are the people who choose the work. Here, they also become an artist; they collaborate. Finally, they also become collectors - because they keep the work after it's exhibited.

In England, contemporary art is viewed with great suspicion. This aims to let these people into that whole world without their having to say, "Respect us because we're worthy." Instead, *we're* saying, "Don't fight against it. Join this club, because you're already part of it."

What's the largest piece you've done?

Thus far, the biggest urban event we've done has been Roadworks, in 1996. We commissioned ten practitioners from different disciplines - graphic design to photography to architecture - and we gave them each a bus shelter. Basically, they could use it as an installation, bring together public art and public transport. One artist, John Isaacs, made his shelter into a festival booth; he got dressed up in a gorilla outfit. He had music in there by Speedway and Pusherman and, every day, he performed karaoke. Bank, who are another group of four young artists, made their shelter into a lump of snow - with an effigy of [explorer] Sir Ranulph Fiennes on top.

All of them collaborated with musicians, to produce some audio for the shelters. So the bus shelter, a familiar object, became changed - by people's perceptions and by their participation. We produced a catalogue which came with a tape of the music done for the project. It ranged from people like Billy Bragg to bands like Acacia. Camden Council gave us £10,000 for it and J. C. Decaux - who build bus shelters - gave another £10,000. Plus, we got £10,000 from a business sponsorship scheme. But none of these people censor you. Not like when you work within the confines of a gallery. Because the gallery always want to know if your product is *worthy*. Sponsors are the opposite; all they worry about is public insurance and liability. They don't even want to see the work!

We're often asked, "What happens when you get assimilated?" And, at this stage, we have an answer because, in terms of funding our projects, we prefer to work in the private sector. *We far* prefer to work in the public realm. Because people there are so much more diverse and responsive. Their reactions make it so enjoyable. And they're certainly not afraid of expressing objections! They're really, really vocal - it's a very emotional presence. It's not just some cold lineage penned by a critic.

If readers want to engage in a similar practice, what would be your advice?

Phone us! Quite a lot of people do that and we just send them all the information we can. I can't speak about cultures outside Britain, of course. But we do have a Web site and we also have e-mail (http://www.fat.co.uk and fat@fat.co.uk). We would encourage anyone to have a go. What we have learned, through particular projects, is how to negotiate with institutions. We've learned how to manage it so they can't ignore you, nor can they marginalise you. Essentially, Fat isn't into destroying anything; we don't want to burn down all the galleries. What we try to do is make people question their relationship to those institutions. That's not always a negative thing; in fact, it can be quite positive.

Are there any limitations on your aims?

All our projects are very specific. So when people ask, "Have you got ideas for other ones?", the answer is "Yeah, we've got thousands of ideas". But we have to wait for the right political moment, so those ideas will be legible - and relevant. Or a context that, when they are placed against it, or inside it, they will be understood. Our only real limitation is we're few in number. At any one time, only five people can be full time, which sounds like a lot but, at any given moment, we'll be doing lots of different projects. All of those require huge amounts of input, huge amounts of paperwork. So your production level has to be realistic.

AVI is the brainchild of two London friends, "David" and "Gavin". This pair intervene on billboards to make political statements. They have also ventured into other realms, but maintain that public billboard alterations are important, cost-effective, and challenging. Here they tell how, why and where they manage their unique business.

What are AVI's requirements?

David: In terms of an intervention, one of the prerequisites is simple. We need a situation where a small amount of text can transform the whole billboard because our resources are limited. It's easier to re-orientate a picture with a small amount of text than to intervene on a photographic level.

Give an example.

David: One of my favourites was this huge image of an open landscape. A car ad with no car, nothing automotive. Just this giant, panoramic shot of Monument Valley. A completely ecologically sound car advert! At the top it says, "Open your mind" and, at the bottom, "The Volvo Estate". We changed the latter strip to "Buy A Bicycle".

Gavin: The site-specificity was important there, because next door was the Kensington Car Pound. And this is a one-way street and there's a traffic light here. Everyone paying £150 has to stop by this. So you're actually giving people quite an intimate message.

AVI:

on advertising their beliefs

Although they have been widely photographed, you haven't shown the billboards in a gallery setting.

David: Really, it's just not work one can exhibit. It's very sort of art historical and not really the point, somehow. I mean, if you started to think only about the resonance of it, you could get in a situation where you'd say, "Why the hell put it up on a billboard? Let's do it digitally." Just have it exist as a kind of resonance but not resonating anything but pure information. Whereas in order to make it work, we had to prioritise which was the main audience. Our priority had to be the public sphere, because on the billboards themselves, they are unauthored. When they're in a book or a magazine, they never are - because it's always tied to someone, even if it's just a pseudonym.

By contrast, when it's up on a billboard, you've just got to imagine that it has no author. Because it's not even graffiti, it's not even like here is a disenfranchised voice talking over a billboard. Plus, it's in that very slick, highly rhetorical style. Really, the billboards are all about hijacking, about almost making the board speak in a different way. That's why it is supposed to look seamless.

Gavin: We never pushed to be called art. Our first press was more about spectacle. You know, "God, someone's got the brass to do this on Oxford Street at rush hour". No one used the word art. Then, people started interviewing us in an art context and we got labelled as art terrorists. *Campaign* talked about us in terms of the copy - they speculated about whether or not we were bored copywriters.

You had a billboard commissioned by the ICA - they show you putting it up in their film on public artists. What is it like doing commissioned agitprop?

David: It was difficult because we tend to address the existing content of the work that's on the billboard. So we tried to have a nice, inane kind of image, which was a cloudscape and a sort of a bright red writing over a cloudscape background. It just said, "imagine a world without adverts." And in the bottom right-hand corner, which is where the name of the products always go, we just had "AVI" - with a little sort of a globe logo that kind of looked like the PanAm logo, a sort of empty signifier of corporate advertising.

People laughed. But people also said, "Oh, yeah, what's it going to be for? What is the product?", which I don't think you can escape. I think this is the whole problem for people being commissioned to do "art on billboards". I think, in the end, the context is too strong and people do just go, "Well, what's it for? What's the advert for?" Even if you have a billboard that says, "This is not a billboard. It's a piece of art." People will still say, "Well, what's it *for*?" It's quite curious. So many artists are being asked to do public work, as if art can extend its hand everywhere. I don't think you can effectively do that everywhere. Things can be done, but they're better not called art.

You've never minded *really* being anonymous.

Gavin: We want to deal not just with the issues we directly address. We want to make people think more generally about power. About the geography of the streets - and the real ownership of public spaces.

David: Also, all those people who work anonymously, their ego always seems to surface at some point. You think, "That's quite cheap, you just can't resist!" But, at the same time, I think it's important that people know the work's being done. And that somehow it's claimed. When artists talk about work and things, you know, to groups of other artists or film makers or so on, they're happy to know that you're working under a pseudonym. But they're *also* happy that they can meet you, happy to be aware of the humanity behind the action. Otherwise, in a strange way, it ends up being as corporate and as anonymous as the work it tries to critique.

Gavin: The question of subversion is all about the context of a thing and the dynamics of how you use it. If it's in a book, then the main point is it's tied to an author. You have captions and it says, "This had an origin, it's this work and has this motivation". But the most potent stuff avoids that altogether. In a book, all the questions of politics become problematised. To a certain extent, everyone who's in it becomes enfranchised. But that may not be the actual status of the work.

David, are you still doing those photo-pranks: where you stage-manage the situation, then capture what happens in still pictures?

David: I still do those. But it was only recently that somebody made the connection between that and the billboard work. They called it a theatrical use of public space, then they linked it to the photos on the billboards. It's strange for us because the billboards always have two lives. It has the sort of initial thing you do for that audience. Then, if it gets in the media or if people talk about it, it has another one.

In David's photo-pranks, he is anonymous. Plus, no one who participates knows they're being staged.

David: Yeah, like when I was photographed from afar falling down in the road. The people who actually "rescued" me and took me to the side of the road, there was no way I could let them know what I was doing. Which is sort of a cheat on their good nature. So as far as they were concerned, they'd done a good deed. They were going away, and I was sort of fooling them. When interventionist work gets recorded and mediated, something completely different happens with its authorship. That audience - the audience which is seeing it through the media - relates to it in a different way from the primary audience.

Gavin: The street has to come before the *Guardian* or the *Independent.* There it's not contained. It's not explained. It's more disturbing. Plus you know its motivation, its politics, its vested interests.

David: This is kind of why we always go for big sites with the billboards, because those viewers are our primary audience. You *could* just do it on some billboard in the middle of a little village or something. And just say, I chose it for photogenic reasons because it's going to be all about the photography. Well, that's not the case for us. I mean, the photography is absolutely vital - and we'd be foolish to overlook that audience. But, you know, doing one in the middle of Oxford Circus or the Hammersmith Roundabout is important to us. So that a billboard will be seen and perhaps not understood - or not thoroughly understood. Rather than the very explained format that always happens once things get known about.

Gavin: Referentiality becomes a thing in itself. The hip guy's going, "Oh yeah, *this* relates to *that*". Reference becomes a smokescreen for lack of hard-hitting context. Do it too much, it's like a Peter Greenaway film.

David: Which relates, in a strange way, to this stuff. Because you train in graphic design by consuming it, and the access to it is not difficult. The same goes for film. Now that it's all visible on video we're all ace technicians. All of us feel we could "do" a Scorcese film. But could we do something brilliant and original? Or are we not too saturated in the stuff?

Gavin: A media career does rely on gatekeepers. If you do work that you can't quite say where it's coming from, the chances of you being in a volume like this one are slim. It's nice to be in the papers; you can't be an outsider all the time. On the other hand, our giving you the images is a trade-off. In the media, you're always there for your "graphic-ness", or for your "counter-culture-ness". Whereas, if we do a billboard around privatisation or something like that, it exists in a context of real actions and consequences.

Is it an either/or situation? Either work is kept out of the media or altered by it?

David: You can't shut off one or the other. I think you need both. But you need to have some sense of proportion, otherwise it just goes into this strange, needy spiral. Something which, at the time, actually didn't have much effect can suddenly take on huge proportions.

Right before the election, lots of people asked us if we were planning to do stuff. But we've just never been keen. I mean, at the time of the last election, we were actually doing billboards. But it's not currently an area that we're interested in. Not that we're apolitical; we certainly aren't. But we came at politics more in relation to capital and the marketplace. We're more interested in showing the latent politics behind advertising. Rather than head-on looking at the explicitly political. That kind of politics never really appealed to us; it never actually engages us on either an intellectual or artistic level. But I love it when I see it. It's great stuff.

Gavin: The boards that work best are when it's confusing and people don't know that it's agitprop. The problem with something that's already labelled "agitprop" is that it pacifies. People will see it in a book, or in the paper, and feel glad that someone else is getting up and saying something. And they'll feel there's enough of a consensus that they don't need to do anything.

David: You have to forge a consensus with people. It can't be so agitprop that people go "OK that's good, but you just carry on". Or, maybe it's actually offensive to you - and it forces you into a solidarity with other people. So it's not just who's speaking on the poster. It's tricky; it's all about questions of consensus.

But you don't consider yourselves, by extension, a part of that picture?

David: I think that one has to be graffiti in the proper sense because billboards are kind of slick - and not too subtle. I think there's definitely a place for the aerosol can. And I think it's where politics itself is declared within the message. That, particularly in the public sphere, that kind of response is really appropriate. To draw or paint on a Conservative billboard, it's entirely appropriate. Rather than getting your computer out and getting incredibly sophisticated text and tweaking it. The question is "Who is actually saying this?"

David, explain your photograph of the woman in Piccadilly.

David: I hired an actress and I had her stand, actually in the middle of Piccadilly Circus. This time, you could see the background, all the neon text and all the lettering. She was just standing there with a sandwich board I had made up, which - to the public - just read as gobbledygook. But, when the photograph was printed, I got the negative flipped. I had it printed huge, 7 foot by 8 1/2 foot. In the flipped one what it says on the sandwich board is, "There is no longer such a thing as society", which is Margaret Thatcher's big quote, something she said in '89.

Thatcher said, "There is no longer such a thing as society, just individuals and their families." Yeah! That was pretty strange, and it's come back to haunt her now. She actually said it first of all in *Woman's Own* magazine, where she was just trying to appeal to the family thing. The kind of matriarch image. But people latched onto it as somehow being an unconscious summary of Thatcherism: such a kind of rampant individualism that it ends up with no idea of "society".

It's strange because when you print it the *wrong* way around, she makes sense - this woman who's standing there in the sandwich board. But then all the other text in the background is back to front. And it's shot like a very straight street photograph, so it looks totally realistic. She's there with this slogan, and everything behind her, it's clearly giant signs and logos for McDonald's, Coca-Cola, Sony. You kind of recognise it, even though it's now backwards, because everybody knows Piccadilly Circus. You want to flip it around in your head but, as soon as you do, she doesn't make sense. You have one or the other, and you can't have both.

What about your show in Bristol, at The Leadworks?

David: For that, I was trying to do a piece about economic exchange - without photographing people in stripy shirts or a screen full of numbers. I settled on a series of shots taken from quite far away, so it produces an observant, distant look. There are sixteen people photographed. There's any two in each photograph and each person's in two photographs, never with the same person. So you can connect everyone up between all sixteen. And there's an implied relation. It's not really said what's going on between them, but all the shots are titled. They're called things like "The Interest", "The Withdrawal", "The Speculation", "The Collapse".

Have you considered switching your medium, into photography?

David: I'm still interested in photography. Although, before I get this backwards thing out of my system, I'm doing a piece which is a video projection. It's the whole of Alfred Hitchcock's *Rear Window* projected backwards. It runs in real time and you get sound and everything. It still runs from the front end of the film to the back end, but left is right and right is left.

I think lots of people are familiar with the film, but it involves the question of whether Jimmy Stewart's memory is a true one or not. Here, everything's literally the other way round. Jimmy Stewart is looking out the window left to right rather than right to left. His bed's on the wrong side or the kitchen's on the wrong side. And the little alley-way on the courtyard is on the right rather than the left. On the one hand, it's a complete intervention. It's a complete sort of turning the thing on its head. But, at the same time, it's completely uninterventional. I'm not re-editing the thing, I'm not putting my name on it. It'll just have a title card on the installation - and that title will just be written backwards - but it will still say, "Alfred Hitchcock's 'Rear Window'".

What keeps you doing interventions on the billboards?

David: Well, the economics, for one thing. The billboards used to cost us about 50 pence each. Yet the prime billboard sites in London rent for between £500 and £1,000 a month. If it lasts for a day, you get a whole billboard for only 50 pence. Some of ours have lasted over a month. It's sort of maximum effect for minimum effort, really.

Gavin: Plus, they involve big-budget adverts. We hijacked that photograph of Monument Valley! It's David and Goliath. You use something very small, not only to knock out an existing meaning, but to put another meaning in its place. But the moment it collapses, you are the Goliath.

You're content with this language?

David: Well, you know, things change. There was a time when the expensive, slick technology that defined mainstream was only available to these big institutions. With the advent of the computer, the whole idea that oppositional culture has an aesthetic that's different - that's rougher or defined by an aerosol can - that's gone. We use exactly the same tools. Within the culture, the status quo and the opposition are speaking in the same visual language.

Gavin: Of course, it's one thing to use the same visual style but it's another to use the same vocabulary in verbally expressive terms. There's still a "language of the Left" which has to do with wiping away the smog of consumer seduction and countering it with hard-hitting facts.

Will you keep doing billboards?

David: Well, we've got better and better. The last one we did was the one for the ICA. Of course, that one wasn't an intervention - and we had the whole thing printed. But even that was an elaborate photocopy. It was a photocopied black-and-white image with white printed text - then we printed the text red and it cost like £60.

It came out in strips, strips about 4 feet wide. Mounting that one took about a quarter of an hour, because we're not professionals, and we hadn't pasted up a *whole* billboard, so we took our time. The ones where we're just having simple banner texts and placing those at the most vulnerable point, the Achilles heel of the poster, those would take a minute at the most. The strange thing is, whenever people turn up to film us or we try and film ourselves, we actually have to do it quite a bit slower than usual. Otherwise it's just absurdly fast. That's the biggest compromise we make for film!

Gavin: One used to put it up at the beginning and the other one photographed. Now, we like to use both photographs and video. When we used to have just photos, the trick was to take a lot while it was being put up. Because it's fast work, plus you get more loose, more comfortable after a while. In fact, we used to go too far in one respect. We used to wear overalls, which was sort of an innocent's idea of what bill-posters look like. Actually, they just wear jeans and T-shirts.

What determines the plans for your work?

David: To a certain extent, the approach we have is dependent on the graphic aesthetic of what exists on the billboards. Sometimes it's just not possible to intervene in that very, very small way, just adding the odd word here or there. It was really interesting when our work came to the fore: at the beginning of that whole kind of '90s sort of stripped-down aesthetic. All the billboards in the '80s were big and garish. They had all those elaborate graphics.

Gavin: But then we started getting billboards which would just have a single-figure picture. A photo of someone on a white background with a piece of text. It was a kind of lean'n'mean capitalism. If the advert looks simple, that means it's common sense. That means it's no bullshit. And that, actually, allowed us to develop that work.

David: Of course, graphic fashions change. At the moment, we're not quite able to do it. We look all the time and sometimes we're just not able, aesthetically or graphically or rhetorically in terms of the sort of language that we like to use, to actually work on the billboards. I mean we could tear our hair out, running around in circles thinking, "Oh my God. Oh my God! We can't do any! We can't do any!"

But you intend to continue?

David: It's just an ongoing practice and it peaks and drops. Occasionally, we have quite an assertive spirit - like, in the past, around the privatisation campaigns. You know, those campaigns are all about a notion of public and public ownership. So, addressing privatisation on billboards is quite interesting - because it is in the public sphere. And they are the kind of billboards that say, "I am talking to you, everybody."

Gavin: Whereas a car ad, even though it's in the public sphere, may not do that. It may just be talking to some potential car buyers. The privatisation ones had that bogus sense of the public that share ownership has. In the end, it *doesn't* benefit everybody.

David: I think that's why a lot of the most successful ones we've done have involved privatisation. In terms, that is, of how they've worked for us: the feedback we've got from people who saw them or people who know someone who has mentioned it to them. Or the ones that the media pick up on. So, while we're hoping more privatisation doesn't take place, we'd certainly do it again.

That's the problem when you have an anti-establishment practice. If your views really do become popular and the political pendulum swings, then you're actually left with no material. I mean, what will happen now? If it's for the good, then that has to be fine. Because, where are your cards? Are you interested in just having your practice or do you want to have the better world your practice is vouching for? I think in the end, that's what slips through the publicity, that idea you're putting the goal out there. I know that I've seen work that's imitating us. I've seen a lot of it. And I'm happy. Am I supposed to think that we're the only ones with a monopoly on appropriation?

But is it ever annoying?

David: Only when people do it badly. You have to be very careful. It's not a spray can. If you're rolling out letters to exactly the same as other letters up there, you've got to get them straight. You see bad stuff and you think, "God, that's worse than not doing it."

I remember this billboard for *The Economist*, their billboards just used to be red and with a catchy sentence in the middle written in white. Then in the bottom right hand corner, it just used to say "*The Economist*". Gavin and I were just walking along the road and there was this guy flyposting posters for *Socialist Worker*. And he put about four, in the middle of the poster, right at the bottom.

Gavin: And we just said, "Why don't you just put one over *The Economist*, where it says *Economist*, and ruin the billboard as well?" But to him it was just a surface. He didn't really feel for what he was pasting up, which was just that month's ad for *The Socialist Worker*. He didn't feel any sense of juxtaposition with the billboard.

We were going, "Why don't you do something that kind of looks like '*The Economist*', but says '*The Socialist*'. That would work!" But he was like, "Mate, this is what *The Socialist Worker* looks like. This is how we paste it up. We put it in the middle so everyone can see it." We were just at total cross-purposes!

Since her initial training at Goldsmiths' College, Karen Alexander has worked in video, film, criticism, film-programming, distribution and multi-media. But a constant has been her interest in the nature of representation. Alexander both directs and produces, lectures and curates. Often, her topic has been the black presence in culture. She also serves on juries at many festivals: from FESPACO in Burkina Faso to celebrations in Brazil, Montreal and Martinique. In 1995, Alexander was recruited into multi-media by Peter Gabriel's Real World Interactive. (Visit them at http://www.realworld.co.uk).

What got you interested in the things you later pursued?

I was born and brought up in Acton, West London, of Guyanese parents. London was a territorial place then and my friends and I never went east past Oxford Circus. Later, talking to friends who grew up in East London, *they* never went past Oxford Circus to the west. So the meeting place for like souls and minds was probably Top Shop! Another determining factor was your Saturday job, and my first proper one was on the Kings Road. I had to travel on two buses to get there and there was something about that journey which got me thinking. Thoughts about who was allowed to be where and why; where you did and didn't see other black people. My gang from Acton was mainly white girls and a few white guys. To be honest, I used to talk the talk but couldn't walk the walk.

What kind of difference did education make?

My school was a local comprehensive which, years later, was featured in a BBC documentary as one of the roughest, most undisciplined schools in London. I think we were being educated as factory workers or, at best, maybe BBC secretaries. The big turning-point at school was a Marxist sociology teacher who had us read Stuart Hall, read some work on feminism and popular culture. Really basic things, but they resonated with me. One Saturday morning, on television, this black person came onscreen and his name-tag read "Stuart Hall". I screamed at my mother; I kept saying, "Mum, Stuart Hall's black! Stuart Hall's black!" For me, it was an absolute revelation - that someone whose work I had engaged with so much was black.

Karen Alexander:

on making the media answer

I thought I was too stupid to go to college. Instead, I got an editorial job at Fodors Guides. But a friend of mine was at Warwick University, and she was having a great time - so I thought I should try. I ended up at Goldsmiths' College, where I did communications and sociology. Basically, those studies changed my life. We were based in the school of art and had people teaching us theories like semiology and structuralism. Also, the individuals I met there were incredible - very diverse and strong people, very creative. They have had a lasting impact on my life. Being around and working with people who can engage with progressive ideas has been important to me ever since, no matter what medium they are working in.

How did you first become involved with making film?

After college I went to work at a video workshop, The Albany. There we made short, community-based productions with local groups - and The Albany's in-house theatre. I got over my phobia about equipment because there I was always showing other people how to work everything.

The Britain that faced me when I left college was really exciting, so I was full of radical thoughts and ideas. I wanted to make films like Godard or Chantel Akerman - with a touch of Douglas Sirk. But no black women were doing anything in film then. For me, feminism became very important, because I worked in an all-male environment. And, because of where I worked in south-east London, race became increasingly important as well. I felt I needed black people I could talk with - about issues of representation and the media. But still go shopping and clubbing with, as well. Sankofa Film and Video became that group. Inspiration came from talking and reading and working on ideas with other black people away from the white gaze.

Because we were so visible, however, we were always being asked to perform - talk at a conference, show our work, etc. So we needed those discussions amongst ourselves. We felt some sort of black presence had to be stamped on the world of British film-making. Around this time, I also met the critic Kobena Mercer. Together we ran a course called "Race & Sex" at Goldsmiths' College. We had a great time talking about the black image, in work by people like Prince and Eddie Murphy - and in film, books and magazines.

What prepared you for actually making film - was there anything which especially helped?

Nothing can really prepare you for the magic, chaos and sheer will-power you are going to need to make a finished film. At college, we did talk about ideas and work through problems. Because we had few resources, we had came up with creative solutions. My studies helped me have a sense of responsibility, especially to others in the film-making process. College definitely helped me develop an aesthetic appreciation. But you only start really learning about the processes - the hard-nosed realities - once you leave college.

At the time I left, in British television, a very journalistic bias had taken hold. It was the rise of *The Late Show*, and things like that. So there were less opportunities for crafted work. Plus, black film-makers hardly get a look-in, because, for television, race is problematic. The controllers want music, comedy and sport - or work made by and about African-Americans. Contemporary life, also, never seems to be our preserve. Even in the late '90s, it's pretty ironic to read in *The New Yorker* about "black British film" - as if it was some huge, ongoing movement.

Sankofa Film and Video did help black British film-making be seen as unified. So did the Black Audio Film Collective. But the reality was always a few people trying to intervene in mainly white alternative practice. Their funding came from the Greater London Council and then, later, from Channel Four. I think what really distinguishes the work of that era - pioneering work from film-makers like Maureen Blackwood, Martina Attille, Isaac Julien, John Akomfrah - is their efforts to develop an aesthetic. An aesthetic that was black and British, in form and content. But one not ignorant of the black presence in other art forms, either at home in Britain or abroad.

Sankofa and Black Audio came out of an arts background, so there was a real desire there to engage with theory. It gave them contact with other avant-garde practitioners. Plus the GLC brought film-makers here from Africa and the diaspora. So, for the first time black and white Britons could see work by people like Ousmane Sembene - or US film-makers like Charles Burnett, Haile Gerima, Marlon Riggs, Julie Dash and Larry Clarke. This opened up great dialogues with black film-makers all round the globe, which remain ongoing today.

Has electronic communication helped with that?

Actually, that has changed hardly anything. Recently, I was reading that just over 2 million PCs have been sold in Britain - as opposed to 22 million TVs. So, although it *will* change, we have a way to go. I am starting to think about doing work on the Internet. But the problem is that, at home, so few people have it. Mark Boothe of Nubian Tales - a high-profile, London-based, black exhibition venture - is always trying to make the technology more public. He's done events like Digital Slam and Digital Diaspora, which link British artists to artists in New York, Johannesburg and Dakar. But, on a general level, because of contractions in funding, black film-making groups are now pitted against each other. For me, though, this age has an over-riding benefit: even when face-to-face contact is less possible, you don't feel as alone as before.

What have you done to earn your living at different points?

I've only had two real full-time jobs, in the sense of being employed permanently. But I've worked as a freelance TV researcher; I've taught at places like University of Westminster, Maidstone Art School, St. Martin's School of Art. Even if I haven't been directly working on production, I've tried to put myself in environments where I had contact with it. Also with thinking through ideas, which is very important. Even when I worked in distribution, it was creative. Because one had to find the words and images to sell a new film - or re-sell an old one to a new audience. Getting films to an audience is the last stage in film-making. Arguably, it can be the most important. After all, films are made to be seen.

From 1993 until 1995, I went to work for the British Film Institute. I had been a script reader for their New Directors scheme and was very involved with the education division. I had also worked on packaging some short films, by black and Asian filmmakers, into the series we called "Black by Popular Demand". So, I applied for a job in Distribution. The BFI is a civil service department which deals with film; they provide a range of services like archives, library, education. They also finance films and their distribution and their exhibition department offers support for a string of regional film theatres. Also, they have a great film archive for scholars.

One of my first jobs was a 7-hour German film, Hans Jurgen Syberberg's "Hitler". Which was great because it couldn't have been further from my usual involvements. I mean in terms of gender and race. The BFI was in a position to do things others couldn't; it brought a lot of shorts and animations into distribution. It launched the first dedicated gay video label. On the whole, the BFI is quite stuffy, but there are groups of people in different key departments who are adept at working from the inside. They get progressive projects and ideas moving.

Talk a bit about your own first work - how did you form your aims?

From looking at a lot of films, and reading lots of feminist and cultural theory. Aesthetically, I like work which formally challenges, from people like Bruce Conner, Michael Snow, Wiseman, Godard. As black women film-makers, Julie Dash and Cathy Collins were great inspirations. My first film work tried to be experimental with content, not form. I was concerned with who was being allowed to speak. I did a lot of work back then with young women, both white and black. As someone who felt I never had a voice when young, I really wanted to capture that spark - that cockiness and confidence - that pre-teenage women have. Jo Spence's photographic work was very influential for me, because she really did put herself in the picture. The author bell hooks maintains that, as black people, we're never going to get progressive images of ourselves unless we are prepared to do that. I absolutely agree.

Of course, you learn that finance - or the lack of it - shapes everything. Especially in Britain, raising the finance for filming is a thankless job. After dealing with Channel Four and the BBC as an individual, I would say, "Try and get an enthusiastic producer". Look for someone who makes the type of work you like. Then look at things like where does that work get shown. Did it have theatrical release or was it made for TV? Is it still available on video; what is the deal with its copyright? What happens to the production fee - how does it break down?

How did you first come into contact with new technology - or, more properly, multi-media?

Like many of my friends, I came to new technology late. I always thought of it as being too tech-y for me. It was the boys-with-toys stereotype. But it became less frightening when I started thinking of it as a delivery medium, a vehicle for ideas. In all my work I've been as interested in content and meaning as I have been in the medium. So things flying across the screen just for the hell of it, that does nothing for me. With multi-media, however, there's a sense of bringing your own individual order to a chaos of diverse ideas and practices.

In the type of multi-media done at Real World, form and content are very closely woven together. The interactive director works quite closely with the design team. It's a bit like doing a jigsaw, making the pieces as you go. At times, it can seem too technology-led, because programmers get the Tarantino syndrome. That is, they want to design things for other programmers. Something can look inane to you - but because ten things are flying around the screen at once and the background is changing, they'll say "Great!" It's still very much a look-at-me industry. So that is a point to emphasise: make sure you have a good and tested team around you.

Multi-media is very different from film. To say the director is in charge of what you see and the producer of what you don't see isn't true. Because the creative side of programming isn't seen, either. And those engines are what drive everything. Programmers are like modern-day magicians. Film is a very much more collective process; you follow one vision, try to make it the best it can be. In multi-media, different elements come together - for me, at the moment, in a less satisfying way. Also the possibility for personal interaction with crew and participants is diminished in multi-media.

How do you "plan" a multi-media project?

"Drum", the enhanced CD we did, had a certain history. It revolved around one question: how to turn a series of TV programmes into a CD-ROM? One which will be engaging and exciting? Our development period was very long; a lot of good ideas bit the dust. Our essential problem was to replace an anchoring voice-over with meaningful interaction. At its simplest, that could mean giving interactive characters loops - loops which would represent different parts of a type of music. Then, when you moved these characters around, you would learn about how that music was constructed.

This is a good example - it sounds simple enough. But, to do it, you have to shoot blue screen with musicians who are going to do believable movements. Then you have to arrange for musicians to record the loops. All the rights to everything must be cleared. And rights are an ongoing problem in multi-media, because of the perception "there's gold in them virtual hills". For us at Real World, it was about trying something different - and pushing artistic mediums to their limits.

Will new technology make itself vital to everyone?

Now that Labour are in power, people are more optimistic. There is a new guard in place, people who, I think, probably learned a lot in the past 15 years. But there is also a generation who have been encouraged to think of nobody else. I think that will change, but I don't know about technology. What roles will it play? That's hard to say - just because, for most people, it's still relatively expensive. For other people, it is more affordable, but they are spending so much time trying to earn a living they haven't got time or energy. To learn about new things, you really need both.

For someone like me, with lots of interests and skills, I think collective work is still the best way forward. Working in groups where people have specialist skills and interests, which are appropriate to specific projects. Together, you can make work be more than its many parts. The process of making a film gives you that feeling. Multi-media really doesn't - not just now. But I think there should be cultural development centres, or technological sandpits, where artists can try such mediums, work on ideas together, get their heads round new technologies. There should be centres like this in all our capital cities and a set of bursaries for three- and six-month periods. I don't want just to be at work. I want to make work!

Karen Alexander's Twelve Trade Secrets

1. See as many different types of art and product as possible, especially from other cultures.

2. Listen closely to everyone. But listen most closely to people who do what you want to do.

3. Get as many skills as you can and learn the tricks of your trade.

4. If you go into some institution from being a freelance, go in at a high level where you can be in control.

5. Take nothing for granted. Ask questions, both of yourself and others.

6. Always be willing to try something new and different.

7. Learn to give credit; it is too easy to criticise.

8. Work on what you would like to see yourself. Not on what others think would be good.

9. Don't fall victim to an investment mentality. Give because you want to, not because you think it will "pay off" later.

10. Take risks. If you don't, you'll regret it later.

11. Be as free as you can - but remember: real freedom always comes at a price.

12. Have people you can call in the middle of the night.

While his schoolmates were busy with computer games, Daniel Pemberton was making records. He also put together an elaborate Web page, one which publicises his brand of ambient music. Thanks to other, bigger names on the scene, he left school with a musical future. He tells how he got this "career" together while still in his teens.

How did you start off; get the money for your equipment?

Writing. That's how I funded it. Although I had this really shit keyboard that I got for my 9th or 10th birthday. You know, the kind of thing you say, "Hang on, I want some keyboards" to old people, and that's what you get. I have a lot better stuff now than when I was 10. In 1992, I got my Korg Wavestation. At the beginning of '93, I got a four-track. Before I had that I did everything live; no overdubs. I didn't have a mixing desk or anything. Since I was eleven, I was into computer games; I used to love reading *Zero* magazine. I didn't even have a computer then, I just liked reading it. So, when they published a new magazine called *Game Zone*, I wrote to them. The editor of *Game Zone* offered me a column. I just compiled things, like cheats in computer games. That was it, basically, I compiled them every month. I worked from letters and from stuff I knew.

How did you go from that to other writing?

In 1994, Future Publishing closed the magazine. So, I started writing for other people. I got featured in *i-D*, so I started writing for them. For *i-D*, I write mainly about technology and music. I also write for *Wired* and *Harpers & Queen*. I also re-write some technical manuals for Sony.

Daniel Pemberton:

technological whizzkid

What sort of music excites you?

When the house music boom of the late '80s hit, I got my hands on vocal-free electronic music. I've got lots of stuff that was in the charts then: M/A/R/R/S, Bomb the Bass, De La Soul, 808 State. I was into those things, but also weirder stuff. I used to listen to concrete music, for instance. I've also been into electronic music a long time. When I was eight, I liked Jean-Michel Jarré. That said, I haven't been listening to much of that lately. I spend a lot of time listening to stuff like the Beach Boys - plus, I've gotten really into film soundtracks, from John Barry to spaghetti Westerns.

With your writing, do you get assigned reviews?

A bit of both, but it's more me choosing. It's not always exciting, though. The last exciting thing I did was the computer game called *Wipeout*, which is made for Sony Playstation. It's totally amazing, but that's still computer games. I did do a feature on this Web company, Obsolete. They do a Levi's site, which is quite impressive. They also do lots of underground things which are more interesting.

But, despite your Web pages and your music, you still don't have your own computer, right?

No, and that's terrible. I really want a computer. But I don't know whether to get Mac or a PC. It's quite awkward, because I need it for music, I need it for writing. And, if I get a PC, everything's cheaper. But I've always liked Macs and I've always hated PCs. I should sort this out before another year.

How did you happen to get on the Web?

What happened was David Toop [the critic, author and composer] suggested that I go and meet up with him. Originally, we were going to do an online interview. But I got really interested and wanted to make it a whole project, to try and make the interview truly interesting. I got help from a lot of people, like Tim Leighton-Boyce, who used to publish *Phat*. Eventually, it evolved into a big site - which still carries my music but not my writing. I keep wondering what I should do with that Web site, whether I should make it sort of cool and funky, or keep it personal.

How did you come to put your own music together?

The first stuff I was doing, seriously recording, was when I got my Wavestation. I was doing stuff with a friend of mine who plays guitar. It was all pretty nasty, sort of instrumental fiddling. But one track was actually good. I still think it's good now; I'd quite happily use it on my album - although, obviously, I'd remix it. I didn't really know what I was doing. Then, I heard "Blue Room" by The Orb - when it came out - and that I found exciting. Because it didn't have any structure; it didn't seem to follow any rules. So I started off trying to make things like that. Kind of more what people call ambient music. From that point, my music started getting noticed. So, I concentrated on that side of things.

Didn't you have a sort of patron?

I corresponded with Richard from The Grid; I sent him a tape. But, you know The Grid split up. However, I met Mixmaster Morris at a gig - and gave him one of my tapes. He was the one who really got everything going. He gave those tapes to people on the ambient scene. Then it was down to me going along to gigs, and meeting people, keeping up the contacts. But it was Morris who got them enthusiastic. Then, my "Bedroom" album came out. I did a remix of the MLO track "Wimbourne"; it was on their album "Io". That remix was part of something called "Wimbourne Revisited". I also started doing a project called 2-Player, a collaboration between myself and John Tye of MLO.

Basically, I've just kept on doing stuff. Right now, I'm doing two EPs for Massive Attack's label, Melancholic. Once more, they're recorded on no-budget equipment. I've done more than that, though, I've made loads of albums! There is a 2-Player track on the Freezone compilation and there was a summer '96 single called "Sometimes" on Ninja Tune.

What have you called the albums for Melancholic?

The first one's called "Industrial Light and Magic", so I'll probably get sued by George Lucas. The other one's something techier, like "Techno Takes You to 3-D". But I don't know quite what's going on with them at the moment. Still, I think they could be quite exciting; they're low budget, but they sound like cool film music.

People are interested in how DJs "see" music.

Well, to me, strings are always yellow. And a lot of this new music, image-wise, there are lots of lights flying about. Neon everywhere. It's influenced by huge cities, all kind of turned on at night, with just lights all over. I think of swirly things too, but it's hard to describe. I don't think it's because of music video, but probably that's helped influence it. So has album packaging.

When I first got into music I dissected everything. When did Nirvana's "Nevermind" come out? That was about the time I started analysing everything: drums, bass, whatever, on every record. I couldn't listen to a record without pulling it apart. I don't do that quite as much now, I kind of know. I sometimes forget there's so much going on. But I like records to have a lot happening. I listen to other records and - one forgets - they're really boringly produced, really *clean*. When I hear a record I probably hear five times more things than the normal record listener. That's not necessarily good. It just is; that's what happens when I listen to records.

Are people who grew up with a DJ culture different?

Older listeners maybe listen more to hooks. But I listen to both. For the last year, I've been obsessed with the Beach Boys. I'm still into pop music. I can write melodies easily. I mean, not *really* easily, not necessarily good ones. But I write loads of melody-based stuff, I just never play it to anyone. But I've gotten into playing the Beach Boys, I'm really into playing that surf stuff for myself. I'm also getting more interested in songs. I was writing something last night which - if I put a John Barry guitar in, with a break-break, it would be sub-Portishead. But it would sound good. I'd also like to try harpsichords and harps and strings. So the DJ culture is not destructive!

But how do you find a sound of your own - with all the cutting and pasting and sampling?

Well, my new stuff's definitely got a sound to it. It's not my only sound, either. I've got another album which is short, avant-garde pieces - weird, sort of two-minute atmospheric works. I want to put it out, but I'm worried about it. I need to differentiate it from my EPs. Because it's different, plus it mustn't look like an album coming out. I've got to come up with a clever way of making it different. But as far as finding my sound: the reason my music sounds like it does is that it's the best I could do on my equipment.

What about your life as a DJ?

My first live appearance was in '94, at the ICA's Electronic Lounge. I did original music that I had written specially. My first "DJ date", though, was at The Big Chill club, in December of 1995. I had CDs, DATs and records - plus some homemade stuff that gave out oscillating feedback. That day, I also made tape recordings of the venue, plus some taped TV stuff and some answerphone sounds. There was even a live radio playing beside me.

The thing I like about ambient DJing is that you can play three different records at once. No one would really care, apart from yourself. I know a lot of people who see ambient DJs and think, "Oh, they're just up there twiddling knobs". People always want a beat, and I kind of agree with them. But my other half thinks that they should listen to more stuff! At the moment, when I play out, I tend to play lots of hip-hop records, old '60s records, and Easy Listening soundtracks.

Do the people you were at school with now know more what you do?

They sort of know now. But when I was at school, almost no one knew. School was weird. I mean, I even did tracks using the school toilets. But, still, no one knew. Most of them found out when MTV Europe came and filmed me. But they didn't really know *what* I was doing. At school, I always wonder what their perception of me actually was. One person asked me - seriously - if I was a millionaire. Which was really worrying! I certainly hope lots of other people don't think that. Honestly, it wasn't "Are you a millionaire?" in a mocking way. It was "Hey, someone said you were a millionaire. Is that true?"

My years at school were really awful. They got better towards the end of '96. But no one there - not many - had identities. Not as individuals, not really. Lots of my friends seem to do virtually nothing. I just hope they'll sort themselves out some day. They seem to have nothing they really want to do. But don't get me wrong. I got on with everyone and I liked them all. They just didn't seem to think independently. It was all based round what other people thought.

Why do you think you developed a range of tastes? Is it because you met a wide range of people?

That's kind of weird. People much older than me seem to think that I know lots of people. But, really, I just like knowing more interesting people. Plus, it really isn't hard to meet them. I mean, I'm just trying to improve my music. I don't do enough work musically. I'd like to get in touch with more film people, for instance.

Have you done music for film or television?

I did some stuff with Channel Four a couple of times. The first one was the National Trust "Without Walls", which was a bit like you couldn't do too much. So the music wasn't very exciting. The second one was this Channel Four documentary - about school - which was an absolute *nightmare*. It took me ages and I cued it all up in time. Then they re-edited it, and had to chop my piece up. They fucked it all up and really pissed me off. The other time was another "Without Walls" piece, which I wrote in only half a day. I now think, given more time or a better project, I could really do something. Oh, I also did an MTV ident. But that wasn't through MTV, it was through a friend. He did stuff for them but it never got used. I'd still like to try doing one of those.

How do you feel about the idea that every music has to have a label?

That's *really* annoying. It's one of those things artists always moan about and yet, it helps them. I mean, I use it as well. But it's only useful in guiding you, in giving a rough idea. I can't label the music I do at the moment. It could fit in anything from techno to ambient, to dance, to classical film music - even maybe *indie*. In some respects, it could fit into any of those. Those labels are one thing about the press which really annoys me. That also worries me about my next record, because there is no real label for it. Everything here is still drum and bass, drum and bass - which is now quite boring. But everyone in Britain is label-obsessed. That's why, in some ways, I'd rather be stuck with an indie label. And I'm pleased it's coming out on Melancholic. Because if you're on an electronic label like Warp, you're just treated like an electronic act. Everyone sees you as an electronic hack. But I think if you're on a separate label, one which deals with rock bands or whatever, and you're an electronic act, you'll get more interest.

If you want to work with people, do you just approach them?

No. Well, maybe. It depends what you mean. It depends on your motives. At the moment, I haven't got enough equipment to approach people properly. Because I could say, "Let's do something", and then get caught, when they say, "OK, where shall we do it?" I'd like to work with so many people! But I have to work on my own stuff first.

How do you feel about the music business?

I've a lack of faith in the general record-buying public. Because the more I start doing music, the more I start to see how everything works. I've come to the conclusion that most people don't buy records because they like them. They might *end up* liking them, which is good. But it's more that they've been told to buy them. Everyone's like that; even I'm like that! I've been influenced by that - and it's depressing.

As you get more into the business, does it change your opinions - or your profile?

Sometimes I'm really known for doing weird records; other times, I'm knocking out loads of records. You know, just by doing that you'll come across. But, in a way, I wish there were more ambitious records around. You know, really exciting records; records you know people have spent ages on.

I mean the Future Sound of London one is fine. So is DJ Shadow's. Because you know they've spent a long time on them, you know they've thought about the whole record - rather than just knocking out some tracks and stuck them together. But I'm sort of different.

One thing which does really disappoint me is the way people with the least imagination - like The Chemical Brothers - get the most attention. I mean, they're all right, I quite like them, I might go see them live, but their records just aren't very imaginative. They're not exciting, they all sound the same. Yet, they'll sell ten times more than a better act.

So you have reservations about major labels?

I think when a group's signed to a major label, they can just push out whatever. I think if you're signed to a major these days, then you've got to have a non-exclusive contract. Just have an outlet for the music somewhere else. That's what lots of people seem to be doing nowadays. You sign to a major. You get your money. You get your security, whatever. You do what you have to do for them during two months every two years. But the rest of the time you do whatever you want.

Would you sign to a major?

Oh, yeah. I don't have problems signing to a major. But it would depend in what sense I signed to a major. You know, at the moment, I'm just doing my music through a major - because Massive Attack are on Virgin - and it's perfectly cool. Because I'm going to get more attention paid to my music than I would normally. And the labels seem to be more into my music than any indie. So that's the main factor. They seem to be more into it. And I'm not watering it down or anything. It's not like I'm trying to make anything more accessible. It's not a deal at the moment, anyway. I was going to do an album. But it was too weird for Virgin. So I'm just doing two EPs. Then they can see what happens. There's some things about major labels which suck. But to be honest, in the long run it's better. I mean, I'd rather lots of people heard my record than not. Plus - I get more money spent on the artwork.

Final Memorandum

What will the '90s mean, in the end, for our young talent? Not only are there malls in English hamlets, there are now Internet cafés in many malls. The Spice Girls are the veterans of Pepsi ads; Tony Blair has energised our image around the world. Bill Gates has bought into Cambridge with cyber-dollars, Paris couture is largely in the hands of Britons. But are an individual's creative chances any better?

Certainly, his or her potential audience is different. Oasis, Lee McQueen and Stephen Hawking share one thing: a moment when the world is reaching for information . This need - for "content" - has not yet reached critical mass. But it already generates insatiable drives for image and novelty. Attitude has always been a pivotal force in British business. These days, attitude can provide both impetus *and* identity.

This is because it unites newly desirable qualities. At one time, value was created through scarcity. Now, in the "information", "knowledge" or "network" economy, value "is derived from plenitude". So claims *Wired* executive editor Kevin Kelley, in a '97 tract, "Rules of the New Economy". Like Judy Blame, Kelley sees plenty of room at the top. But communication and connection, he feels, are keys to the kingdom.

For many young creators, the emerging environment - networked or not - still appears a very harsh one. For them, Britain's current landscape remains one of absences. There is no housing they can afford, and few business premises. There is little commercial guidance or efficient management. Yet two assets persist: the aforesaid attitude - and a special kind of *human* connectedness.

For the latter, just look at two signal '90s moments, not as different from each other as one might think. First came a national mobile phone explosion, the consequence of One 2 One's initial free calls. This united a young nation via handsets. Suddenly, on every corner, in every supermarket, on every Roadmaster bus, Britons started chatting. Linked in a fresh and immediate way, they started phoning home from the grocery queue, engaging in romantic rows on street corners, even taking business calls in the cinema. Everyone knew other Europeans loved to talk but, for the English, this was a revelation. Transport, living and software might be pricey. But talk - that basic fuel of creativity - got cheaper. Even when the prices rose again, this effect remained.

Princess Diana's death exposed equal changes. At the time, much was made of the vast communal feeling, the acres of flowers and the oceans of mourners. Few who participated failed to call the experience special, no matter what their actual thoughts about the Princess. Later, when Diana's visage appeared omnisciently, like the Virgin Mary in a Catholic country, it put the stamp of arrival on a modernist shift. For Diana epitomised communication: no matter what the roadblocks, her story told itself. Her trajectory had bridged cultures, continents, classes - and was comprehended in many different ways.

More than any other action, though, it led to talk. Coming to terms with Diana meant conjecture, gossip, discussion, opinion. There were the extant interviews, the iconic footage, the re-televised confessionals and the tabloid inches. But there was also a posthumous hunt for meanings which raged wildly on the Internet. As the Diana phenomenon played itself out globally, one perceived how cross-cultural knowledge had distinct limits. But, more to the point - more telling of the '90s - was the sheer saturation of noise and image.

In this atmosphere, with this barrage of stimuli, many would-be talents are overwhelmed. Yet Britons are accustomed to a media culture; it existed in the 18th-century coffee-house. From The Clangers and Mr. Blobby to Teletubbies, this is a nation with rapid turnover in its *topic du jour*. Creatively, it can embrace the sublime alongside the silly. Thus, British talent may abound in media savvy while, at best, surmounting media cynicism.

"What other people have to understand", says Tony Farsides, writer and editor of *Record Mirror*, "is that in Britain, everybody is a critic. Not just a consumer, but an actual critic. So we don't just go out and buy an album. We discuss and evaluate the whole campaign. We know everything is sewn up and sold to us, so we criticise the packages from every angle."

MTV Europe's house designer Paul Ayre agrees. Ayre is the London-based station's head of on-air graphics. Trained at TV-AM and the BBC, he also works independently on "cross-media" projects. From 1996 to 1998, Ayre helped author a book on trainer culture ("Size Isn't Everything") for Booth-Clibborn Editions. From the beginning, this undertaking - which had six editors, one based in Paris - included CD-ROM components and documentary film. The project was initiated as "international", and much of its material came from the Internet. Yet its collaborators always intended it to be "British".

"People don't always realise," says Ayre, "but Britain is the most visually literate culture on earth. This comes at a moment when visual smarts are it. What are today's primary symbols of world communication? Things like the MTV logo and the Nike swoosh."

This characteristic of the "network economy" benefits Britons. "Because we've experienced the gamut of media. People who've grown up here can manage in the mainstream, and they interact well with other cultures. They also understand the things which are emerging - the new promotional tools such as ambient media."

"Ambient media", Ayre explains, "is like sending your commercial message sideways. It combines persuasion with projection." He describes the strategy as "tiny hints", which collude to send a larger message. "Like if you know someone who has a Chinese takeaway. You get a flyer for your product put in all their orders."

Ambient media is a reversal of advertising. Instead of being pushy, loud and brash, it is casual, low-tech and provocative. It can range from rave invitations to altered hoardings; from MTV "stings" to bus shelters dressed by artists. But it is always highly interactive and relies on observers to connect the dots. The emergence of ambient media is another signifier of the networked mindset.

Theories, of course, abound around our high-tech future. What will it mean for makers and for exports, for support and investments in creativity? What new resources will be made available? Will British talent flower in light of its changes? Or have we already been penalised as "late starters"?

As a multi-media producer for Real World Interactive, Karen Alexander listened to all of these theories. But she also knows the actual practice of the moment. All Alexander's creative experiences - art college, film-making, even the clearing of copyrights - came into play when she entered multi-media. For two years, she produced and assembled "Drum": at first a CD-ROM, finally an enhanced CD. "Drum" is an "interactive introduction to world music".

Initially, Alexander was intrigued by its promise. She liked the idea of a non-linear format, "a way in which ideas can be complex yet not seem confusing". But she soon discovered very concrete problems. Even with full support, long time-lines and generous funding, frustrations still abound on the new frontier. Behind the techno-rhetoric lurk old-fashioned challenges. One is the competition between disparate skills and their egos; another, the unavoidable march of time. "You put aside what seem like insane amounts of time - for development, programming, testing. Then, even when you have a 'rough cut', you don't really know: can it actually do what you said it would? Only much, much later do you find out."

It's hard to balance technology with "creative direction". And that's only one of the problems. Unless one is making games or teaching tools, there are few paradigms in which to operate. Alexander: "Programming-led projects are still experimental. But it's deceptive; they can seem like other media."

"Take a CD-ROM, for instance. The organic nature of production on it seems like film. You can do things like incorporate the unexpected. But it's frustrating in some very different ways. Because there's no control over certain aspects, things like how long the debugging takes. Nor is it easy to take something *out*. To a non-programmer, the actual whole is intangible."

Although Alexander emphasizes stumbling blocks, she did find herself adapting rapidly. More and more, this is typical of young Britons; the '90s saw their talents necessarily gain in fluidity. From digital sampling to mobile phones, through video and e-mail, interfaces and Web sites, a different psyche is emerging. And it is already busy finding rules to break.

Meanwhile, our vexed relationship with new technology continues to emphasize both ties and differences - ways in which we are both like and unlike others. As with most of Europe *vis-à-vis* North America, it is the differences which matter in the end. This is especially clear as, more and more frequently, Britain faces North American business models with her own. Most North Americans, as critic Adam Gopnik notes, draw their identities from the things they buy. Most Europeans draw theirs from what they do.

Nothing has yet made them swap those characteristics - not Ted Turner's "globalised television" or American soccer or the World Wide Web. Certainly, "British style" is transformed when packaged for export (neither Posh Spice or The Prodigy are the same in Ohio as they are in Soho or in Essex). But, at home, British style retains a unique coherence. While the UK plays its part in global fads - buying Nike trainers and yukking at The Simpsons - Britons do put a special spin on how they do it. We can now communicate with anyone anywhere. But, on the street, we maintain a hermetic vernacular.

That vernacular is consistently constructive; it will reliably provide us with "bumsters" and "alcopops". Who but modern, young Britons can truly decode these, much less transmute such constructs into art? Britons, in the end, will remain comptrollers of their exports. For only they really understand "Scary Spice", Direct Faction or a DJ "rinsing the samples". What may seem like a random accretion of slang - scraps of multi-cultural life meeting multi-media - is in fact a singular cultural circuitry. It picks and chooses, imports and cannibalises, trades and uses...and continues to move.

It is that movement, that vibrant, constant change, which provides the nation's healthiest resource. For in the new or "networked" economy, as Kevin Kelley reminds, we are all immutably linked. Moreover, "The wonderful news about the Network Economy is that it plays right into human strengths. Repetition, sequels, copies, and automation all tend toward the free, while the innovative, original and imaginative all soar in value." He is joined in his views by *The Economist* who, in 1997, described the "knowledge economy" as "one in which ideas, and the ability to manipulate them, count for more than the traditional factors of production".

Imagination. Innovation. Seeing fresh angles. "Human capital" which is keen to trade both tools and visions. Certainly, Britain has a plenitude of talents. But their willingness to share is her greatest asset.

Afterword & Acknowledgements

During the week of October 1993, my friend Tony Cooper committed suicide. He chose to close the book on his private catalogue: the hopes, fears, longings and sorrows which were his own property. Tony remains one of Britain's most inspiring graphic designers. At the age of 30, after just six years of work, he had progressed from mundane employment (chicken packer, work at Tesco) to an impressively complete command of graphics. His resumé displayed success after success.

"Agent" Cooper was witty, irreverent, stylish, proud and brave. In a field where people live off one idea for years, Tony rarely repeated even one project. Coming to terms with Tony's choice, writing his obituary, were all part of deciding to do this book: a book about opportunities, tenacity and survival. Five days before I completed the manuscript, I heard an even closer friend, Gavin Hills, had died. There are far too many things to say about Gavin, and it is too soon. But when we last spoke, only twelve days earlier, our conversation reiterated those things central to Gavin's being. He believed in optimism, in true love of country, and in responsibility for the widening world. During Gavin's short life, he saw pain and suffering: in Somalia and Angola, in Northern Ireland and in Sarajevo. He also saw it in the lives surrounding him. It did not ever make Gavin sour or cynical, but it increased his determination to make a difference.

Gavin always fought for things I, too, believe in. Whenever I think of him, or of Tony, I hope I will always think of what Pasternak had to say about Mayakovsky, "Even in this sleep, he was going away from us, in a stubborn endeavour to reach something."

This book would not have been possible without the love and support of Steven Sampson, for which I am grateful beyond any expression. Also absolutely crucial was the help and support of Victoria Rose, Colleen Sanders, Matthew Best, Ian Wright, Simon Emery, Phil Bicker, Carla DeSantis and Tim Leighton-Boyce. I give very special thanks to Karen Alexander, Tony Farsides, Terry Tazioli, Jan Even, Nyan Bushan, Isaac Julien, Philip Crewsden, Paul Sanders and the Black Audio Film Collective. Thanks go, too, to the patient folk at Thames and Hudson, especially Thomas Neurath and Helen Scott-Lidgett, as well as my wonderful host of doctors and physiotherapists: Dr. Maureen Johnson, Dr. Scott Mindel, Maura Dillon Cronin, Norma

Curulla and Patricia Rodgers. Appreciations, Larry Reid, Tracy Rowland, Tom Corddry and my 66 Bell compatriots. And, for MTV Europe, gratitude and love to Lorraine Alexander, Eric Kearley, Paul Ayre, Naomi Sesay, Alastair Connelly, James Hyman, Juan Gelas - and Steve Blame. For the Honest Jon's Massive, as always, shout-outs to all, especially Alan, Tony "Al Capone" and Mark. Memories and thoughts rest with my late friend Kathy Acker, who passed away between writing and publication. Last but not least, of course, many, many thanks to all of the artists and photographers who gave their time and shared their secrets.